NARCISSISM, CODEPENDENCY AND GASLIGHTING EFFECT BIBLE:

2 IN 1:

THE RECOVERY GUIDE ON HOW TO PROTECT YOURSELF BY EMOTIONAL ABUSE AND MIND MANIPULATION. DIVORCING & HEALING FROM A NARCISSISTIC ABUSE

Dana Parent & Melody Covert

TABLE OF CONTENTS

NARCISSISTIC ABUSE SYNDROME

TABLE OF CONTENTS
NO MORE CODEPENDENCY AND GASLIGHTING

NARCISSISTIC ABUSE SYNDROME

A SURVIVAL GUIDE FOR HEALING FROM A RELATIONSHIP WITH A NARCISSISTIC MOTHER OR PARTNER.

DIVORCING A NARCISSIST AND PROTECTING YOURSELF AND YOUR KIDS

PART I

Introduction

The myth of Narcissus is a more favorable one to portray a narcissist's dressing table and self-absorption. However, a deeper conversation concerning the roots of this full-fledged character disorder is missing. It is correct that narcissism is climbing in our civilization, but how does it manifest, particularly as a character disorder? There are many theories concerning how narcissism appears in a person - by a "narcissistic wound" in youth, a routine of idealization and devaluation from a parent, or maybe a neurological perspective that focuses primarily on the way the narcissist's brain develops structural abnormalities associated with empathy.

Yet there's still no obvious answer concerning how Narcissistic Personality Disorder appears in a person. In "The Cracked Mirror: Characteristics of Narcissistic Personality Disorder in Children," Dr. Karen Barden Stein (2009) notes there are particular risk factors regarding children developing the disease. The children who become narcissistic tend to contain one of more of the following characteristics: children of narcissistic parents, adopted children that are overindulged by their parents or confront a contest with their siblings, the children of active parents, particularly when the child lacks the same skill because of their parents, overindulged wealthy children, or children of divorce, especially a divorce where the child is vied over and treated as a thing to be "won." Narcissists might have endured something damaging as a child - psychological neglect or physical neglect, as Kernberg (1975) implies, with a vital parent.

This severe injury in youth, what psychologists call a "narcissistic wound," might have caused them to close off the pieces of themselves that may empathize with other people as a kind of intense self-protection. It might have been brought on by a parent who failed them, mistreated them, or invalidated them, resulting in exactly what Million (1981) calls "compensatory narcissism," an independently fictitious self that permits a child to feel an illusion of excellence to hide feelings of low self-worth. On the opposite end of the spectrum, narcissism could be generated by the overvaluation of a child, allowing the child to stay as a child forever with no consequences or with no foundation in objective fact due to their assumed perfection.

This pattern of overvaluation instead of devaluation might lead a child to arrested emotional growth - in other words, a child who's spoiled to the point that they create a sense of abuse and dismissiveness for the feelings of others. A 2015 study from the Proceedings of the National Academy of Sciences found that parents who overvalued their children could produce narcissistic children.

Children appear to get narcissism, in part, by internalizing parents' enlarged views (e.g., 'I'm superior to other people' and 'I'm entitled to rights'). This new study contrasts with Randi Kreger (2012), who predicts the differentiation between "vulnerable" narcissists and "grandiose narcissists." According to Kreger, grandiose narcissists are created by parents who spoil them, leading them to believe how superior and qualified they can be, while exposed narcissists are normally the product of parenting. As somebody who has taught young children of brighter backgrounds, I certainly watched this burgeoning feeling of entitlement in the children whose parents permitted bad behavior, permitting their children to float upon the bounds of other people without apology.

Parents who educated their children with an excessive sense of entitlement had an indifferent attitude and coddled their children to the extreme even if they overstepped borders. Parents who educated their child's healthy boundaries and self-esteem were more likely to demonstrate empathy, guilt, and responsibility for their behavior. Narcissism tends to arise if parents treat their children as prizes or live vicariously through them - degrading and objectifying them, teaching them that they're items - which educates the child, in turn, to see others as objects. There may, therefore, be a double "overvaluation" and "failure" occurring inside this circumstance, which generates narcissism in a child; the parent might overvalue the child, but might also instill a feeling of worthlessness by not supplying the child with feedback that confirms that they are important and valued. It is because the narcissistic child is overvalued as "ideal," and this kind of comment isn't balanced with realistic expectations.

It puts pressure on the child as a decoration instead of a three-dimensional individual. Additionally, it creates a sense of entitlement, instilling in them the idea that they're deserving of items they have not earned. Because this parental overvaluation isn't balanced with the opinions of everyone else in the child's life, it causes that child to develop a feeling of grandiosity which vacillates between feelings of worthlessness and a hyper-inflated self - in other words, narcissism at the area of a wholesome self-image (De Lisle, 2015). Additionally, it may lead the child to tremendously emphasize one feature more than others – for example, intellectual capability or a different talent - instead of healthy self-esteem and self-acceptance.

That said, parents may not be accountable for creating narcissism within their children, and there are lots of parents with narcissistic children who do supply their children a loving, supporting house.

That is where we need to think about biological predisposition being handed down in families. Twin studies have proven that narcissism is a more typical, heritable characteristic (Livesley et al., 1993). There's also a neurological and biological perspective that requires us to take into consideration how the mind of a person with NPD differs from somebody who doesn't possess NPD. Studies have found that there are structural abnormalities associated with empathy and compassion in narcissistic people, which can be intriguing to note. Psychopaths may also show brain abnormalities, but not merely in compassion; they also show abnormalities in the processing of pro-social feelings like guilt and ethical rationale (Schulze et al., 2013; Sethi et al., 2015). While every concept is persuasive and contains its indicators, I worry that clinicians are still not entirely sure exactly what causes NPD.

The solution is probably more complicated than any single concept. In my view, psychopathology is frequently brought on by an interaction involving biological predisposition and surroundings. Additionally, there are multicultural elements that could make certain ailments more inclined in particular nations or across different contexts. We must consider that there are protective factors and risk factors that decide whether narcissism presents as a full-blown character disorder. It is generally not nature versus nurture, but instead a combination of nature and nurture - many ailments are a result of the interaction between environment and chemistry instead of just one or the other. These variables consist of a strong support community, accessibility to therapy/medication, upbringing, religious beliefs, society, press, in addition to some other experiences beyond their family unit such as sex, sexual assault, witnessing violence, and other traumas that can weaken or reinforce the predisposition involving pathology.To put it simply, narcissists could most likely be created through quite a few different methods and may come from various backgrounds; their narcissism could be created via an interaction between biology and environment. I have witnessed narcissists from all kinds of backgrounds: stabbing ones in addition to overvalued ones whose parents taught them a sense of entitlement from quite early on. I believe that it's important to admit that narcissists may come from many different backgrounds. Psychopathology is generally produced via the interaction between biological predisposition and surroundings. While survivors cannot be 100% sure what triggered their spouse's NPD, Australians can be sure that having a spouse with NPD can be dangerous and catastrophic because of their lack of compassion and tendency to become exploitive. I find that the questions of "why?" and "how?" are less important. If somebody has a disease, it doesn't mean their misuse isn't hurtful, they are not accountable for their violent behavior, or their misuse doesn't affect the sufferer.Quite the opposite. Somebody who has a disease and doesn't secure expert aid in altering the behavior that hurts others, instead using that disease as an excuse to carry on mistreating people, can nonetheless be liable for their activities. Yes, we could be compassionate toward the fact that our abuser might have been contested. Still, we cannot let this empathy blind us to the reality that if they're reluctant to change or get therapy, as most narcissists are, we will need to make self-compassion and pruning a priority to detach from them. Inside this kind of same-sex connection, you may finally be utilized as a vehicle to provide respect, praise, focus, and anything they might want at the moment; this is exactly what Otto Fenichel (1945) calls a "narcissistic supply." Should you be in a relationship with a narcissist, be cautious; the false self is frequently so magical and so distinct from the authentic self that you might fall prey to a vicious cycle of real abuse which will be exceedingly tricky to extricate yourself from.

The cognitive dissonance that leads to being in love with a psychological predator is improved from the false mask that the narcissist gifts to the world. A relationship with a narcissist frequently includes mental, emotional, and sometimes sexual and physical abuse based on where the individual falls on the spectrum.

Chapter 1
The Cycle of Abuse

Abuse of all kinds is cyclical. It involves a series of steps in which tensions escalate, abuse happens, there is some sort of reconciliation, and finally, the honeymoon stage in which the abuser showers the victim with love and affection, promising things will not happen again. This cycle repeats constantly, looping from stage to stage, and is almost impossible to stop without one person leaving the relationship altogether or through some serious, intensive therapy on the abuser's part. The abuser has to seriously want to change for therapy to work, and even then, therapy is not a guarantee that the abuse will stop. The ONLY definite way to end the cycle of abuse is to leave.

Remember: NEVER attend therapy with your abuser, particularly when your abuser is a narcissist. The narcissist is likely to learn more methods to use to control you rather than learn how to better the situation. The only time in which couple's therapy would be recommended is after the abuser and the victim have both attended intensive individual therapy to understand what caused the situation to happen and how to prevent from that situation occurring again in the future.

The abuse cycle follows five steps: Idealization, devaluation, discarding, destroying, and hoovering before returning to idealization.

Idealization

Idealization is when the narcissist or abuser puts you on a pedestal. He tells you how wonderful you are, that he cannot live without you, and how important you are to him. This stage typically involves plenty of gifts for you and involves an emotional high. You feel loved, valued, and wanted, and you thrive on this feeling. This is the stage that you look forward to. It is what keeps you in the relationship even through the other four, far less pleasant, stages. It involves a whirlwind romance, seduction, love, praise, and adoration.

This stage oftentimes involves promises about the future, such as marriage, buying a house, or children. The promises made here are meant to appeal to your desires and meant to make you want to stay in the relationship. You want to feel wanted, and you become addicted to the feelings during this stage. Think of a marriage—this is the honeymoon stage. This is when everything feels like you are seeing and experiencing it in a new light.

If you have already gone through this cycle before, the idealization stage is filled with apprehension, as you know what likely awaits you. While you love the feeling of being wanted, you also recognize that there is a danger if you happen to offend your partner in any way. You understand that the devaluation stage will happen if you do even the smallest thing wrong, and you seek to avoid that at all costs. You do what you can to stay in your partner's good graces.

Devalue

During the devaluation stage, abuse starts to make its way into the relationship again. You are right back to how things used to be as if nothing had ever changed. It may begin with verbal abuse, with your partner shouting at you for small mistakes that are not a big deal in the grand scheme of things. Even buying the wrong butter that rang up as $0.39 more expensive could be enough to make your partner seethe in irritation. Your partner may accuse you of having grabbed that butter on purpose, although you had just grabbed the first one in a pile under that particular sign. He accuses you of wanting to fight.

Gaslighting might follow next, involving trying to convince you that you are wrong about your perception of events. He may cheat on you again, if cheating has been one of the issues in your relationship, or it might be gambling or drinking more than you are okay with.

During this stage, your partner wants you to remain silent as tensions rise. Silence is acceptance as far as the narcissist is concerned, and he will work with that if he has to. He wants to teach you to accept the abuse, and remaining silent would be saying that you do, as far as the narcissist is concerned.

During this stage, you are put in a position where you can escalate things further by calling the narcissist out on whatever abuse he is attempting, or you can remain silent. Neither of these is particularly good options, but ultimately, you need to maintain your boundaries. It is okay to defend yourself during this stage. If you feel that you are being disrespected, it is acceptable to leave, either temporarily or permanently.

Discard

Next comes the discard stage. This is typically what happens if you refuse to allow the abuse to happen. If you call the narcissist out on his behaviors, demanding to be treated with respect or expecting to not be cheated on, he is likely to grow offended. Remember, the worst thing the narcissist can imagine is being discarded altogether, ignored, and rejected, so this is what he does to you, instead. Thinking that you operate in the same way as he does, he chooses to toss you aside in hopes of teaching you a lesson.

The discard stage frequently involves some sort of silent treatment or abandonment. He might break up with you or refuse to acknowledge your existence at all. He feels as though by not putting up with his abuse, you have disrespected him, even though his abuse was disrespectful to you and upholding boundaries is something that should be expected. After all, in a loving relationship, you are not cheated on or called names. You were well within your rights to stand up for your boundaries and refuse to put up with the narcissist's abuse.

Destroy

If the discard period ends with some sort of conflict, or you continue to try to call the narcissist out on his behavior, the next stage is the destroying stage. This is when everything explodes. The narcissist has a blowout, and the abuse escalates further. It may turn physical or sexual, or it may involve threats. Either way, this stage is meant to emotionally, and quite possibly physically, shatter you into submission.

The narcissist will escalate his behaviors, choosing whatever his typical methods of abuse are, and he will not stop. He will do whatever he can to hurt you, as he wants to make you suffer for the pain he believes you have inflicted on him. He feels so wronged by you that he wants you to hurt the way he does, although he only perceives himself as a victim due to his distorted perception of reality. This is enough of a reason, to him, to justify his actions.

During this abuse, he is likely to isolate you, either physically keeping you locked somewhere, or taking away your keys, phone, money, or anything else you could use to call for help. He wants to ensure that you are stuck, and he wants to leave you there to think about what happened and about how it was your fault.

Hoover

The hoover stage is named after the vacuum, referring to the fact that the narcissist is going to try to suck you back. He knows that he has done some serious damage to the relationship, and particularly if he sees that you are not engaging in trying to save the relationship, he will try to do so instead. During this stage, he will try to deny the fault for the attack. He will blame it on you, or on some other external cause. Perhaps he will say that he was sick, or he was stressed, or he was under the influence of drugs and alcohol, and therefore, he feels as though he is blame-free. What matters is that he is the victim at this point.

He may say that he is so sorry to you and promise to do better. He will probably cry and tell you that you are the best thing that he has ever had in his life and that he cannot believe he ruined it. The important thing to remember is that he does not mean any of it during this. He is saying whatever he has to do to save face and get you back in line. He does not feel bad for what he has done and simply wants to make sure you are willing to stay in a relationship with him. Perhaps he does not want to deal with the publicity of a divorce, or he wants to avoid moving or losing his children, but whatever the reason, he is desperate to reconcile here. There will probably be some token of apology at this point: A lavish gift, a heartfelt (but not really because a narcissist does not love) letter apologizing, or even doing something for you that he would not normally do. He wants you to think that he is trying harder so you will agree to continue the relationship.

Repeat

After hoovering has been accomplished, the relationship returns to the idealization stage. You are back to feeling like everything is perfect in your relationship and that things will be okay. Still, you cannot help but feel a sense of foreboding knowing that your partner is capable of doing what he has done. You worry that he may lash out again, and while you are enjoying the time you have at the moment, you also feel incapable of relaxing.

During this stage, the narcissist usually does behave, at least for a little while, and he follows through with what he has promised. He does not cheat, hurt you, yell, or do anything else that he has promised not to do. However, this never lasts. Just as before, you will eventually do something, or he will blame you for something, and the relationship will again move toward the devaluing stage in response to a threat.

Chapter 2
Narcissistic Personality Disorder

N arcissistic personality disorder (NPD) is the proper medical diagnosis for a narcissist. This is a very real, very insidious personality disorder that has no cure, no medication to alleviate the symptoms, and the only treatments that are available for this disorder are frequently rejected by the narcissist. It has become somewhat trendy today to call people narcissists if they act vain at all, as a sort of joke, but true NPD is no laughing matter. Those with NPD have a very dangerous personality type due to the nature of their disorder and the narcissist should always be approached with the same caution you would use to approach a bear or other deadly predator.

Diagnosing Narcissistic Personality Disorder

Ultimately, the behaviors a narcissist exhibits can be reduced into one of three categories: A lack of empathy, a propensity for grandiosity, and requiring attention. If you had to describe a narcissist in the fewest words possible, it would be, "attention-seeking, grandiose, and lack of empathy." Though this is technically correct, to garner an actual diagnosis of NPD, one must meet at least five of nine criteria, as dictated by the fifth edition of the Diagnostic and Statistical Manual of Mental Disorders (DSM-5). The five behaviors must be pervasive, meaning they occur regularly and repeat in a wide range of different situations. While it requires a minimum of five traits to earn a diagnosis of NPD, people with less than five traits could still be toxically present enough to be a problem in your life. The nine traits of NPD are delusions of grandeur, an obsession with power and success, delusions of uniqueness, entitlement, manipulative, lacking empathy, envious, arrogant, and constantly requiring attention from others.

Grandiose

Grandiosity is probably the most quintessential trait of narcissists. This is the belief that the narcissist is better than everyone else. He wholeheartedly believes he is the best gift that was given to the world and he expects everyone around him to agree. As far as he is concerned—therefore as far as you should also be concerned—he is perfect exactly how he is. However, he does not mean that in the sense that everyone is perfect in their inherent imperfection. He means he is perfect. He does not believe in having to prove this perfection, either— it is simply a matter of fact within the world that he is better than those around him. No matter what happens, he will always believe he is better than those around him, even if he fails or someone happens to beat him out in a competition, get chosen for promotion over him, or gets the result he wanted. Even if you happen to do better than him at playing chess and beat him three times in a row, he will assert that he is better at chess and that you had cheated to win.

Obsessed With Fantasies of Success or Power

Because the narcissist inherently believes in her perfection through delusions of grandeur, she also believes that she deserves nothing short of perfection. She feels that she deserves to get the perfect spouse because perfection deserves nothing less than perfection. She deserves the perfect house, the perfect vacation, the perfect job, the perfect family, and anything else she dreams up. As the best person in the world as far as she is concerned, she deserves nothing less than the best as well, no matter how unrealistic or unattainable. She could convince herself that she deserves to be the ruler of the world and believe it.

Unfortunately for the narcissist, many of these desires are unattainable. Nothing in this world is perfect, although the narcissist may believe otherwise. Her delusions eventually become her downfall, as things frequently go wrong in the real world. Plans fail sometimes, people get short-changed, and perfection in the truest sense of the word is little more than an idea; a concept that people everywhere may strive for but never actually reach. Because perfection is impossible, the narcissist is never satisfied. She is constantly feeling her delusions of perfection challenged, and she often reacts quite poorly to such a slight. She becomes irate because things do not go her way, and nothing short of perfection is ever satisfactory.

Belief of Uniqueness

The narcissist sees his superiority as inherent support for being different than everyone around him. He sees himself as unique, and that uniqueness means that he cannot relate to other people, which entails the belief that he cannot relate to anyone else either. His uniqueness is used as justification for other people being unable to understand him, particularly when others try to call him or his behaviors out as being delusional. If someone questions a choice he made, he finds comfort in being able to write that opinion off as someone who is not smart enough, cultured enough, or informed enough to understand the workings of his mind. Someone who is less grand than he can never hope to possibly understand his innermost thought processes, and therefore, those opinions that were made are worthless to him.

This same belief that other people cannot possibly understand him comes with the belief that he can also choose to ignore another people's displeasure. If someone comes up to tell him that he angered them, he can shrug it off and wholeheartedly believe that the other person is unable to understand what he did. For example, if he decided to fire a person who worked for him, another coworker may come over to complain, to which he would respond that he had plenty of good reasons to fire the person. His judgments should not be questioned. He does not feel the need to justify such a decision to someone else and chooses not to. Instead, he goes about business as usual, believing other people's displeasure too trivial to pay attention to.

Entitlement

The narcissist has a deep-seated belief that she is entitled. As briefly touched upon when discussing delusions of grandeur, the narcissist believes that perfection inherently deserves whatever perfection desires. Her entitlement does not require any sort of proof, as she believes she is inherently entitled, and inherency does not require proof. She believes that whatever she desires, fame, fortune, love, beauty, and anything else, are automatically owed to her and that they will just appear in front of her without her having to put in the effort to earn them. She wants it all without having to lift a finger.

For example, imagine a narcissist applying for a job that she wants. It comes with prestige and power and she wants it, though she severely lacks in credentials. She expects wholeheartedly to get that job without having to earn the degree it requires. She assumes that she will get the job because the interviewer ought to recognize potential and perfection when he sees it. When she is sorely mistaken, she is likely to lash out at anyone who dares question her, saying that they had it out for her, or they discriminated against her for being a girl.

Manipulative or Exploitative

Since the narcissist's perception of the world is so strongly distorted, he has to manipulate others to get what he wants. He has mastered the art of manipulating others to make them see what he sees and does so convincingly. If someone dares to question his perception of reality, he will not hesitate to blatantly lie about the situation. He may even tell the other person that she is insane and imagining things, even though it is truly his perception of reality that is skewed.

Narcissists even manipulate others with their personalities—they pretend to be perfect and present themselves in a confident, perfect manner, despite the fact that internally, they are quite broken and lacking identities. They literally wear masks to skew people's perceptions of them in hopes of getting what they want. The narcissist is a master at doing so in a covert manner, making sure that the manipulation tactics can always be denied if necessary. If ever called out for these tactics, he will deny, deflect, and distract the accuser using any means necessary.

Lacking Empathy

Empathy is incredibly important in human societies. It is used to communicate wordlessly and understand how other people are doing in order to ensure that other people's needs get met, even if someone has to help. When you can tell at a glance that your child is hungry, your empathy and understanding for what hunger feels like encourages you to act to provide your child with food to assuage that suffering. This is the basic concept of empathy: Understanding how other people feel as though you are feeling that particular feeling at the moment.

Narcissists lack this empathy. They can see how other people are feeling but do not feel it themselves. Though the narcissist may look at you and see you crying, she does not care that you are, unless your tears happen to be staining her clothes or preventing you from doing whatever it is she wants or expects from you. The fact that you may have just lost someone and are grieving that loss is irrelevant to her. This is why narcissists have no qualms about using others—they do not feel the pain of being manipulated. While they can see that there is pain involved, they do not feel that pain upon looking at the person who has been wronged simply by looking at them. That feeling of pain is a good deterrent for people who can feel empathy—they feel that pain and guilt kick in, causing them to stop. The narcissist has no such skill.

Envious or Believing Other Are Envious of the Narcissist

Because narcissists feel as though they deserve the best, they will often look at other people and feel envy when someone else has what they have. If he applied for a job, but someone else got it, he will feel envious. If someone else gets the girl he wanted, he will feel envious. If someone happened to win the lottery, he would feel envious. He will attempt to avoid the person he envies, and certainly will not ever congratulate the other person. On the other hand, he will take his own envy and attempt to spin it around onto the other person in a tactic known as deflection. He may downplay the other person's newfound achievement or success, and instead spin it around to say that he should be the one envied.

For example, imagine that the narcissist was not picked for a new promotion. He may say that he is lucky to not get the new promotion because the new position had so many more responsibilities, and the slight increase in pay did not make up for the added work. He would insist that not getting the promotion is clearly the better position to be in and lament the fact that the one who did get the promotion will be so busy that he will never see his family since he will have to stay behind at work longer now to make sure everything is done. Instead of voicing that he is envious of the other person, he presents the situation in a way that implies that the one who did get the promotion should be envious of him.

Constant Need For Admiration

Finally, narcissists thrive off of attention and admiration. They feel the need for these incessantly, and that particular attention they yearn for is referred to as narcissistic supply. The narcissistic supply comes from other people fawning over the narcissist and positive attention. He needs to feel as though those around him are constantly paying attention to him and he will absolutely do things that will draw attention to him in the way he wants, even if that involves lying or manipulating the situation or even breaking laws.

Chapter 3
What Is and What Isn't Narcissistic Abuse

Narcissists don't accept blame.

The truth is, a narcissist can never accept liability, mainly because all they see is two choices: either perfection or worthlessness. In other words, they rarely are willing to accept responsibility for their wrong decisions. They see taking the blame as admitting that they are flawed and worthless and this can cost them their self-esteem because they are vulnerable to self-hate. Deep down, they unconsciously expect you to despise them and make them feel worse about themselves than they already do.

The following day after they get up in a better mood than they were, they will hug you. But then you might reject their show of affection. Instead of showing remorse for how they reacted when you left them on the sofa to get something from the kitchen, they will start wondering what is wrong with you! The fight you had is entirely out of their conscious mind because now they feel good. You may go ahead and blame them for their ridiculous and annoying behaviors and for ruining a perfectly beautiful evening.

But the truth is, the narcissist that he/she is will not take responsibility for their actions. If you try to bring it up, he will blame you for his actions. 'If you did not get up to leave, we would not be in such situations in the first place' is what he/she would say.

A narcissist will not apologize.

The reason why a narcissist does not accept responsibility is that they think that it is humiliating. They feel as though taking blame will crush their ego and self-esteem. Hence they are not willing to apologize for their mistakes and poor choices even though they know perfectly well that it was all their fault. It is, therefore, something entirely unrealistic to expect them to apologize.

What is shocking is, as time goes by, they begin to make reparative gestures that are almost like an apology except that they do not express it openly. They will do things like taking you out for dinner or buying you a gift, among other gestures. Therefore, one piece of advice is that, if you are going to be in a relationship with such a person, take the reparative gesture as an apology and do not demand a verbal apology lest you make them annoyed again.

On some level, your narcissistic partner might realize that he contributed to the fight and had overreacted to you getting up and leaving in the middle of an ongoing TV series. He might buy you a bracelet or any other gift that you like. You will take the gift filled with excitement, and everything that had happened goes out the window just like that. You allow yourself to accept the gift and keep your cool because the next time something similar happens, you also get more jewelry, and you keep reminding yourself of that whenever there is a fight between the two of you.

The truth is, it is wise to pick your battles well. If something minor has just happened, let it go. Because when you tell your narcissistic mate that he hurt you every time he does, the relationship will be sour, and you will always be at war. You will not gain anything from it. It is better that you save those small fights for when something big and intentional goes down. That is when you will stand up to defend yourself by merely walking out of the relationship especially when he refuses to accord you the respect that you deserve. Simply put: a narcissist will do anything that they feel like if you allow them. The choice is yours!

Narcissists are not at free will to process past fights.

Once you have fought with your partner, you may see it necessary to go back so that you both can discuss what went wrong and how you can behave better next time if something similar went down. The truth is, a narcissist will refuse to do this because they feel as though you are 'rubbing it in' all over their face about their past mistakes.

The best response is for you to approach them with gentleness and to use the word 'we' rather than using 'you' so that it does not send them a message saying that you blame them for what happened in the past. You can tell the person something like 'I know that we both love each other and want things to go back to the way we used to be. I think that we can both find a compromise and choose to be kind to each other and to be mindful of what we say when caught in such a situation as that last one.'

Narcissists do not respect others' boundaries.

One thing that you have to do when you are with a narcissist is that you have to be very clear about what you can tolerate and what you consider intolerable. Because if you leave them to have their freedom with no boundaries, they will cross the line that you respect.

For instance, you will find them criticizing everything that you are from the clothes that you wear to your relatives and family to the beliefs that you hold so close. They will often hit below the belt whenever you are fighting and end up saying hurtful things and later act as though nothing happened.

Let's consider an example of Jack and Lydia and cheating. Jack is Lydia's boyfriend. Two days ago, Lydia found out that when Jack went on a trip, he reconnected with an old girlfriend. When Lydia confronted Jack about it, he said to her 'you are a fat ugly bastard, and I'm just doing you a favor by being with you and having sex with you. Instead of being grateful, you are coming here to threaten me. Shut your dirty mouth!'

Lydia was so surprised when Jack, her boyfriend uttered these hurtful words. What was unfortunate was that Jack did not seem to realize that he was crossing the line. Lydia never wanted to see him again. When Jack realized what he had done, he started begging her to stay and give him another chance. She kept thinking over and over again what her family had warned her against from the very beginning of the time she wanted to marry him. In Jack's mind, these things did not mean anything, and that was receiving punishment for nothing.

Narcissists do not mind humiliating people in public.

This is something that is quite annoying. Sometimes a narcissist will insist that you get up and leave a restaurant because they have a feeling that the services offered are poor even though you are happy staying. They will often yell at you on the streets and walk away as if nothing happened.

The most important thing for you is to decide if this is something that you can live with for the rest of your life. If you are willing to live with that, you have to determine where the line is for you. The truth is, if he or she did it once, there is a high chance that they will keep doing this repeatedly with no remorse. Because doing this is part of how they cope with what they perceive as insults to their person.

Let us consider the case of Mary and David on a date. Mary was so beautiful, and she knew that. However, she was highly narcissistic and felt as though she was entitled to doing and saying whatever she pleased whenever she wanted. She had the idea that men liked her company and the opportunity to have sex with her at the end of the day.

David said that on their first date with her, whenever she got insulted, she got up and walked away leaving him sitting all alone at the restaurant. What Mary expected was that David would run after her begging for her forgiveness and for her to come back. Instead, David remained seated, calm and collected and ordered more drinks. He merely sent her a text message telling her that he did not mean to insult her and would like to start over. She came back, and they carried on with a lovely evening. They pretended as though nothing had happened at all.

The truth is, by not chasing after her, David had earned Mary's respect because he remained calm and wise in the manner, he handled the entire situation. For David, the boundary was so bright, and he had done what he was willing to. Which means that, if Mary continued belittling him or chose not to come back, he would end the relationship right there.

With a narcissist, verbal abuse often escalates to physical abuse.

One of the typical things about narcissists is they often use verbal abuse and end up physically abusing the other person. Unless you draw boundaries around this, you will end up with bruises all over your face and body. Unless you enjoy a beating, I suggest that you stop that narcissist before you get hurt.

Let us consider an example of Clare and Geoffrey at dinner. They had been married for a year when he started yelling at her, and soon this progressed to grabbing her arm and slamming her against the wall. Clare convinced herself that it was just a mistake and she was not hurt so much. The next time it happened, they were out on a dinner date with another couple who were their friends. Geoffrey took offense at what Clare had said and stumped her foot hard under the table. She shouted out loud 'stop hurting me.' Embarrassed at that, Geoffrey ignored her for the rest of the evening pretending as though nothing had happened.

Clare realized that Geoffrey was crossing the line and she decided that she had to put a stop to it lest it hurt their marriage, making it a living hell. That evening she said to Geoffrey 'I love you and I want this to work. We need to know when we are crossing the line and hurting each other like you did to me before and repeated it in front of our friends at dinner. It doesn't matter how angry we are at one another; there is no excuse for laying a hand on someone else. If there is any problem, we have to be willing to discuss it and apologize whenever we are in the wrong.'

Geoffrey tried to make excuses blaming her for his actions, but she insisted that no amount physical violence would be small enough to allow their marriage to stand. That is when Geoffrey realized that Clare was serious and if he did not change, she would divorce him. And so he realized he should be careful about the kind of treatment he was giving her. Of course, being the narcissist that he was, he forgot twice but Clare reminded him where the boundary was, and he respected it henceforth.

The point is this: it is not comfortable being in a relationship with a narcissist. However, if you have chosen to stay with this person, you have to ensure that you educate them about what you expect from them realistically. You have to learn a couple of tips on how to deal with them and make the decision where to put a boundary and be willing to defend it no matter what.

It is essential that you understand that a narcissist does not love themselves. Feelings of shame drive them. Deep within them, they feel the gap between the fake self they show the world and their true shame-based self. They choose to fill this gap within them using destructive defense mechanisms that are killing their relationships and causing other people pain and hurt.

Chapter 4
What Are the Types of Narcissism?

Talks of narcissism are very common today. People throw around the word narcissist and narcissism without thinking about what it means. In fact, in modern culture, these terms have carved a life of their own, and their meanings might be slightly different from the traditional concept in psychology. Narcissism can be used as an insult today, or even a subtle dig to describe someone, especially celebrities.

Classic narcissists

Classic narcissists are identified as grandiose, exhibitionist or high-functioning narcissists. They are the basic definition of a narcissist, and the type that comes to mind whenever someone is talking about narcissism. These are people who feel too good for everyone else, yet at the same time, they still have a burning desire for everyone else to make them feel important (Casale, Fioravanti, & Rugai, 2016)

Classic narcissists are attention seekers. Most of their discussions are laced with stories about their achievements. They believe that they deserve attention and special treatment because of who they are or what they have achieved in life. Like many of their kind, most of their stories are full of half-truths.

They love to be flattered just as much as they love to flatter themselves. For a classical narcissist, a boring avenue is one where no one pays attention to them. They feel entitled and if they cannot get this for gratification, they are disappointed. A classical narcissist will also not like to share the limelight with anyone else. If they have to, they will go out of their way to make sure they do something that makes them stand out.

Vulnerable narcissists

Vulnerable narcissists also identify as a closet, victim, compensatory or fragile narcissists. This category is for narcissists who don't like attention, but still feel they are better than everyone else. Instead of seeking attention like classical narcissists, they prefer to intertwine their lives with other people (Hart, Richardson, & Tortoriello, 2018)

One of the common traits of vulnerable narcissists is to play the pity card. Their attention comes when they present themselves as wounded individuals who need to be cared for. Some vulnerable narcissists are too generous with people around them, so that you don't forget who they are, or what they did for you. What they need is admiration and attention to boost the image of their perceived worth.

Malignant narcissists

Ever heard of toxic narcissism? Well, those are malignant narcissists. Malignant narcissists are the most exploitative of the lot. They will stop at nothing to manipulate their victims into submission. A malignant narcissist is guilty of many antisocial tendencies, which might not be present in classic or vulnerable narcissists.

The simplest description of a malignant narcissist is a psychopath or a sociopath. Upon careful analysis you will realize that they are sadists and take pleasure from their victims' pain. While the other narcissists might seek attention and approval, a malignant narcissist is always after control and domination (Trifu, 2013)

If they have to, they will be aggressive and deceitful to get their way. Anything or anyone that stands in their way will always meet their wrath. Malignant narcissists feel no pain, no remorse and are not apologetic, especially if they inflict suffering upon you in order to gain what they seek.

Overt and covert narcissists

Overt and covert narcissism is about the kind of methods the narcissist uses to get what they want. Some narcissists might be very open in their approach, while others are secretive and stealthy. Overt and covert narcissists will take advantage of someone for their personal gain (Huszcza, Berenson, & Downey, 2006). However, as their definitive names suggest, overt narcissists will be upfront about their approach. They are visible and you cannot mistake them for anything else. Their intention is clear.

Covert narcissists on the other hand are behind-the-scenes kind of people. You might not know you are under their manipulative spell until it is too late. Some covert narcissists use tactics that are so stealthy, it allows them credible cause to deny responsibility if they are caught.

Malignant narcissists have perfected the art of both overt and covert narcissism. Classical narcissists are generally overt, while vulnerable narcissists tend to be covert.

Somatic and cerebral narcissists

Somatic or cerebral narcissism is about value proposition (Y. Lee & Park, 2016). What does the narcissist see in themselves that they hold in high regard, or what do they see in someone that they want so badly? Tragically, none of these subtypes will allow their partner or anyone else to enjoy the limelight. However, they need someone around them to prop their shine. They look good, but they need someone to make them look even better.

In a relationship with such narcissists, you might assume they love to show you around, and feel special, but in a real sense what they need from you is an object they can flaunt for people to see. It gives them pleasure when people see how good you are and praise them for making you shine. You are no more than an item in their collection.

Somatic narcissists are more attracted to their personal appearances. Their focus is on their youth, their body and what they look like. You will notice this in their selfies. You can also find many of them at the gym, and their favorite place on earth is in front of a mirror.

Cerebral narcissists believe they are the think tanks of this world. They are loaded with all kinds of information, some of which might serve no purpose. What appeals to them is the knowledge or perception that they are the most intelligent people in any gathering. A cerebral narcissist will stop at nothing to remind everyone of their accomplishments. They believe they command and demand respect because of the powerful position they have, or the powerful connections they have. Find them in any altercation and the first thing they throw at you is who they are, or the important person they can call to shut you up.

Vulnerable, malignant and classic narcissists can be either cerebral or somatic narcissists.

Inverted narcissists

Inverted narcissists are a special lot. They are covert and vulnerable in nature. They are predominantly codependent individuals. They cannot stand on their own, and always need someone to whom they can be attached.

Satisfaction and happiness for inverted narcissists come when they are connected to or are in a relationship with other narcissists. Most of their trauma can be traced back to childhood issues, like abandonment. Because they grew up in a dysfunctional system, they are more comfortable around other dysfunctional people, hence their affinity to other narcissists.

Chapter 5
Narcissistic Personality Symptoms

Generally speaking, those who suffer from NPD tend to exhibit personalities characterized by an excessive need for admiration, a sense of grandiosity, and a sense of disdain for others and their problems. It can be easy for some people to mistake this sense of grandeur for self-confidence. The best litmus test for this is to simply look at the reality of the person's situation and then see whether such behavior is earned in any way.

While disdain for others is never justifiable no matter the level of achievement, having this as a standalone characteristic is not indicative of NPD. The simplest way to express this point is to say some people are just assholes. Being an asshole, by itself, is not a sign of NPD.

The key point I'm trying to make here is that the sense of superiority is extremely distorted to the point where the person is unable to view reality anymore and accept any form of negative feedback or criticism. Over and above again, a person suffering from NPD will seek to devalue others around them or even use those others' achievements in order to prop themselves up.

There is also an expectation of wanting to be treated in a manner that is superior to those around them, and if this need is not met, a tantrum of some sort follows. Bear in mind, all of this is far easier to observe in an overt narcissist. Someone who is covert needs to be observed more since they tend to be passive about all of this.

Further symptoms that narcissists exhibit:

constant belittling or bullying of others.

being intensely jealous of others.

thinking others are jealous of them.

complete lack of empathy for others.

expecting obedience from others.

thinking themselves unique or superior to others.

constantly needing praise or admiration.

obsessed with obtaining power, success, attractiveness and so on.

seeking to exploit others for personal gain, without regard for consequences.

Occurrence

NPD usually manifests itself during childhood to late adolescence and can be observed in children. While a child's behavior might not cause as much damage as an adult's, the symptoms remain the same, and there is no difference in terms of how a person will behave. Also, men tend to exhibit more of these characteristics than women.

This actually strengthens the case for the environment playing a far more important role than genetics since if it was entirely up to the latter, men and women would have an equal chance, statistically speaking, of exhibiting NPD. However, given society's focus on men achieving and becoming financial successes while minimizing the importance of that success with women, it seems natural that a lot of boys develop NPD.

Add to this the fact that boys are expected to somehow ignore their emotions, and it becomes easy to see why a boy might think that emotions are somehow invalid and that it is ok for him to succeed at all costs, no matter the harm he may cause to those around him.

The symptoms listed above are constant and stay true no matter the environment and manifest similarly no matter the situation. An important point to emphasize here is that cultural norms play a big role in all of this. If a culture uniformly exhibits such behavior, then an individual's behavior can hardly be said to be unique. The standard method of diagnosis requires the patient to exhibit behavior that is a deviation from the norm.

Secondary Features

In addition to the above, people who suffer from NPD tend to exaggerate their connections to people who are in a position of importance. Mind you, this is done not with a view to cheat someone but because the narcissist genuinely believes this to be true thanks to their own sense of self-importance.

Monopolization of conversation and visible impatience when someone else talks are also tell-tale signs of someone with NPD. A key difference between someone who is simply insecure of their identity versus someone who is a narcissist is that while the insecure individual's reactions to a slight or criticism might be emotional and will largely be the same, the narcissist is far more deliberate and calculated when retaliating.

Another point to note is that the self-image of the narcissist is actually stable, unlike that of someone who is insecure. A narcissist's high opinion of themselves always remains high, extraordinarily so, while a person who is insecure tends to oscillate somewhere between needing approval to feeling somewhat content and being able to take a joke at their own expense.

Routinely blaming others for any of their own failings and insisting that those around them view them the same way as they view themselves are also classic signs of NPD. A narcissist will go to any length to protect the integrity of their own self-image, and such behavior is completely in line with this. Given the importance of the self-image, the first reaction of a narcissist to a defeat or setback of some sort is one of anger, humiliation, and embarrassment, no matter how trivial the setback might be.

It is not always possible to view these symptoms since the narcissist will cloak them from the real world but watch out for any behavior such as isolating themselves from everyone or by faking humility. These are covert tactics. Overt tactics would simply be rage and a desperate desire for revenge.

Once again, it is important that I emphasize something here: A lot of people in successful or high positions within society will exhibit these symptoms. The key is to check whether this behavior impairs or hobbles their ability to function in society or if it causes distress of any sort to those around them. Only when it does, does a diagnosis of NPD make sense.

Key Things to Look Out For

It is impossible to ascertain what someone is thinking inside their head at all times. Even if you know someone personally, this is indeed often impossible. Thus, the best way to look for such behavior is to look at the person's surroundings and evaluate their environment. This will give you a lot of clues about who the person really is. Narcissists are no different.

A narcissist, thanks to their constant need for self-validation, will only surround themselves with people who stroke their ego. This will often be cloaked with terms like "loyalty" and so on. Such relationships are not based on things like friendship but on whether or not the other person can be of some use to the narcissist.

Constant drama within the so-called friend circle is another tell-tale sign. The narcissist will test those around them to see whether they can be relied upon to provide ego reinforcement which is like oxygen to the narcissist. Thus, there will be cycles of approval and disapproval which keeps everyone around them on edge waiting to see how the narcissist will react.

Observe them in situations where they have nothing tied to the result and you will often see them react with indifference and outright contempt for another person's situation.

They will also routinely take credit for other people's work, and they have no issues attaching themselves to the positive results of others. While this practice is relatively common in the workplace, the narcissist will often take things a step further by making themselves the prime reason for the success. They have no qualms about shoving the person who is actually responsible to the side.

The other side to this coin is that they will belittle others in order to make themselves look good to those in power. Such a display can be overt or covert.

One of the biggest behavioral characteristics of a narcissist, however, is the so-called love bomb. It is very important to understand the psychology and symptoms of this since a lot of people are thrown off by this behavior.

Chapter 6
Who Does A Narcissist Target?

You eventually found a man who is not only good, however amazing. For the first couple of months, everything has been amazing. The connection was fantastic. Sure, you struck a few minor lumps that looked like they might be red flags, however, you thought everybody has bad days and he'd never meant to become such an idiot. In any case, he triumphed. Except lately, you are the person doing all of the apologizing.

You do not always understand exactly what you did wrong, however, it is just simpler that way. He lets you know which you activate his moodiness, even though he will not tell you just what you did or why it upset him. Actually, there is a lot he is secretive about his feelings.

The Second thing that now you know it's that over time the situation worsens. He gets angry more and more often and for no apparent reason, so you finally decide to leave him. He says he understands and maybe apologizes for his behavior, so you feel free to leave because you have gone away for a few days, but he insists he continues to look for you, so you start thinking about forgiving and giving another chance.

You get back together and after a short time, everything starts all over again.

He had been an emotional illness. The sort of person who took good advantage of your kindness, as well as in the worst manners, attempted to capitalize on these. Deep down you know he is wrong for you; however, you can not help but feel that the need to stand with a guy who has been through a lot of time with you.

Here is the fact: None of this was your own fault because narcissists are the greatest psychological predators.

It may almost look like YOU did not get concerned in HIM, but instead the HE got involved YOU. The day you had been flirting with this man you believed seemed amazing, and the next thing you knew you had been in a fast extreme and dedicated relationship, and also you cannot remember precisely how that occurred.

That is because narcissists are masters of success. It is like they possess a sixth sense of identifying the folks most likely to drop because of their visionary personality and stay around and treat them after they show their repulsive inner selves. That is why understanding how to take care of a narcissist is going to help you in eliminating them from your life.

However, Can you understand the narcissistic personality disorder signals? If it is possible to identify with all the qualities at the 7 statements given below, you might be at greater than average risk to be targeted by a narcissist.

7 Traits That Make You A Superb Target To Get A Narcissist

1. You've got something the narcissist needs (money, energy, location, lifestyle).

In a Relationship in which a narcissist is demanded, there is a recurrent dynamic that comes to play. It starts with a hook a fantasy, frequently one you believe is all about you, but for your narcissist is about control. On occasion the narcissist will encounter as useful when things do not work out, the table has turned onto you. As soon as you've captured on, or attempt for him to accept responsibility, the strain only calms.

2. You own a caregiver's personality and also a strong desire to assist others.

For a moment, the connection appears to be a match made in paradise, but it is a quick ticket. In the first phases of the connection, the generosity and kindness of this caretaker is expressed. The giver has somebody to dote on, and also becoming the middle of this world works out nicely for the selfish demands of an emotional vampire. Yet, since the relationship becomes more intimate, the narcissist absorbs the connection's time, resources and energy while still gaining control.

3. You get a compassionate, empathetic personality.

Narcissists Have a reason behind everything that occurs in their own lifetime and nothing is their very own fault. Obviously, you pay attention and wish to assist, but if you catch yourself saying, "I was only looking for nice..." more and more frequently, and when part of it feels employed, odds are there is an unhealthy dynamic during play. Actually, empathetic personalities and caretaker forms are prime candidates to get psychological vampires.

4. You grew up in a darkened environment.

Your Past will make it tough to spotting border crimes when they occur, which could lead one to dismiss your instincts when someone violates your confidence. Narcissists do not like bounds. If an individual has a chance to set them, keep them, or take the blame when a person has been broken, then a predator-type sense the weakness and also utilizes it for their benefit. From time to time, narcissists will execute hero-like functions, but instead of promoting liberty or empowerment inside their spouse, they utilize their aid for a means to make dependency.

5. You're lonely and feel a dire desire to find love.

"Locate a need, fill a need" will be the narcissist's mantra. Someone that has reduced self-esteem is simpler to control than somebody with a high awareness of self-confidence. In the beginning, the seriousness feels great since it can be mistaken with enthusiasm, but a narcissist is incapable of isolation. Gradually the intensity a cold, calculated mood leaves you wondering exactly what went wrong and trying to obtain the loving man you thought you understood.

6. You willingly to take the blame -- even for items, you did not do.

The connection deteriorates, narcissists utilize blame and guilt to "establish" that you're the issue. Empathetic and sensitive people are really vulnerable to this blame game due to their visionary nature.

7. You avoid confrontation and conflict.

Narcissists feed off of fear and use it to make smoke screens and aroma. Non-confrontational individuals frequently are frightened of jealousy, remorse, or whatever may cause the reduction of a significant connection. When narcissists react liberally they activate those fears in those who'll bend over backward to keep things calm and calm. Counter-intuitively, the further you avert battle, the more attractive you become to some narcissist.

Do not need to become a victim. Build on what you've learned in the experience and enable your instinct to ensure in the future you will understand how to prevent another narcissist, do you agree? Listen to your gut, and follow your instincts, and also keep in mind that if it is too good to be true, odds are, it's.

Chapter 7
Narcissistic Manipulation and Abuse

Narcissistic Abuse

Narcissistic abuse is insidious and painful for those that suffer from it. Those who get victimized oftentimes find that they have no choice but to go along with their abuse because of the way it is presented. Others never realize that it is happening at all, leaving them feeling like they are drained, exhausted, and miserable without ever realizing why they have those feelings in the first place.

The abuse that the narcissist shells out is usually meant to serve very specific purposes—ensuring that the narcissist is able to meet his need for narcissistic supply. The best way to do this sometimes is through abuse, or at least, that is how the narcissist sees it and will always see it. The abuse can make attaining that supply easier, especially if the narcissist uses methods that are inherently frightening. The narcissist may threaten to leave their target, for example, if they are threatening not to allow the narcissist to do something. If the target resists, the narcissist may then decide to lash out in other ways as well. The narcissist will attempt to browbeat, or sometimes literally beat the victim into submission. They do not care about legalities or even moralities involved—all that matters is that the narcissist gets what he wants.

Much of this happens because the narcissist is coping with their personality disorder—their coping mechanisms become inherently abusive because they are the most emotional, visceral responses that could be had. The narcissist may want to get their supply, for example, but be told that they cannot have it. The narcissist is not going to take this well—instead of being accepting of the situation, the narcissist is likely to blow everything up. The narcissist responds in this way because it is easier than using other methods, such as trying to find another target. If the narcissist is already invested, they see no reason not to try to make sure that they still get that desired end result that they wanted. They will start to lash out with abuse because they feel threatened. They feel the threat of not being able to get that narcissistic supply that makes them tick and keeps them going. Just like an addict starved for their next fix, the narcissist will do anything to make it happen.

Narcissists and Manipulation

Sometimes, the abuse that the narcissist uses is manipulation in particular. Manipulation is something that is meant to be difficult to track—it should be done in a way that it goes entirely undetected. In doing so, the narcissist makes sure that no one suspects him of being abusive at all. Generally speaking, manipulation is behavioral sets that are meant to make the other party feel like they want to change their current position on something, but it should be their idea rather than the idea of anyone else. In order to manipulate someone properly, it must be undetected. The individual must believe that the idea that you have implanted is one that was their own, otherwise they are much more likely to reject it.

When you engage with a narcissist, the narcissist must meet three different criteria to determine how successful his manipulation is likely to be. It must be:

1. Covert: The victim should never realize that it is happen—the manipulation should be hidden underneath a few layers of deniability. The narcissist needs to make sure that the victim never notices or realizes that it is happening. If the narcissist were to realize it, it would lose out on most of the magic and would no longer work properly, meaning that the narcissist would need to find new tactics to use.
2. Involves vulnerabilities: Another factor that must be met in order to ensure that the abuse is effective is to make sure that the individual doing the manipulation is looking for and utilizing vulnerabilities for the target. The narcissist is aware of this, and this is a major reason why the narcissist regularly listens in the early stages of the relationship. The narcissist wants to listen just to get to know you and your vulnerabilities so they can be exploited later.
3. The narcissist must not care: One final rule that is needed is the idea that the narcissist does not care about the abuse. If the narcissist were to care about abusing other people, there would be a major problem. The narcissist would be

ousted, discovered as the manipulator, and when this happens, you run into other risks as well. You run into a problem of being discovered. For this reason, it is better for the narcissist to simply not care at all about the victim than to care enough to interfere with the process.

The Impacts of Narcissistic Manipulation and Abuse

The narcissist is so skilled at presenting himself to other people that most do not realize the truth—that he is a dangerous narcissist. They hear the story from the victim and come to the conclusion that it does not line up with their own perception of the situation, and they decide to disregard the victim's testimony altogether. Instead, they side with the charismatic narcissist, who probably has some harebrained argument as to why he did not, in fact, abuse anyone at all.

As the victim attempts to process the abuse that was endured, usually, they will realize that there are several very real warning signs that must be considered and recognized. In particular, you can expect to see the following in victims of narcissistic abuse:

- Dissociation: This is the emotional and sometimes even physical detachment from your environment. You feel entirely numb, and you might find that you struggle with your memory. When you dissociate, you are responding to trauma—your mind cannot continue to grapple with the abuse, so it instead dissociates from it to try to suppress the traumatic aspects. You are looking for any and all ways to avoid the trauma when you do this.

- You constantly walk on eggshells: Whether you are around the narcissist or by yourself, you will find that walking on eggshells is one of the biggest side effects that you will suffer form. No matter who you are with, you will constantly watch what you are doing in hopes that you can avoid accidentally upsetting the narcissist and triggering the narcissistic rage that you would otherwise be exposed to. Unfortunately, however, this does not always work. You will still probably end up upsetting the narcissist at some point and will have no choice but to figure out how best to cope with the abuse the best you can.

- You ignore your own needs: You oftentimes will put the narcissist's needs before your own. You have been taught to give in to the narcissist's demands just to be able to keep yourself safe, even if just temporarily. Your dreams slowly wither away. Your happiness dwindles. You feel miserable most of the time, but you do not dare to say a word, lest you unintentionally bring about the wrath of the narcissist. You allow your entire life to revolve around the narcissist instead of focusing on yourself and what you want.

- You have sudden unexplainable health problems: Stress can wreak havoc on every aspect of your body. When this happens, you wind up with all sorts of unintended consequences. You find that you are going to struggle immensely—you may suddenly have migraines on the regular, or you might feel like you are suffering from other pain. This is your body's response to all of the cortisol in your system.

- You mistrust everyone: You find that you cannot trust that anyone around you actually has your best interests in mind. You will note that people around you become threats to you—you are constantly expecting and assuming that someone around you is preparing to betray you and you cannot cope with that. You would rather go through life without trusting a single person than allowing yourself to make yourself vulnerable again

- You isolate yourself: After spending so much time being abused and ashamed of what has happened, you may find that you are more likely to self-isolate than anything else. You do not want to go through the process of actively interacting with anyone and you do not want the risk of being betrayed again, so you decide that you will isolate yourself. You do not want to be blamed for the abuse, as happens all too often in today's world.

- You may consider suicide or self-harm: The abuse that you endure from the narcissist can be entirely debilitating pretty often. When it builds up to the point that you can no longer take it anymore, you may decide that life is no longer worth living. You may feel like you are entirely helpless and like you have no possible way in which you can survive the negativity and abuse. Instead, you start turning to more destructive methods to attempt to cope.

- **You blame yourself:** The narcissistic abuser is skilled at teaching their targets to fear and blame themselves for the abuse that occurs. You start to internalize the blame for the abuse, and you assume that it is your fault. After all, the narcissist has said this. You may have spent time dwelling on the abuse as well, desperately trying to pick apart why it happened and what made you so vulnerable to it in the first place. You find that you repeatedly asked yourself why it happened, and the answer came down to you—it could not have played out any other way and you assume that you are at fault. After all, if it is not the narcissist's fault, then the only person left in the equation is you.

- **Your self-sabotage:** Another common impact of the narcissist's abuse is the self-sabotaging attitudes that are taken. The narcissist is skilled at trying to condition their victims into doing what they want, when they want. Some of these people, especially after being shamed for so long and broken and battered, may begin to self-sabotage. After all, they are already in that position—what does it matter? Why should they pursue their goals if they are already worthless? Why bother trying if they do not deserve it in the first place?

- **You fear success:** Nothing creates an angry narcissist faster than you are succeeding at something. That is the perfect way to drag the narcissist's attention back to you, and you can then be certain that you are going to be punished. The narcissist will not approve of your success and instead will berate you for it and make you feel bad about it. This then teaches the victim to fear success. Instead of joy, they feel fear because they are so accustomed to being met with aggression if they do succeed.

- **You protect your abuser at all costs:** Yes, the narcissist has abused you. However, your mind often has a way of minimizing the abuse in order to avoid facing reality. Your brain is in survival mode, so while your proverbial house is burning down all around you, your mind is happily sitting there, sipping at tea, and insisting that everything is just fine. The victim does this to avoid setting themselves off or upsetting themselves. They do this to protect themselves from the endured trauma. If it wasn't so bad by their own admitting, then why did they leave? If it wasn't so bad, why couldn't they have worked it out? Nevertheless, it becomes easier for the mind to completely disregard reality and instead crate this idea that the abuse was not so bad, protecting him and avoiding the potential consequences altogether.

Chapter 8
The Narcissistic Relationship Pattern

Not all relationships are toxic and imbalanced, and even so, a majority of relationships, even platonic or work-related ones, will develop patterns. Patterns are evident in our daily life activities: the pattern of your workday, the pattern when you come home, the routine with your spouse or partner about who cooks and who cleans after supper, or the routine or pattern of when you go to sleep and your nighttime rituals.

All patterns begin somewhere and develop or change over time, and in any relationship, you have in your life, a lot of patterns will change while many stay the same. If you tend to date men or women who have certain tendencies or attributes, in this case, NPD, then you will already be comfortable with these patterns, and perhaps, not realize that you are repeating the same patterns over and over again by being drawn to similar types of people.

Patterns are the life grooves that get worn into our consciousness and mental state. They are the basis of how we think, react, feel, and treat others and ourselves. Patterns, like bad habits, can be broken and will only require that you acknowledge what the patterns are in the first place so that you know what needs to change.

As with any relationship, typical narcissistic relationships will follow a general pattern that causes the partners involved to exist in a repetitive cycle. Otherwise, the pattern is the general rule of thumb for how the narcissist will operate in every relationship. The usual pattern has three stages, including idealizing the partner, devaluing them, and finally discarding them. It is an emotional rollercoaster, and it can repeat itself, depending on how many times you are willing to go on this ride without facing the truth of what is going on.

Let's explore the stages so that you figure out what stage you might currently be in with your partner, or if you can recognize a common theme in your relationship from these patterns.

Idealize

In the first stages of the romantic partnership, a narcissistic person will create a reality with their partner that involves a feeling of infatuation and otherworldliness, almost as if it was destiny that the two of you came together. The sensation is of true love and a beautiful and inspiring courtship coming into being. Some people have described this part of the stage as intoxicating or like being on a drug and the high lasts for weeks, months, and occasionally longer than that.

It is not abnormal to feel the love high in the beginning stages of any relationship, and it is greatly common for couples to inspire this feeling in each other as they get closer and form the love bond. In the case of the narcissistic relationship, the following stages offer a broader explanation of how it is different than other love relationships in their blossoming stage.

People who have reported being in narcissistic relationships have described the "idealize" stage like finding a soulmate and are on a cloud of beautiful life possibilities with their partner. The sensation is that you will never fall apart and that you are meant to be together. This connection is offered greatly by the narcissist who will "drug" their partner with loving words, dedications, praise, courting rituals, intense sexual relations, regular vacations or trips, promises of creating a future life together, and the admonishment of being the most important and special person they have ever met.

It sounds amazing, doesn't it? And who wouldn't want to have such a whirlwind romance right from the get-go? Isn't that what every romantic comedy is selling to you? The "love bomb" phase of the relationship feels like a dream come true, and the reality is that anyone who experienced something like this would probably have a hard time being skeptical, especially when they are being promised the world and that love will last forever.

The next stage creates the platform for understanding the true nature of the narcissistic relationship after the "honeymoon" phase has worn out their ability to gain "narcissistic supply."

Devalue

As the relationship enters a more realistic and comfortable rhythm, the intensity may not be as extreme, and some aspects of the connection may start to wane or grown faded. There are moments of disagreement and possible attempts to confront the narcissist about their attitude or behavior, with a reaction that is not what you might expect from someone who is so deeply in love with you, as they demonstrated before.

The large, red flags on the tropical paradise, love island you created together start to paint another picture of reality. It happens slowly and subtly and can sometimes even feel stealthy, cunning, and deceptive. The objective of the narcissist is to devalue their partner in covert ways to attain a level of emotional superiority, in effect, causing their partner to establish an urge or desire to rekindle the level of affection that they had experienced in the first stages of becoming acquainted with each other.

The narcissist quietly bullies while their partner, or the victim of narcissistic abuse, works tirelessly to bring the sensuality and love back into the courtship by falling for the game and asking the narcissist what they can do to change or "fix it."

In a lot of situations, a person might see these red flags and not feel attached to the narcissist, choosing instead to let the relationship naturally dissolve into the final stage (discarding). However, in many cases, the partner of the narcissist will want to remind themselves of how magical the opening of the affair was and that it must be true love, and therefore, worth seeking out solutions to whatever issues are arising.

The patterns will continue in the "devaluing" stage, as the narcissist will not want to comply with any kind of growth and will create emotional and mental (occasionally physical) abuse in the form of gaslighting, putting down their partner with verbal comments, avoiding or withdrawing emotional or physical intimacy as a form of punishment, disappearing for periods of time without word, withholding seduction or affection, and blaming their partner for anything that might be an issue with them (projecting).

This stage can continue for a while, but eventually, if the partner of the narcissist is not complying with their demands, needs, and expectations, then they will be discarded and cast off.

Discard

If the partner of the narcissist cannot provide them with adequate narcissistic supply, then they will be discarded without emotion or need for debate. If the partner asks for a kind of compromise, honesty, relationship counseling, healthy boundaries, or mutual exchange, then the narcissist will likely determine that they are no longer with the "perfect partner." What they want is someone who can always feed their ego without the demand for anything else in return, and so, if you are not able to meet these demands, you are no longer a viable partner for the narcissist.

Keep in mind, as you read this that it is totally and completely normal and healthy to ask for reciprocity, balance, comradery, communication, and compromise in your relationships. These qualities and attributes, however, are not commonly practiced by the narcissist and so you will be throwing bricks at a brick wall for no good reason if you ask them to compromise or see your side of things.

In a codependent partnership or a situation between a narcissist and an empath, the relationship can be a lifelong pattern (idealize, devalue, discard - over and over again) that will never fully reach a full discarding of the relationship. However, the act of discarding can occur as a result of not meeting the narcissist's needs, and it will be an emotional discarding and punishment that can only be rectified by the partner of the narcissist succumbing to the emotional needs and demands of the narcissist's ego.

Either way, the discarding stage can feel like a huge shock to the victim or target of narcissistic abuse, because it began with such passion, love, and admiration. How can such a loving and amiable person become so different and not even care about your special bond? The answer is that they never truly cared, and they were simply looking for someone to feed their ego and offer them narcissistic supply. If you can't meet that demand, then you're out.

Unfortunately, this can happen all of the time, especially if you don't know what patterns or flags to observe when you are getting involved with someone. It can be very hard to tell at the beginning of a relationship if someone is a narcissist, and they may be a healthy narcissist at that. The key is identifying the patterns in the devaluing stage so that you don't end up shocked, confused, and alone with a stack of insecurities and neuroses about yourself that you were convinced of having by your narcissistic partner.

The effects of this pattern over time can be exhausting and detrimental to you. If you have already engaged in this type of pattern before and you keep going through it with certain patterns, stop blaming yourself for the relationship ending after such a whirlwind start. Odds are, it's not your fault and whatever your narcissistic partner told you about yourself is not true.

Chapter 9
Narcissism In Families

The narcissistic family structure can be just like living in a so-called "haunted house". Each family member that isn't a narcissist will innately feel that something is wrong in the family, but the truth may never be revealed from its place lurking within the shadows. Children who are raised in a home with narcissists learn to become familiar with an underlying feeling of anger, as well as fear. They may have a constant sense of doom and foreboding. After a while, however, these children, as well as adult family members, learn to constantly ignore their instincts, because they are taught that the only reality is the one woven day and night by the narcissistic family member.

Sometimes, both parents in a family will be narcissists; it's not unusual for narcissists to fall in love with each other, feeling as if the other is the only person they've ever met who can understand them. In this case, children are often merely there to serve their parents. There will be a strict set of rules in the family dynamic, as well as an over-attention to appearances of the family outside of the home. Children of these families will know the so-called "rules" perfectly, because it's their survival that's at stake if they disobey them. Adult children of narcissistic families often express a chasm-like feeling of abandonment and neglect, as well as betrayal: after all, the people they instinctively loved the most and who were supposed to provide love and care for them did just the opposite. There is no actual, humane love in store for kids of a narcissistic home.

Non-narcissistic family members of a narcissistic home carry the burden of keeping a great secret from the rest of the world: from their classmates, best friends, romantic partners, other family, and coworkers. Even if they tried to share this information with others, the fear that the narcissist (or narcissists) would a) find out, and b) turn this ally and source of comfort against them is usually too strong, and the victim remains in secrecy.

Usually—and especially in a household where both parents are narcissists—kids are made to believe, groomed, even, that their family is superior to all other families. This reality only exists outside of the home, however. Within a narcissist's house's walls is the undeniable truth that only the narcissist is superior. A non-narcissistic partner and any other family members or children will also know that they do not share in this esteemed reputation; at home, they are just like everybody else, or worse, if they are the direct targets of the family narcissist. These suppliers to the narcissist are there to serve, amuse, and control. They do not get to enjoy the spoils that come from being on top. If they do excel or succeed at something, the narcissist may be quick to sabotage or undermine that achievement, due to feelings of inadequacy and jealousy.

In a narcissistic family, the parents do not care for the kids, the kids care for the parents, in the sense that it becomes the children's responsibility to keep the narcissist or narcissists on track and feeling as if they are in control. The children must wear many different hats: they are faux therapists, the narcissist's biggest fans, master spies, and keepers of secrets. They must show performative affection, love, and support at the snap of a finger, and often have to take on an abnormally long list of chores. The narcissist doesn't look at other people and think "what can I do for them?", he or she wonders how they can make their victim more useful. Menial housework would take away from the time the narcissist has devoted to achieving and conquering.

Triangulation. Inevitably, in a narcissistic family, other family members will be used to deliver messages—even when all parties are sitting in the same room. The narcissist takes special pleasure in shaming his or her subservient and having control of other people to such a degree as setting them against each other is of particular satisfaction to the narcissist.

Triangulation also works for the narcissist when he or she is giving another family member or spouse the silent treatment. While seated at the dinner table, a narcissist might ask their older child to "Tell your mother the roast is cold, and that she needs to heat it up before we eat it." Small jabs create micro-aggressions and toxic environments, and the narcissist needn't end his stonewalling just to get a hot dinner.

When a narcissist uses this passive aggressive form of communication, it's because they're in a rage, usually. Direct communication is often only reserved for special occasions, such as when one of the children or the spouse of a narcissist pushes back against their treatment by the narcissist or says or does something that the narcissist has understood to be a personal attack.

Boundaries in a narcissistic family are meant to be broken. Children will enjoy no physical autonomy; a typical narcissistic parent will often ask embarrassing questions, sometimes in front of neighbors, friends, or other family members, pertaining to private subjects such as menstruation, masturbation, and physical development. Many children develop their own disorders as adults and carry trust issues onto their own adult relationships because of the constant invasion and disrespect of a narcissistic parent.

Siblings in a narcissistic family are often used "for sport" and made to compete against one another for affection and attention. Typically, one child will be treated better than the other, to give the impression that one is the "favorite" of the family. Children who grow up in this toxic environment are usually quite distant to each other, harboring feelings of animosity and resentment towards one another.

Emotions are never to be expressed in a narcissistic family, unless they are performative professions of love towards the narcissist, who may simply turn around and say "yeah, right" or "I don't believe you for a second". If a child reaches out to a narcissistic parent for reassurance, they will get none. No number of nightmares, skinned knees, or broken hearts will enable a narcissist to feel empathy for their child. Many children run the risk of becoming narcissistic themselves in such an environment, having never been taught the important lesson of empathy in their formative years.

If there is more than one child in the narcissistic family, typically at least one will model themselves after the narcissist, while the others may go on to be the constant victim in their adult relationships. The former learns how to manipulate others from their parent; the latter learns how to allow others to manipulate them. The child being groomed towards narcissism will often assist the narcissistic parent in gathering intelligence about other family members and take pride when those family members are punished for any disobedience or challenge.

Refusal to change. While spouses, siblings, and children of narcissists may implore them to seek professional, clinical help, a narcissist will rarely submit themselves to therapy. Even if they do attend a session or two, the narcissist is completely incapable of understanding that they are in the wrong. To admit fault would be akin to psychological suicide.

What's worse, after returning home from a therapy session, the family of the narcissist will typically have to endure great retaliation for betraying their narcissistic spouse, parent, or family member.

Chapter 10
Narcissism in the Workplace

There are people who may exhibit some tendencies especially in competitive and high-pressure business situations, but the pathological narcissists are found in the following personas:

An interrupter and hoarder of conversations – Most narcissists like to talk about their accomplishments, projects, or personal life constantly. They think that everyone is interested in their doings and what they're doing is more interesting than anyone else. Of course, there is absolutely little interest in other people's lives or a show of empathy. When you do express your opinions or talk a bit about yourself, the narcissist usually changes the focus back to themselves. They love the sound of their voice (Ni M.S.B.A., 2015).

They're name droppers – Hoarding conversations is not the only annoying habit of a workplace narcissist. Along with manipulating the conversation around themselves, there are narcissists who like to name drop. They also have a habit of status dropping.

They'll repeatedly remind people of the degrees they earned, the prominent school they attended, the celebrity names they know and mingle with, what significant projects they're working on, the praises they recently received from the head of the company—the list goes on and on and on. They need to continually make themselves appear important and have an exaggerated sense of themselves.

They love the spotlight – Narcissists love to be the center of attention. They dominate phone conferences, marketing meetings, client presentations—you name it, they're right there hogging the spotlight. And during all these functions that turn into the Narcissist Show, they like to remind everyone of their accomplishments, why their proposals and ideas should get special treatment.

They like to keep the facade up of how powerful they are and their importance to the company (Ni M.S.B.A., 2015).

They steal ideas and take the credit – There are those narcissists who are famous around the office for swiping ideas and work from their co-workers. Then they'll claim a disproportionate amount of credit for the work or take total credit although they had little to no input into the project.

In situations involving teams working together, narcissists put in the least amount of work or is not a major participant to a project but will argue to have their name added to the list of contributors.

Another tactic of a narcissist is to go around and "chat up" members of the team about the project and then use their ideas to write up a project status report to upper management under their name alone. They don't even bother to copy other team members who, if questioned about certain aspects of the project, are clueless as to how management was informed of the project's status. They "know it all" – Some narcissists who rise to levels of management not only take credit for other people's ideas (how do you think they got to management?) but they know everything about everything. How? Because they spoke to someone for five minutes, picked their brain, and made the information they derived from the conversation as their own.

This can be maddening, especially if it's you they're talking to and picking your brain. It's difficult to cut someone who exhibits this narcissistic trait, especially if they're your boss.

They may be charming, but do they follow through? – Not so surprising but narcissists make for charismatic salespeople, even when they're not working in sales. They are capable of turning on the charm and creating positive impressions. Of course, that's how it begins with a narcissist—they can charm birds from trees if they needed to in order to get what they want. They can coax others to believe in the ideas they present and people who they feel will be beneficial to their cause will find themselves unwittingly manipulated by the narcissist so they can get what they want.

The problem for those who actually believe a narcissist is that they lack substance and their big ideas become missed deadlines, broken promises, overspent budgets, and complete failures.

Then, when the dust settles and there is blame to lay, the narcissist will turn it all around by pointing fingers at the actions of others that caused the failure. They couldn't have caused the failure because remember, they're too superior to have had a hand in that fiasco (Ni M.S.B.A., 2015). Breaking the rules regardless of what they are – Narcissists think they're special, entitled, and beyond rules and regulations. They think nothing of taking advantage of people and inclined to take short cuts. They're entitled attitude includes handing in incomplete or false reports to management, creating business situations and schemes that are illegal and unethical, stealing office supplies and perpetrating deplorable white-collar crimes. These narcissists truly believe that anything they do, even if it is blatantly illegal, should be pardoned. They truly believe they should receive special treatment and are above the law regardless of what they've done.

Blaming others for their failures and averse to criticism – Pathological narcissists are extremely sensitive and averse to criticism. The narcissist's delicate sense of their flawless self is threatened by negative feedback, even when it is correct and justifiable. This can trigger their narcissistic injury.

Their usual reactions to being criticized are excuses, anger, and indifference that is pretended because they really do care about being criticized! That's the only thing they do care about and not about what they are being criticized about.

And let's not forget the masterful ability that narcissists have in turning the blame onto others for their own shortcomings. Someone else is always at fault and they make sure to let everyone who'll listen know about it.

Unable to relate to others – Many narcissists do not have the ability to relate to their co-workers as equals. They will either take a superior position and postulate that they're better than you in some way or will adopt an inferior stance and submit to you.

Both of these postures are premeditated to influence you to give them what they want. That is the purpose of any relationship to them. Their lack of humanity and empathy to positively interact and treat others as equals.

Passive-Aggressive traits – The passive-aggressive traits of a narcissist in the workplace are frequently done to put others down, elevate their own self-esteem and "superiority" and to get away with as much as they possibly can.

Their workplace behavior can include sarcasm, hostile joking that's veiled with a follow up of a just kidding remark, negative gossip, social and professional elimination, stonewalling, repudiating personal responsibility backstabbing, acting like a victim and premeditated acts of weakness to produce favor and sympathy from others.

How to Deal with a Narcissist at Work

- Keep your cool – No matter what the intimidations, gaslighting, verbal threats, twisting of the real truth or trying to project a guilt trip on you, remain calm, cool and collected. This could be thought of as a way to exercise self-control and you will be able to react more tactically when your emotions are lessened.

Since narcissists lack empathy or compassion, they can be ruthless in attacking anyone who they perceive as a threat. Someone who has healthy relationships with co-workers is a prime target. Realize that any form of attack from a narcissist is to undermine your standing to bolster their ego and perceived superiority. Remaining cool will also annoy the narcissist who is not used to being out played.

- Take a moment before responding – Talk a breath and pause for a moment before reacting or responding to any demands the narcissist may make. A brief pause is effective as well. Narcissists like the immediacy of action or, in their minds, crisis to bully others to be on their side. Let your actions be seen as slow rather than making a decision that is forced or too quick.

- Disregard aggressiveness – Narcissists like to use a usual ploy by using body language that's aggressive because they don't have to say anything and let their posturing do the talking. They use tactics such as looking down on a person when they're speaking to them, leaning forward, puffing up their upper body or blocking a doorway in order to attain control.

- Ignore them. Don't call attention to it because it assures them that what they're doing is effective. Act casually and naturally. Don't allow them to intimidate you.

- Watch your body language – Some people have physical habits that give off signs of anxiety or nervousness like fidgeting, picking on their nails or skin, pulling on their hair or turning red. Narcissists often use the moments when their target is exhibiting these traits to strike harder. Remember that narcissists lack empathy or compassion so they use someone's nervousness against them and attack.

- Speak quietly – Every narcissist has an area that they feel insecure about and can be used to embarrass them when they need to have the line drawn on their behavior. So, in order to fend off attacks that narcissists like to instigate for their own purposes, do as Teddy Roosevelt, the 26th President of the United States proclaimed to "Speak softly and carry a big stick, you will go far."

- The big stick is for protection from those narcissistic attacks, but it is a figurative, not a literal one (Hammond, 2017).

- Look out for their roller coaster of tactics – Narcissists use a pull in/push away approach that is, for them, a natural way of dealing with people. They praise and idealize a person and then follow it by devaluing them. Sometimes, they do both in the same sentence. Watch out for this type of tactic and reject the idea to agree with either so you can remain neutral.

- Set your boundaries – All of these points are important in how to deal with a narcissist in your workplace but this one has special importance as it is you who have to set the boundaries and you who has to enforce them.

In general, narcissists have no respect for boundaries. Initially, when boundaries are presented or declared to them by others, they take pride in ignoring them, showing no respect for them at all.

However, when a boundary is enforced consistently over and over again, they will eventually give in. There may be resistance in the beginning but keep your stance regarding your boundaries and stay firm. Over time they will acquiesce, and their behavior will get better (Hammond, 2017).

- One last thing about boundaries – continue to stand firm. No matter how a narcissist exhibits "good" behavior, they won't stop trying every once and a while.

- Attempt to bond with them – If you challenge a narcissist you will be instigating an attack against you. They are extremely sensitive and hate to be embarrassed and made to look bad. Rather than challenge them, try aligning yourself with them, partnering with them. This will be better received.

- Speak clearly and concisely – Communicating with a narcissist can be frustrating. A conversation with them seems to always be steered in other directions by them. Since there is work to be done, and a brief period to relay instructions and communicate with them, you need to speak directly and clearly about what needs to be done. Be concise in discussing any goals or expectations.

- Don't entertain any of a narcissist's "what's in it for me" agenda.

- Devise an exit plan – If for any reason and at any time you feel unsafe when speaking with a narcissist, seek someone outside your department to speak to about your feelings. If you speak with co-workers the narcissist will turn any situation about your feeling unsafe about you being disloyal to the department.

- Co-workers aren't the only narcissists you may work with. There is also a dilemma if the narcissist is your boss (Hammond, 2017).

Chapter 11
Narcissistic Mothers

Common Traits of Narcissistic Mothers

While narcissistic parents do share some common traits in general, there are some traits that are more common in mothers or fathers. Narcissistic mothers employ drastic back and forth methods that result in psychological and emotional whiplash for their children. This back and forth is largely due to the way a narcissistic mother present herself to other people versus how she is at home. She can be charismatic, friendly, and personable in public, but critical, insulting, and controlling at home.

Narcissistic mothers are often outwardly sociable. They portray an air of confidence, success, and act as if everything in their life is seamless and perfect. Whatever they do looks easy: working sixty hours a week, owning a lavish home, being on the PTA, and appearing involved in their kids' lives. Narcissistic mothers appear to be able to do it all and make it look so simple! Their friends, colleagues, and other parents adore them and might even feel envious of how simple and perfect a narcissistic mother makes her life look.

The only problem is, it is all an image, an inflated self-image that isn't anywhere close to what a narcissistic mom is truly like. At home, a child raised by a narcissistic mother knows the difference. Mom is controlling, critical, angry, and demanding. That face of perfect happiness and constant ease goes away. She uses an abusive tactic of withholding to make her children compliant, dependent, and insecure, all while forcing them to show her gratitude and praise.

It is worth noting that success does not mean narcissism. Most career oriented, financially successful women are not narcissists. Extroverted and involved moms are also not automatically narcissists. These traits are common in a narcissistic mother, but they are not defining. The major differences between healthy moms and narcissistic moms is seen in how they are at home.

When a narcissistic mom comes home, she will want to control her children and micromanage them. A healthy mother comes home to support and nurture her children. When they are at home, narcissistic mothers continue to need and demand gratitude, affection, and attention, even at the expense of their children's needs. Narcissistic mothers lack empathy towards their children and are angered by any kind of independence that their children may try to gain for themselves. A narcissistic mother is always right, because she has to be right.

When the socially engaged, publicly adored narcissistic mother comes home, her smile fades. She diverges from that "perfect" image and becomes controlling, manipulative, and demeaning towards her own children, as well as a romantic partner if there is one in the picture. This shift can be very confusing to adolescents and isn't entirely understood until adulthood in most cases.

Narcissistic mothers rely heavily on manipulation for control. They expect you to do what they want when they want, and if you do not, they will insult, belittle, and degrade you. Any time that you are not fulfilling mom's needs or doing whatever she wants to make her think her needs are of the utmost importance, then her attacks are going to come in the form of vicious criticism.

One of a narcissistic mom's favorite manipulative lines can sound a lot like, "If you really loved me, you would do what I want. If you do not do it, you do not love me." She is easily offended and will resort to guilt if she does not get what she wants. Accusations of not loving her, not valuing her, or taking her for granted will be used frequently.

Since a narcissistic mom has an image to keep up, you might see her being friendly and accepting in public. Then, when you get home, you will hear everything she has to say that is negative about a person she was just smiling with and agreeing with earlier that day. Mom is opinionated, but not at the expense of her superficial image.

Narcissistic mothers are going to find faults and negativities in anything you do that does not please them. They will demean and insult you, and even when you go to great lengths to make it right, you will never get recognition for that. Apologies mean nothing and are never going to be enough. Actions to make up for what you did wrong in your mother's eyes are not going to be adequate either.

Everyone enjoys praise and validation on some level. Children are no exception. However, since narcissistic mothers lack empathy, you won't be getting praise from her. If anything, she will minimize your accomplishments or achievements, unless they directly fluff up her own ego. She will make you feel anxious with her lack of praise and constant marginalization of what you do.

If you were raised by a narcissistic mother, you know that mom needs to be the center of attention at all times. She will expect you to love her, adore her, shower her with praise, take care of her, and wait on her and all her needs. She never returns any of these sentiments or favors, because to her, she is the only one that matters. This expectation is entirely one sided, which can lead to resentment as well as feelings of low self-esteem and lack of confidence in children. Constantly feeling like they do not matter makes them think they do not matter. Narcissistic mothers are great at making their children feel like they do not matter.

The crux of the situation is that every human is biologically programmed to want and seek maternal affection. A child raised by a narcissistic mother who is deprived of that affection or is given praise and affection on a conditional basis, is going to develop a lot of emotional and mental problems that extend into adulthood. Most children who discover that they were raised by a narcissistic mother continue to seek her approval and affection, even knowing on some level that she cannot give it.

Narcissistic mothers are master manipulators when it comes to playing on the emotions, vulnerabilities, and insecurities of their children. It becomes normalized in the family dynamic. Narcissistic mothers also use emotional manipulation to play family members against each other in an attempt to remain the focal point of attention and the one who receives the most love and affection. Siblings fight, they confide in mom, and offer her their love while harboring resentment for their siblings. If siblings or a child and father attempt to form a closer bond, narcissistic mothers can get jealous and will further try to damage that relationship.

Narcissistic mothers rely heavily on emotional manipulation for control. They seek adoration and validation from within the home and from external sources as well.

Father Enabler

Since it is difficult for narcissists to maintain long term relationships, it is not uncommon for fathers to be absent when there is a narcissistic mother involved. An absentee father becomes an enabler by avoidance. This father might only be partially involved in his children's lives or might have disappeared altogether. While he isn't purposefully enabling the narcissistic mother, his lack of action is considered a type of enabling.

A father who isn't in the picture at all obviously does not have any ability to influence his children's lives. He gets to be blissfully ignorant, out of sight out of mind, so to speak. While he may still care about his children and just have to be as far away from the narcissistic mother as possible, he is still damaging his children by allowing them to remain in the full custody of a narcissistic mother and not being around to give them any semblance of normalcy or positivity.

A part time father who knows that his children are primarily with a narcissistic mother has the ability to be a positive role model to his children. However, it is not uncommon, given the controlling nature of narcissistic mothers, for the mother to manipulate her children against their father. This creates a divide where children might not respect their father, think he is weak, or otherwise grow resentful of him. A narcissistic mother won't accept that their father left because of her, and children pick up on the contempt.

As a part time parent, the ability to influence his children will be limited. Not to mention, trying to compete with a narcissistic mother's self-centered delusions is hard, especially when the children buy into them. This kind of father is an enabler in the sense that he is around, but he does not change the custody situation. By allowing the children to stay with the mother and allowing the mother to continue her treatment of the children, he is an enabler.

The most harmful kind of father enabler is the father who is present in a relationship and in the house but does nothing to interfere with a narcissistic mother's abuse. There are several reasons for a father to "turn a blind eye" towards a mother's narcissistic abuse. One reason is that the father has been conditioned and has also been suffering from narcissistic abuse. He is so far in that he does not see what is wrong with the relationship or the way the mother behaves. This can be especially true if he has not needed submissive personality type by nature.

However, fathers that remain in a partnership with a narcissist and do nothing to support their children or remove their children from the situation become secondary abusers. Their devotion to a narcissistic mother and her needs surpass that of his own children. Again, this can be a cause of years of narcissistic abuse and conditioning, or because the father has his own issues.

Many fathers who are stuck in a situation with narcissistic mothers essentially learn to say nothing so that they can maintain harmony with their spouse, or even defend their spouse's behavior to their children to show their support and loyalty to their spouse. Most parents who are enablers for an abusive partner have some kind of personality disorder or mental health condition of their own. This is true with enabling fathers as well.

Enablers can come in a few different fashions. If they are gentler enablers, or subjected to the same abuse and conditioning, they are, by and large, kinder and more affectionate to their children, even if they wait until the narcissistic mother isn't around. There are father enablers that are classified as "true enablers" who can be equally as horrible to their children as a narcissistic mother. Maybe they will gain some kind of pleasure or satisfaction from witnessing the abuse. Whether it is physical or emotional, true enablers will establish their own dominance in the abuse cycle towards their children. These types of enablers might not participate in abusive acts on their own, but having a narcissistic spouse encourages them.

Chapter 12
Narcissistic Fathers

Narcissistic fathers affect the lives of their children; as a child and as an adult. Their relationships, work, and entire lives are negatively affected. The critical part is that adult children with narcissistic fathers may not easily decipher what is wrong even till death.

In most cases, the narcissistic dad suffers from NPD (Narcissistic Personality Disorder), which might not be detected early. A father with NPD exposes his child(ren) to a world of abuse, which can be mild and extreme. A Narcissistic father sees his child as a means to boost his ego; he sees him/her as an extension and not a person.

Now you have someone who does not know how to function in any other capacity, your father!

Even as the child grows, the dad, being a narcissist, feels the need to gain control over his child. This leads to competition and extends to jealousy. Since the narcissistic dad is interested in gaining control, he might view his child growing independence as a threat. Therefore, the threatened narcissistic dad decides to bully and abuse the helpless child. What seemed like love and admiration from a narcissistic father suddenly turns to anger and resentment. In some cases, a narcissistic rage can become violent or physical, leading to physical injuries in the case of boys or rape in the case of girls.

To stay out of trouble, most children decide to adhere to the rules of their narcissistic dad. They avoid the narcissistic rage by trying to adjust their lives to suit the needs of their father. Most times, the abused child is made to believe that the cause of the problem lies in him/her. He thinks, "well, maybe I am a bad person, after all."

The child lives through this emotional trauma for most of his life. He knows something is wrong, but since he can figure out what it is, he concludes that maybe that is how parents are.

However, the picture above is just one manifestation of narcissistic dads. Some fathers can be nice, friendly, kind, and loving to you. But, a narcissist love comes with conditions. Narcissist fathers are always self-centered, and their needs come first. If they show you love, on the one hand, they will make you feel guilty or beholden on the other hand. The child grows up feeling that all forms of love are conditional.

The major problem with the children of a narcissistic father is the confusion that stems from not understanding what the problem is, yet they know something is not right. Even when some children are exposed to the traits and find that it is similar to their father, they still feel that they are the cause of the problem. This is the extent of child abuse and brainwashing done to them while they were young.

How did this develop over the years?

1. Children whose dads are narcissistic have been taught, over the years, that all they do is a reflection of their father. So, if the narcissistic father had shown, conditional love, he/she is compelled to fit into his lifestyle. Also, if the narcissistic father had shown anger and contempt, he/she is afraid to be like him.

2. Both mentalities further increase the problem and makes the child extremely anxious. The child is scared of what he wants. On one side of the narcissistic father, he is anxious to measure up. On the other side, he is eager to get away from any path that reveals his father's character.

3. This identity crisis becomes confusing to the child, and he/she concludes that everything is his/her fault. The shame of the abused child increases further since he/she has never had unconditional love.

Coping and Protecting Yourself

If you are an adult child of a narcissistic father, you might have started to realize just now how toxic the environment was while you were growing up. You are probably learning that you have absorbed all the negative opinions about you even though they are not true. You accepted the wrong opinions as valid and true because you felt guilty about rejecting your father's false view of yourself. He made you believe that you fit the negative profile he fabricated to make you feel insignificant and worthless.

It has taken years to come to the realization, but you may feel a little bit triumphant for the opportunity to get your life back. Hopefully by now you are realizing that you have to start seeing yourself as you are and not the picture that your narcissistic father painted you to be. You acknowledge that change needs to happen if you want to reverse years of emotional neglect and abuse.

Change will not come easy because your narcissistic father will not change his ways just because you are now wiser about the relationship. If you want to be treated differently, the change must start in how you present yourself with him whenever you get the chance to interact.

You know how narcissism can make you feel, so even if you and your father have not seen each other for long stretches of time, you can recognize it the moment he opens his mouth to give you a negative aesthetic evaluation of yourself as a form of greeting.

A narcissistic father will always find something to attack you with, no matter what you say. He has enough ammunition to cast judgment on you to make you feel stupid, weak, useless or something else. It has been his approach for the longest time, so there's no way he's going to change knowing full well that his tactics have been effective in demolishing your self-esteem, or whatever's left of it.

It is difficult to respond properly to a demeaning comment if you are oversensitive to critical comments. The way your father makes you feel depends on how sensitive you are to hurtful words. Even if you respond defensively and change the topic of conversation to your strength, the offensive comments thrown at you will always hurt.

Working on your hypersensitivity is one way to prepare yourself to deal with your narcissistic father. Judgment will always be present, but if you learn to acknowledge that everyone has shortcomings, you wouldn't think of yourself as a worthless human being that your father makes you out to be.

The problem with children of a narcissistic parent is that they automatically gravitate toward the negative. It is a learned behavior caused by long years of emotional abuse. The negative comments about appearance and performance, even if they are not accurate, stay with the children and gnaw at them. The feelings of unworthiness and unlovability deepen when there is nothing to contradict the parent's false image about their children.

In a toxic relationship, such as the one you have with your father, affirmation of your positive traits and abilities are probably hard to find. You just don't measure up to the unreasonably high expectations of a delusional and self-absorbed father. What you probably for a long time failed to realize (as children of narcissistic father do) is that a father does not fit the image of Superman. For so long, you believed in the perfection of your father because that is the image that he projected to you and to everyone else. The same perfection makes it difficult to find errors and limitations, which only fortifies the notion that your father is, indeed, perfect.

Learning to think that your father is not infallible can make the negative words less hurtful. They don't sink so deep and they make you feel less affected. The less affected you are, the more you can focus on finding ways to respond properly.

As an adult child of a narcissistic father, you grow older and try to make a life for yourself without the parental pressures and definitely without the manipulations. However, even as you grow older, you still fall prey to your father's manipulations. You still do what he expects you to do even though you can choose not to do so. But there will come a point where you're no longer willing to tolerate the manipulation.

Living with narcissism is like training to feel inadequate. You learn to hate yourself because your father's demeaning remarks constantly reminded you about your flaws. Even though you know that having flaws is normal, you still feel bad because the way your father treats you magnified your flaws unnecessarily.

Chapter 13
Your Parents' Problems Are Precisely Those Of Your Parents

Okay, I know this sounds pretty obvious, but if you grew up having to deal with emotional weight from the problems of your narcissistic parents, it is not so easy to understand. So, let's say it like this: if Laura (or Juan, or Ines ...) comes and tells you her dramas, you don't need to solve them. Most people tell about their problems by sharing them and nothing else. And if for your bad luck Laura expects a solution, tell her to find a therapist; that you are not paid a turkey for solving their problems. And if you still feel an urgent need to help Laura (or Miguel, or Pedro ...), read about what the FOG is (in Spanish it would be something like MOC: Fear, Obligation, and Blame), which is one of the effects long term narcissistic abuse.

Reduce or End Contact If Necessary

Pigs do not fly. And narcissists do not change. And no, your little friend of the unit who came with that sermon that everyone can change with therapy has no idea that not even a battalion of psychologists would make your daffodil parents from being so. Julia Hall says that "narcissists rarely change, and if they behave more friendly than normal, it is most likely a manipulative maneuver." So, do whatever it takes. If you think you can deal with what it means to maintain reduced contact (and all the guilt that will be thrown at you), do so. If the damage is too great and you can no longer live with that psychological torture, end the contact. The narcissist does not get tired of being narcissistic. He doesn't stop being narcissistic, neither asleep nor awake. And if you are concerned that the abuse extends to other members of your family, as a couple or children, then you already know what you have to do. These pigs are not going to fly, but you can already leave once and for all. It is one of those things for which it is cool to be an adult.

Effects of Living with Narcissistic Parents

Talking about a narcissistic father or mothers may seem strange, since it is difficult to imagine a person who essentially only thinks about himself and satisfies his wishes, with the need or desire to have and raise a child with love and care. And it is even difficult to think that they can meet the needs of a child, as any parent would. However, there are narcissistic parents, and the effects of raising them on children can sometimes be frightening.

The truth is that, when a narcissistic person by definition has a child, he does not necessarily do it to love and care for him properly and expected, rather they do so to raise that child as an extension of himself. This means that narcissistic parents only have children so they can have someone to control, who can satisfy all their personal desires, and also so that in this way, they can fulfill through their children, all those goals that they themselves had when they were young and were not able to reach.

This is how the effects of being raised by narcissistic parents soon appear. Commonly the children of narcissistic parents present various difficulties to build their own personality because, at an early age that is when the personality is built, they are forced to reach all the expectations of the parents, to behave as parents say they should do it, and to satisfy their wishes no matter what. So, instead of building their personality, children adopt what their parents expect them to have, giving away their freedom of expression.

The saddest thing about this kind of situation is that it is not until many years later, that these children realize that they have been raised by a narcissistic father or mother, probably when they are teenagers and begin to hear comments about it from their friends, showing them what is not normal. Although even, they may not realize until they are already adults.

And, while they realize, they have lived a lifetime trying to satisfy their parents and probably failing in the attempt, because a person who according to the characteristics of a narcissistic person, will never feel completely satisfied and will always want and wait for more (and they will ask for more).

This leaves the children with a feeling of guilt, and as if they did not feel part of something, inadequate, thus destroying their self-esteem, if they ever had it, because they feel they are not good enough for their parents to want.

But that is precisely what a narcissistic father or mother seeks, destroy or not help build their child's self-esteem, so that they have someone to control, because children feel that the only way to be loved is by satisfying all the needs of their parents, and, as parents will never be satisfied by their personality structure, a vicious circle is created from which it is difficult to leave.

And although for this type of parents everything seems very normal, if we think about it enough, we will know that this whole situation can be considered as psychological abuse. In many of these cases, even this type of parents can commit physical abuse, because when a child does not meet his expectations, he is severely punished, with lack of attention and care, and physical abuse such as slapping or beating.

The effects of living and being raised by narcissistic parents are not limited to childhood, most of them in the long term continue to wreak havoc on the lives of these people, continuing through adolescence and adulthood. They are teenagers and adults with poor social skills, to start and maintain romantic and interpersonal relationships.

They tend to associate or get together with people as narcissistic as their parents or even more because they have learned that the only way to be loved is to be extremely complacent. And, if by any chance they are able to find a person who loves them for what they really are and not for what they can do, they eventually feel uncomfortable and inadequate, causing in most cases, the end of the relationship.

On the other hand, there are those who, like learning is basically given by imitation, learn that the way to establish relationships with others is by being narcissistic like their parents. They do not learn this consciously, rather it is something that remains attached to their personality structures. So, it is equally common for children of narcissistic parents to become narcissistic adults.

It should not surprise us then to find more and more people in the offices of psychologists and psychiatrists, people who fail to establish lasting relationships or maintain them, because they always find a defect in the couple no matter how good it is, or on the contrary, extremely submissive people who They don't feel good in any relationship, because they haven't learned that what they are is enough.

Either way, the effects of living with a narcissistic father or mother hardly disappear over time. It is necessary in the first instance to realize that you have had a narcissistic father, and then make the personal decision to attend psychotherapy and face the ghosts.

Other people can overcome these situations when they have experienced a significant experience in their lives that has made them put everything in perspective. One way or another, building healthy relationships in adulthood after being raised by a narcissistic father requires a deep inner journey, which, although not easy, will be liberating.

Chapter 14
The Surprising Impact Narcissistic Abuse Has on Your Brain and Reversing the Damage

Narcissistic abuse is one of the most damaging abuses out there because it affects you emotionally, and mentally. It can come in forms of physical, verbal, and mental abuse, so the quicker you catch the signs, and the faster you identify the narcissist, the better off you will be. Believe it or not, this kind of psychological abuse leads to the physical changing of the brain, according to recent studies. Because narcissists don't feel empathetic toward anyone's feelings, they don't see the consequences they cause or the damage they implement. It is proven that with long-term narcissistic abuse, part of your brain actually shrinks, and changes its shape. This leads to cognitive problems and mood disorders such as anxiety, depression, and even bipolar.

The two parts of the brain that change their form or shape with continuous narcissistic abuse, are the hippocampus, and the amygdala. The hippocampus is the region of the brain which focuses on memory and learning. The amygdala is the region of the brain that is responsible for forming and development of negative thoughts and emotions such as guilt, shame, fear, and envy. Over time, with constant abuse, comes the physical shrinking of the hippocampus, and swelling of the amygdala.

The Hippocampus

The hippocampus is part of the limbic system in the brain. The limbic system focuses mainly on processing and developing feelings and responding with actions or reactions. The limbic system also included the amygdala and the hypothalamus. The hypothalamus works together with the amygdala and creates the nervous system and the endocrine system. These systems regulate, balance, and control body functions. So, if the hippocampus is damaged, or the amygdala becomes disrupted, you may experience more suicidal thoughts, panic attacks, and flashbacks, or nightmares. This is out of your control when you have experienced such abuse for long periods of time. However, you can fix this by escaping your present nightmare and managing ways of dealing with stress and preventing yourself from enabling this type of relationship again. Short-term memory is the first step to learning; without it, we wouldn't learn anything. The hippocampus stores these short-term memories, then later converts it into long-term memory or "permanent" memory. Stanford University and the University of New Orleans implemented a study, which found that there are strong links between high levels of cortisol (a stress hormone) and damaged or altered hippocampus. This means that the more damaged the hippocampus is (shrinking, swelling, etc.), the higher the possibility of high cortisol levels will surge through the nervous system. When we have high surges of cortisol pumping through us, we may feel things like dizziness, experience panic attacks, become moody, overthink, worry, fret, etc. Basically, the more stress you have, the smaller your hippocampus is, which is not a good thing.

Hippocampus is the core of our memories. We have two types of memories, which includes the declarative memories, and the spatial memories.

- Declarative memories relate to facts and events. An example would be learning the lines to a play, the lyrics to a song.

- Spatial relationship memories are more in-depth memories that involve pathways and routes. Some may say the spatial memory is our photographic memory. So, an example of this type would be that you memorized how to get from point A in a city you don't know to point B.

As talked about before, the hippocampus converts our short-term memories into long-term ones, then finds a different place in the brain for these long-term memories to be stored. What is interesting about the hippocampus, is that it is always generating new nerve cells, and continues to develop on a daily basis. So, it makes sense why long-term abuse would frustrate, or damage the development and shrink.

The shrinking of the hippocampus has been linked to long-term stress, or abuse, which then leads to trauma, which involves PTSD signs, and sometimes schizophrenia. Since evidence shows in recent studies that stress is one of the main causes for the shrinkage of the hippocampus, it makes sense why escaping narcissistic abuse is beneficial to start lowering stress and reversing the cortisol levels; you may experience when under this amount of pressure.

The Amygdala

The amygdala is mainly responsible for controlling our instinctual, core emotions, and functions. These include lust, fear, hate, love, along with heart rate, body temperature, breathing, and sugar levels, and blood pressures. When the amygdala is on high alert, it implements physical symptoms to the rest of the body, which is where the "fight or flight" response comes in. The fight or flight response is a response the body reacts to sending symptoms like trembling, sweating, feverish, dizziness, etc.

These symptoms can be alarming, but most of the time, they are "false alarms." Narcissists keep their victims on high amygdala alert, making it difficult for their victims to manage stress. So, when the hippocampus shrinks, it produces excess cortisol levels, and then the amygdala becomes triggered, it also sends out the same response that cortisol will apply. With this in mind, the hippocampus has now stored short-term memories into long-term memories, which are triggered by the abuse resulting in PTSD. When the amygdala is swollen as a result of the narcissistic abuse, anything can trigger this "fight or flight" response. So, you are stuck in a downward spiral of panic, and fear over the smallest things, which can be smells, sights, and even feelings. This is because what we see and experience, our brains are trying to relate to what has happened from before - pulling from our memories - and if those memories are traumatic, it triggers the amygdala to apply uncomfortable, disabling symptoms. In short, the amygdala is the reason we are afraid of things or the reason we love things. It controls how we react or perceive the world around us. Based on our experiences through life, the amygdala is our control for how we respond to events that cause our emotions. If the amygdala is swollen, we will most likely react to everything - or small things - with fear and see them as a threat.

So, say you managed to escape the wrath of a narcissist. If you were in the relationship (parent, spouse, employer, etc....) for a long period of time, you would have developed PTSD, heightened fear, phobias, panic attacks, or depression. This is because the stress that the narcissist caused, caused your amygdala to swell, which then the amygdala has gotten used to living with heightened awareness, and seeing everything as threatening. While in the relationship, the victim (you, for example) will use coping mechanisms such as bending reality defense strategies. These are as follows:

- Projection: You may convince yourself that your abuser has goodness in them and that if you try harder, be better, or "bow" to them more, they will treat you better, but you are just struggling right now. With narcissists, this is rarely the case, and all you are doing is making excuses to stay in the relationship longer.

- Compartmentalization: You may only be focusing on the positive side of the relationship, completely ignoring the abuse and the negative, thus still defending your abuser. By doing this, you are telling yourself that this type of behavior is okay, thus training your brain that this way of heightened fear and the way you are living is normal. Hence the lasting effects of the narcissist.

- Denial: Because you feel it is easier to live with the abuse, rather than confront it, or escape from it, you may make excuses for yourself like, it's not as bad as it seems or as it feels.

The process where your brain has to create new neural pathways comes strictly from the hippocampus. Everything we do, learn, know, read, and understand is all the responsibilities that the hippocampus takes care of. With a shrunken hippocampus, it becomes harder to focus, takes longer to understand and learn, and we have to put more effort into doing things that were easy to us before. We may lose interest in things that we loved, partially because we don't have the drive, motivation, or energy to do it. This can all happen from narcissistic abuse.

The hippocampus shrinks due to the increased hormone surges of cortisol (the stress hormone response). The cortisol then stimulates the amygdala or triggers it, which is the cause for our thoughts to become fretful and anxious. So, it is essential to learn stress-reducing techniques to prevent this from spiraling - even if you aren't associated with a narcissist.

Chapter 15
Disarming the Narcissist

Feed their ego

A narcissist needs a lot of attention, affection, praise, and adoration to thrive. So, by complimenting him and feeding his fragile ego, you can easily handle living with a narcissist. You must be prepared to keep feeding his ego, if not, be prepared to deal with his tantrums. This is something you will need to get used to if leaving the narcissist is not an option for you. A couple of simple compliments can go a long way while trying to deal with a narcissist. This is not manipulation. Instead, it is about understanding his personality disorder and using it to help smooth things out.

With narcissists, it is very easy for us to shift our focus onto them, mainly because we often we feel like we have no choice and as if we are being forced into those frustrating interactions with them. There is no way of navigating our own feelings and emotions when a narcissist is around because they are so vindictive and demanding of our undivided attention that it becomes increasingly more difficult for us to function at a normal, clear-minded level. We find this mentally destabilizing and the hardest part about interactions with a narcissist is the normalization period after where we sit in utter bewilderment, struggling to comprehend how such a person can take such a mental toll on our minds.

Narcissism - or rather people who have Narcissistic Personality Disorder – is not just a personality disorder. It is an array of traits and characteristics in which congregate and formulate within someone's identity. A narcissist's identity is an infliction in itself. They have a heightened sense of identity, meaning that they are individuals who only see the best in themselves, although exaggeratedly, and cannot see their own faults and flaws. Like with Narcissus, his successors only see their best reflection, one that only reflects positivity, beauty, and success, and this develops, in their minds at least, that they deserve recognition from us for all of that. They embody an unnatural yet common persona of "gods amongst men". And this, though buried deep within a narcissist is a sensitive being, affects us – people who are not narcissists – even more. A narcissist's words and way of exuberant bragging degrade us and that degradation is unhealthy for us. It breeds self-doubt, it impairs our ability to succeed because we believe the judgment of someone who themselves cannot stand – or even believe – judgment. They are critical of us and we need to learn how to deal with them.

Let us go back to that word. Sensitive. Narcissists are sensitive individuals who lack empathy and outward emotion towards others yet possess such a deep and in-tune emotional connection with themselves. This makes them highly oblivious to their own faults and flaws which, in turn, when pointed out to them, they simply cannot believe you. So creates a grudge which can often linger for months to years to a lifetime. Narcissists are, staying with sensitivity, incredibly reactive to rejection. This could be towards how they look, what they do for a living, what they have said, and their opinion. Remember, a narcissist is "always right" and for you to challenge that stance often has a more hurtful outcome for you. Why? Because we cannot win against or challenge a narcissist and that is something we must deal with.

However, with this said, do not make promises with a narcissist. To rephrase that – do not allow yourself to believe that a promise made by a narcissist will be seen through and kept. Though a narcissist will never forget a grudge or a person who "once said something about me", they will almost always "forget" a promise made. A reason for this could be that we have already given the narcissist what they want, and they have simply moved on. The best piece of advice for this, if a narcissist has made a promise with you, is to be persistent in order to make sure that their word is kept. Yes, in a way, this is challenging the narcissist, though this route is not challenging their credibility.

Dealing with narcissists is something we have all done and gone through and through those interactions we know now that dealing with narcissists is like dealing with a hostage situation; something can always go wrong and we will feel the effects of that for a very long, long time. Narcissists have this austere and gravitas about them that sometimes, when dealing with relationships, can come across as them being charismatic, which at first is true. However, this is an effect of them being the one in control of every possible outlet and outcome of the relationship through their campaign of strong manipulation. How can we tell when they are manipulating us? Assess the situation as a politician would when dealing with a conflict resolution crisis in some foreign country-look at the situation, how it has benefited you, the narcissist, and then see who it really has benefitted. The answer will often shock you.

Acknowledgment

When we are dealing with a narcissist whose opinion seems to be the only one that "should be taken into account" we can simply acknowledge the narcissist, thank them for their opinion, and then to make sure that we have made certain that they seem sure that we appreciate their opinion. We can thank them and do whatever we want with that information. By acknowledging the narcissist's opinion, we have navigated a safer route around the definite feeling of scorn that would have otherwise been directed towards us by the narcissist. By doing this we have been the "adult" in the situation and have seemingly heightened the narcissist's self-esteem by making them think that we will use their advice and suggestions, even though to a degree we will not be taking it into consideration. Avoiding the conflict which comes from challenging the narcissist's opinion allows us to show an interest in what the narcissist has said.

Understanding

Though acknowledging a narcissist implies that we listen and do not take into consideration, understanding the narcissist is by actually listening to them and taking into account what they have said is a little bit more complex. Though this tactic can usually save us from the wrath of the narcissist, understanding their opinion takes a little more nous. We need to make sure that we let them know that we value them and then listen to what they have said, keenly listening until, from underneath all that self-absorbed theory, we can piece together our own picture of what they have said. This can be entirely frustrating, but it is something that sometimes we should do. Behind their mask is someone who has gotten to the top quickly, despite stepping on everyone to get there. Often, when we dissect what they have said and omitted the spotlight fever connotations we can actually get a clear picture of what they are talking about, thus meaning that the advice they have given can actually be applied to a certain situation in which we are going through.

Staying Calm

If you are not a person who can easily deal with a narcissist then staying calm is by far the most difficult practice for you when they start going on about this and that. It irks you, creates this massive bubble of steaming water that wants to spill over. We all have been there, don't worry. It is that feeling when what they have said is so mean or just dumbfounded that we ball up our fists, sigh, smile, and nod our heads; that frustration that is about to explode; the emotion of complete and utter anger that fills us and consumes us. But we can deal with that emotion. It takes time to perfect it but staying calm, especially when the narcissist you are around is persistent in his or her presentation of themselves, can be a life-changing tool in being at peace with the situation or interaction. Sure, it is extremely difficult but acceptance of that situation or interaction with the narcissist and then finding a small piece of calm within you can certainly go a long way. For instance, a narcissist starts explaining all that you did wrong, whether this narcissist is someone at work or your loved one, and you become awash with anger but know how the narcissist will react, do you shout and go off and get nowhere with the narcissist or do you try your best to stay calm, listen, and then just move on? Everybody snaps eventually and that is our human nature, our survival instincts kicking in. It is a normal reaction. It is the pressure building up and our tempers becoming unhinged. But, we do need to be aware that by arguing with or retorting back at a narcissist only affects you and not them.

Channeling the Narcissist Out

This is the opposite of acknowledging and understanding a narcissist. channeling out the narcissist is the basic term for I do not want to be around you because you make me feel worthless for your own personal gain. Another way of saying this could be that you have taken the decision to cut out the narcissist in your life who has had a negative impact on you mentally and physically. Although, yes, the attachment to them is quite strong and the process will be difficult, the step forward for you will have such positive effects on your life. However, channeling out a narcissist can also be someone at work who you have chosen not to listen to because of their self-centered nature. This could have a big impact on your work life, whereas before you had to deal with the feeling of doubt and hurt, you can now flourish in an environment where you are more comfortable, at peace, and at ease without the mental strain of being around the narcissist.

When you first begin to realize that you're with someone who's a narcissist, it can be devastating. You may spend more time agonizing over the fact that you fell for your partner's act than even trying to figure out how to get back on your feet. "How did I let this happen to me?" you might ask yourself. The first thing to understand is that the fault is not yours to claim: it belongs solely in the lap of the narcissist. The only mistakes you made were believing that people were capable of love, which they still are. You fell victim to a master mimic and manipulator.

Defend the Borders

Remember that you have the right to say no. It's your body, your heart, your mind. If any of your rights are being violated, say so, neutrally and assertively. If your words are ignored, have consequences ready in place to be invoked. Consequences are not punishments (although your abuser may say otherwise); they are meant to protect you from being harmed any further. If you must leave to go to a friend's house, calmly explain why. When you return, reiterate why you chose to leave if the narcissist brings it up.

Living with a narcissist or implementing a real relationship with a darker personality disorder person can leave you second guessing everything. This is because you no longer trust yourself or others around you and is why it is so crucial to heal through personal growth, to get past this. The biggest reasons why trust seems so difficult after a narcissistic relationship is because you are fearful that it will happen again, being alone has now become very new, and new things can be scary, and the narcissist has damaged your perception of life, and so you see everyone as a narcissist. If trust already doesn't come easy to you, then learning to trust again, may be even more difficult.

Chapter 16
Handling Narcissistic Abuse

Always Try to See Them for They Actually Are

The narcissists, when they need to, are very good at turning on their very own charm, which can actually attract others towards them. You might even find yourself to get attracted to their grandiose promises and ideas. This particular characteristic of a narcissist can also make them famous, among others. But, right before you get drawn into it, try to look out for them when they are not on stage and how they treat people during that time. In case you can catch them manipulating, lying, or even harshly disrespecting others, there is nothing to support that they will not be doing the same with you. Despite everything that is being said by the narcissists, your needs and wants are mere of any importance to them. And, in case you try to bring up this very issue, you are most likely to be met with utter resistance from their side.

So, the very first step that you can take while dealing with a person who has the tendency of imparting narcissistic abuse on others is by trying to accept their actual self. The moment you are going to believe their true self, you can easily cope with them.

Try to Break out of the Spell and Do Not Focus on Them

Whenever there is any narcissistic personality around you, all forms of attention are most likely to gravitate to their way. You cannot do anything to it as it is by design, no matter if it is a positive or negative form of attention. The individuals who suffer from NPD tries really hard to always keep themselves in the spotlight, whether it is the light of good or bad. You might eventually also find yourself into their tactics in which you will be pushing away all your needs, and you will do everything for keeping them satisfied all the time. In case you are waiting there for a break in the behavior of such attention-seeking individuals, that day is never going to come in reality. No matter to what extent you try to adjust your own life for suiting their needs, they will never be going to find it enough.

So, if you have to deal with an individual who is having narcissistic personality, do not ever allow them to indulge your senses of your very own self or to define your own world. Everyone in this world is important. Try to remind yourself regularly about your very own desires, strength, and goals. Take charge of your life and try to take out some time for yourself. This way, you can easily break away from their spell by simply not only giving all your focus on them.

Learn to Speak for Yourself

There are many times when simply ignoring something or just walking away from someone is actually the appropriate form of response. But, a lot of it actually depends on the form of relationship. For instance, dealing with your parent, boss, or with your spouse might call out for some different form of strategy rather than just dealing with your sibling, child, or any of your co-workers. Many of the individuals who are narcissist by nature actually love to make other people squirm. If that is really the case, start by not to get visibly annoyed or flustered, as it will only be urging them to go on with what they do. If it is with someone who you really need to keep up close in your life, then you are really required to speak up for yourself. While doing this, try to do this in a gentle, calm, and loving manner. You are required to tell them how their behaviors and words are actually impacting your life. Try to be consistent and specific about what is not being accepted by you and how you are expecting to be treated by them. But, you are also required to prepare yourself for the very fact that they might simply not get what you are trying to say, or they might simply not care what you say.

Start Setting up Boundaries

A person who comes with narcissistic personality is most likely to remain self-absorbed. They might also think that they are always entitled to go wherever they want, get through all your personal things, or might also tell you the way in which you should react or feel. They might also be providing you with unsolicited forms of advice and then will also take credits for all the things which are actually done by you. They can also pressurize you to talk about any of your private stuff in public. They may also have a very small sense of personal boundaries or space, and that is why they are most likely to cross most of the boundaries. To be precise, they cannot see or do not want to see the personal boundaries. That is when you are required to clear them about your very own boundaries, which are actually of importance to you.

You might think that why would the results matter to them in actual? This is because the narcissistic individuals start paying attention to everything when something actually starts to affect them personally. Make sure that it is not just like any idle form of threat. Try to talk about all the consequences only when you are absolutely ready to carry all of them out, just as stated. Otherwise, they will not believe you from the very next time. For instance, you have a narcissist co-worker at your office who always parks their big car in the way of your car parking. It would generally make it hard for you to back out. As being a narcissist, they might not agree to you when you ask them to leave a space for you gently. Then, it is the time to state the consequences to them for not actually respecting your needs or wishes. If you are not able to back out safely, just tell them that you will have their car towed down to the police station.

Expecting Them to Go Back

In ace, you are standing out to a person who has a narcissistic personality. You can also expect them to respond in actual. Once you open up and set up all your boundaries, you can expect them to come back to you with some demands of their own. They might even try to actually manipulate you into believing that you are the actual one who is being controlling and unreasonable. They can even play out their cards of sympathy. Just be prepared to stand out where you are, firmly. In case you try to take one step backward, they will not be taking you seriously from the very next time.

Do Not Let Anyone Take Away the Truth from You

A person who is suffering from NPD is most likely not to admit his/her mistake or actually take up the overall responsibility of hurting you. Instead of doing this, they always tend to project all of their negative characters and behaviors onto you or some other person and tries to play the victim card. You might find it hard to keep calm at such situations by accepting the blame of someone else, but you are not at all required to belittle your very own self for salvaging their ego. You are the one who knows the actual truth, and so do not let anyone take the fact away from you.

Try to Find out for a Support System

If you are not able to avoid a narcissistic person in your life, the option that you can opt for is to try to build up some healthy relationships along with a network of support of those people who are close to you. When you spend excessive time with a person in an abnormal relationship in which the other person comes with the personality of a narcissist, it can actually leave you completely drained emotionally. Try to rekindle up all your old bonds of friendship and also opt for nurturing the brand-new ones. Start getting together with your family as much as you can. In case the social circle of your life is not that large, try to opt for some new classes for exploring some new kind of hobby.

If you are looking out for a healthy form of relationship, try to look out for the very signs of the same:

- A relationship in which both the parties listen to each other and also make efforts to understand each other properly.

- Both parties have the ability to acknowledge their own mistakes and also have the guts to take responsibility for their mistakes.

- Both the parties can actually relax and also be their actual selves when in front of each other.

Try Insisting on the Immediate Forms of Actions and Not Promises

The people who actually suffer from NPD are very good at making false promises. They will promise to do exactly what you want and not to do all those things which you actually hate. What they promise is generally for doing better. You might even find them being very sincere with the promises that they make. But, in the true sense, the promises are only the means for the narcissists to achieve what they want. Once they have received what they need or want, all of their motivations will be gone. You will no longer be able to count on all of their actions, matching with what they said.

You Need to Understand That a Person Suffering from NPD Requires Help from a Professional

The individuals who are suffering from NPD will not be seeing any kind of problem, at least not with their very own selves. As a result, it is always very unlikely of them to ever ask you for a professional kind of counseling. People who suffer from NPD will also be having some other disorders like mental health disorder, personality disorder, or substance abuse. You can suggest them to opt for professional help by pointing out their other disorders and not by directly pointing out their traits of NPD. However, it is absolutely their very own responsibility to opt for professional help which can't be made to them by you.

The Narcissistic Addiction to Supply

The individuals with narcissistic personality always feed on the feelings of the third parties. They tend to grow more stronger simply by making others feel very weak in front of them. The only thing that matters to them truly is their very own gratification. No matter what kind of relationship it is, a narcissist will try to dominate and manipulate you for keeping up the grand vision of themselves. You are nothing more than a mere source of adulation and attention.

So, the best way in which you can deal with such individuals is by not giving them the attention of which they are hungry. When you stop giving attention to a narcissist, they will tend to change their attitude towards you but do not fall for that. Try to stay where you are, and this way, you can easily cope up with a narcissistic form of abuse.

Do Not Start to Feel Bad

There are many people out there in the society who might think that the strict form of approach for the narcissists is a form of aggressive behavior. But, little such people know that doing this will not only be doing good for themselves but also for the narcissists. When you try to move on from such a form of relationship by cutting down all the ties, the narcissist will, for a very short time, at least will be having some degree of pain. This pain is necessary for them to understand that what made that person go away from them. So, there is absolutely nothing to feel bad about. First, learn to think about your own good.

Chapter 17
Awakened From the Nightmare: Why You Should Not Waste Your Life on Certain People

At what point are you reminded that life is precious? Do you have to wait until you go through a near death experience to understand this? The one awakening call you should consider is that no one knows what life is like beyond the human existence. Further, our days are numbered in this world until we're gone, and no one really knows about tomorrow. That alone should remind you to enjoy being human and existing right now. You are not going to live forever, so the best you can do is live in the now.

In making your life a worthwhile experience, you should seek to love yourself and not allow anything that threatens your peace have a chance in your life. One of the key principles you ought to apply is decluttering your life. Yes. you may have already accumulated so much in your life, much more than you need. You may have already allowed toxicity and negativity in your life, and you may be holding so much that you think you cannot get rid of. But what do you do? Are you going to live your life stuck in the same mud that you got into long ago? For someone who loves their life, the answer would be No. Seek to say "No" when something bothers you. De-cluttering does not only refer to removing material clutter from your living space. It refers to so much more, including getting rid of fake friendships and toxic relationships. Appreciate the people that are there for you and get rid of the rest. You do not need everyone in your journey, and you cannot make everyone happy. With the myriad of distractions in the modern world, even people you thought loved you can forsake you and may be using you strategically for their advantage. But realize that people who are real and true to you will never forsake you and neither will they maliciously take advantage of you.

A toxic relationship is among the greatest causes of a miserable life. It not only denies you peace of mind when you are together, but it also disorients your life once you have parted with your oppressor. Do not fret too much about the minor things; most people care too much about minor stuff. Be reminded that life is so precious and so insignificant things should not have space in your life. Cutting off on these small things will allow you to focus on the things that matter, including enhancing your livelihood, relationships with family and friends who matter, and establishing whether your romantic relationship is with your perfect match or you are in a relationship with the wrong person. No one is so important that they should come into your life to make you miserable. You have to brace yourself to face everyone as they come so you can identify what they are bringing into your life.

The worst mistakes you can do in the dating scene today are to not show boldness and instead show desperation. You cannot afford to be desperate. This is what will make you think that someone is coming into your life to fill in a blank hole, and that is where all the misery begins. The only person in a good position to manage issues in your life is you. You are the only one who understands you the best. You are your best cheerleader and you are the only person who can look out for you. Until you are an adult, your family exists to help and support you in everything you do, but in adulthood, you are expected to make your own decisions. Whatever decision you take has its own consequences. But the good thing is that we can always learn to eliminate the negative influence of people who do not wish us well and even protect ourselves from such influence by not allowing other people's idealism and thoughts to rent space in our minds and hearts.

You should be in control of your life. You should take it upon yourself to be the only person who decides what to take with you and what you should leave behind, starting now. Your ultimate goal in life should be to find your purpose and aligning with your purpose allows you to live a meaningful life where you are happy and fulfilled. Keep in mind that a meaningful life calls for careful planning, owning your own actions and being ready to defend yourself. Knowing where you are in life, where you aim at getting to in the future and whatever it is that you need to get there, you stand in the best position for living a rewarding life. The key to achieving a rewarding lifestyle is living the best way you can in the present and not procrastinating on doing something that is detrimental to your wellbeing.

Remember, your body is your best tool in going about your daily activities, and your mind is the best tool in showing you how to carry out your daily tasks and the decisions. Therefore, take care of your wellbeing, both mentally and physically. Do not allow anyone to waste your time that could have been used in activities that count in your life. Realize that every moment counts. Most importantly, realize that you are important. No one can do you better than you, and thus no one has the right to dictate what you should do. That which makes you happy, go for it. Do not let anyone with a contrary opinion have space in your life. Always be reminded that you are unique and important.

Sometimes, especially when dealing with a narcissist, the lines may be too blurry such that you do not realize when someone has crossed them and is truly controlling your life, denying you the chance to make everyday count in living a meaningful way. Therefore, watch out for the following things, which should let you know that you are in a place you don't want to be in.

You Complain About the Same Thing Over and Over Again

The basic rule of thumb you should know is that if you have complained about something about 2 to 3 times, you are in a position you do not want to be in. It is upon you to accept it or change it. Whether it is frustration at work or with your partner, you should not take complaining as a mere release of defeat. Rather, this should serve as a sign that you are subconsciously rejecting something in life.

You Are Made to Feel Ashamed About Your Past

Frequent reminders that you have been a failure in the past may get you feeling ashamed. There are partners who are ever ready to remind you that you have made mistakes in the past. They make you forget that your past is who you were and that does not define who you are now or whom you want to be in the future. A narcissistic or toxic partner will make you open up about your past and will always use it to drive you to the corner and empower themselves. When you start feeling ashamed of your past because of your partner's constant reminders, this is when you realize that you are in a situation that is not good for your personal development and happiness.

You Are Beginning to Think That Changes Are Bad

Embracing change and leveraging opportunities as they come counts as among the most significant principles to thrive in this life, especially in today's world. If someone is influencing your opinion about changes and making you feel afraid of change, then you should not entertain them, since this is not where you need to be. As long as you are taking calculated moves, change is what brings you where you want and need to be.

Your Partner Has Made You Abandon Your Favorite Hobbies

Whenever you do something that you deem important to you, it gives you joy. You know that you are headed in the right direction if you do something every day that makes you happy. However, if your partner criticizes your hobbies and makes you see how unreasonable, or wasteful they are, this is not the ideal situation for you to be in. No one is justified to stand between you and your happiness.

You Barely Have Time for Yourself to Rest

You want to show how much you can achieve in a day, but you are always complaining about how unappreciated and exhausted you are. In all sense, we all have 24 hours and some of these are meant for sleeping, in which you rejuvenate your mind and go on with your work. If you are not able to get enough rest, you are always bitter and resentful. Such things sweep off your happiness and sanity eventually, in ways you could not expect. You are not a superhero that you should always be active. If you are in such a position, you are most probably trying to please your partner because they have conditioned you into this. Perhaps, it is your toxic partner who wants you preoccupied so you do not have time to alleviate yourself from their control. Clearly, you do not want to live in such a condition and achieve a rewarding life.

Chapter 18
10 Tips to Help You Get Your Life Back

N ow that you have recognized all the ways that narcissistic abuse has impacted your relationship, it is time to start thinking about how you can get your life back. Fortunately, it is not as difficult as you think. Countless people have survived narcissistic abuse, and so can you. Here are some tips to help you do this.

Tip #1: Take steps to regain your confidence

One of the more powerful aspects of narcissistic abuse is that it breaks down your confidence. That is the goal: to tear you down in such a way that you become totally dependent on the narcissist. Therefore, one of the more important steps you can take is actually regaining your confidence. As you start to feel better about yourself, you will come to see the narcissist for who he or she is.

Tip #2: Keep your guard up

The narcissist uses the tools you give them against you. In other words, the narcissist knows how to manipulate you because you have taught them how to. They know all about you, even how your brain processes information. Although you cannot take back all the data that you have given this person, you can learn how to protect yourself in the future. Being a little reserved can go a long way.

Tip #3: Question the motives and intentions of your partner

The narcissist knows how to use emotions and words to establish rapport with people and to control them. Indeed, the narcissist does this so naturally that most people don't even notice it. What you can do to protect yourself is to start to question the intentions of the other person. The goal is not to make you paranoid, but to teach you to take the step of questioning why the other person wants this or that. This will make you a little more proactive in doing what the narcissist wants, and there is no harm in that.

Tip #4: Use your intuition about when something feels off

It is okay to listen to your gut when something does not feel right. With narcissists, you can become so used to putting the needs of the narcissist above your own (and seeing the narcissist as superior to you) that you naturally do what they wish even if something feels wrong. Once you start to listen to your intuition, you will begin to see the ways in which the narcissist works for themselves and not for you.

Tip #5: Start doubting the negative language of the narcissist

The narcissist used demeaning and untrue language to make you feel less than them. They do this because they have a personality disorder that requires them to see themselves as superior to you. The negative language serves to reinforce this dynamic of them being the "great" one and you, "worthless." You may come to accept this dynamic subconsciously, but now is the time to throw a wrench in the works. What the narcissist says to you about yourself is not true, so learn to start doubting their words.

Tip #6: Start questioning the inflated self-image of the narcissist

The personality disorder of the narcissist involves the construction of an image that may bear no resemblance to reality. In other words, narcissists frequently see themselves as more talented and more capable than they actually are. You are the tool they use to reinforce this image, so in addition to questioning their belittling language, you should also start questioning the things they say that place them above you. These things probably aren't true either.

Tip #7: Start spending more time around other people

The narcissist seeks to isolate you, so they can keep you in the codependent relationship. This is an aspect of narcissistic relationships that some people do not understand. As cruel as the narcissist can be, they actually need you around because you serve an important function for them. So, what's the best way to disrupt their narcissistic pattern?

Start spending more time around other people. This will give you a sense of your self-worth and help break the control the narcissist has over you.

Tip #8: Regard your needs as important, too

Your needs are just as important as those of your partner. You are not a robot who just needs a little bit of oil and some fuel, and that's it. You have physical and emotional needs, too, and your relationship should be meeting those needs. You are one of two people in a relationship, not the unfortunate person in chattel slavery or indentured servitude. Start regarding your own needs as important as those of your partner's and not secondary.

Tip #9: Do not let yourself be talked into things you do not want to do

The narcissist is oh, so suave. He or she knows just what to say to reel you back in. Just when you thought you were angry and were ready to confront them about something, the next thing you know, you are laughing, kissing, and making plans for tomorrow. What happened? Well, what happened was that the narcissist turned on their manipulative charm, and you fell right into the trap. You will need to learn how not to be talked into things. Pay attention to what the narcissist says they want you to do, and if it is not something you want too, then don't let them talk you into it.

Tip #10: Spend less time around the narcissist, or leave the relationship completely

Sometimes, the simplest course is the most effective. Breaking free from the narcissist may mean that you spend less time around them. In fact, it might just be time to walk away. Although this may seem to some like the only course of action to take with narcissistic people, sometimes it is not easy to leave someone you love, especially if you have spent a long time with the narcissist. However, you may need to put some serious thought into leaving the relationship, especially if it is an emotionally abusive one.

Chapter 19
Practicing Daily Affirmation

You must understand your experience the best you can and accept your part in the matter. Once you have done that, there is no point in begrudging yourself for the part you played. The only productive next step is to move forward.

The way to move forward is with daily activities and daily affirmations that will undo your negative sense of self. The following reading is not comprehensive. It is only the start. You can find more affirmation readily available on the world wide web. The point of this part is to get you warmed up to the idea of receiving daily affirmation from yourself and acknowledging its importance to your recovery.

You Are Good Enough

Everyone is their own starting block. If you're reading this, you like to turn to resources that help you tease out the intellectual secrets to life. You must believe that there is hope for you to feel better than you do right now. This is true.

Yet, this does not mean you are not already good enough. The fact that you are reading this means you are better off than a lot of people who do not believe in their own ability to improve and recover. You obviously believe in yourself and want to feel better. That means you are good enough already.

Tell yourself that you are good enough where you are to take the next step. You are always good enough where you are to take the next step. There is never a point where thinking you are too far behind will lead you to the next step.

You must understand that the only way to take the next step is to know that you are exactly where you need to be to take it. And, the truth is, you are. You are where you need to be to take the next step, always. That's the beauty of steps. You are right where you need to be to move forward. It's only a matter of doing so.

You Deserve to be Happy

Tell yourself that you deserve to be happy. Why? Well, for one thing, if you were in a relationship with a narcissist, you might not have thought about your own happiness for quite some time. You were more concerned with someone else's happiness, weren't you? You put the happiness of others before yourself. Good for you. You're not a narcissist. BUT you deserve to be happy, too.

Start thinking of yourself as someone other than yourself. Think about how you would go about making yourself happy if you were someone else. Then, go about doing it. Think about what makes you happy. Tell yourself that there is nothing wrong with making yourself happy in the same way you make others happy.

I trust that you don't go around making others happy by hurting other people. The same rule applies to making yourself happy. If you can make yourself happy without hurting anyone else or creating negative consequences for yourself, there is no reason not make yourself happy in the healthy, appropriate way in which you have been making others happy for a long time. It's your turn. You deserve it.

It is Okay to Feel Shame Sometimes

Unlike the narcissist you were with, you know the feeling of shame pretty well. You know it because the narcissist you were with made you take on their shame. This was very generous of you. This shows that you have empathic abilities the narcissist does not possess. Yet, you took on a lot of shame that wasn't your own. This is not the appropriate way to feel shame. Your shame should be your own.

The narcissist saw you as an extension of his or herself because that's how narcissists approach the world and they passed their shame onto you because they could not feel it in themselves. It is time for you to reclaim your shame. Feel shame; that's fine.

Don't overcompensate by taking up the narcissists tricks to avoid shame. Make your shame your own. If you feel ashamed of something, ask yourself if the shame you feel is your own or someone else's. If it's your own, good! Feel it, and then move on. That's all there is to it. Be proud of the fact that you can feel for yourself again, regardless of whether or not the feelings are good or bad.

Check in to see what you're feeling. Don't avoid all bad feelings. You won't recover in avoidance. Do give yourself credit for feeling your own feelings, though! This is the pathway to your recovery. Feel things but ask yourself whose feelings you're feeling. It may have been a while since you were sure you were feeling for yourself and not for them. Be proud of yourself for every feeling that you know to be your very own!

Love Yourself for Loving Others (Even Narcissists)

Do not get down on yourself for loving someone who turned out not to be the person you thought they were. Do not get down on yourself for loving anyone. Be proud of yourself for having the capacity to love.

Be proud of yourself for putting so much of yourself into that relationship. Be proud of it, accept the reality of it, and then move forward and look for something new.

The appropriate response to loving someone that turned out to be bad for you is to try to find someone to love that will be good for you. Now, you have a better idea of what is bad for you. That's a very good thing. Love yourself for loving them, even if you decided in the end that it was too draining.

Enjoy the fact that you are full of so much love that you could be with a narcissist but then take steps to be with someone who can give that kind of love back to you. It is so good that you are capable of loving. You deserve to be loved back by someone else who is just as capable.

Be Proud of What You Learned from Your Experience

There is nothing helpful about thinking negatively about yourself because of this experience. You will only gain from positive thinking about your experience. Think about what you have learned. Be glad for that. Imagine you had not learned it yet and you were about to fall victim to the love of a narcissist next week! It is good that you learned what you learned.

Tell yourself this every time you start to think negatively about what you went through. Tell yourself that regardless of the pain caused by the narcissist, it is good that you learned enough to avoid suffering the same pain again in the future.

Be Proud of Who You Have Become

Think about who you were when you met the narcissist you were in a relationship with. Are you different now? How so? Instead of beating up on who you were, be proud of you are now! Think about who you have become in addition to what you have learned. Tell yourself that you are glad you have changed in the ways that you are in fact glad that you have changed. Find ways to compliment yourself for being exactly who you are today.

Stop coming up with reasons to blame yourself for actions taken in the past. Start coming up with reasons to compliment yourself for the actions you are taking right now.

Be Proud of Your Boundaries

You have boundaries. They were violated for a long time. Think positively about the boundaries you set for yourself. Acknowledge them every day. Own them. The narcissist you were in a relationship probably neither respected nor understood your boundaries. This might mean you need to protect your boundaries with extra force right now. Maintain them as needed but the most important thing is that you respect yourself for having them.

You simply need to respect yourself for having them the way the narcissist did not respect you for having them. You should also understand them better than the narcissist could. Maintaining them may or may not always be a possibility. Boundaries are violated all the time. People do not always understand the boundaries of others. You cannot control these facts.

You can, however, control the way you feel about your own boundaries. The worst offense of the narcissist you were in a relationship was not violating your boundaries. They didn't know any better because they didn't understand your boundaries. The worst offense by them is that they made you feel negatively about your boundaries. What you can control at this point is how you feel about your boundaries. You can decide which of your boundaries is worth maintaining and, in general, whether or not you feel good or bad about your boundaries. The point is to make up your own mind about the value of your boundaries. You no longer have to evaluate their merit by the standards of a narcissist who cares little for them.

Be Proud of Your Ability to Feel Shame

There has been some intentional repetition on this particular aspect of recovery because it is more difficult than affirming oneself, but the two things are not necessarily desperate. You can allow yourself to feel shame and accept the reality of your situation without thinking negatively about yourself or your situation. Once you have allowed yourself to feel shame, be proud of yourself for feeling it. Then, allow yourself to move on from it and respond appropriately.

Take the next step to feel better within the scope of reality. The narcissist you were with liked to take the easy way out of shame by imagining a new narrative. Love the narrative you know to be true even if it involves feelings like shame. Shame is part of the human narrative, but you can feel good about yourself for being able to feel shame and overcome it without escaping from it through fantasy and denial.

Be Proud of Your Desire to Know Reality Over Fantasy

Seeking fact over fiction separates you from the narcissist you were with. You've endured the emotional abuse of their manipulation of your reality. Now, you get to choose reality and think positively about it. The narcissist you were with made you feel your fact seeking was negative (when the narcissist turned out to be wrong about something), but now you get to return to your love of reality. Be proud of the things they made you feel bad about.

Love the fact that you love the facts. Recall all of the times that they had an outburst because you simply corrected them with the facts. Appreciate the fact that you did that. It is not a bad thing that you want to know the truth. It is unfortunate that the narcissist you were with could not handle the truth when it was against them.

Be Proud of Who You Are

This is pretty close to being proud of who you have become, but as you get closer to changing your negative thinking to positive thinking you should be thinking less about the past.

The difference between being proud of who you have become and what you learned from the experience and simply being proud of who you are in the absence of having to look back upon the relationship you had with a narcissist.

Eventually, you will want your daily affirmations to move completely away from having anything to do with the relationship you were previously in. It is important that you start by directly affirming yourself in the ways the narcissist denied you, but the next step will be affirming yourself without even thinking about the narcissist you were in a relationship with.

Chapter 20
CBT, Yoga, Self Hypnosis, and EDMR For Narcissistic Abuse Recovery

Cognitive Behavioral Therapy for Narcissistic Abuse Recovery

Over the years, CBT has proven to be pretty effective for helping trauma victims. The aim is to bring improvement by systematically changing the pattern of thoughts, feelings, and behaviors. CBT revolves around the fact that the three are connected and an improvement in one can trigger an improvement in another.

With CBT, patients can learn:

- Helpful coping mechanism with stress and how to handle trauma

- To interact with their trauma in a new way that does not trigger a negative reaction

- How to develop an objective understanding of their relationship with the narcissist. This can help revive their sense of control and also develop healthy coping skills.

The therapist helps victims to reconsider their thinking patterns to detect unhelpful patterns. These are patterns that might have occurred due to continuous exposure to the abuse. For instance, victims might think they are bad people for attracting a narcissist. Unknown to them, narcissists do not take an interest in weak or insignificant people. They prefer to go for strong and powerful people, people that can soothe their ego, people that they can exploit. Victims, however, does not know this.

With this therapy, victims can begin to see themselves in a new light. The aim of this is to help bring the traumatic experience to a new light. This way, they get a new perspective about the incidence as well as their ability to cope.

Many times, victims of narcissistic abuse avoid and suppress memories of the abuse or anything that triggers their time with the abuser. CBT can help reduce this by assisting patients in healthily embracing the occurrence. This involves a planned and controlled exposure in a way and pace that the patient is comfortable with. This helps bring control and confidence, rather than resorting to avoidance behaviors.

Yoga for Narcissistic Abuse Healing

Over the years, yoga has grown in popularity as a means to connect the mind and body. A mindfulness exercise that uses various breathing and relaxation techniques combined with physical movement; yoga has proven to help treat mental health issues as well as trauma from past occurrences.

Continuous exposure to stress and potentially life-threatening situations reconfigures the body into fight-or-flight mode. Even though this is the bodies way of saving us from danger, excessive stress raises the cortisol level which we know triggers mental health problems.

Yoga has a soothing effect on all levels of stress in the body. It can calm the body and transport it to a state of tranquility. A common factor with victims of trauma is the inability to adequately process and heal from their experiences. This is why traditional therapy alone is not very helpful.

Introducing Trauma-Sensitive Yoga

Trauma-based yoga stands out in that it directs the body awareness of the present moment to take care of any symptoms arising from abuse or trauma. This emphasizes the internal experiences of the victim intending to get in touch with their body at the present moment.

The helpful feelings could be anything from how the cloth hugs their body to the movement of air through their lungs. The aim is imbibing how they can take action about their experience. With this yoga practice, students can learn to get in touch with their body and mind.

Yoga, in combination with psychotherapy, can help reduce the aftereffects of trauma and narcissistic abuse while reinforcing positive emotions such as acceptance, compassion, and empowerment.

Self-Hypnosis for Healing

Hypnosis is a way of reaching for memories that are out of consciousness. Self-hypnosis tries to provide positive restructuring to dissociated traumatic memories. In other words, with self-hypnosis, victims can face their fears and the traumatic time spent with the narcissist. Rather than being hindered by the memory, patients embrace these memories in a new dimension. This is done with the aim of re-moralizing memories like self-protection and at times, pity for the abuser.

With this, victims can access the traumatic memory in a controlled way while viewing them from a broader perspective. There are many forms of self-hypnosis, but we will run through the eye fixation self-hypnosis method. Be sure you are in a quiet room without distractions.

Get into a Comfortable Position

Make sure you are well seated without crossing your legs and feet. Your clothes should not be too tight, and we suggest no shoes.

Look Up and Take a Deep Breath

Pick a point on the ceiling and direct your gaze, without straining your neck. With your gaze fixed in this position, breathing in deeply, pause, and exhale. Repeat this for sometimes and relax. Close your eyes and feel every tension in your body drift out.

Allow Your Body to Relax

Let go of all tension in your body and sit in a relaxed position. Countdown from five and let your body relax deeper with every count. Direct your attention to your breath, note the rising and falling of your chest. The key is not in trying to relax your body. Rather, it is in allowing your body to relax.

Bring Back Your Consciousness

Count from one to five and open your eyes. Open your eyes at the count of five, stretch your arms and legs

You might not feel as calm as you would want. The key is growing with practice as there is a learning curve.

Using EMDR to Heal Narcissistic Abuse

With Eye Movement Desensitization and Reprocessing (EMDR), victims can unlock past hurtful experiences. It is not a traditional therapy and works best over a few sessions. It has healing effects on the thoughts, feelings, and memories of the past, and in this case, narcissistic abuse.

EMDR is an intense form of therapy in that it seeks to unlock painful memories, associated with the abuser. It is a psychotherapy that helps people heal and recover from the emotional distress of a traumatic event.

Humans generally have either the left or right brain hemisphere dominant. However, EMDR with bilateral stimulation helps activate both sides. Since they both work at the same speed and capacity, there is rapid processing. This reconfiguration makes it easy to identify trauma by highlighting the affected area. Rather than the trauma being stuck, it gets processed in a healthy manner.

Many victims of abuse, specifically narcissistic abuse, react to the memory of the trauma like it just happened. Part of the aim of EMDR is to curtail this. For instance, you remember how your abusive partner yells at you. Nothing you did was good enough which made you sad and angry. The difference now is that even though you remember every detail; you do not feel the anger.

This is what EMDR is trying to achieve. It helps reprocess the memory such that even if you remember how hurtful the experience of the abuse was, you no longer feel the physical manifestation. Not only do you have a renewed approach to these memories, but you also have to let go of the hatred and resentment you had for your partner.

Chapter 21
Is There A Light At The End Of The Tunnel For Narcissists? Solutions?

To understand whether there is hope for a narcissist then one should understand what a narcissist is. That brings to the question at hand of who or what a narcissist is? A narcissistic person is a person who is self-centered and thinks of himself or herself to be more important compared to others. Narcissism is a personality disorder and is more profound in men than women. Some of its symptoms include the excessive need for admiration, inability to handle criticism and not considering someone's feelings and ideas.

Is It Possible To Cure 100% A Narcissist?

Narcissism is a psychological disorder in man thus can be controlled and curbed to the core. This may be through some psychological means this must be through a psychiatrist obviously. Talk therapy is always the best in this case but it may not always work. This therapy helps to deal with interpersonal relationship and their functioning. To deal hand in hand with a narcissistic person then one has to get into his personal life and also specific relationships. A narcissistic person's treatment is slow and always ongoing until they get better.

Since we have established that narcissistic people go through a slow and long-time treatment to attain a possible normal life. The possibility of full recovery is fully dependent on the cooperation of the patient. So, what are some ways in which one can treat a narcissistic person?

First one must learn on their communication with others. These skills help to improve communication if they are used properly. These skills are listening, verbal and non-verbal skills. When these skills are not natured communication becomes very difficult. So, these skills are working progress every day to day life. Understanding these skills and their purpose is the most important starting point of working towards them. Researching also helps one to develop one's communication skills. This research should be about communication and how to go about it at large. Every person has a duty to learn these skills to keep the conversation between him or her with other people going.

Learning how to listen is another way since a narcissist does not consider one's opinion hence should learn listening skills. Listening skills are important in every social institution that is: school, work or even marriage. They help one person to understand others. They are also key to solving problems since listening to someone's grievances is what makes someone to work on them. Communication is mainly about listening to others and also responding to them. When someone rarely listens then most of the problems between him or her and others are rarely solved. Good listening skills earn someone other people's trust and affection. Listening skills are also essential when someone is given a high-ranking job. This is because he or she has to listen to the grievances of other workers.

Another way is by telling others like your friends and family for them to be able to help you monitor and keep a check on your progress. The goals or intentions are to be followed for one to progress to perfection. Friends and even family will help one by giving advice and also helping one to keep on going to whatever one wants. This also enables one to rely on friends and family on anything that they may need to keep them going on the journey. Family and friends are the best way to keep things going for everyone.

Also, accepting and maintaining the relationships that a person has already. So how does one do that? This is done by listening more to the people around you like family, friends and even workmates. Maintain relationships is easy but a narcissist has trouble doing that hence he or she should focus on making the people around him or her are happy and satisfied by their relationship with him or her. This is done by a lot of talk therapy and a lot of discussion on how their behavior gets in their relationships in all social institutions.

Another way is by tolerating criticisms and failures. One is supposed to know how to accept that people will always have a say on things. The first and most important thing for one to achieve happiness is by one ignore what others think of him or her. When someone listens to others opinion it gets to their head. When this happens then one wants to change themselves so badly. This then becomes their life mission and it is pretty much low. One then should not listen to others' opinion especially if they are rumors. One need to focus on what he or she thinks of himself or herself at all times for maximum or full happiness.

Spending time with nature. Nature is what is provided outside by the mother earth. These may include; trees, rivers, springs, waterfalls too. Nature has a calming effect especially if one sits and stares while enjoying or taking in the sceneries. They are supposed to be very calming and exciting to watch for all its viewers. It should be a great distraction for all those who take time and view all nature's interests. When they busily give someone the distraction they so needed it helps one forget his or her troubles even if it is only for some amount of time.

Another way of finding inner peace is by doing good deeds. What good deeds then? This is helping someone who needs your help or helping someone who is a great deal of trouble. Have you ever noticed when one does bad things on to others then they keep replaying it in their heads? This then causes one to stress out every time one does a bad deed to another person. So an easy fix for this deeming problem is by being good to everyone regardless of how much of a jerk that person was or is to you. How does this help a narcissistic person? This helps him or her to maintain his or her relationships with other people at all times by having the charm of being a good and kind person. A narcissistic person may need to learn how to be a kind and caring person.

Meditation is another way. Meditation is the increase of attention, but one focuses on nothing. The difference between meditation and mindfulness is that meditation attention is increased by focusing on nothing while in mindfulness attention is increased by focusing on the task. These two things are so similar but different. They both inter-relate with each other. Meditation easily clears one's head and allows them to live freely without being chained to their thoughts. Meditation is an easy way to unburden oneself from are the thoughts and misery that comes with it in life. It is important to meditate in order to clear one's mind.

Knowing one's self-worth and another self-worth is important. Self-worth is a trait in which one sees themselves and also opinions to be very important. It keeps one confident and elevated in true self form. When one feels self-worthy then they are able to do anything they wish to accomplish. One must learn to appreciate oneself and to also feel good about oneself too. It is important for one to feel like that so that they can live a life of great bliss and also peace. Self-worth makes one very happy and proud person in life. Self-worth of oneself and others should teach the narcissistic person the value of each and every person. It shows how one can be important in life and in all social institutions. This is an important virtue to teach the people suffering from this disorder. It is a way to tame their self-centeredness.

Another way is by doing what you love and loving what you do in return. These refer to hobbies, work, education, friends and even one's family. In basic terms, one is supposed to pick up what he or she loves and throw out what makes him or her unhappy. This also means that one is supposed to choose the things he or she loves. Like picking a marriage partner one loves or a career one loves or a job one loves and enjoys to actually do. It is important to remember that loving something means that you will cherish it and keep it. When one loves someone or something they become less self-centered. They then allow things or people in their lives.

Lastly, people of this disorder should be taught how to express gratitude to others is a very important step to achieving happiness. When one thanks others for their contribution to one's life then they feel appreciated. With that maybe done unto you since you appreciated others in their works for you on your behalf or stead. Feeling or being appreciated makes one's self-worth to increase or expand. This then improves on one's confidence thus brings out a very creative side of the person at hand. A confident person is not afraid of doing anything they want to achieve. This then helps them achieve all their goals which makes them happy.

Chapter 22
Quick Fixes To Get Through The Day

When you are in an abusive situation, every single day can seem like it lasts forever. You stress about every word you say and every move you make. And that can last several months, or even years, after the relationship has ended.

The most effective way to distance yourself from your abuser is emotionally. There is a tactic called "Grey Rock," and it is one that you will need a lot of work practicing as it will not be something you are comfortable doing. The Grey Rock method is a way to deter toxic individuals from escalating any situation. The point of it is for you to come off as boring, unengaged, and as uninteresting as possible. This will take some practice; however, keep trying to be the most boring person on the planet so they leave you alone. The items to focus on are as follows: Answer in a neutral tone, talk about boring topics, give generic responses, do not make eye contact, and give very short answers. This will deter any and all interaction with you by the toxic people in your life.

Some other quick-fix ideas that you could try including:

• Call them out on their behavior

• Find a way to increase your self-esteem

• Practice your assertiveness

• Analyze your codependency

• Do not try to fix your abuser

Calling them out is more so just letting them know that you are aware of what they are doing. For example, if you notice that you are experiencing gaslighting, inform the abuser that you are completely aware of that tactic.

You cannot fix your abuser; it is a waste of time to even try, and it will do more harm to your emotional status than it would do it any good. Take a deeper look at whether or not your codependency is hindering you from avoiding toxic individuals. At this time, it is important for you to shift the focus to yourself and your own care in order to become a strong, independent person.

How To Build A Support System

Most likely, since you have been isolated for some time, you have lost touch with most of your family and friends. Your main goal at this point is to reconnect with those you were once close too.

When the wife sat in her chair, after she caught her husband having an affair, she realized that she had lost touch with just about everyone and that put her in a very vulnerable state. She had a few goals in mind, but they were dependent upon those she was reconnecting with.

Goal 1 - She began by reconnecting with her immediate family first. There was a lot of conflict because of the anxious state of mind and pitting of her against her family by her husband, so the first goal was to apologize and reconnect with immediate family members.

Goal 2 - The next goal was to reconnect with old friends, friends that she knew for many years, but lost touch with due to the severity of the isolation.

Goal 3 - Maintain the relationships that are being rebuilt.

Goal 4 - Find others who have been in abusive situations and connect with them on how they have handled everything. Also, learn how to trust family and friends again to discuss issues with them as well. The local domestic violence center can assist with finding groups and may also offer counseling to victims.

Once the goals are met, there should be a decent support system put in place for the victim of abuse. You need people who will openly listen to you, allow you to vent, but also give you the advice you need to hear in order to move past the trauma. If you start by focusing on your family and friends who you were close too and branch out from there, you will find that there will be plenty of people who will be happy to help you, even if it is just to offer a listening ear.

If you are unable to figure out where to start building your support system, reach out to your local domestic violence center, and they will be able to either counsel you or give you a schedule for group therapy sessions that they may have available. There are plenty of options available to you through your local domestic violence center, and they will be able to offer you free counseling to help you leave your abuser as well as when you have left your abuser. They also offer group counseling where the victims will share about their experiences with abuse, how they are coping with it, the steps they took to remove themselves, or the steps they are taking to get out. They may also have art groups where you will be able to meet other survivors of domestic violence, you can draw pictures about your future goals, and you can talk openly about struggles that you have been through. If you are worried about childcare, most shelters also offer childcare so the mother can attend a therapy session.

Finding something that works for you will be the key to your future; many enjoy group settings, but others may need one-on-one sessions. Think about your comfort level, what you want to accomplish, and what you want for your future, then contact your local center to discuss options.

If you do feel stuck in your situation—and there are plenty of us out there who do—the domestic violence center can also meet with you to discuss ways to increase your self-esteem, ways to make sure you are safe and secure in your home, as well as ways to safely plan an exit from an abusive relationship.

People in your support system can be the following:

- Close family members
- Friends

- Therapists and counselors

- Domestic violence center advocates

- Survivors of abusive relationships

Take a look at who you used to be close with, who you are close to currently as well as who you would like to speak to in the future. A combination of any of those options would make a successful support system.

Relaxation Techniques To Get Through The Day

If you are able to relax at any time during the day, that will be a huge relief for you. If the abuser is always around you, they may not want you to relax, so try to find time or a place where you can go to focus on yourself for a few minutes. A few ways that can help you relax throughout the day include:

1. Take a shower or bath,

2. Go for a walk,

3. Practice deep breathing techniques,

4. Yoga and meditation,

5. Aromatherapy,

6. Listen to music, and

7. Talk to a friend or family member.

Take a shower or bath. If you need alone time and need to relax during the day, if you are able to jump in the shower or tub, it is a great way to unwind. This will also give you some time to be alone and clear your mind.

Go for a walk. A brisk walk is also a way to relax and clear your mind, it will allow you to focus on your surroundings as opposed to what you have going on in your situation.

Practice deep breathing techniques. Deep breathing exercises are very helpful and can be done almost anywhere. If you are unable to step away, focus on breathing in through your nose and out through your mouth. Make sure you are focusing on breathing slowly.

Yoga and meditation. Yoga and meditation are ways to re-center your mind and body. If you cannot find the time during the day, try to focus on one pose that may be easy to do anywhere. Or if you have to sit in a chair, focus on your body touching the chair as opposed to what is going on around you.

Aromatherapy. Aromatherapy can have a calming sensation for many people. Lavender and chamomile are the two most popular aromas that people use to relax.

Listen to music. Music is a great way to drown out everything around you and focus on the song and words that you are hearing.

Talk to a friend or family member. When in doubt, talk it out. It sounds cheesy, but it does work. You will feel better when you are able to let it you with a confidant.

If you can find ways to unwind and destress throughout the day as well as refocus away from any issues you are facing, you will find that the days will become less dreary. If nothing seems to work for you, head to your doctor or speak to your therapist. It may be recommended that you are put on a low dose of anxiety medication to help you take the edge off and get through each day peacefully.

It is extremely important to focus on making time for yourself each and every day so you can avoid falling into a deep depression. In abusive relationships, even after they end, it is all too easy to become depressed.

If you want to coach ice hockey, go to the casino, get your hair colored at a salon or bungee jump off of a building, you can do so. You are a human being, and you can do whatever it is that makes you happy. Do not let anyone make you feel guilty because you are doing something that you love or want to do. Abusers will try to twist things in a million different directions, so you are deterred from going anywhere; stand your ground and maintain your freedom.

Chapter 23
The Victim Cycle

Each person who ends up with an abusive narcissist is going to deal with these steps as well. However, in addition to the abuse cycle, there is also going to be a victim cycle.

The victim cycle is going to be the one that starts because of the abuse, and it is the goal of the abuser for the victim to become trapped in that cycle as well. The narcissist wants the victim to go back and forth between these two stages, the cognitive dissonance and the co-dependency. This is the perfect scenario when it comes to the narcissist and their point of view because it leaves the victim weak and always coming back for more.

Cognitive dissonance

The first stage that we want to look at when it comes to the victim cycle is cognitive dissonance. This is going to be any and all of the mental pain and discomfort that the victim is going to experience when a new contradictory belief will clash with their original belief, by some new evidence. After you are under a belief for some time and then that belief is gradually taken away, it can be painful. Not only is this going to end up being pretty painful, but many victims find that this is overwhelming, and it can be hard for them to accept the new reality, even though they are seeing it. It becomes even harder when there is a lot of emotion that is attached to that original belief that they had.

In a heathy scenario, this kind of process is going to be a great way for us to learn more about ourselves and to help us correct bad behaviors and beliefs. But when the scenario is unhealthy, such as with abuse from a narcissist, this process can be really painful for a victim. It can cause so much pain that the victim is going to refuse to change their beliefs, despite seeing new evidence that contradicts what they believe.

Even though the logic should serve in showing that the original emotions and beliefs that the victim had to the narcissist was wrong, it is hard to override the original beliefs. The victim is going to struggle because of the pain and the tragedy that are going to come from that experience. For many, it is basically too much to bear letting go of the narcissist, even if they are dangerous to be around, and so, the victim is just going to stay.

The battle with this cognitive dissonance within the mind of the victim is going to go on for months, and sometimes even for years. As the abuse grows from the narcissist, and they see their mask start to slip little by little, this just gives the victim more and more evidence against their original believes. Even though it is going to be really hard for the victim to do, they need to be able to detach themselves, somehow, from those original beliefs about the narcissist so that they can free themselves a little bit.

Co-dependency

After the narcissist has slipped up and shown the victim a glimpse of their true self behind the mask, the victim is going to start fighting in order to make it back to that first phase, the idealize phase. When this happens, the narcissist is going to do everything that they can to use this to their advantage so that the victim becomes co-dependent on the narcissist.

This is going to be a part of the greater cycle because the victim is going to begin to seek validation and affection from the narcissist, and they will go through the other phases of the abuse cycle. The narcissist are the ones who are in control here and they are able to pressure their victims into feeling like they are incapable of doing anything and that the narcissist is needed. The abuser wants to fee like they are the lifeline to the victim, and that the victim is not able to do anything without them.

When the victim is in an abusive relationship and they have entered into the state of co-dependency, it can sometimes feel like they are unable to step away on their own, without the narcissist. This means that the narcissist is winning, and they have their victim right where they would like them at this point. The victim is going to feel incomplete, and the narcissist is going to insert themselves here as the missing piece.

The co-dependency is going to be the result of abuse as a psychological disorder that is going to be pushed further down each time that the victim goes through the cycle. Unraveling this issue and realizing what you are capable of, and that the victim is able to have their independence, no matter how mad it makes the abuser, can be challenging, and it often takes some time. Remember that you are fighting against someone with a lot of skills in manipulation, against someone who is trying to keep their own needs met, and who doesn't have a care in the world about how this affects other people. It is a hard battle to win.

So, how do you know whether you are co-dependent in your relationship? You can tell this by looking to see where your own personal needs are going to lie in the relationship. If you feel that you need the other person to make you feel happy, if you feel like you are absolutely nothing without them, or you are not able to make decisions in your life, no matter how big or small without their approval and validation, then it is likely that you are co-dependent.

Feeling guilty

A state that a lot of victims of this kind of abuse are going to deal with is a sense of guilt. When the narcissist is able to manipulate their target, it is going to lead that target to always think that they are the ones who are wrong. The narcissist is able to take some of the evidence that you gave them from spending time together and go through your past in order to validate why you may be the attacker, while they are the victim, even though the roles are actually reversed. The victim is going to be manipulated into feeling guilty for harming the narcissist, even though it is really the narcissist who is the one to blame here. It is possible that this will go so far (and at some point, it will get here), that the victim is going to take the responsibility for the relationship failing, and they will feel like they were at fault for falling out with the narcissist, while the narcissist gets to sit there and feel like they are the superior one.

The reality of this is that the victim actually didn't do anything wrong. They never earned the abuse, even if they had made a mistake, and often the only mistake they did was falling in love with the narcissist and not being able to leave. This is another symptom of the narcissist successfully being able to abuse and manipulate the victim into seeing the narcissist as the one who needs attention and care.

When the narcissist does this, they do not have to come out and admit that they were wrong in any case, and they don't have any reason to apologize. Why would they be to blame or why would they try to apologize if it was the victim who did everything wrong. The victim, on the other and, is going to feel like they need to do far more than what is actually reasonable in order to get forgiven by the narcissist. The narcissist will get a lot of attention in the meantime as the victim tries to make up for their wrongs, and this makes them happy.

Fear of being alone

Many of those who are victims to narcissistic abuse are going to have a fear of being alone. Since they have been told over and over again that they are worthless and that no one would ever love them, it is easy to see why the victim is going to fear loneliness. Of course, the narcissist is going to work hard in order to make the victim feel as lonely as possible. The two ways that they are able to do this include

In the bigger picture, it is common that the victim is going to be afraid of being left on their own and never being able to find the right love again. Because they worry that no one else is every going to love them again it is likely that the victim is going to cling to the narcissist and to that relationship in order to avoid a lonely fate. The narcissist is doing this on purpose, because they know that if the victim feels this way, they are less likely to leave and go somewhere else for love.

When it comes to the day to day life, it is possible that this fear is going to change to just being scared of loneliness, even for a short amount of time. The victim may feel that when they are alone, they could be neglected and abandoned. They may start to sit alone with their thoughts and notice how toxic the relationship really is, and then they will feel some pain for these thoughts.

Even worse, there are times when the victim is going to sit on their own with their thoughts and have a fear that their partner, the narcissist, is cheating on them or spending time with one of the people they have brought in for the purpose of triangulation, rather than doing what they told the victim they were doing. This fear and this lack of trust is something that the narcissist worked hard to put there, but which is going to torture the victim.

Fear of the truth

While it is possible that some of the victims who are dealing with narcissism are going to be hungry for the truth, it is possible that some of these victims are going to have a fear of knowing it. This is going to tie in with the battle that we talked about with cognitive dissonance earlier on. Even when the facts are clearly presented to us, it is sometimes easier for the victim to ignore it and cling to their original beliefs. Learning the truth, and accepting them, can affirm a lot of painful information to the victim, and this can make them feel shame, heartbreak, and embarrassment.

For example, learning the truth here is going to confirm that the victim has allowed someone to come in and abuse them, exploit them, and lie to them, for however line they were in that relationship. Perhaps learning the truth confirms that the narcissist has been cheating on them for some period of time.

Now matter what the truth revels, it is painful to admit. It is even more painful and shameful to think that the victim allowed this to happen to themselves. The thing to remember here is that the only reason that the victim allowed this to happen in the first place is because the narcissist was so good at what they were doing, the victim had no idea of what was going on.

Chapter 24
Why Recovering Can Be Hard?

Recovery is not easy, but when you look into the intricacies, it should actually be easy for you to walk away from someone who had abused you emotionally, physically and psychologically. The person didn't respect you for who you are and therefore it should be easier to never turn back, but why doesn't it happen that way? Why is it harder to come out of an abusive relationship than it is to overcome a divorce or break-up? It is because you don't have the Casablanca effect. If you remember the scene in the movie Casablanca where the lead actress is asked to get on to the plane with her husband and she asks the lead actor – "What about us?" He says, "We'll always have Paris." The lead character is able to understand why she left him earlier and comes to terms with reality, yet he feels the pain of being abandoned but, he could regain the love and experience by revisiting their Paris moments.

Now, this is never going to happen with a narcissist because there was really no "We'll always have Paris" moment. Why is it so? Everything you ever believed in him, every connection, every promise, every moment spent together doesn't make any sense because you doubt if there was any reality in it. It is completely burned to ashes. When you walk away from a narcissist, you are not recovering from a failed relationship, but you are recuperating from warfare.

Love Patterns of a Narcissist

Did he ever love me – at least once? Will he be thinking about me now? Will he realize his mistake and come back to me? It is natural for you to ask these questions a hundred times in your head if you were truly and deeply in love with a narcissist. After all that he had done to you, you still have a faint hope somewhere in the corner of your heart that he will return to you.

It is not difficult to understand the patterns of these men and women, as they are quite predictable. Their relationship behavior is almost the same with all the people they have been with. It is easy for you to predict his behavior with you if you know their love pattern with their ex. This will give you more clarity as you begin to realize how they actually saw you, and if the relationship really meant anything at all to them.

Certain love patterns exhibited by the narcissist are so common that you can distinguish it by giving them names:

- The Hater

- The Romantic

- The Recycler

- The White Knight

- The Big Game Hunter

- The Novelty Seeker

Unfortunately, most women want their narcissist ex-partner if he displayed 'The Romantic' pattern often. Why is the loss so distressing for women that they long for him to come back? The fact is whatever your ex-partner had told you when he was in love with you was what he actually meant to say. Yes, you read it right. You are not crazy. He really meant it when he said he loved you.

He was in love with you – yes, he was in love with his idea of a perfect partner that he saw in you – a romantic fantasy of both as an ideal couple. The narcissist romantic loves the idea of a perfect romance – mesmerizing candlelight dinner, long car rides with you by his side, moonlight walks by the beach, perfect weekend getaways to a cozy cabin in the middle of the woods and the amazing passionate slow sex. His ultimate goal is to make every single moment romantic and intimate. He makes you feel that you are the most beautiful and loveable woman he has ever come across in his life. He makes it sound perfect by introducing you to his friends and social network as for how blessed he is to have you.

And then when you are so sure that you finally found your ideal partner and think about taking a step ahead, he backs off. You get to hear excuses on why he couldn't call you or meet you. You are confused and have no idea what is happening. Ignoring your emotions and feelings is the best weapon a narcissist will use to hurt you. If you were in a relationship with a normal guy, all these romantic moments and the passionate sex might have built a greater trust and led to genuine intimacy. In the case of narcissistic men, the moment they realize that the fantasy is becoming a reality, they go mute and start getting frustrated.

Some just walk away without paying heed to your emotions, while others torment you by breaking your confidence.

I Miss Him Badly – What Do I Do Now?

It is depressing to go through a break-up with a narcissist since it will test your patience and strength. You get thwarted by your own boundaries and all you feel is exhaustion – at all levels. You are unable to look at this as a relationship that is over as you yearn for the person to come back. Your grief and anger come bubbling at full speed, taking you away from reality. You expect things that are far from reality. You are overcome with mixed emotions where, at one point you want him, and the very next moment you never ever want to see his face in your life again. The feelings begin to get intense as it stretches from disgust to desire. Why does this happen?

The bond you had with the narcissist is traumatic, that you fail to see the difference between reality and fantasy. It is referred to as the trauma bond. The characteristic feature of trauma bond is you revisit your past so often that it takes up almost 100% of your brain energy resulting in controlling your nervous system not just for months, but for years together.

Your mind keeps churning all the memories that there comes a point where you fail to differentiate between the present and the past. Instead of being in the present, you get obsessed thinking if your ex-partner really cared for you, and if he is thinking about you at this very moment. You don't stop here - you go through a list of what-ifs in your head so that you soon lose yourself in the past.

Remember, a trauma bond is not love, but a form of emotional addiction. It takes you through a series of roller coaster rides that gives you the feeling of getting high. Confused? Often, the narcissistic partner abuses his victim with distressing arguments, spiteful insults and intensifies the fear of abandoning. Soon enough, this is followed by an extreme act of intimacy, soulful apologies and awesome sex.

So, when you think about the fights and arguments you had, instead of the agonizing pain, you end up thinking about the good moments that followed. You think he really cares or cared, but the truth is that was not love. Look at it from a third person's perspective; the moments you thought were breath-taking were actually not real. The feelings you are going through now – self-doubt, unworthiness, fear, etc. were created by the narcissist.

Strategies to Move On

How do you do work on yourself and move on?

- Let truth be your best friend
- Practice mindfulness
- Heal yourself by reconnecting

Let Truth be Your Best Friend

Stop fantasizing and get back to reality. Make truth your best friend. Use a voice-recording app and record all the things you are able to recollect about your ex-partner (the abuses he hurled on you, the ways he tried to hurt you, etc.). You can also write them down in a diary. Go through the list and summarize it into a list of points. Put it up in a place where you can see it regularly. Your last exercise will be to boil all the points down to a one-liner. For example, "The person is a leech who sucks my soul every time he enters my life, and I am in no mood to encourage him any further." Every time you are overcome by his thoughts, repeat the phrase to yourself.

Practice Mindfulness

You can break his spell and recuperate your attention by practicing mindfulness. It is impossible to wipe your thoughts completely but, instead, you can watch it from a neutral safe point. You don't allow the thoughts to consume you but become an observer of your own mind who isn't judgmental.

Write down the list of things you would like to do for yourself – one or two things for a day. These can be simple things that help to nourish your soul and live in the moment. For instance, it can be walking your dog, preparing a meal, enjoying a spa massage, watching your favorite movie or doing yoga.

But remember, whatever you do, do it with all your heart. If your mind replays thoughts of your ex-partner, just repeat the one-liner you had written.

Heal Yourself by Reconnecting

After all that you had to go through, it is quite natural to want to stay away from people. You will need time for yourself – for your mind, soul and body. You need to click the reset button and start afresh. Trusting yourself will become difficult; forget trusting other people but tell yourself that it is okay, and it is quite normal to go through such experiences.

Tell yourself that your intelligence has nothing to do with being victimized by a narcissist abuser. It was just bad luck that you fell into the hands of the perpetrator. The moment you realize this, you will find it easy to connect to yourself. All you wanted was to be loved, but things didn't go the way you expected it to. Give yourself some time to forget and forgive yourself. Take a deep breath. Get to the analyzing mode. Be calm and begin to find an answer to the whys. This is needed so that you don't fall into the trap of a narcissist again. If you need to do this, you need to get connected to your inner self. Get out of the toxic environment and find a breathing place. Spend more time with animals and nature. Go dining with your trusted friends. Analyzing and over-thinking are completely two different things. You will be able to analyze only when your mind is clear and free of unwanted thoughts. Over-thinking is dangerous – you end up thinking about stuff that might not even happen. Go out for a movie, chat with your best friend, or plan a trip – anything that can stop you from over-thinking. Try new things – learn to play the piano, hug a tree, if that's what works for you, watch a squirrel eating his food, etc. Come out of your comfort zone and break all the barriers. Be open to new relationships – don't raise a wall and shun away people. Go with the flow and give time for new relationships to grow on their own. Don't go investing too much of yourself emotionally. This is not just for partners, but for friends too.

Self-healing is important for you to overcome your emotional wounds, especially after narcissistic abuse. The wound can become fresh and raw if left unattended, which can make you a victim of another narcissistic relationship or rekindle your old abusive relationship. Invest your energy and time in learning about yourself and your behavioral patterns. Understand the characteristics of your narcissistic partner and use the experiences as a tool to prevent yourself from getting abused again.

Learn to say NO when you are not interested and practice it more fiercely. Connect with your deeper self. Now that you are holding the keys of your life, don't hand it over to anyone else again – however genuine the person is.

Chapter 25
Recovering from the Narcissistic Parent and Partner

Recovering from the Narcissistic Parent

It's a parent's job to give their child their needs like:

- Consistent Attachment;

- Mirroring;

- Attunement; and

- Positive Regard for their primary caregivers.

Without these, it is difficult or impossible for the child to develop a stable and cohesive sense of self that is positive and leads them to develop secure and rational attachment.

Parents with a narcissistic personality disorder cannot provide for these needs and so, instead of helping their children to thrive, they interfere with their emotional and mental development. As a result of these traits, the child can develop a number of problems, including:

- Absorbing a twisted and dysfunctional notion of love;

- Learning that their only worth is in what they do rather than who they are;

- Failing to understand or set healthy and appropriate boundaries;

- Being romantically drawn to narcissists;

- Seeking validation from caretaking and people-pleasing;

- Neglecting or even nullifying their own needs and wants;

- Mistrusting the validity of their own thoughts and feelings;

- Despairing that their needs will ever be met;

- Struggling with self-esteem and their ability to maintain a stable sense of self;

- Coping through addiction and self-destructive behaviors; and

- Following in their parent's footsteps by also becoming narcissists.

In addition to the general steps listed above, healing from the effects of narcissistic parenting involves building up your personhood as well as ensuring that you don't follow in the footsteps of your parents, stopping the cycle of abuse with you.

- Confront Your Abuse and the Effect It's Had on You. You were abused as a child and an adolescent, and that abuse very likely continued into adulthood. In fact, it may still be going on. You need to own it and you need to take a hard look at yourself and your relationships with others. Do your best to fill in the gaps in your memory to get as complete a picture as possible, but don't be surprised if you cannot get honest answers from your immediate family as they may still be under the influence of, or have their own trauma from, the narcissist. This may involve confronting your abuser, which you have every right to do. Bear in mind, however, that such a confrontation may leave you far more frustrated than vindicated because the narcissist is unlikely to accept that they have done anything wrong. To help you get an idea about the damage done, ask yourself the following questions:

- Are you repeating the patterns you saw as a child?
- Are your notions of a healthy relationship similar to the notions of those around you?
- Do you attract, or are you attracted to, narcissists?
- Do you find yourself covering for your own inadequacies with grandiosity?
- Is your sense of entitlement greater than it should be?

- Are you an inveterate people pleaser?
- Have you diminished or nullified your own wants and needs?
- Work Through Your Missing Milestones. The children of malignant narcissists are often not allowed to develop into fully functional individuals with their own identities, tastes, needs, and desires, often missing out on many developmental milestones along the way. As you confront your abuse, examine what you missed out on and with the help of your therapist and work through what's missing.

Healing from a Narcissistic Relationship

This is much closer to healing from a stereotypical abuse situation, so the steps will be a little more straightforward. They all deal, on some level, with safety, responsibility, and release, and the key is to be consistent in how you carry them out.

- Remove them from your life. That's right have no contact with your narcissistic abuser. The rationale is simple: If they don't have access to you, they cannot harm you, and since they don't need to be right in front of you to inflict damage, that means no physical contact, no phone contact, no email, no text, no social media stalking, no messengers, no smoke signals, no skywriting, no carrier pigeons, no nothing. If you share a child together, you will have to have the court establish strict protocols that reduce contact to the absolute minimum, preferably with someone from the court acting as a go-between.

- Why so strict? Because the kind of abuse committed by a malignant narcissist tends to be more mental and emotional than physical, even though that happens as well. As long as you are still being preyed upon by the narcissist, you will not be able to begin healing. Any contact, or any more than is absolutely needed under a parenting plan, can seriously undermine your recovery. Beyond that, however, there is a real similarity to kicking an addiction. There is a bond between you and the narcissist that developed through the trauma they inflicted on you. This connection is hard to break, and if you give in to the withdrawal, like a smoker or an alcoholic, you could wind up right back where you started, which would make any future recovery that much more difficult. The only real cure, then, is to go cold turkey.

- Own It. You need to own your pain. You might be asking why, since you were the victim of something that was done to you, do you have any responsibility for it? Because laying the blame at the feet of your narcissist for all the abuse, pain, and suffering they rained down upon you for the duration of your relationship is, in reality, only half the battle. You can blame them, hold them responsible, demonize them, and try to force them to heal you, and at the end of the day, none of that will make you well. In fact, if you go that route, you will retard or even completely stop, your recovery.

- To recover, you need to leave your abuser in the dust and take personal responsibility for your own healing. You are the only one who can confront it, you are the only one who can do the work necessary to get rid of it. Your therapist will be able to assist you on this journey, to give you the tools you need to regain your power, but in the end, it will be you standing against your demons.

- Let It Go. If you want to lay all that to rest, you will have to let go of the trauma, but how? After all, you have incorporated so much of it into your persona, and it has been there for so long that it feels a part of you. Some will tell you to talk it out, others will say that ridding yourself of it requires a radical shift in the way you see things, a mental and emotional growth spurt to make you over into someone new, someone who has evolved past the old patterns of abuse and can finally shed them. In other words, it means finding your authentic self.

- There was an authentic you before the narcissistic abuse, but that version was buried under layers of abuse and pain. Recall that early version of yourself, dig them out, clean them off, and invite them back. Rediscover the things that went into creating that version and embrace them with a new, more experienced spirit. Accept what had happened to you, learn from it and add those lessons into the arsenal of the authentic you. Your therapist will help you through this process and when you are done, you will be stronger and wiser, ready to once again take on the world.

- Ensure it Never Happens Again. The things that made you susceptible can still linger, and people will occasionally fall into the same traps even though they know what to look for.

- The problem is one of balance. You have to balance the need to keep your guard up with your equally important need to live a life, develop relationships, see the good in people once again. These things are not necessarily mutually exclusive, but they can and sometimes do fall out of balance and that leaves you vulnerable.

It's not foolproof and you have to accept that there is always going to be some risk. That's just probability. The key is to do the inner work that will recover and strengthen your authentic self, to learn the signs and do your best to spot them, and to develop the self-love you deserve to be able to act when you do.

Chapter 26
Gaslighting

Gaslighting refers to a type of psychological abuse used by narcissists to infuse in their victim's an extreme sense of confusion and anxiety to the extent that they no longer trust their perception, memory, and judgment.

Gaslighting techniques used by narcissists are similar to those used in interrogation, torture, and brainwashing. These techniques have been predominately used in psychological warfare by law enforcement agents, intelligence operatives and other clandestine agencies for decades.

It is intended to systematically target the victim's mental stability, self-esteem, and self-confidence so that they are no longer capable of functioning independently.

When a victim is being gaslighted, the abuser systematically withholds factual information and replaces it with false and misleading information.

Gaslighting is a subtle manipulative tactic, thus, it is difficult to detect, and with time it completely undermines the psychological stability of the victim. It is a very dangerous form of abuse because it results in some major damages (victims lose the sense of their self). When they've been gaslighted over some time, they lose trust in their judgments, and even degenerate to the point of questioning the very essence of life. They don't only second guess themselves, they also become highly insecure when it comes to decision making.

Furthermore, the victims fall into depression and are withdrawn, making them dependent on their abuser for their sense of purpose and reality. Gaslighting takes away the victim's identity and purpose and replaces it with self-doubt and emptiness.

Gaslighting in Relationships

The people that use gaslighting the most are abusive partners in relationships. A narcissist in an abusive relationship will try to convince the whole world that it is love and intimacy, but the truth is, it's nothing but manipulation. Gaslighting in itself negates genuine love and affection.

Narcissistic relationships follow a pattern, and when it gets to the stage where the abuser begins to show his true colors, he will begin to dish out some gaslighting techniques. For example, let's say you guys had plans to go out over the weekend, but when you called to remind him a few days later, he backtracks, saying something like "I can't remember having such discussion with you, are you sure I'm the one?"

It looks like an innocent response, and at this stage, you won't read too much meaning into it because you're still in a state of bewilderment and perhaps it might look like you even remembered wrong or you misheard.

When something like this happens in isolation, it might not be gaslighting; it could be that you truly forgot or there was a mix up somewhere. However, when it becomes a consistent occurrence, then questions need to be asked.

As time goes on, you'll start to notice more inconsistencies between the things they say at different times. For example, you may suggest the idea of visiting a spa for massage because they've said in the past that they love going to the spa. But this time, they might say something like; "I hate going to the spa. Let's go to the beach instead."

Now, it gets a little bit confusing and you begin to doubt yourself; was it someone else that said they like a spa? Or has the story changed? If you're convinced that they made the earlier statement and are now saying something else, this might be their way of suppressing and manipulating you into believing that you're not attentive enough.

When the gaslighting moves up to the next level, the abuser will now begin to insinuate that you are the one that is now backtracking for your earlier assertions. The manner at which the narcissistic abuser would present the matter depends on the stage of the relationship, but this is an example of such conversation;

Victim: I just informed my mum and dad that you're attending our Christmas dinner. They can't wait to see you.

Abuser: Hey, but we agreed that we need to take some time before we involve family, didn't we?

Victim: But we had this discussion some days ago and you said you were more than happy to attend

Abuser: I would love to meet your parents, but I told you that we should give it some time. You even agreed. However, the deed is done, and I won't disappoint your parents, so I'll attend.

If you study the conversation above, you'll realize that, by agreeing to attend, the abuser is acting to be nice and accommodating. As the gaslighting progress, the abuser will continue to explore new methods, and from dishing out lies as a response to your statements and questions, they'll begin to start conversations with lies concerning things that were done in the past. For example, they'll say something like;" You told me I can borrow your credit card, right? Well, I have just bought some items online. I'll make a refund next week.

This time, they cooked up a conversation that shows that you permitted them to spend your money. However, you're convinced that you never did, and they know you didn't, but if you decide to talk about it, they'll concoct more lies, and ultimately cloud your mind with some believable stories. Again, this is just a way of proliferating your self-doubt, in other for them to assume control over your possessions, feelings, and life.

Finally, when the abuser starts to notice that your resolve is getting weaker and weaker, they'll substitute covert deceptions for straightforward lies. Thus, they will lie about things they/you did or didn't do, and things they/you said or didn't say. For example, let's say you started heating water for coffee and had to leave to take care of something else. But when you returned, you saw that they've used the water for the same purpose. They'll insist; "I heated the water a few minutes ago, but if you say you did, then it's obvious you're imagining things. Perhaps you want coffee because you saw me having it."

This might sound funny, but it works like magic and as time goes on, the victim's self-belief is depleted gradually, until the final stage where it dies.

Gaslighting at Work

Gaslighting knows no bounds, and you can find yourself being gaslighted at your workplace, either by your boss or a co-worker. Most times, the perpetrators use it as a tactic to gain or maintain power, but that's not to say that it can't drive the victim crazy.

For example, you were given a particular task, and you'd put in so much of your time to get it done, however, when you approached your boss, his response was; "but I told you to X instead, why did you waste your time doing this?

Considering the amount of time, you've put into the work and the fact that you're sure you did what you were asked to do, you might get a little agitated and even try to be on the defensive. However, you might get a familiar response like; "Are you sure you're not over-reacting?

Or let's say your boss promised to give you a raise if certain conditions are met, and as a dedicated worker, you've even exceeded those conditions. However, when you brought the matter to his notice, he responded thus; "I did not promise to give you a raise. I only said I might consider giving you a raise if you met certain conditions, and so far, you've not met any."

Let's say you have a co-worker that is jostling to get promoted ahead of you and decides to gaslight you. From time to time, you'll realize that they'll say certain things specifically meant to undermine your self-confidence, and even make you doubt your worthiness, as per career path and grow. For example; "Someone said that director isn't impressed with the report you submitted. Trouble is looming." "Weren't you selected to join the team? Well, I figure you're not good enough to join." "Why are you mad at me? I only said you need to improve your skills." Gaslighting from abusers isn't limited to words only; sometimes it comes with actions too. For example, you've spent most of your day working on a file on your computer. So, you decided to step out to get some air, but when you get back, you realize that the project has been mildly edited – however, you're confused because you're not sure whether you did it yourself.

Gaslighting is all about perpetuating confusion, as well as insecurities in the lives of the victims, and there is a plethora of ways to go about it.

Gaslighting in the Family

As explained earlier, gaslighting is a term used to describe a poisonous form of psychological abuse. The methods used in gaslighting are subtle, thus victims are always unaware, and the end product is the distortion of their self-belief and self-confidence. Gaslighting is used by people of different origin, race, religious and even ethnic affiliations. It is also used by friends, lovers, co-workers, bosses, students and family members.

In the family settings, some narcissistic parents use gaslighting techniques to manipulate their children and this goes a long way in destroying their mental development. When children are manipulated into believing that their instincts are wrong all the time, they learn not to trust themselves. Narcissistic parents groom their children to lack any sort of belief in their sense of reality.

It is sad when you think of the thousands of children that depend on their narcissistic parents for teachings and support, only to poisoned and hindered in the development of their self and their reality.

When these children grow up to be adults, they become what is referred to as a "victim narcissist," who are known to have difficulties in decision making and lack every sense of self-belief.

They constantly seek validation and approval from other people because their instincts and individual voice were silenced many years ago.

Whenever they think about themselves, rather than having feelings of internal strength and a strong sense of self, it always results in internal criticism and belittlement. The internal criticism results from the abuse they suffered in the hands of their narcissistic parent as kids. Even when they have regular thoughts, they might see it as "being stupid," or in regard to being upset, sad or angry, they may believe they are undeserving of these emotions or even "overreacting."

They have been gaslighted to believe that they're always wrong, thus they doubt their very own perception of the world. The saddest part of the situation is that they see nothing wrong in the way they hand things and their entire thought process. They cannot differentiate their genuine thoughts from their projected ways of reasoning.

Chapter 27
Healthy Narcissism and Pathological Narcissism

Each and every person has a little narcissism in them, and that is perfectly normal. Not having any narcissism at all is actually unhealthy and is related to codependency. But you have to know how much narcissism good and how much is bad. Your psychological well-being will depend on the level of narcissism you possess and act on. There has to be balance and a limit on any individual's narcissistic tendencies. If there is too little narcissism, this person might have very little confidence and low self-esteem. This will cause the person to be fearful and feel inferior to others. If there is too much narcissism in one person, they will have a huge ego and stand out at the cost of social cohesion.

Balance with a healthy amount of narcissism will help the individual to be confident, but not so much so that they fail to identify their own shortcomings and failures. They will recognize and accept their negative aspects along with their positive ones.

Healthy narcissism will allow a sense of self-awareness where they will have realistic expectations from themselves in relation to their abilities. They will not be threatened by being different from others and will not keep comparing themselves. They accept that they are different and have their own strengths to play on. They use their healthy level of narcissism to make sure their needs and desires are met. However, they do not do this at the cost of someone else's well-being by disrespecting or disregarding them. This is healthy narcissism that people can channel by maintaining a balance in their give and take with others.

This will allow them to have relationships that are mutually satisfying and not selfish or abusive. The person will be respectful towards others and allow them to have their needs met even while they fulfill their own needs. It does not have to be at the cost of someone else's needs. A healthy narcissist will treat others as their equal and not have any need to show they are superior. This will apply in any relationship they have at home or at work. You will see how contrasting pathological or unhealthy narcissism is with this healthy narcissism.

A healthy narcissist is confident and practices self-love. They tend to be independent and are comfortable in their own uniqueness. Such people have the ability to make decisions in the right way. They are empathetic towards others and share emotions. A healthy level of narcissism will benefit the person as it allows them to grow well and develop healthy relationships with others over the years.

When there is too much narcissism in an individual, it will manifest as a personality disorder. This NPD prevents such people from having any true bonds in their relationships with others. They always need to prove themselves to be superior and try to outdo others. This is usually done in an underhanded or negative way. They have an excessive need to assert superiority with every person in their life. A pathological narcissist will hurt others with their actions. Their idea of self-love goes beyond what is healthy since they always put themselves first. Other people do not matter to a pathological narcissist. They see others just as an extension of the self and focus primarily on themselves.

When a pathological narcissist is close to someone, they expect that person to be perfect constantly. They fail to sympathize or empathize with others. Healthy narcissism will allow people to share emotions, but pathological narcissism does not allow his. They tend to prey on people who are not very narcissistic and have low levels of self-esteem. These are the people who end up being victims of narcissistic abuse. Such codependent individuals fail to protect themselves from pathological narcissists. The narcissists' needs are placed above their own, and they like to accommodate them at the cost of their own well-being.

A pathological narcissist will lie and manipulate others and especially un-narcissistic people. They do not understand or accept that it is okay for others to have different views or opinions. They take it personally and are angered by it. They like people who agree with their personal views and opinions. Someone who actively tries to change narcissists' opinions is seen negatively. A healthy narcissist will be accepting of such differences in opinions.

So how do you know when you go from healthy narcissism to pathological narcissism? Well, if you notice that you or any other narcissist is abusive towards others and belittles them often, it is unhealthy. This kind of person is at the point where they don't think or care about others. They stop at nothing to get what they want and to protect their own ego. It is not of consequence to them if others are harmed due to their words or actions. They fail to maintain healthy relationships with anyone.

Most connections will only be at a surface level, and deep level connections are rarely if ever present. They are scared of being vulnerable to someone if they allow them too close. They are unwilling to face any criticisms that may come their way if they truly reveal themselves. Such people take it personally when they are criticized and often seek revenge for the slightest things that would not matter to others. They don't have real self-esteem and are just self-absorbed. This is why they have to need to exercise control constantly. They lash out at anyone who tries to take this control away from them. A pathological narcissist is very set in his ways and is inherently unwilling to change.

Chapter 28
The Light at the End of the Tunnel

One of the hardest things for us to deal with when we are healing from this kind of relationship is the idea that in the eyes of a narcissist, we are only a tool to use or a kind of obstacle that needs to be destroyed. We may have been head over heels in love with that person and would have done anything for them. But in their eyes, we were just a tool to use for their own gratification, and nothing more. Everything else that happens in between with them is going to be their charm or their harm in manipulation to keep us caught in their game. And this game included you giving it all, and then taking it all, with no reciprocity.

Before we are able to move on, we have to be able to get this. We have to understand that the narcissist doesn't really care about us or our feelings. The narcissist is only going to care about how they can use the target as a tool for their own needs. When the narcissist finds that their target no longer wants to be used, or that they have no further use for the target, then the relationship is over without a backward glance. We have to understand this before we are able to move away from the narcissist and make our life so much better.

This is something important to remember because it is going to be true no matter what kind of relationship you have with a narcissist. All of the people the narcissist deals with are going to be objectified and categorized to use for a special purpose. And when they have met with their purpose, they are going to get rid of that person. Everyone with a narcissist is going to have some kind of expiration date. We are either an obstacle or a tool, and we are not worth more or less than this.

One of the biggest defining characteristics that come with a narcissistic personality disorder is that they do not have a good perception of reality. The narcissist is going to see the world through a lens of being self-absorbed and assuming that others around them are just tools that they are allowed to use in any manner that they want. Others are just there to serve and support them, and they don't understand why someone would not want to do this.

Those who are attracted back to the narcissist are going to be dazzled by the fake self-confidence, the shocking persistence, and the charming personality that come with this. The non-narcissist is often going to change themselves and turn their lives upside down in order to follow what the narcissist wants. They will change their own values, morals, standards, and even their own personal beliefs in order to stay with the narcissist and keep peace in that relationship.

The sad thing here is that this is where the seeds of dysfunction are going to be laid. The non-narcissist is going to be unaware that the desire to maintain peace is slowly going to corrode their own identity. As the person becomes relationally entangled with the narcissist, the distorted view that they get from the narcissist is going to start their reality. The more that the target is going to follow the rules that they get from the narcissist, the less clearly they are going to be able to see what is right and wrong, and what is the true reality that they should follow.

Once the target realizes what is going on, and they start to make the changes that are necessary in order to leave the relationship and regain their own identity, the stages of recovery are going to be slow, but in the end, it is well worth the effort. It is going to be really hard to work with, and sometimes it may feel like you are not making any progress at all. But rest assured that you are going to be improving and that one day, you will reach the light at the end of the tunnel and see the results that you want.

When it comes to the foundation of your recovery, you want to keep at it and see that it is going to get better. There are a few steps that you need to go through, and if you are able to do this, you will find that you will get to the end of things and regain your life without needing to have that narcissist back in your life.

One of the models that are used to help with recovery, and which can help the path to recovery look a bit brighter and easier, includes Erik Erikson's Eight Stages of Psychosocial Development. This is the foundation for many forms of recovery because it is going to highlight how important it is to start in the beginning, and then try to rework pretty much all of the aspects of the target's life after they have been in a relationship for some time with the narcissist. A summary of the eight steps that you should follow based on this model will include:

Mistrust vs. trust

When the target is in a narcissistic relationship, the target is conditioned in some manner so that they are going to just trust the narcissist, and no one else, in all their ways of emoting, behaving, and thinking. If there are any different opinions in the target during that relationship, then this is going to be shot down and torn into shreds so that the target let's go of it and goes back to just following the narcissist.

The recovery of the target has to begin with learning that they can trust someone other than the narcissist when it comes to life. They need to be able to trust the perception of others, especially those who actually understand what is going on in the relationship. Taking the control of the perceptions of the relationship away from the narcissist can be one of the ways to start seeing what is going on, can help them to see that things are not going the way that they should, and can help the target learn to mistrust the narcissist (as they should), and start trusting others in their lives.

Doubt and shame vs. autonomy

The next thing that we are going to take a look at is the idea of doubt and shame versus autonomy. The narcissist is going to love using shame and doubt in order to subdue their partners. This is often because at the heart of the narcissist is going to be someone who has been struggling with their own shame for a long period of time. Reversing this pattern means that the target has to make some of their own decisions, even if these decisions are not that great in the beginning. The natural discovery process of learning from their mistakes and being able to suffer from the consequences that come with this, rather than just blindly following what the narcissist says, is going to develop some autonomy.

Guilt vs. initiative

When we look at the ego from the narcissist, it is rarely going to appreciate it when their target starts to take some initiative in that relationship. Instead, the narcissist is going to try and keep this to a minimum and will be mean and belittle the other person until they give in and give up their own ideas and thoughts.

Instead of letting this initiative happen, the narcissist is going to accuse the target of trying to take over or control them. If there is even one tiny hint of truth to these statements, the target is going to feel a lot of guilt in the process. Gaining back the initiative is going to involve trying new things, engaging with different people, exploring creativity, and then rediscovering some of your favorite pastimes again. This is hard to do sometimes, but it is going to be critical to helping you see the results that you want with getting out of that relationship.

Industry vs. inferiority

During the relationship, the target is going to quickly start to see that what they do, what they think, and the emotions that they have will always end up inferior to what the narcissist says, thinks, or feels. The narcissist has to be superior all of the time, and this ego is not going to tolerate a partner that is equal or better than them. Reversing this pattern and allowing yourself to do better than the narcissist would allow before, is going to require a new form of thinking. The target may have to spend some time to remind themselves that they are good enough and that they do good work.

Role confusion vs. identity

Narcissists don't like anyone having any kind of identity around them. They will take their target and strip them down to having no personality at all. When you have a personality, you have opinions, thoughts, and feelings that are not going to be consistent with what a narcissus wants. The target is just there to do what the narcissist wants, and so the narcissist is going to take it away. If you would like to recover from the narcissist, you will need to remember your own identity and remember that you are able to make your own decisions and be any person you want.

Isolation vs. intimacy

The narcissist worked hard to take away the friends and other connections that the target has during the relationship. The more isolated the target could be, the more power the narcissist was able to have. When the relationship is over, it is important to start adding in some more intimate relationships instead. You have to first accept and know who you are, which is why the step above is important as well.

But once you drop the narcissist out of your life, and focus on developing your own identity, you will then be able to make new friends and relationships that can help you to reach the level of intimacy that you so desire.

Stagnation vs. generativity

The nature of self-absorption that comes with the narcissist is going to prevent them from giving anything back to others, which is unless there is some type of outward benefit to the narcissist. Even when they are in a close relationship, the narcissist is going to expect a lot more than they would even dream of giving back. Once the target is out of the relationship, you may find that the target is going to find pleasure when it is time to guide others out of the narcissistic fog and into the new reality.

Despair vs. wisdom

A person who decides that they need to stay in the narcissistic relationship for the long term is going to develop a sense that, even though this is bad and not much fun, it is as good as it can get for them. They will put aside their own desires and wants in order to fulfill the wishes of the narcissist. Their sacrifice is going to be a type of silent surrender that few are going to appreciate and realize. However, when the target can get out of that relationship, the wisdom that the target was able to gain from that ordeal is going to be so staggering. Not only have they been able to see some relief from the fog lifting, but the perception they gain is going to be crystal clear.

There are a lot of things to appreciate and look forward to when you are trying to break free from a narcissist and live the life that you would like. Once you get through this recovery, things are going to be so much better, and you will finally reclaim the life that you want.

Conclusion

Narcissistic persons do not do what they do out of thoughtful motivation. The danger, harm, and disturbance that they force unto others is an unavoidable product of their condition. Narcissism, as a personality disorder, should be handled from a medical perspective instead of misguided condemnation and finger-pointing against ailing individuals.

Everybody bears the responsibility of understanding the causes of narcissism and be sufficiently armed to deal with any undesirable impacts that arise from that condition. Of magnanimous significance is the ability to effectively cope with people who exhibit narcissistic behaviors.

Furthermore, the ability to understand that narcissistic behavior is a potent force in souring relationships. It is important in figuring out proper ways of mitigating effects of the behavior. That is, in more comprehensible terms, essential in providing a conducive environment for narcissists as well as devising ways of coping in cases of narcissistic abuse.

By understanding the different forms of narcissistic abuse, it becomes highly manageable to come up with person-specific approaches towards handling persons who exhibit given narcissistic traits. Besides, it is evident that though treatment for narcissism exists, there is no medication for the cure of narcissistic personality disorder. But, medications are necessary for the cure of other mental and physical health condition that may exist alongside the narcissistic personality disorder.

In a nutshell, narcissistic abuses are diverse. One narcissist may not necessarily be as abusive as another. This is plainly true considering the fact that narcissism manifests itself in a number of variations. It is, therefore, wise to have the moral power to handle each case of narcissistic abuse in a unique way that guarantees desirable outcomes in the form of sustainable stable relationships in spite of the challenges that arise from destructive narcissistic behavior.

The next step is to practice regaining control and recover from your relationship with someone with Narcissistic Personality Disorder. Having read the first couple of parts of this book, you have equipped yourself with knowledge of the basics of Narcissistic abuse, its causes, its signs and symptoms, as well as its different forms.

Gaining this understanding has hopefully shown you that the abuse you have experienced was not your fault. The following parts should have provided some much-needed affirmation of what you have been through and why you deserve the time to recover. Further, you should understand that you are not alone.

Anyone who has had a relationship with someone with Narcissistic Personality Disorder has experienced narcissistic abuse in some capacity. None of these explanations condone the abuse but hopefully, it has helped you understand that what you can do to start you're the journey towards your recovery and better yourself.

Your path to recovery involves understanding, acknowledgment, affirmation, and perhaps therapy. This book should have explained the benefits therapy will have on your recovery process in addition to giving you plenty of tools to work with on your own. Good luck on your way to recovery. Remember that regaining control must be practiced until it becomes natural once again.

PART II

Introduction

With increasing awareness of mental illnesses, there is now a pattern noticed among the people who toss it around and diagnose others and sometimes themselves, with mental disorders for minor inconveniences. Temporary sadness is often labeled with depression or nervous breakdown. Similarly, temporary annoyance with things out of order is labeled with Obsessive Compulsive Disorder or OCD. And similarly, self-love or self-acceptance is also sometimes confused with narcissism. People are self-obsessed and sometimes vain in the 21st century, especially when the world is driven by celebrity culture. Yet as every other disorder misunderstood, self-love is not the only criteria to fit in the puzzle of what narcissism is. Other aspects of the disorder often goes unnoticed. This part is dedicated to understanding exactly that. They are in love with a theatrical and idealized image of themselves that they keep in their mind.

What goes behind the head of a narcissist?

One might ask why they would keep such fantasies of unlimited and uncontained importance or power. Why is there an undying need for special treatment and admiration for every little task they do or things they say? How can someone love an image of themselves so much so that they delude themselves into thinking that they are that person? When probed deep inside their minds, one would find hidden among that layer of perfection. These insecurities are dark and ugly enough to cringe at the exposure to light. From the inside, narcissism is tainted with unstable self-esteem that many people consider to be high. People often mistake it to be high due to genuine reasons because many psychologists have conducted studies where they measured the narcissist's self-esteem and found them to score high in that area. But of course, judging the book by its cover might have been a good business idea, but it doesn't work well in science. After digging deep into this matter of interest, psychologists found out that people have two kinds of high self-esteem: secure and fragile. Narcissist belongs in the latter category with their high self-esteem relying on self-deception and external locus of validation. Consider a parasite that latches onto their host and sucks admiration, attention, and validation out of them as their nutrition. That picture you just made in your mind; it is exactly how it's like to deal with them. Because the stage they build to perform their act on is built on the foundations of dysfunctional behaviors and attitudes.

The volatility and impulsivity in their behavior that ultimately leads to the arrogant, self-centered thought process and behavior often result in a display of zero empathy, which subsequently develops into an unstable interpersonal relationship. The prevalence of this disorder in the communities is rare, ranging from 0 – 6.2 percent. But around 50 – 75 percent of people clinically diagnosed with NPD are males. No wonder most women are victims at the hands of these men. A mesh of demanding, patronizing, selfish, shameless, manipulative, cocky, and unsympathetic entity garbed in human flesh is always ready to hunt for a host.

They also tend to turn a blind eye to their behavior, because let's face it, the grandiosity they worked so hard to build up cannot tumble down at the slightest criticism, can it? But what if it's causing them problems and people are still standing up to them for their unjust erratic behavior? They hold up a Captain America shield and deflect the avalanche of criticisms to others; mostly to those who are standing up to them in the first place. In their world, the walls they built can never be penetrated. So the disagreements or criticisms are a pathetic attempt at personal attacks by others. Because in the end, the mirror on the wall tells them that they are perfect, they are beautiful, and far beyond the intellectual and emotional capacity of normal people. Mostly, if someone, unfortunately, falls in love with such a person, they tend to play along with their set of demands, just so they don't get to be the victim of their rage and coldness. It's easier that way. Easier, unless their poison becomes toxic.

Many faces of Narcissism

So, to get a better understanding of why they are the way they are, let's delve deeper into the many faces of narcissism. Narcissism is a spectrum, so there is no one way that it will manifest itself. But the two most important distinctions of narcissism are grandiose and vulnerable narcissism, which sometimes blends as well.

Grandiose narcissism is often considered a subclinical or mild form of narcissism because it fuses positive and negative aspects of the spectrum. The positive being high self-esteem, extraversion, charm, self-efficacy, self-confidence, and assertiveness. But obviously, it is not without its negative manifestations that might come in the form of exploitation, entitlement, disagreeableness, dominance, antagonism, and aggressiveness. For them, they have to maintain that grandiose by various means; if someone happens to befriend or court them, they often become the main object to that display.

The reality is often different than what a grandiose narcissist would consider it to be since it does not always share the grandiose version of him. To counter that, from the very start, they would start training their mind to live in a fantasy world where their supremacy, in everything, be it looks, be it intelligence, or be it social acceptability, is greater than anyone else's around them. This training doesn't happen in one day if that is what you are thinking. You can't just one day begin to think that your supremacy exceeds everyone else's, and it happens the next day. Nope. These fantasies are made to strive to become a version that is greater than everyone else, and to achieve that, a narcissist would not have any hurdle to come in between. If it does so, it is met with extreme rage and defensiveness, with their charm dwindling into rubbles.

Even in this realm of grandiose narcissism, two dimensions define whether or not they would be tolerable to their partner or general society. This concept is called in scientific terms Narcissistic Admiration and Rivalry Concept (NARC). If I am to break it down and take the former chunk of the name called Narcissistic Admiration, it epitomizes the assertiveness and self-improving aspects of a narcissistic individual. In this case, the narcissist would have fantasies of grandiose, an aspiration for uniqueness, and self-enhancing behaviors that will exude a positive aura of admiration for that person, ultimately boosting his narcissistic ego.

The second dimension, however, is where the trouble begins, for that is composed of narcissistic rivalry that is constantly striving for antagonism and defense. A person overpowered with narcissistic rivalry would exude a red or black, (whatever you consider dangerous) aura, for these people will strive for supremacy via a display of hostility, and negative speech, which might belittle others in most cases. The devaluation of others gives them a sense of value. Or, if I may add, their eyes light up with excitement when they see the light diminishing from someone else's eyes. The result is nasty, more often than not, resulting in fights and conflicts.

So at one point where the first dimension leads a narcissist to have their goals directed on self-stimulation, hedonism, self-direction, achievements for which they will manifest lower distrust, forgiveness, gratitude, benign envy, grandiosity and high self-esteem; the second dimension, on the other hand, will direct the narcissist to a strive of power achieved by malicious envy, low self-esteem, the nonexistent concept of forgiveness, low trust, zero empathy, loneliness, impulsivity, and low self-esteem.

Honestly, if the second dimension weren't so cruel, it would almost be an object of pity. And since it is a spectrum, the lines to these distinctions are often blurred with time.

For example, a grandiose narcissist at the first meeting would be considered popular, competent, alluring, and charming. This deception often deludes people into thinking they are of the amiable kind, and that is how people fall into the trap of getting into a close relationship with them. But once the acquaintance turns into friendship and more, that's when the veil of charm starts to fall down and out comes the narcissistic rivalry dimension of that person, revealing their exploitative tendencies that will be festooned with the traits I mentioned above. It's mostly a deception of the evilest kind since people almost always do not see them for the person they are because they never cross that door from acquaintance to a close relationship. They don't know what happens once the veil uncovers the actual person. They haven't seen them. And those who have had good reason to be distant to them. Now that I have broken down the grandiose narcissism, I will uncover a darker form of the disorder that is a more clinically expressed form, called vulnerable narcissism. The roots of this form extend down to pathological fragility and distress. A vulnerable narcissist has interconnected negativity both in themselves and in their relationship with others as well. If you cross path with this kind, you will first notice anxiety, depression, mistrust, borderline traits, neuroticism, and negative temperaments in general. If you are wondering how along with all these features, do they manage to love themselves, then you might come to the right conclusion after a while, which is, they do not. And that is exactly why they feed importance and affirmation from others to absorb that nutrition of validation by others. Their minds are conflicted with poor well-being, lower self-esteem, passive aggression, hostility, avoidance, defensiveness, anxiety, incompetence, vulnerability to depression, shyness, introversion, and hypersensitivity. This emptiness that they are confronted with in their minds makes them feel entitled (rather falsely) of the validation nutrition.

Now an interesting difference between the two forms exists. A vulnerable narcissist, with all its miserably vulnerability, cannot be expected to have extraversion in their trait list. It takes guts, after all. So, you cannot be deceived into thinking otherwise, as is the case with grandiose narcissism that will first lure you into their trap, only to suck the life out of you. A vulnerable narcissist, on the other hand, would trap you in his lure by the constant display of neuroticism garbed in the self-proclaimed love/care. This self-proclaimed love and care of this narcissist often delude you into feeling guilty for any negative feelings you might develop for him. And do note that he will be perfect in his attempt at making you feel that way only, for they do have secret grandiosity harboring inside them. Where one form plays the guilt card, the extrovert grandiose would belittle you and play with your self-esteem. Both forms of abuse are profound. Moving forward, there is also a stark difference in happiness levels among these two narcissists. The vulnerable narcissist is often more clinically pronounced for the very same reason that they are challenged with more comorbidities. Anxiety and depression often come side by side, along with an extreme need to feel validated and entitled. Whereas a grandiose narcissist has lower depression levels, extreme satisfaction with themselves, and of course, a heightened love. It's almost a dream for a vulnerable narcissist to jump to the other side of the spectrum. What connects these two separate distinctions is low agreeableness. Both are intolerable at one point. It takes time to realize that. Some people detect it earlier than others. But it does become apparent somehow. People can take bullying, threats, insults, and attacks to a certain level. The saturation capacity of every person is different. The defense mechanisms are different. The bubble that they live in so large that they think that is their world since that is all they have seen. If someone is to pop that bubble, the real world might become too much for them. To pop the bubble, or not to pop the bubble, that is the question that you have to ask yourself now.

Chapter 1
Psychological Manipulation Techniques

Emotional Manipulation Techniques

Gaslighting. To gaslight, a person is to cause them to doubt something about themselves that is real. Though covertly, they tend to ask questions that would make think twice about even the things you have often held to be sacrosanct.

For you to combat this emotional technique, you need to document your experiences and life happenings, and you should often refer to them. This will help you not to doubt even a single of your experiences.

• Projection. Manipulators use this tactic to shift their shortcomings or deficiencies to another person. Instead of them taking responsibility for their errors, they would rather place the blame to someone else. It is an abusive technique that seeks to take the burden of guilt from them to another person. Their main purpose is to paint themselves clean while the other person looks unfortunate and dirty.

They aim to make you look weak while they appear to be strong. You should check out for people who easily notice wrongs in others: they are only projecting their negative selves.

• Intimidation. When a manipulator considers you to be a threat, he or she tends to silence you. They tend to stay close to you and talk in a manner that combines subtlety and aggressiveness. Manipulators will tend to look into your eyes with strange body language so that you can forget your train of thought or end an interaction with them.

To combat this technique, you need to get over your fears and learn to stand up to intimidation. As a precautionary move, you should prevent yourself from revealing your weaknesses or fears to someone you cannot trust. Ask for help from other people where and when you need it, but you should never make the manipulators feel that you are afraid of anything, even them.

• Magnify their problems while diminishing yours. They pretend that they are so sorry for what you are going through, and they would also put on a show of short-lived empathy, and this is to hide their true intentions. However, they will quickly bring up their difficulties too and magnifying them so that yours look insignificant.

• Intellectual Bullying. They will tend to overwhelm you with intellectual facts. They may not be so accurate, but they know that you do not have the chance or access to verify the authenticity of their claims. To an extent, manipulators place themselves before you as an authority of some kind to have their way with you.

To combat this tactic, you need to be informed. You do not have to know everything about everything but endeavor to know something about everything. When a person approaches you with an alleged fact, apart from you not being swept off your feet, you can predict its authenticity or not correctly.

• Intentional Digression. It refers to deviating from the normal course of interaction to something completely irrelevant to the issue at hand.

• Name-calling. A major characteristic of an emotional manipulator is that they have an exalted but always false opinion of themselves. They tend to be often right while everyone else is often wrong. Most of the people who practice emotional manipulation tend to be narcissists. So, when you try to challenge their ego, be prepared to get some more names in addition to those on your birth certificate.

To combat this technique, you should state frankly to them that you take exception to them calling you names.

• Stalking and Gossiping. The main purpose of manipulation is to create Byron you. But when it seems controlling you might be very difficult; they can change their technique to controlling how people see or view you. Manipulators seek to achieve this by them spreading falsehood about you behind your back. In some situation, they may even be forced to stalk you: that is monitoring you around. The main reason is to intimidate and give people a bad impression of you.

• Conditioning. This is a psychological method of training a person towards a specific taste or trait that the trainer wants. The purpose is to make you get rid of your initial values and embrace those of the manipulators.

How You Can Manipulate People (Strategies)

Every single tactic you need so that you can manipulate the minds of others. Always try to be smart about using the tactics, practice a lot, and soon you will be able to influence how other people behave and think.

• Fear and relief tactic. This technique involves playing a bit with someone's emotions. While it's a fact that this tactic can cause a great deal of anxiety and stress, this tactic is very efficient.

This technique had two parts: First, you should make another person to fear something. By doing so, you will make the other person vulnerable to the illogical behavior that you can use for your advantage. Secondly, you offer the person relief of the fear that he or she is experiencing.

• Mirroring Tactic. This technique involves two parts. First, when you are trying to mirror the person, you are trying to manipulate. Secondly, the person you are trying to manipulate will be mirroring you. Mirroring establishes trust between you and the other person, and it also helps you create a connection that you will finally begin to exploit. The tactic is quite simple all that you need to do is to copy the behavior. Always take a close look at the person's body language, hand and face gestures and the tone of their voice.

• Guilty Approach. Do not underestimate the potential of making a person feel guilty about something. If a person tends to feel guilty about something, he or she will do anything possible to compensate for it. At this point, is when you start planting your ideas into someone's subconscious mind and wait for them to flow with it.

• You are playing the victim card. This tactic goes hand in hand with the guilty approach technique, and you should consider combining the two do you to achieve the best outcome. But remember to be more careful when you are using the playing victim technique because at times it can be a double-edged sword and it can work against you if you overdo it. You pretend to be the victim in a situation, making others to feel sorry for you and make them feel bad about how they are treating you. This occurs by allowing your targets to feel like they are the one trying to influence you.

- Bribery Technique. This tactic is widely used, and it often works like a charm whenever you try to make someone do what you desire. When you reward someone, they will feel compelled to return the favor. Always make sure to use it in your best interest when they return the favor.

Try and figure out what your significant other needs and just give it to them, make sure that you suggest something in return. Always be careful that it does not sound that you are blackmailing them, as that may not end up well.

- Be a good listener. Developing trust between you and the other person is a very important aspect of influence. If someone does not trust you, he or she will not want to interact with you, and you will lose the opportunity of influencing them. That is why it is very vital actually to be friends, and one of the best ways to do so is by being a good listener.

Benefits of being a food listener:

- It creates an illusion of friendliness at the prices of the interaction. You will seem to be trustworthy and appealing when people see that you are interested in what they have to say

- It strengthens your trust when you, after some time, mention what they had told you before. This shows that you actually cared and genuinely listened to them.

- Learn to interpret body language. Most people will tend to express themselves more through their body language than their real words. When you find it challenging to decipher a person, what you have to do is to pay close attention to their body language. For you to effortlessly influence a person, you must figure out the person's emotional and psychological makeup, and you can't do that without considering their body language.

- Make use of your looks in your best interest. Whether you like it or not, human nature is very shallow to a specific extent, and you are naturally attracted to charismatic people. If you are a good-looking person, then you can make the best out of it and influence others. You have to be cheerful, positive and have an approachable and welcoming body language. Make people feel very special and ensure that you are often confident about yourself.

Chapter 2
The Benefits of Divorcing a Narcissistic Husband

Being single is difficult after you have been in a romantic relationship even if that relationship was nothing to be desired. We as human beings require connection with other people and that need is more so apparent by the formation of romantic pairings. This is because of the psychological needs that we have. These needs include:

- Needing to feel loved. This need for love starts from the moment we are born. A baby needs to receive love from its parents to develop healthily. A child who does not receive this basic need typically has social, emotional, mental, and behavioral problems growing up and this extends to their adulthood.

- Needing to feel important. We all want to feel that our existence matters to at least one other person. This need manifests itself in doing meaningful tasks, contributing to the community, acquiring wealth, and starting a family. The last item needs a partner to accomplish. Also, simply having someone to come home to and knowing that someone misses tur presence is basic but has a huge impact on making a person feel wanted.

- Needing security. We want to feel safe and comfortable in our environment. Knowing that we can obtain healthcare if sick, having a home to shelter up and knowing that someone is in our corner allows us to rest easy.

- Needing to contribute. Beyond our own need to grow and develop, we want to be part of someone else developments. It is human nature to leave a mark on the world in some way and helping the person with whom we have a romantic engagement will do that.

We enter romantic relationships to have these needs and others met. While, of course, no two persons or any relationship is perfect, a healthy

174

relationship is one where both parties are having the majority of their met consistently by entering and remaining in the union. The victim of a narcissistic marriage does not have these needs met consistently and if they are being met, there is some trade-off that is not healthy.

You did enter into this union and now that you have realized that you are better off without it. Here are a few reasons to reinforce your decision and to make you realize that you will be all the better off without having this narcissistic personality in your life.

- Having this time to yourself will give you a chance to focus on you without the demands of anyone else intruding. You will no longer have to walk on eggshells and can freely be who you are.

- You will learn to rely on yourself more so that you do not feel the need to be in a relationship to be happy or fulfilled. This will show you that any relationship you contemplate entering is simply a complement to the life you have built for yourself rather than the focus of all your attention.

- You will realize just how strong you are because you would have come out of this relationship a survivor. Being able to survive a relationship with a narcissist and also set in motion a brighter future for yourself will make you realize that you can indeed to anything that you set your mind to.

- You will be able to control your own life and destiny without the input of someone who does not have your best interest at heart.

- You will learn to set healthy boundaries so that you will not tolerate unacceptable behavior from anyone else in your future.

- You will realize that there is a lot more to be gained from being your authentic self rather than closeting your true identity away to please someone.

- You will learn to appreciate life and success on your terms.

- You will begin to learn more about yourself as you and fully embrace the fact that you have the freedom to do as you please, think as you please, and be free to be the person that you are.

- You will love yourself better and as such will demand better love from anyone else that you let into your life. This will give you the power to walk away if that unconditional love is not given a lot quicker and easier the next time around.

- You will gain a better perspective on what you want out of the marriage so that if you contemplate the union another time around, you will not be persuaded by someone who will provide you with less than you deserve.

Chapter 3
Five Theories on Psychological Manipulation

1 Cognitive

There are many well recognized psychological processes in theories regarding the art of persuasion. One of those is the Cognitive Response model, developed by Anthony Greenwald in 1968. It is still relevant today for determining some factors in persuasion. It is also a model used extensively in the world of advertising.

Greenwald suggested that:

It is not the words of the message that determines the success of persuasion, but more the emotions of the receiver. The internal monologue of the one receiving the message will be deciding factor on how easy they are influenced. Such internal thoughts will include positive and negative aspects, according to the individual's personality. This not a learning process, but more based on whether the person already views the message with favorable or unfavorable thought processes (cognitions).

Overcoming any counterarguments will rely on the expertise of the persuader. They should stop their target from having sufficient time to construct any counterarguments. The persuader must encourage positive arguments to come to the forefront. This gives the "persuasion effect" a better chance of success.

Persuasion can be more difficult if the intended target has been forewarned. It allows the target time to build their counterarguments, if the "message" is counter-intuitive to their present cognitions. The importance in pre-warning can be seen in research conducted by Richard E. Petty, in 1977. The study showed that students given notice about a certain event were less likely to be persuaded that those who had no pre-warning.

2 Reciprocity

Another well-studied explanation for how we might be open to the power of persuasion is the Rule of Reciprocity. This is based on a principle related to social conventions. If someone does you a favor, or does something good for you, then you are more likely to feel obliged to return the favor.

The Rule of Reciprocity can also happen subconsciously. Without even realizing it, you may agree to an action or favor asked of you by the requester. All because at some point they had done something for you, and you feel in their debt. You may feel obliged even if the request is something you would normally decline.

It is an effect widely used by companies who are looking to make sales. Often companies give out free samples, or time-limited trials. This is not without a motive. It is in the hope that the customer feels obliged to return the favor and buy the product or continue with the agreement.

Reciprocity is a recognized psychological process. It is an adaptive behavior which would have increased our chances of survival in the past. By helping others, it is likely that at some later point they will help you. Though, it can also have negative effects. If someone does something bad to you, then you may be driven by the rules of reciprocity to exact your revenge.

The Rule of Reciprocity is well supported by academic research. Burger et al (2009), suggested that a group of participants were more likely to agree to a request if the requester had previously done them a favor.

3 Information Manipulation

A powerful tool in the manipulator's armory. This is a method of being outright deceitful. It is a means of providing limited and confusing information to the victim. The effect of this will unbalance their way of thinking, making them vulnerable. It can also incorporate the use of intentional body language, to persuade and manipulate someone.

A study by McCornack et al. (1992) showed the different ways a message can be falsified to assist in the manipulation process. McCornack's theory has a premise of four maxims, in a truthful statement. A breach of any of these will render the message as intentionally deceitful. The four maxims are:

Quantity

This is the "amount" of information provided. Most of us seek to provide the right amount of information so that the receiver understands our message. Not too little, or too much, as that might confuse. A manipulator though would play with that quantity of information. They may omit certain pieces they consider irrelevant. Most especially if it is likely to work against their argument. This is known as "lying by omission."

Quality

Refers to the "accuracy" of the information provided. Truthful communication is one of High Quality. If we were to violate this maxim, then the receiver hears intentional mistruths. This is "outright lying," to gain the manipulator power.

Relation

Here, we talk about the "relevance" of the information to the message. To confuse or sidestep an awkward question, the manipulator may go off topic. This is a way of changing the subject, for the sole purpose of misleading. It could be to hide their weaknesses. Or even to over-emphasize on something that will give them more power over their listener.

Manner

The "presentation" of the message. An important aspect of this is body language. We read inflections and facial expressions as we listen. A manipulator may exaggerate these to mislead the presentation of the message. This is all in the aim to emphasize their agenda.

Lying to manipulate or persuade someone is not a new concept. It is though, a method that is becoming particularly potent in the modern world. Online communication and social media do not always involve face-to-face contact. This makes it easier to tell mistruths or exaggerate information. A manipulator may in their elements with such communications.

4 Nudge

Not all manipulation is sinister. Sometimes we may be manipulated to help us make the right decisions for our good. To do this, the Nudge Theory is particularly useful. The Nudge Theory expands positive reinforcement, by using small nudges.

Skinner's studies or behaviorism show how useful this theory can be. With positive reinforcement, such as rewards, it can manipulate people into behaving in the manner that you are hoping to encourage.

One example of "nudging" can be seen in this example. Adding exceptionally high-priced items on a menu may seem counterproductive. Yet, the result of this increased the sales of the second highest priced item. The customers were given a "nudge" in the right direction, but for the benefit of the restauranteur.

Richard Thaler, considered the father of the Nudge Theory, was awarded the Nobel Memorial Prize in Economic Sciences. His contribution to behavioral economics was considered quite momentous. Nudge Theory gives positive reinforcement, or as Thaler described it, it gives "nudges."

The Nudge Theory is not only effective in economics. It can be used to encourage behavioral changes and influencing personal choices. Even accepted social norms can be manipulated to changes, in this way.

Nudging is so successful, that in 2010, the British Government set up a Department Behavioral Insights Team. This was to help develop policies. The department was referred to as the Nudge Unit.

There can be obvious benefits of using "nudges" to influence people. It is still a form of psychological manipulation that can infringe on an individual's civil liberties.

5. Social Manipulation

This type of manipulation is also known as psychological manipulation. It is often a tool for politicians, or other groups of powerful people who are used to advancing their own interests. In its worst form, it is a means of social control. By taking away individuality, it coerces the populace into accepting what is given to them. Though it can have a positive side when used to help with personal issues, such as improving health and wellbeing.

Those in power who use social manipulation may use distractive techniques to deflect from important issues. They would argue that their proposals are for the benefit of the populace, and the benefit of your family and its future. Anything you think personally, that might be different, is wrong and selfish. This type of persuasion is very paternalistic, almost treating individuals as if they were all children. This "system" will strive to make the crowds believe the things that have gone wrong are, in fact, their fault. The only way to resolve the problem is to listen to the guidance of those who know better.

Such a political strategy would bring to forefront one social problem, only to hide another. It is a tactic to cause social unrest and panic among the populace. By creating unease in society, the populace will begin to demand changes. An example could be that the department wishes to hide the problems health care. So, they decrease the budget in crime prevention, causing crime statistics to rocket. The populace will receive information to coerce them into believing the best way forward for the crime problem. The politicians will feed propaganda, by disseminating their truths and facts. It may not always be true, or it may be information that is exaggerated, such as misuse of statistics. This type of social manipulation could take years to get the result that the manipulator requires.

The use of psychological manipulation is all a part of social influence. Professor Preston Ni, Communication Studies, published an article in Psychology Today. He indicates that one party recognizes another's weaknesses. They deliberately set out to cause an imbalance of power. This enables them to exploit their victims, for their agenda.

Does this make us all social puppets? To some degree, it does. Most of us comply and conform to what is expected of us to avoid a society of chaos.

Think for a moment, what is the latest gadget or home improvement product that you would like to buy? Is it something a friend told you about, or a neighbor owns? Chances are it is something that someone else has, or you've read that it's popular on the internet, and that makes you desire it. This is another side of social manipulation. We can be so easily swayed if we let our guard down. Whether that is a good or bad thing, depends on how you view it.

As mentioned earlier, not all social manipulation is a bad thing. it can have positive aspects. The word "manipulation" might conjure up thoughts of a criminal individual/s bending you to their will. But, used correctly, social manipulation can help the populace, as a whole. Good examples of social manipulation are the "5 a day campaign." Health specialists attempt to convince us to eat more fruit and vegetables. Or even the "stop smoking campaigns," which have resulted in reduced numbers of smokers. The result of which is a reduction in smoking-related diseases. This is coercion at its best.

Chapter 4
Narcissistic Strategies of Manipulation

You may already have an idea of the strategies that your narcissistic mother is using to manipulate you. All narcissists share more or less the same strategies to exert control over their victims but also to not push them too far where they leave. There needs to be a balance created which will keep their victim wrapped around their finger. Narcissists use a large range of tactics that work to distort the reality of their victims and to shift responsibility to them rather than themselves. Although other people who may not be narcissists also use these tactics, narcissists use these tactics to an excessive extent.

1. Gaslighting

Gaslighting is probably one of the most talked about manipulation tactics out there. Gaslighting is easily described using these common phrases; "Are you crazy?", "You just imagined that" or "That never happened!". Gaslighting works in a way to erode and distort a person's sense of reality. It takes away a person's ability to believe in themselves. It will prevent you from coming to terms with the abuse and mistreatment. When a narcissist is gaslighting you, in this case, your mother, you may end up gaslighting yourself to close the gap between the cognitive dissonance you may have. If your narcissistic mother has been gaslighting you for some time, it begins to erode at your sense of self-trust. You end up believing that everything they say is right, and your perceptions are likely incorrect or you need their approval to confirm your thoughts. To resist and recover from gaslighting, you must ground yourself in your reality and write down things as they happen and reiterating it to your support network in order to have other people confirm your perceptions. Having a support network is really powerful when it comes to re-learning what reality is and how to guide yourself again.

2. Projection

A prominent trait within narcissists is when they are unwilling to see their own mistakes and shortcomings and does everything they can in order to avoid accountability. This is called projection. Projection is a defense mechanism that narcissists have in order to deflect responsibility away from themselves by putting the blame on another person. It is a technique that helps them avoid accountability and ownership of their actions. Instead of acknowledging their own mistakes and flaws, narcissists will put the blame of their mistakes onto their victims and have them take responsibility for the behavior of the narcissist. This is how narcissists put the shame they feel about themselves onto other people. Narcissistic abuse works in a way where the world is to blame for everything that is wrong with them. You are responsible for babysitting their ego while they make you doubt yourself.

3. Playing Mind Games

Having meaningful and thoughtful conversations with a narcissist is nearly impossible because they will likely play a lot of mind games in order to boost their own self-image. Narcissists often use a lot of projection, gaslighting, and circular conversations in order to throw you off track, distract you and get you to agree with whatever they're saying. This technique is used to confuse, frustrate and discredit you so they can distract the attention away from the actual problems and make you feel bad for being a normal person with real thoughts that may differ from their thoughts. In the eyes of a narcissist, if there is a problem, then you are responsible for it. If you have spent time arguing with a narcissist, you should know that it always ends with you wondering how the argument even began in the first place. You probably disagreed with them about something crazy like the ocean is purple and now your entire life, career, choices, family, and friends are under attack. This all happened simply because your disagreement hurt their sense of self-image and inflated confidence which resulted in a narcissistic injury.

4. Generalizations

Narcissists aren't the masterminds that we tend to think they are. In fact, a lot of them aren't even that intellectually strong. Instead of trying to look at things from a different point of view, they will make blanket statements or generalizations that don't take your argument into account despite the different perspectives that you may have explained to them. In addition, the generalizations they make tend to invalidate a lot of the experiences that you may be sharing with them; this is used to maintain their status and to dismiss any achievements or experiences you may be proud of. For instance, sexual harassment accusations against famous people or well-liked public figures are often retaliated with the statement that false reports of sexual harassment happen all the time. While those DO happen, they are very rare, and this statement fails to acknowledge the actions of the accused person. These types of situations also happen in relationships, especially ones between a mother and her child. For instance, if you point out their narcissistic behavior or a negative action they've done, they will often retaliate with a generalization such as 'you're just too sensitive' or 'you are never satisfied' rather than talking about the issues at hand. It may be true that you are someone that is sensitive at times, but it is also true and possible that your narcissistic mother is also the one being cruel and insensitive most of the time.

5. Misrepresenting your thoughts deliberately

When you are dealing with a narcissist, your personal opinions, feelings, and experiences get translated into flaws that you have. Narcissists will retell your experiences as a way to make your opinions and thoughts seem absurd. For instance, if you are talking to a narcissist about a friend that is behaving in a toxic manic towards you, the narcissist may respond with, "So you think you're perfect then?". They will use what you tell them and twist it into a way that makes you look like a bad person. This allows them to invalidate your feelings and opinions regarding inappropriate behavior of any kind so they can use it to make you feel guilty when you try to set boundaries with them. From a psychology point of view, this manipulation tactic is called 'mind reading' and is a form of cognitive distortion or diversion. Narcissists will jump to conclusions based on what you say instead of taking a step back to properly analyzing your situation. They will put words into your mouth and make it seem like you have a crazy point of view so that they can use it to discredit you in the future.

6. Nitpicking

There is a huge difference between destructive criticism and constructive criticism. Constructive criticism is used to help a person improved, whereas destructive criticism is usually a personal attack. Narcissists never want to help you improve, all the way to do is nitpick at you and pull you down in any way possible. Narcissists, especially mothers, like to use a technique called 'moving the goalposts' to ensure that they can keep being dissatisfied with you. They will ask you to provide evidence to validate your opinions and then they will just set up another expectation and demand more evidence for that. If you are doing well in school, your narcissistic mother may nitpick at you and ask how come you got 9 As instead of 10. Once you hit 10 As to please them, they'll ask you how is it that you don't have a good job yet. The goal posts always change and may not even be related to the previous one at times. However, they don't do this logically; they do this in order to get you to keep seeking their approval and validation. By raising the expectations higher every single time, narcissists are able to convince you that you are unworthy and never 'enough.'

7. Evading accountability by changing the subject

Narcissists never want to be held accountable for anything, so they will purposely redirect and reroute conversations in order to benefit themselves. For instance, if you have a narcissistic mother and you are confronting them about their neglectful parenting, they will bring up mistakes you've made in the past in order to change the conversation to one that puts the blame on you and not them. This diversion technique has no limits when it comes to subject or time; it will often start with "Well, what about the time when you…" Narcissists use this diversion tactic in order to derail conversations that may challenge their status quo or their perception of their self-image. Anything that may threaten their appearance will be redirected in the form of bringing the attention on to another person by placing blame. If this happens to you, don't let them derail you. Keep stating and mentioning facts without allowing yourself to be distracted.

8. Threats

Narcissists feel threatened when their grandiose sense of self or false sense of superiority is challenged. They will demand other people of unreasonable things while punishing them for not being able to meet their unrealistic expectations. Instead of properly compromising, they will instill fear in you about the consequences that will happen if you aren't able to meet their demands. They often give ultimatums in the form of "if you don't do this, I will…" This type of manipulation tactic is used frequently in mother and children relationships. It may be in the form of "if dinner isn't prepared by the time I get home, you are grounded for a week."

9. Name-calling

Name-calling is usually a manipulation tactic that is left as a last resort for a narcissist. This is usually used when they can't think of another way to manipulate your actions or opinions. To them, name-calling is a quick and easy solution to degrade, put you down, and insult your intelligence. Name-calling is often used to criticize their victims' insights, opinions, and beliefs. Even if you had a perspective that is well-researched and informed, the narcissist could still spin it in a way that makes you feel as if your thoughts are idiotic or silly. If they can't convince you otherwise, they make target you personally instead and try to undermine your intelligence and credibility as much as they can. It is very important to end any conversations as soon as name-calling is involved as the conversation will likely not go anywhere and you may just end up having your feelings and confidence hurt even more.

10. Conditioning

Narcissists are usually successful at conditioning you to place them first and to serve them full time. They will try to get you to associate your happy memories, talents, and strengths with disrespect, frustration and abuse. They do this by sneaking in insults or put-downs about your good traits and qualities and may even try to sabotage your goals or ruin family/friend gatherings. Some narcissists go as far as isolating you from your family and friends and try to make you financially dependent on them to make it hard for you to leave the abusive situation. They train you to become afraid of doing the things you use to love. Narcissists do this because their goal is to have 100% of your attention upon them and nothing else. If there is anything outside of your life that may threaten their control over you, they will try to mitigate that risk. Moreover, narcissists are pathologically jealous and they don't want anything else to ever come between you and them. Conditioning would be the most damaging if you grew up in a family with a narcissistic parent. As a child, you are easily moldable and conditioned because you don't know anything different.

Chapter 5
Effects of Narcissistic Abuse over Time

O nce the narcissist is able to get ahold of you, it will not take long before they start to do as much damage as possible. And because of their tactics, it is likely that the abuse from this person is going to continue on for a number of years if not longer. This is never something that lasts a few weeks, or a few months only and then is done with for good. The narcissist is not going to give up without a fight. And since the victim often doesn't understand what is going on around them, they will often stay in this kind of abusive relationship for a very long time, and deal with the consequences in the process.

It is important to recognize some of the signs and symptoms that can come into play when someone is abused by a narcissist for any amount of time, but especially what happens when this person is under the control of their narcissistic partner or parent, or even someone else in their lives, for a long period of time. The changes that happen to a person are going to be outstanding and learning how to recognize the signs and try to avoid them as much as possible can be critical.

First, we need to take a look at some of the signs of a narcissist taking over. These signs are pretty much going to be part of the effects that happen with narcissistic abuse over time, especially when the victim does not recognize what is going on. When we think about abuse in most cases, we are going to often think about physical abuse first. But there are different forms of abuse that we may have to deal with, and emotional abuse is one of the worst.

Emotional abuse is going to be about as serious as the physical abuse, and often it is going to come before it. Sometimes, these two types of abuse are going to happen together. If you are still trying to figure out if you are dealing with a narcissist in your relationship, it is important to look for some of the following signs:

1. Yelling
2. Making threats that are either overt or subtle.

3. Isolating you away from the rest of the world, including your friends and family members.
4. Trying to control as many aspects of your life as they can.
5. Punishing you any time that you speak up or choose to not go along with what they want.
6. Thinking that it is perfectly fine to invade your privacy and not thinking a thought about doing it.
7. Tries to make you question your own sanity. This is a process that is known as gaslighting.
8. Spewing insults or ridiculing you in other ways.
9. Name-calling

The first thing to realize here is that if you have been abused in an emotional manner, it is not your fault. There is also not a correct way that you are meant to feel about this situation. Emotional abuse is not something that is going to be seen as normal, but the feelings that you have in this situation are normal.

Now that we have this in mind, it is time to take a look at some of the different effects that can happen with the emotional abuse that you experience, whether it is over the short term or the long term.

Short Term Effects Of A Narcissist

In the beginning, you may notice that there is some denial that you feel at first. It is hard on most people to realize that they are dealing with a narcissist and that they are in this kind of situation to start with. Often we won't believe it, and it is completely natural to hope that you are a bit wrong with this. It is possible that you will have some feelings of shame, hopelessness, fear, and confusion.

This is not where it all is going to end though. This emotional toll, even if it just happens on occasion or for the short term with the narcissist, can come with some other side effects including physical and behavior. You may experience some issues including:

1. Aches and pains in different parts of the body that you aren't able to explain.
2. A heartbeat that is racing
3. Nightmares that just won't go away.
4. Muscle tension from tensing up the body during any interactions with the narcissist.

5. Lots of moodiness because you can't express your feelings and you are anxious about what is going to happen next.
6. A lot of trouble concentrating because you are focusing on what the narcissist is talking about.

When the abuse goes on for a longer period of time, then there are going to be some other side effects as well. Studies have shown that severe emotional abuse, including what we see in a narcissistic relationship, it can be as powerful as physical abuse. Of course, if this goes on for a longer period of time, both of them are going to end up leading us to feel depression and low self-esteem. You may also develop issues including:

1. Social withdrawal (which is going to be something that the narcissist tries to manufacture), and loneliness
2. Insomnia
3. Guilt all of the time
4. Chronic pain that you just are not able to explain away.
5. Lots of anxiety

In addition to the issues above, there are some researchers who theorize that this emotional abuse could end up contributing to the development of other conditions, ones that don't seem to relate back to the abuse at all, including post-traumatic stress disorder, fibromyalgia, and chronic fatigue syndrome.

The longer that the abuse from the narcissist goes on, the worst the symptoms are going to get. And this is how the target gets stuck in a loop that is so bad for them. The target feels low self-esteem, deals with a lot of different health conditions, and starts to rely completely on the narcissist. This is going to ensure that the narcissist is able to get what they want, but leaves the target feeling lost and confused, without a good way to deal with the issues either.

Chapter 6
Is Your Partner A Narcissist?

This is one of the most critical questions in a relationship. Along with questions like, "Am I dating the right person?" and "Am I comfortable in my relationship?" and many other issues.

It is imperative to stay happy and healthy, both physically and emotionally, in any relationship. There are stories of different people coming from a bad relationship with psychological breakdown. Yes, it is true. This is why the question "Am I dating a Narcissist?" is essential and paramount because being in a relationship with a narcissist is a terrible choice.

It might be your worst choice in life. This is another scenario for you. You know when someone is appropriately dressed, walking tall on the street and happy with himself. People keep staring at him, and he thinks they probably think of him as handsome. Suddenly, a beautiful young lady walks up to him and tells him he has dog poop on the back of his shirt. Suddenly, his countenance will change, realizing why those people had been staring at him like that. This is like what this part is going to do.

It is going to enlighten you, shedding more light on who you are dating. Sometimes, you might not see something until it's too late. The association is one of the most delicate topics, and it'd be unfortunate to joke about it because it could affect all other aspects of your life.

Here, we are going to list out the common signs on how to identify a narcissist. It is high time, and we avoided those who're out to disrupt our peace. After several years of reading and studying several psychology materials on personality disorder, psychologists have gained a lot of insight into who a narcissistic individual is and how to identify them. There are some aspects of their behavior that is complicated and hard to understand.

In a lazy man's tone, it is just weird. Do you want to know a little definition for narcissists? They are silent killers or slow poison. They gradually kill you little by little without you realizing the damage they've done to you.

Some people might be thinking a narcissistic individual is psychologically disturbed. No, not really! You won't see them on the streets, homeless, in rags, or begging. They are always well-to-do and self-accomplished. It's hard to tell if they are a narcissist or not. These few commons signs would help you know if you are currently in a relationship with a narcissist or not. If after reading through this part you notice you are in a relationship with one, please pack your bags and run for your life. Don't try to change them because it may be complicated. Note that some individuals may have one of these signs listed below, but it doesn't mean they are narcissists. Please read carefully and digest properly.

Eleven Signs You Are In A Relationship With A Narcissist

Here we are going to be shedding more light on that aspect. It is left for you to make the decision and take the necessary steps if you are a victim. If you are not, try as much as possible to avoid them. Run, if possible.

1 Very Charming And Persuasive At First

You meet this very handsome and rich guy. He treats you very specially, says very loving things to you and makes you feel good about yourself. That's how a narcissist gets their prey. He's quite the catch in the beginning. You could almost say in the first two to three months that he's your soulmate or heaven-sent angel. Suddenly all that stops, and you feel distant and unloved. According to great psychologists, narcissists are very skilled in love bombing their victims for some time. They are what we call, "too good to be true" kind of people. They seem like better lovers than those who actually love you when it comes to gifting, calling, texting, infatuations, and sweet-talking. In my two-years relationship with a narcissist, at first, he was so charming and sweet. My parents knew him quite well to the extent my dad took him as his son. They go out on weekends at times to fish. All this happened only at the beginning of the relationship.

2 Self-Centeredness

After the first lovey-dovey stage they feel you are hooked on love. They start to showcase their true self. This is one of the primary attributes, and you then you see self-centeredness. They act selfish. They think of only themselves. They don't say, "oh! I went by the grocery store, and I got you this or that." No, they only care about themselves and not you. On the outside, while anyone that matter is watching, they are very attentive and supportive, but when it is just you, they switch. So when you complain to your friends, they'll think you're crazy to the extent that you think you're insane too.

3 perfectionists

A narcissist never goes for people who are not accomplished in one way. They don't choose mediocrely; they actually study their victims before going after them. You've to be something before they can approach you: beautiful, a sport or music star, a successful businesswoman, and the list continues. It is always something that would boost their ego or social status. So, while in a relationship with a narcissist, the focus is not on the growth of the relationship. The focus of a narcissist is on their outward image. What people think of them as a power/perfect couple. This is because they like to protect their public image.

4 Bossy

When you first started dating, they loved every damn thing about you. Your love for rap music, funny reality TV shows, country music, partying, and other things. I mean everything. It seemed like he was the perfect guy for you. Suddenly, they begin to boss you around. They suddenly want you to start living the way they want. They believe if you are not doing things the way they want, you're wrong. You begin to wonder whether you were the one who caused their change or if they have some other lady on the side.

5 The Never-Wrong Attitude

It is somewhat impossible to argue with a narcissist. After a while of arguing, you may get confused. This is because they are under the impression that they are never wrong. They are always right. That opinion of theirs is the best and only option for you. So, arguing with them on a matter is impossible.

6 Lack Of Empathy

Now, this part is the saddest. It is quite different from when you see a sad movie, and you don't cry. It is way different from that. A narcissist isn't capable of empathizing with others or you as his partner. He simply doesn't care. All the cares they showered on you at the beginning of the relationship were fake and timely. Don't try to change them because they cannot change. Just opt out!

7 - Lashing Out

When they notice you might leave them, they begin to become sweet again. Of course, they don't want you to leave them. When they get the feeling that you are beginning to do without them, they may get angry and lash out at you. They start to blame you for pulling away from them emotionally, bringing on one excuse or the other. They may lie if necessary.

8 They Make You Feel Bad About Yourself

After the first stage of love bombing their partner, a narcissist switches their behavior and starts to make you feel like a wrong person. All the things he was okay with before, he suddenly hates, and now, you are the bad person.

Maybe he used to be cool with you buying Chinese when you are too tired to cook. Suddenly, he hates fast food and accuses you of starving him always.

9 Compliments

They love compliments from others. It feeds their ego. When you continuously compliment them as a sweet partner, they love it.

10 No True Friends

Narcissists never have real friends. They have colleagues all around, business partners and acquaintances. They actually choose their cliques based on their needs. They don't actually keep real friends. So, when you go out with your friends, they tend to get angry and feel left out. They start to criticize you for the kinds of friends you're hanging out with.

11 You Feel Like A Thing

At a point in the relationship with a narcissist, you suddenly get a feeling you are being used. He just gets what he wants: sex, food, and so on. You are neglecting your own needs. He doesn't even compliment you again, like how beautiful you're, how successful you are becoming, and so on.

I sincerely hope you are not dating a narcissist because it's a toxic relationship. With all these signs written above, you can see that dating a narcissist is not a good thing in any way. They don't actually think they are doing anything wrong so it may be impossible to save them. It's best to look out for yourself and find a way out.

Chapter 7
How To Break Off A Relationship
With A Narcissist

Should I Leave My Partner?

You have to get away from the narcissist because staying is not good for you in the long run. However, there are situations where the narcissist in question is a vital part of your life, and it's utterly impractical for you to leave him/her completely. For instance, he/she could be a spouse with whom you have kids, a family member, or a colleague in your department. In such cases, you can try to put as much distance between the two of you as possible while at the same time trying to limit the harm that befalls your kids, your other family members or your career respectively.

If your lives aren't already intertwined, you can break up with them, leave them, and avoid contacting them altogether. Remember that they didn't really care about you, so don't worry too much about how they are going to feel after you break up.

Don't bother explaining too much detail about why you are leaving. Remember that if you take the time to justify yourself, they are going to try to talk you out of it. Break up in a public place and leave, never to return. Don't agree to be friends with them or to hang out in the future, no matter how insistent they are.

Some psychologists even suggest that you should break up with narcissists over the phone because there is no way of telling how in-person meetings are going to go. When you avoid contact with the narcissist, tell him that he is not welcome into your home, and block his number from your phone. If you leave the tiniest window open, he is going to find a way to crawl back into your life. Don't do any lingering goodbye. Just say your piece and leave.

There are always going to be some mutual friends who are going to vouch for the narcissist and tell you that you made a mistake leaving him. These friends may mean well, but they certainly don't fully understand how much you have been suffering under the thumb of the narcissist. With them, you have to make it clear that the narcissist is persona non grata, and the cost of bringing him up during your conversations is that they will lose your friendship. Tell them that you don't want any updates on the narcissist's life, and if they still talk to him, they shouldn't tell him anything about you either.

When you leave a narcissist, that very same day, write down exactly why you left him. In your journal, put down the rationale for your decision, and all the reasons why being with him was a bad thing for you. The purpose of this is that when the narcissist comes crawling back into your life and tries to manipulate you, you can refer back to your journal and remember why it's vital that you stay away from him. We have talked about gaslighting and how a manipulative narcissist can get you to question your own sanity, so having contemporaneous records of your thoughts and feelings can help you stay grounded on the truth.

If you successfully get away from a narcissist, hopefully, he/she will move on quickly, find someone else torment, and leave you alone. Because the narcissist never really cared about you in the first place, he won't be too hung up on your relationship, so don't question your decision when you see that he/she has moved on too quickly and you start to worry that you may end up alone. Being alone is better than being with someone who sucks the life out of you.

Executing The No Contact Rule Immediately

The narcissist lives to trigger emotional reactions in people because, in their minds, that gives them some sense of power. If a narcissist causes you to lose control over your emotions, it gives him a lot of satisfaction. When a narcissist attacks you verbally, ignoring him can drive him crazy.

You have to understand that narcissists crave attention, so ignoring them hurts them more than anything else. They want to be acknowledged and validated; that is why they start with the conflict in the first place. When a narcissist targets you and destroys your life, your natural instinct will be to get back at him/her by reacting angrily and emotionally, but if you do that, you are only playing into his/her hand.

It may not seem so at first, but over time, you will realize that ignoring the narcissist is actually much more satisfying than engaging with him/her because then, even to third-party observers, the narcissist will just seem like a petty person who likes to pick fights with people, and you will seem like the mature adult who is able to rise above it all.

The narcissist wants to control you and to assert dominance over you, but you have to remember that people can't take power from you. You actually have to give it to them. A narcissist can only have dominance over you if you relinquish control to him/her. As we have mentioned, you are guaranteed to lose if you play the narcissist's game, and that is when he/she is actually capable of dominating you. By ignoring the narcissist, you blatantly refuse to play his/her game, and then he/she has no means with which to get close enough to have any form of control over your life.

In as much as ignoring the narcissist hurts him/her; remember that you are doing it for yourself and for your own peace of mind. When you choose to ignore a narcissist, don't be preoccupied with the effect that the lack of attention has on him/her. Focus on doing something worthwhile for yourself. If after ignoring the narcissist, you are still obsessed with how he/she is reacting to it, then you are still under his/her control, and you are relinquishing your power to him/her.

When you ignore an ex who is a narcissist, don't turn around and start stalking him on social media to see if he is miserable. Now that you have regained control, you should focus on detoxifying from the narcissist's influence and training yourself to be more vigilant in the future.

If the narcissist is someone who is in your life permanently, ignoring him/her is going to be a regular thing, so you have to train yourself so as to get better at it. Ignoring a narcissist is more than just avoiding responding to their taunts. It's about learning to stop caring about their opinions and their criticisms. The first step is to restrain yourself from responding to them even if their comments hurt you, but after that, you have to work on yourself to get to the point where what they say rolls off you like water.

When you ignore a narcissist, you have to keep your safety in mind. Some narcissists tend to turn aggressive or violent when you deny them attention, so you have to be careful not to be anywhere with them without witness's present. Ignoring a narcissist makes him/her feel that you have slipped away from his/her control, and in a desperate effort to regain that control, you never know how they are going to lash out. You have to be a lot more cautious and a lot smarter going forward because the narcissist is going to bring his/her "A" game in order to regain control over you. Keep ignoring them, and no matter how hard they come at you, don't relent, not even slightly.

How To Create A Safety Plan If You Are Trying To Leave

Confide in a friend or family member who you know is not going to confide in your narcissistic spouse. You feel lost and alone after years of emotional abuse from a narcissist. Confide in someone that you know that you can trust.

Find ways to regain your self-confidence and self-esteem that's been taken from you during years of emotional and verbal abuse. Remember your own self-worth and in the future steer clear of abusive, controlling people. However, be aware that as you leave, he may get custody of all the friends and he will go out of his way to make you the bad guy. As someone with Narcissistic Personality Disorder, he cannot be seen as the bad guy in this. He needs the admiration, the sympathy and the support of your friends.

Join a support group like Codependents Anonymous with people who will understand what you have been through. They can help you heal.

Put a no contact rule in place and enforce it on him and yourself. It takes time to heal and if you have contact during that time you open yourself up to being manipulated into going back to him. You need to have regained your self-confidence and self-esteem before you would see him again. This takes years and you are better off never seeing him again if possible.

See a therapist before you leave. You will need all the support you can get so put this relationship in place first.

Once you make the final decision to go – GO! Don't hang around. Don't give him any opportunities to manipulate you.

BE SAFE. You are dealing with a potentially dangerous person. Many people with Narcissistic Personality Disorder can be violent, mean and you just don't know what might happen. If you feel at all unsafe take measures to protect yourself. Have family and friends with you when you leave. In the worst-case scenario, you have to inform the authorities that you are leaving and ask for their oversight.

Watch out for revenge. Narcissists are known for seeking revenge and holding a grudge. Expect something and be prepared emotionally but don't let it affect your new narcissist free life.

Don't answer the door if he comes around after you leave. Maintain the no contact rule for at least a year if you can.

Healing after Ending a Relationship with a Narcissist

The door closes and the narcissist is gone from your life. But not from your spirit. The things they do and say have a way of staying with you for a while, impacting your self-esteem even though he isn't there to do it. It was so hard to walk away and now it will be hard to stay away and begin to heal. The key to staying away and beginning to heal is detachment. You have to detach yourself from everything you thought you knew about him and everything you felt for him. Let go. Detachment is letting go. Step 1: Stop blaming yourself for what went wrong and start blaming the narcissist for being incapable of really loving you. See the relationship for what it really was and see him for who he really is as someone with Narcissistic Personality Disorder.

Step 2: When a relationship ends you go through the stages of grief just as if someone died. In this stage, the anger comes. You are angry at how he treated you and angry at the abuse you endured.

Step 3: This is your stage. It is about how much stronger you are now. You're thinking of positive thoughts in this stage. You feel good about the work you have done. You feel free of the love you once felt for him and now you can't stand the sight of him. You are spending more time with friends and creating a new life.

Step 4: Detachment! Success! You focus on yourself and your life now. You rarely even think about him. You are physically and emotionally free from any narcissist you might know.

Chapter 8
Redefining Yourself After The Abuse

Developing The Mindset Of Getting Ready To Take Back The Control Of Your Life

It is bad for your wellbeing and quality of life to continue staying in an abusive relationship. Surprisingly people stay even when it is seriously affecting their body and mental health. There are various reasons why people opt to stay, but the truth is these are all wrong reasons. If you have been abused for long and you are still in the relationship, it means that your partner has succeeded in manipulating you. You may think that you are staying to save your partner because they made you believe they cannot live without you. Truthfully, they are just saying things to make you believe you are still soul mates and to deflect the abuse. A healthy relationship does not work like that. To prepare your mindset in taking back control of your own life you will need to entertain new thoughts.

Now that you have learned that you are with a narcissist, there are two options: to stay and know how to deal with them or to leave. There are different types and levels of a narcissist and this will determine the extent of harm the one you are with can do to you. If you are with a person who is verbally abusive, manipulative, and shows no sign of empathy or remorse towards you, it is high time that you leave now. The aspects such as denial, self-doubt, and self-blame are core to why you may continue staying in an abusive relationship. It is wrong to feel this way about yourself because the truth is you are not the reason why the relationship is not working or is having problems. Gaslighting by your narcissist is what make it appear that you are the reasons they are abusing you. Thus, you stay trying to change so that you can be the person they want. Unfortunately, they never get satisfied and there is nothing you can do to fully satisfy them; this is the reason why it is important to think otherwise.

It is a trick to manipulate you, it is not that they care. You have to start thinking this way although you may not want to believe it, entertain this thought and you will see it is the truth. You see, in this relationship you are in a limbo where either you leave but then your partner draws you back again or they give you the silent treatment. At times they will leave you confused over what has just happened when they return after few days and start telling you how much they cannot live without you. Your mind takes you back to your first days in the relationship and you buy into these lies and once again you give them a chance. You believe that this time it will be better, and you even give up some of your needs, goals, and priorities to try and make it work only to be surprised later when the trend repeats itself. As much as you may not like it, let yourself consider that you are being used. It is a trick to manipulate you so that you can continue giving them the satisfaction of control and power. You have to accept that they have no empathy towards you which means they do not care about your wellbeing.

Now that you have allowed this line of thought how do you overcome the obstacles then?

Avoid Self-Doubt

It will be hard to overcome the obstacles of a narcissist if you have no sense of self-awareness. It is true that to this point you have given up doing what is best for you in trying to please your narcissist partner: your goals, dreams and even doing what you love to be more successful. It is bad enough that you do not listen and trust your feelings because you are all about pleasing and serving someone else. Even after making all these sacrifices you should know that a narcissist will never honor your feelings. At one time you may have told them that you are sad, but they dismissed this by saying that you are overly sensitive or weak. Narcissists are bullies by nature and when everything that you feel is being dismissed you will start dismissing yourself. As explained earlier, if you do not put yourself first and know that you are not the problem then it will be extremely hard for you to overcome the obstacles. Thus, the first obstacle that you need to escape is self-doubt and self-blame. Disregard what they tell you. Listen to your body and what it tells you. There is nothing wrong with your feelings if you feel sad, disappointed, and angry or any negative feeling because of your partner. Trust what your body is telling you and do not consider any outside influence.

Disengage Or Ignore

The narcissist takes pleasure in provoking you and enjoys any kind of emotion you portray; be it rage or love. Their key focus is your reaction to their behavior. For a normal person, they will determine that you are upset because of something wrong they did to you, but the narcissist will not. They are okay with the emotions you portray either happiness, or anger and they think that this is love. Theirs is a game and they use it to trap you. You are their victim and they need you to feed off of. What you need to do is deny them the satisfaction they gain from your reactions by disengaging. After knowing this and believing it will be easy for you to disengage. Do not be concerned with their annoyance, do not engage them about it and do not try to reason with them. Be concerned about you and what you can control and focus on that. All the other things you have been trying have failed, but by refusing to accept something they have done they will comprehend that they have done something wrong. It is confusing when they use their 'hot and cold' aspects but it is advisable not to fall for it. In case of anything, pause and give yourself time to think, do not engage and do not take the bait. After doing this you will realize that you have started feeling better and you have started to think about yourself.

Think About Boundaries And Set Them

In most cases, when a relationship has arrived at this point you have probably forgotten about boundaries. You have given up the boundaries that at one time you had and have allowed the narcissist to cross them. Think about boundaries, things that a person should not do to you. You can begin by writing these boundaries down, whatever they are and communicate them to the narcissist. It is true that they will not let you have them, and they will try by all means to disregard them. Setting good boundaries includes identifying steps that you will take when they are crossed. This is why it is important to be true to yourself. If you give a warning and they continue to cross take the actions or steps that you had set to take. You should not suggest something that you cannot actually do, because if you fail to do it then it shows weakness. For instance, if you told them that if they ever hit you again you will leave and you fail to do so, it will definitely communicate that you are neither serious nor ready to observe the boundaries. It takes an incredible strength to adhere to the boundaries you set and take swift action when they are crossed to protect yourself.

Stop Using Words Such As "I'm Sorry" And "Fair"

Always remember that narcissists have no empathy, they lack emotions because it will help you in all decisions that you make. A normal person will understand what you mean by stating that they are not being fair and when you apologize. To a narcissist, 'fair' is not a real concept and all they care about is getting what they want. To them what is unfair is if they do not succeed in abusing you to feed their emotional deficiency. When they are calling you words, making you jealous, physically abusing you or even giving you the silent treatment, this is what is fair. Trying to make sense of things with them is a waste of time and will even worsen your psychological wellbeing. Thus, it is important that you stop apologizing because saying you are sorry sends the message that they are successful in whatever they are subjecting you to.

Acceptance

It does not mean accepting abuse; rather accepting they are a narcissist. Maybe the reason why you were with them is because you thought it could work like any other relationship. The truth is they are not going to change; they are not going to give up abusing you anytime soon. There is no sense in wasting your time and life in this. As much as you may not want to believe it, there is no happily ever after. It is important that you accept that you cannot change their personality disorder. If you do accept these things, it will be much easier for you and it will give you a high chance of doing what is good for you. The focus herein is to know that being in an abusive relationship is not good for you and whatever you are going to do is to strictly improve your wellbeing and not to compete or outsmart them. Do not make clear your intentions at this stage as you may end up fueling the fire. Acceptance gives you power over their attempts to manipulate you. It will add to your quest of taking back control of your life.

Chapter 9
Develop Emotionally Intelligent Parenting Strategies

Practice Self-Care

The first tip to becoming a loving and healthy parent is to practice plenty of self-care. This includes such things as getting plenty of downtime to recharge your batteries, eating right, getting enough sleep, and taking time to appreciate the things you have. By practicing these methods each and every day, you will significantly reduce your stress levels. This, in turn, will enable you to become more mindful, and thus, more in control of your emotions, thoughts, words, and actions.

Another important aspect of self-care is to talk to someone when things become more than you feel you can handle. Whether you choose to talk to a close friend, a family member or even a professional therapist the important thing is that you find someone who will both listen to your concerns and help you to find solutions. The feeling of being alone in any given situation can increase the anxiety of that moment exponentially, making your struggles even greater. However, having someone that you can talk to and ask for advice can make all the difference, thus ensuring that you never get overwhelmed by life and become the emotional wreck your parents were.

Give Your Child Time

Once you have your emotional and mental wellbeing taken care of the next step is to help take care of your child's emotional needs. Most children of emotionally immature parents suffered from being neglected for most of their childhood. The best way to heal those wounds is to make sure that you give your child the time they need to feel loved, appreciated, and most importantly, wanted. Spending quality time with your child on a daily basis will ensure that they get the emotional nurturing they need in order to become mentally and emotionally strong as they grow.

Another benefit to spending quality time with your child on a daily basis is the bond that such time creates. The more time you spend with any other person is the closer to that person you become. This applies to your child just as much if not even more so. Therefore, if you want to establish the bond with your child that you never had with your parents make sure you spend regular time with them every day doing something that matters to them as well as to you.

Quality time with a child can come in almost any form, so the important thing is to try several different techniques until you find those that work for you. One common activity is reading. Whether you choose to read a bedtime story, or you choose to read something in the middle of the day is up to you. The act of reading will have the same impact no matter when it's done. Not only will this create a loving bond between you and your child, it will also increase your child's mental development, thereby giving them an edge in life when they start school.

Other activities include playing sports, engaging in crafts or artistic activities, or any other practice that will encourage your child to develop their inherent talents. The important thing is to respond to your child rather than force your child to respond to you. Therefore, if you see them playing with a ball, bat, or other piece of sporting equipment, spend your time developing their athletic skills. Alternatively, if they like to draw, paint or engage in another creative activity such as singing or playing music then join them in that activity and establish your bond while helping them to uncover their inner talents.

Put Yourself In Your Child's Shoes

Growing up is a difficult process, even when you have the best parents in the world. Needless to say, it gets even harder when your parents are emotionally immature. That said, just because you overcome the demons from your past and practice the parenting you wish you had been raised with doesn't mean that your child won't face difficult times throughout their childhood. The best thing you can do in these cases is to put yourself in your child's shoes. This will enable you to better understand your child, and thus offer them the help and support they need. Sometimes they might need time alone in order to work out their thoughts and feelings, while other times they might need you to hold them close and tell them everything is going to be OK. The important thing is to remember that no single remedy cures all ills. Therefore, be attentive to their needs and respond in the way they need you to. This is the essence of developing parent-child empathy.

Another benefit to developing parent-child empathy is that it will serve to heal the emotional wounds from your childhood. By stepping into your child's shoes, and sharing in their pain and struggles, you provide the care and compassion that you lacked as a child. As you give that care and compassion to your child, you, in turn, give it to your inner child, thereby relieving it of its feeling of abandonment. In the end, the effort you put into relating to your child and providing the love and support they need becomes self-serving in a way as you benefit as much from the love you give as they do. Even better, when they show their gratitude for your love and empathy, it will go a long way to proving that you have overcome your past and become your very best.

Avoid Using Authoritarian Behavior

Needless to say, there will be times when your child and you don't see eye to eye on a subject, but you know that your decision must stand as it is in their best interest. The chances are any time such an event took place when you were growing up, your parents played the dictator card, reminding you that you lived in their house, and that meant you followed their rules. While this approach can end an argument quickly, it can also end any chances of a parent forming a loving and lasting bond with their child. Therefore, if you want to be the best possible parent for your child, you have to take that dictator card out of your pack and tear it up. There are always better ways to solve the situation.

One way to solve the situation is to discuss things with your child as though they actually are capable of understanding complex ideas. The important thing is to never treat your child like an imbecile. Being young isn't the same as being stupid. If you take the time to explain things in simple terms, you just might get through to your child and make them realize your perspective. This can help them to make better decisions the next time a similar situation presents itself.

Unfortunately, there will be times when discussing the matter won't get the job done. In this case, you may have to put the proverbial foot down and take charge of the situation. However, this doesn't mean that you have to be mean about it. You can be loving and caring as you drag your child away from making a bad decision. By avoiding authoritarian behavior, you become more consistent in your child's mind. They know they can trust you even when you are preventing them from having their own way. This ensures that they will never fear you, and that will make you a far better parent than the ones you had to endure while you were growing up!

Let Go Of Always Needing To Be Right

One of the most common signs of an emotionally immature parent is the insatiable need to always be right. It's bad enough when you see two grown people arguing for the sake of proving one-person right and the other person wrong. However, when it is an adult arguing with a child, the situation is beyond insane. Who in their right mind would need to prove their point to a five-year-old child anyway?! The chances are you know at least one person who fits that mold all too well. That said, in order to take yet another step away from becoming like your parents, it is vital that you recognize and eliminate any inherent need to always be right. The bottom line is that it is OK to be wrong. What isn't OK is to deny being wrong even when you know you are.

However, if you want to take this to the next level, you have to learn to avoid arguing your point even when you are right. After all, the problem isn't just in needing to always be right. The real problem is in needing to be right at someone else's expense. This is especially true when that other person is your child. It's fine if you and your child don't see eye to eye on a situation. In fact, it should be expected. You have had a lifetime of experiences and lessons that have given you the perspective you have. Your child, by contrast, has not. Therefore, you should never expect your child to be as wise as you. That is nothing more than a sign of emotional immaturity. Instead, accept that your child won't see things the way you do and allow them the space they need to learn the lessons their life has to teach them. Eventually, time will tell who is right and who is wrong on any particular issue. The important thing is to never compete with your child. This only makes them feel bad about themselves, and it makes you look like a monster, one that grows stronger by making your child weaker.

If you really want to have the ultimate experience, you can always join your child on their journey of discovery. Sure, your life has taught you plenty of lessons, but that doesn't mean that your child's life can't teach you even more. In fact, if you take the time to see life through your child's eyes, there's no telling what you might discover. Therefore, in those instances, when right and wrong really doesn't matter, take the time to see things through the eyes of your child. This will give you a fresh perspective on life, one that might open your mind to a whole new world full of wonder and excitement. At the very least, it will give you a chance to bond with your child on a whole new level, thus ensuring that they have a relationship with you that you never had with your parents. Even better, by looking at life through your child's eyes, you can begin to live the childhood you never had. Now you can play in the dirt and not have to worry about getting yelled at by the mean adults!

Chapter 10
Protect Children From Conflict's Damaging Effects and Their Stress and Developmental Skills

Children's Stress And Developmental Skills

At a young age, children are resilient and will learn to adapt to separation, despite the many challenges and hardships they experience along the way. It is important to understand that while every child and situation is unique, most children will need comfort and understanding so that they feel valued and wanted. This is especially a must when the other parent is a narcissist and tries to manipulate the children into a state of codependence. They will attempt to make the child(ren) feel incapable of doing anything on their own, and that they must rely on the opinion and direction of the toxic parent for all their decisions. This can be done in subtle, minor ways, by criticizing or making them feel incompetent, or their opinions unworthy. Comments like "don't be silly/stupid," "you won't make it on your own," and "you are not capable" are just examples of how a toxic parent can make your child's life miserable and cause them to hurt. It can have a major impact on their confidence and ability to feel capable of accomplishing goals on their own.

There are ways to build a protective barrier with your child to help them cope with a narcissistic parent. The following examples are ways in which you can foster a strong bond with your child(ren) while combatting the negative behavior of your ex and its effect on them:

- Praise them for hard work and encourage them to work towards their goals. When they fail or fall short of their achievements, reassure them of their capabilities and give them as much time and effort as possible to accomplish them. Even where they need assistance, assure them that they can do it on their own.

- Show empathy and explain it to them. Demonstrate the importance of caring for others by inviting them to get involved with volunteering, listening to other people's thoughts and feelings. Make it a priority to help them understand the value of feeling empathy for other people, and how to gauge their responses when handling delicate situations. A narcissist parent will not provide any guidance on empathy, as they are incapable of it.

- One of the most important gifts you can provide to your children is unconditional love. This is defined as a love that prevails above all else, regardless of what decisions your child makes and how they live. It is not an easy road for some parents who co-parent with narcissist ex-spouses, as some children will grow to exhibit signs of the narcissism of their own. This can lead to another level of difficulty and conflict. Despite this, you can continue to demonstrate love, even if you don't agree with your children's behavior or how they handle situations. You can always reassure them that you love and support them while explaining disapproval of some of their actions. It can be a difficult yet rewarding way to communicate with your children in the long-term, as they will always know that you are there for them.

How To Explain Separation To Children So They Can Understand What's Going On

Many parental separations occur when children are small and unable to emotionally understand and comprehend what is happening. It can be a scary experience for toddlers and young, school-aged children who are just learning to express their feelings. There are helpful ways to communicate simply so that your children will understand:

- Explain the separation in easy to understand terms: "mommy and daddy need to live apart for a while" or "mommy/daddy will be moving away for a bit." If they ask why just explain in simple terms: "sometimes we fight, and we need to spend time away so that we can get along better"

217

or "we need to live separately to be a better mom and dad to you."

- Let children know that the decision for separating, and divorce, is about the parents and has nothing to do with them. Make it explicitly clear that they have no fault or reason for the split. One of the separations of the most painful effects has on children is when they fear they are the reason for their parents. A narcissistic parent will make them feel this way at some point, either by blaming the child and/or the other parent. Keep explaining that they are not to blame and make a point of reminding them as often as needed.

- Give your children space and allow them to express themselves. It is important that they feel safe in venting or showing their emotions, as holding it in will only cause them more grief later. If they feel angry, and vocalize this to you, validate it for them. Let them know that they have a right to feel this, and other emotions.

Protecting Kids From Alienation And Parental Conflict; Helping Them Recognize And Work Through Their Emotions

As a parent, there is an instinct to want to protect our kids from harm, including emotional hurt and abuse. When a parent reveals their true narcissistic form, it can be difficult to shield children from them, even following a divorce where they are expected to visit the other parent or live with them as part of a custody agreement. When your children are in your care, exercise as much care and kindness as possible. Show your unwavering support for them in all that they do, and make sure they feel comfortable talking to you. They may want to express frustration about the other parent, and explain the hurt they feel, though maybe resisting because they fear you may tell the other parent, or their statements may reach them somehow. For this reason, reassure the kids that anything they divulge is safe with you and that they have no reason to fear any backlash or retaliation at the hands of the other parent. While it may seem easy to convince them, children can have more fear when they don't understand how a process works.

What happens once the separation becomes permanent, and the divorce proceedings begin? Children will need more of an explanation at this point, including what to expect next. Even when kids understand what is going on, they may not be able to comprehend life outside of what they are used to. If they (and you) viewed the separation as a temporary circumstance, a simple explanation can suffice, however, more information is needed when there is going to be a major change in the way the kids attend school, where they will live and how they will interact with family and friends. It's important to "fast-forward" to possible end results of the divorce, so that they know what to expect, and to prepare for it:

- Where are we going to live? In the early part of the separation, temporary arrangements are made. Usually, one parent will leave the household and live separately for a time period, during which both will decide if there is a chance of reconciliation. While the family home remains occupied, change is minimal, and no major upheaval, such as a change in school or living arrangements, is needed. The parent who lives apart may agree to pick up the child(ren) according to a temporary arrangement or find a way to meet with the other parent for access and visitation provisions.

- What if one of the parents is abusive? In severe cases, the parent leaving maybe you, if you've encountered abuse at the hands of your spouse or have reason to believe they are abusing the children. This can lead to a quick decision, such as seeking refuge with family or friends, or living in a temporary shelter or living situation, until permanent housing can be found. Children may already understand what is happening, though it can be a frightening experience, especially when they are not in a stable home and may have to move more than once following the split. During this time, it's important to stress to your children that the reason for the separation is due to their safety and well being. Make it clear that their safety and health are a priority, above all others. It is also important to impress upon them that moving is temporary and that soon, they will have a new home and feel better again. Keep hope and positivity alive as much as possible, even when you don't feel it yourself. Let the kids know that it is not easy for you, and them, but by working together, everything will get better in the end.

- Staying in contact with friends, family, and arrangements where a transfer in school is necessary. This can be a difficult realization for your child(ren), as they will lose contact with friends at school, and family and friends who live nearby. When you have to move, it's important to make arrangements in advance to stay in touch with the people they love, even if it's through online social media, and arranging visits now and again. Make a point of calling them regularly, and video-calling in real-time, to keep your kids connected to the people they will miss once they move. This is an invaluable way for your child(ren) to see that you care about their connections with family and friends by keeping the connection open and continuous. This will also help them to understand the importance of bonding and caring for others, which is not something their narcissistic parent will teach them.

Change is inevitable during a divorce or separation; whether it involves major overhauls or smaller changes, it's going to impact your children in many ways. Being a supportive, stable parent is going to help them anchor their lives throughout childhood and as they progress into adulthood. While the ex-spouse connection will be volatile, it's going to be easier for them to cope with you by their side.

Chapter 11
Says To Choose A New Partner

Loving Again After Leaving Your Emotionally Abusive Relationship

After dealing with a relationship where you were continuously emotionally abused, it can be a difficult task to let someone else in. You will need to let your guard down for your new love interest to come in. However, you are scared that you will be back to someone similar to the narcissist you ran away from, whose only goal is to dominate and manipulate you.

But this does not have to scare you. It may be difficult to open yourself once more, but if you know how to go into it the right way, it does not have to be so complicated. In this segment, we will be looking at how you can love again after you have broken free from the narcissist.

Make Sure You Have Moved On

Consistent emotional abuse like one the narcissist employs on their victims can leave a lot of scars emotionally and physically. If you have managed to break free, you need to be sure that you are already over the past experience of abuse. At this point, you should have taken steps to be over your ex and better still; there should be no contact between you both at this point. Before you think of delving into another relationship, you have to ensure that you are no longer holding on to the previous.

Get More Knowledge

Your past experience with a narcissist should have armed you with as much knowledge as you need. However, learning more is not a bad idea and can be quite helpful. Learn all you can about how to spot narcissistic partners who would abuse you in relationships.

To take it further, you can write down a list of healthy traits in relationships. Also, pen down those traits you will never accept. These could be some traits you noticed in your past relationship. Once you notice the new relationship is starting to get some level of seriousness, take out your list and let your new partner sees it. All couples have to clearly understand the boundaries and weaknesses of others and learn to respect them. This is particularly crucial for those that have dealt with abuse before. The most important thing is to search for a partner who meets the standards you have put in place for yourself.

Follow Your Gut

Once your new relationship has kicked off, watch out for behaviors that do not make you comfortable. The instant you begin to observe any of these behaviors in your new partner, do not let them slide. Ensure you do not forgo behaviors you can't deal with and call them minor. If your gut is telling you a particular situation is not right, then you should listen to it as there is most likely an atom of truth in it.

If you seem like your new partner will be fine if you speak about what you have observed, then ensure you do so. Pay close attention to their reaction when you confront them, and this will let you better understand the kind of individual they are. With the reaction, you can make a properly calculated decision about your new relationship.

Engage In Safe Dating

Even in instances where you have not dealt with a narcissistic relationship, it is crucial to engage in safe dating when you go into a new relationship. There are many ways to remain secure while dating. Some of these include:

- Meet up with your new love interest at a public place the few first dates

- Inform a trusted friend about your destination at all times

- Find your own means of transportation to the venue of the date. You don't want to get stuck in the same vehicle with someone you don't know so well

Doing all of these will help you determine if you can completely trust your new partner, the more serious the relationship becomes.

Do Not Rush Things

This falls under the category of engaging in safe dating. However, it is so essential that you need to focus on it specifically. Invest enough time in ensuring you get to know your new love interest better and vice versa. You should develop a relationship where you can both comfortably tell each other what you think and desire. Be sure that the relationship offers you and your partner mutual benefits and that you both are satisfied and happy.

Give your new love interest the respect they desire and expect similar treatment from them. Take the time you wish and do not be in haste to get into a new relationship. Watch out for signs of danger. For instance, if they seem in a hurry to get things going, then you need to exercise caution. The pace of the relationship should go at one that feels satisfactory to both partners involved. No one should feel coerced or manipulated into going at a faster pace than they find satisfying.

Let Your Present Partner Know About Your Past

A significant step to building a good relationship is to honestly communicate with your partner in detail. This is particularly important if you have previously dealt with emotional abuse in the past like the one the narcissist subjected you to.

Tell your partner how it felt to be manipulated, gaslighted, and controlled. If your partner understands where you are coming from, it will help ensure the relationship goes the way it should. Pay attention to the reaction of your partner when you divulge this information. This will help you determine if the relationship is right for you or not.

Believe That You Can Find Love Once More

Many victims who have dealt with bad relationships, including those with narcissists, believe that they don't have the capacity to get healthy and happy relationships. However, this is not the case. Always remember that there is always someone out there who is suitable and ideal for you. All you need to remember is to learn to love in a healthier manner than what you have been used to. If you can believe, then achieving it becomes easier.

Chapter 12
Narcissists and Marriage

5 Things To Look For In The Narcissist's View Of Marriage

In terms of marriage and partnership, the games and deceptions of a narcissist do not make for the best partner. In fact, there is no partnership present at all; perhaps only in fleeting moments. Partnership implies unity, harmony, and a mutual respect, trust and connection. All a narcissist has to offer is mind games, suffering, confusion and oppression. It can be highly oppressive living and being with a narcissist as they don't like to see you happy, thriving or succeeding in your own personal goals, dreams and aspirations. (We explored this earlier.)

Number 1: The Need To Control

Narcissists are extremely controlling. They see their partner as a target or supply for their deep- seated manipulations and need to control. Fortunately, you can spot this tendency early on, creating better boundaries and inner strength. It can be more difficult once you are already enticed and wrapped around their little finger, but if you can remain strong and centered from the start then there shouldn't be a problem with recognizing this sign that you are with a narcissist.

This control reflects into many areas. It may be the clothes you wear, your beliefs, your daily habits and actions, your likes and dislikes, and your holistic identity and sense of self. Whichever the expression, you are simply not allowed to be you or be free to make your own life choices.

Number 2: Emotion- Phobia!

Quite simply, narcissists are terrified of emotions. This is not in reference to manipulation or using negative and harmful emotional intents to cause pain or chaos, but it is talking about real and sincere emotions and connection. Unlike in normal relationships where love, care and affection are prevalent, narcissists are incapable of true intimacy and subsequently see marriage as a way to exert their dominance and emotional superiority. Of course, the narcissist is not in any way, shape or form emotionally superior- however they see themselves as better than you in some way. This is because of the distorted view that emotions and vulnerability are weak and inferior.

Earlier on you will recognize the need to use emotions to control, manipulate, dominate and suppress and will further realize that these personality traits are a recourse to married life.

Number 3: A Fragmented Family History?

There will always be some aspect of childhood trauma, repressions and family stories with your narcissistic partner. Most people see childhood or family related wounds as a way to self- develop, heal and transcend wounds and pains brought from childhood. Yet a narcissist is so afraid of vulnerability and looking to the core of themselves that the patterns and wounds brought from childhood will show their ugly face in your relationship. Your partner will use projection as a means to hide from their own issues, also masking their inner securities and wounds with negative and hurtful displays, words and behaviors.

In terms of what they look for, your partner essentially uses you as their scapegoat, perpetuating the cycles they are yet to heal.

Number 4: Projection: You As Their Mirror

You are essentially their mirror. Like with projecting their family traumas and childhood wounds, the narcissists perceive you as their mirror or shield to their own ignorance. Many things which require patience, understanding and compassion; a desire to help and heal one another, are instead met with projection. Imagine throwing a ball at a wall. Regardless of how many times the ball hits the wall, it will always bounce back. The ball is symbolic of the narcissist's intentions, motivation and inner turmoil and the wall is you. You are simply their shield and structure to bounce off and keep their games in play. Regardless of the negative trait, situation, story or (destructive) intention, the narcissist will always see you as someone to stand by their side or in front of them to take their 'stuff'.

Number 5: Insecurities Masked As Arrogance (And Other Less Than Favorable Qualities)

You will know you are with a narcissist when their deeply buried insecurities start to come to light. They will always be masked as arrogance, a false sense of superiority, self- centeredness, an inflated ego, and other less desirable personality traits. Real displays of vulnerability, raw emotion, and low feeling or moods which are natural, and a part of our humanity will never be shown. Wounds, traumas, doubts, fears, and general self- discovery or self- development are all covered by a need to appear the best, all together, omniscient and forcefully superior. There is no sense of room and space for healing and in the narcissist's eye they are already perfect. They want you to believe they are perfect too, and anything which threatens their sense of self- created status is met with abuse, manipulation or projection- like tactics.

In the narcissist's eye, you are less smart, less accomplished, less capable and less deserving, in all areas of life.

Reason Why A Narcissist Gets Married

This brings us onto why a narcissist gets married. This segment may be heard to understand and comprehend, as; let's face it, narcissism is a pretty severe and distorted personality to embody. But the truth will set you free and hopefully further prevent a future marriage or relationship with a narcissist.

A Scapegoat

Unfortunately, you are their scapegoat. Like in the signs and things to watch out for, a narcissist sees you as their mirror to project all their stuff on. You will be blamed for all of their own wrongdoings, judged and persecuted for the narcissist's mistake, faults, and negative traits. This is how narcissists fundamentally view marriage; they see their partner as a tool for shifting blame and passing responsibility. The sad truth is that they need this. They need to have someone in their life, hence why they choose to get married. Once they have found someone who is enticed by their charm and immersed in their illusions, they have hit the jackpot. The fact that anyone who does not have Narcissistic Personality Disorder is or has capabilities for compassion, kindness, care, intimacy, patience, and a general sense of 'niceness' signifies that they will make the perfect scapegoat.

To Perpetuate Their Own Insecurities/ Traumas/ Emotional Wounds

It may seem like something out of a psychological thriller or drama movie, but one of the reasons why a narcissist gets married is to perpetuate their own insecurities, traumas and wounds. Remember that narcissists have some deep vulnerabilities which they are too afraid to admit. Narcissists can live their whole lives in states of inner depression, chaos and turmoil, and with further repressions and unresolved wounds and pains; without ever healing or transcending from them. Their narcissism is simply a cover and a shield to hide them from their own wounds. Like with anything in life, we are social and family- oriented creatures. (Yes, even narcissists!) This means that they need someone to bounce off, be with as a support system and mirror. Of course, the narcissist will never change or even wish to heal or transcend their narcissistic ways, but they need someone all the same. You will be their rock and gem, just unfortunately in a way which drains you, depletes you, and leaves you feeling psychologically and mentally abused.

To Keep Their Illusions Intact

Narcissists get married to keep their illusions intact. They need you to stay fooled and enticed in their games and manipulations. The saying there is "support or power in numbers" applies here. In marriage, the narcissist receives your love and support which further empowers them and keeps their narcissistic ways in a sense of acceptance. If there is no support, then there is no acceptance. Something cannot exist without the energy, awareness and thumbs up from people. It is we human beings who create and shape reality as we know it. This is one of the key reasons why a narcissist gets married, because they know that their illusions will only survive and thrive through the support of another. Again, you become like their rock or gem. This support may be unconscious or based on you being fooled and stuck in their games, however it is still a green light.

For Peers And Colleagues

What better way to keep one's social illusions of charm and eloquence in play then to have a level- headed, normal and sincere partner on their arm? Having a husband or wife is the cherry on top of the cake to a narcissist, and also the foundation which keeps their personality and self- created identity at play. To peers and colleagues, the narcissist appears normal and even kind, wise and beautiful (in an inner beauty sense) when they have a sane partner by their side. Their partner provides a justification, grounding and acceptance. The narcissist also knows that any moments of their narcissistic personality which may come to light will always be supported, backed up and justified through their partner's compassion and love. It is like you (the husband or wife) perpetuates and makes their innate narcissism OK and acceptable; they know that you will always have their back and make their shadow look like shine. This is because this is what a real partnership and marriage looks like, you are supposed to support your partner and be there for them in times of need. Yet, it is not reciprocated and leaves you clinging onto the idea and false reality that your partner is charming and is capable of a real social grace, kindness and companionship. When you are alone again, you will once again be the target of their games and abuse.

For Their Sense Of Success: Self Identity And Appearance

Furthermore, they need a partner for their success, self- identity and appearance. Their professional and personal life are fueled by your love and sanity. Companionship and intimacy are a natural and fundamental part of life and the narcissist knows this- even if they can't display real intimacy and companionship themselves. They hide behind you and your favorable beautiful qualities, always making them appear in a positive light. In fact, their self- identity and public or professional/ personal persona depends on this. If you were to withdraw your support, who would they be? They could be exposed in their real character, or their hidden intentions and motivations could be brought to the surface. Marriage to a sane, sincere and non- narcissistic partner is the perfect shield.

'The Charm Illusion'

Most people would not choose a partner or lifelong companion if they knew they would be psychologically and emotionally abusive, manipulative and holistically speaking lacking in such empathy. So, this is the precise reason why a narcissist needs a marriage partner. Who would want to be married to a narcissist and enter into such a formal and long- standing agreement? The answer is no one- no one would willingly or consciously choose this. It all therefore comes down to the charm illusion, the illusion from the start of your connection that your partner really is charming, decent and sincere. If their husband or wife sees them as beautiful, kind and worthy of a loving and supportive marriage, why wouldn't others see them as worthy in other aspects of life? A narcissist depends on the support and love of friends, peers and colleagues, so having yours is the first and main step. You are like the anchor, cement and seed all in one. Without you, the narcissist is nothing. "The charm illusion" is essentially the delusions and harmful stories your partner can keep through your own acceptance and compassionate, yet self- detrimental, support.

Chapter 13
Divorcing A Narcissist

"It may be difficult at first but divorcing a narcissist is worth it."

I sn't this a statement you tell yourself every day!? It plays in your mind like a mantra, the self- affirmation reminding you that going in the right direction will be worth it in the end. It should be so easy- why stay with someone who has no empathy, care or kindness towards you and who wants to see you suffer? Yet it is not as easy as it seems, hence why you need to repeat statements such as this.

This is one thing that many people don't tell you when taking the steps to divorce a narcissist. You need mantras or affirmation- like statements to keep you on course, remind you that this really is in your best interests, and that it will be worth it in the end. The psychological, mental and emotional abuse and trauma you have suffered are real, and regardless of how many times you have been gaslighted, or made to appear crazy, in the wrong or losing the plot, you know the truth in the core of your cells. Being with a narcissist is completely detrimental to your health.

Luckily there are many steps that can be taken. A covert narcissist is exactly this- covert; still in the shadows of their own manipulations, delusions and shady- hurtful character. They are not (yet) in the open or publicly acknowledged, and is this because you have not yet made the decision to allow them to be seen in their true light? Taking a stand and choosing, with your own free will, inner strength and sheer conviction, that you will no longer allow yourself to be abused, victimized or manipulated allow your partner to be seen, and for you to subsequently finally take the steps necessary to be free from their abuse.

Of course, all of this is something you know- so see these words as a reflection of your own psyche and conscious mind telling you exactly how it is. The fact that you are reading this and have chosen, consciously, to align with your true self and leave your narcissistic partner for good implies that you are already well on course. This is confirmation, and you are heading in the right direction! You are strong beyond measure.

Divorcing A Narcissist: Stop Reacting!

Reaction. Reaction is not the same as response. When you respond to someone or something, you provide a space, wisdom and awareness to connect on a mature and responsible level. Responding allows for authenticity, calmness of thought and clarity in communication. Yet, reacting is something completely different.

The key to your narcissistic partner's success is in your reaction. They need people to become emotionally entwined and engaged with their stories. If there is no reaction then there is no exchange- no one is appeasing or empowering them. Power is a great word to be aware of here. Reaction provides a narcissist's empowerment, or more accurately faulty sense of empowerment. Causing pain, hurt and manipulation to others is not empowerment. Regardless, reacting provides the sustenance that a narcissist needs, so the best way to heal and begin your own journey of empowerment is to stop reacting and start responding.

Things To Be Mindful Of: How You May Be Reacting!

Your partner attempts to provoke a reaction and you allow it. Instead of taking a moment to slow down, be calm inside and recognize the intentions of causing destruction, chaos and harm; you play to their manipulations. Thus, a vicious and highly repetitive cycle can begin and continue for hours or even days on end. The key is to detach and not get caught up in their games. It can be easier said than done, however, the tips and techniques for effective response below can really help with this.

'Snide remarks.' Expanding from example 1, at this stage your partner should know you very well and therefore know your triggers. Snide remarks or specific comments are a very effective way to get a reaction from you and subsequently enable them to continue in their ways.

'Awareness goes where energy flows!' If you don't give your attention, time or energy to something, how can it perpetuate? The answer is that it can't. The intentions and motivations of your partner require energy and attention, otherwise they are formless.

Watch out for the signs. Assuming you have been with your partner for a while you will know the signs to when they are going to begin their games. If they are bored or displaying signs of frustration, stimulation or boredom this is a sure warning that you will soon become their target for their stimulation. A narcissist needs that 'spark' to feed their egocentricity, self- centeredness and feelings of self- worth. Without it, their illusions start to crumble down and they have no choice but to look within, seek help and ways to change; which are of course very rare for a narcissist.

If you feel yourself becoming stressed, anxious, nervous or heated inside, these are sure signs that you are on the verge of a reaction. Unlike in partnerships where narcissism is not present or a key theme, and where most people are allowed a few moments of blowing off steam or showing weakness; in this relationship, you are not provided the patience, compassion or support necessary. This means that even when or if your partner does happen to be in a serene, kind or non- narcissistic space you may unfortunately spark them with your own reactive behaviors. It is extremely rare for a true narcissist to see you becoming upset or worked up on your own accord and not use it as a chance for drama, or further manipulation.

A Deeper Look Into Divorce And Reaction

Divorce is a serious thing. The process inevitably means that you have decided to part ways, restart your life and take back your individual resources, belongings and physical necessities. This in itself is a major red flag in a codependent- narcissist relationship! Your partner's entire identity is merged in the reality that he or she can feed off you, use you as their hidden and subtle yet powerful support system, and bounce off your kindness, empathy and positive attributes. So, once you started responding this destroys their world. They can no longer keep up the facade once you make the decision that their actions are not acceptable. This can only happen when you begin to respond.

How To Start Responding

The true response begins when you start to slow down and become an observer of both your own thoughts and feelings and your partner's. This is best achieved through meditation and mindfulness. The significance of these two self- help methods cannot be overlooked. They are both extremely powerful in helping you to live your best life, be free from narcissistic abuse or targeting, and start responding.

Meditation

Why is engaging in meditation one of the best ways to learn how to respond and thus change the way you perceive and feel about the situation? Because, meditation allows you to detach from overactive thoughts and feelings, further becoming the observer. When you observe you are not caught up in the emotions or drama associated with your partner's intentions. You can calm your mind, control your feelings and responses, and feel more peaceful within. Clarity of mind and thought can also result, and you generally become more insightful, patient, wise and loving with meditation.

Mindfulness

Linked to meditation is the power of mindfulness. Mindfulness is exactly what the word implies, it allows you to become more mindful or conscious. Being conscious simply means embodying a higher awareness and level of integrity. You won't want to react when you start to integrate the lessons and vibration of mindfulness as you will not want to lower yourself to such levels. There is an innate dosage of eloquence, self- respect, grace and personal integrity associated and developed with mindfulness, and your viewpoints and perspectives will change for the better. Any action or behavior of your partner can be met with a greater conscious reaction and response. Further, you will start to feel good about the situation, regardless of how testing it is, and will see the positive.

In essence, mindfulness can help you see the light and recognize that your mind is a powerful tool. You are not responsible for your partner's thoughts, behaviors or in/actions, but you do have control over your own.

How To Manage Conflict

Managing conflict is the same if not similar to learning how to respond. When dealing with someone with deeply buried narcissism, you need to know how to respond appropriately and in a way that doesn't cause further harm to yourself. Once again, you are not responsible for the narcissist's energy. You may have spent years being the most patient, loyal, loving and understanding or empathetic partner, yet these qualities are all lost on them. Managing conflict during or after the divorce proceedings should not be viewed as any different.

Please do not make the mistake of thinking that now you are finally free, or soon to be free, that your partner will suddenly 'see sense' or have a heartfelt awakening. They will not. A narcissist will always view you as their scapegoat and wall or mirror to project their stuff onto, so now you are taking the correct steps and working towards your own wellbeing and happiness; they do not want to let go or give you up so easily.

The following steps may seem simple or effortlessly implemented, yet they are not! Narcissists will do everything in their power to maintain their illusion of power and try to keep you entrapped in their games until it really is all over. So, in order to combat this and manage conflict successfully, do stay committed and completely aligned to the following. They are all necessary for your happiness, peace of mind and success.

Chapter 14
Co-parenting With A Narcissist

What if you end a relationship with a narcissist, but you have children together? This complicates the situation, but it isn't hopeless. Your child can still grow up healthy and happy; you will have to be the responsible, consistent figure in their lives. Unfortunately, you cannot depend on your ex to pull their weight in this way. This part explores what your child might be going through, how to prioritize their well-being, and how-to co-parent with an ex who will never cooperate the way you want. This will seem overwhelming - how can you embody the role of two parents at once while combating your ex's toxicity? - so you will also learn some methods for self-care.

What It's Like Being The Child Of A Narcissist

You know what it's like to be the partner of a narcissist, but what about a child? It's important to understand what your kid is going through if their other parent - your ex - is a narcissist. Depending on how long you were with your ex with a child or children in the mix, you've probably noticed the unhealthy aspects of their parenting style. Here are some common consequences:

The child's needs and wants are ignored

Just like with their partner, a narcissist won't pay attention to what their child needs or wants. The narcissist's needs always take priority, so the child learns from a young age that what they want doesn't matter. They are never nurtured and taught to feel safe. They feel small and insignificant. These kids may not even know how to express what they want and need, because that type of thinking has never been encouraged. Their sense of self can be very stunted.

To counter this messaging, encourage your child to pursue their dreams, and show interest in what they're into. Ask them questions about how they feel and what they think about things, whether it's movies, friendships, or the separation from your ex. If your kid expresses a lot of insecurity and self-doubt, gently guide them, so they feel like they have support, but also freedom. This guidance can be applied to finding a hobby or having conversations about what they're feeling about their life.

The child has a lot of anxiety about their worth

Narcissists frequently put very high expectations on their kids. They believe their kids reflect back on them, so they push them to succeed. The child won't feel loved unless they're doing something well, looking a certain way, or thinking certain things. The narcissist might be very critical, judgmental, and withholding when their kid inevitably "fails." The child will feel like nothing they do is ever good enough. It's very common for these kids to have low self-esteem and very poor self-worth because they believe love is conditional.

Pushing back against the belief that love is conditional is arguably the most important thing you can do as a parent. Parents should always be the people a child can rely on for love, no matter what. If your ex isn't capable of being that, it's all the more important that you take on that role wholeheartedly. Always celebrate your child, especially when they "fail" or don't meet the expectations your ex set up. Let them know your love isn't dependent on their successes; you love them because of who they are, not what they do. You can still encourage them to improve and set goals, but never attach your attention and affection to an outcome. Be sure to actually tell them you love them no matter what, too. Words are powerful.

The child is the one taking care of their parent's emotional needs

From a very young age, the children of narcissists learn to always tiptoe around their parent. They figure out pretty quickly that their parent's emotions are unstable and prone to quick change. The parent will start looking to the child to help them work through things. This can result in telling them things that are too mature for the child to deal with and expecting support. The child becomes the responsible one - the voice of reason - way too soon. Their own emotions are neglected, and the child isn't able to develop healthy self-care skills.

How To Deal With A Narcissistic Co-Parent

Recovery from a relationship with a narcissist is complicated if you have kids. Odds are you won't be able to stick to a non-contact rule or cut them out of your life completely. Hopefully, you can if there was abuse in the relationship and the law protects you, but even then, things don't always go the way they should. If your ex wants to be involved in your children's lives, there are certain things you can do to make the process easier and safer.

Set communication boundaries

As a co-parent, you will need to talk to your ex. However, you can decide when you talk and about what. Your ex will always try to push the boundaries and use any opportunity to get under your skin. They may even try to get you so angry that you lose control, which gives them leverage over you. Avoid talking on the phone or in person if your ex likes to go on rants, emotionally abuse you, or otherwise try to get you worked up. Stick to emails, which gives you more control over what you say, and it keeps everything in writing.

It's impossible to control what your ex says when your kid is with them. However, when the kid is with you, you can set more boundaries. Expect your ex to want to talk to the kid a lot. Set a schedule and stick to it. For example, no phone calls on school nights later than 8pm, and only after homework is done. Your ex will probably try to break these rules, so stand your ground. If you believe your ex is using phone calls to emotionally abuse your child or disregard any other agreements made in court, consider recording them. In many places, you must tell your ex their call is being recorded. Talk to a lawyer before moving forward.

If things are too complicated and difficult, get a parent coordinator. Judges appoint these people, and they basically act as a mediator between you and your ex, so you don't need to talk to them unless absolutely necessary. The parent coordinator handles scheduling visits and any other communication.

Protect your child

If your ex has custody or visitation rights, it's hard to control what your ex says or does. However, you should never use your child as a messenger pigeon. Don't ask them to communicate with your ex on your behalf or ask them to spy. This puts the kid in a very awkward and possibly scary situation. You can find out how they're being treated and what they're doing just by having normal conversations. If you're concerned by something they say, ask them a question like, "How does that make you feel?" It can be hard to know what to say and there are certain things your child might not want to talk about with you, so getting your kid to counseling is an excellent idea.

Be especially aware of how your child's milestones might affect your ex. As healthy kids get older, they will become more independent. Narcissists typically resist this aspect of child-rearing because they want to keep control. Anticipate your ex becoming stricter, more critical, or more emotionally unstable at these times. Be ready to encourage your child and set more boundaries with your ex if necessary, so your kid feels extra secure and supported.

You will feel a lot of emotions, especially negative ones, during a co-parenting scenario with a narcissist. Don't use your child as a sounding board for your frustrations with your ex. This not only makes the kid feel like they need to comfort you and manage your feelings it makes them feel torn about their love for their other parent. They might instinctively resist your criticisms and jump to your ex's defense or become angry and even scared of their other parent. This puts them in your ex's crosshairs while also making your ex angry at you for turning their child against them. The already-fragile co-parenting situation becomes even more volatile and stressful for your child.

The more written detail, the better

Co-parenting with a narcissist is complicated and every situation is a little different. One of the best things anyone can do is keep detailed records. Right at the beginning, when you start seeing a family law attorney, tell them what's going on with your ex. Tell them they are a narcissist and are "high-conflict," which is a legal term for these types of custody scenarios. In your custody agreement, write down every detail, like who pays for what, the days and times they have visitation, holiday visitations, and more.

Having detailed records is also important as life continues, because your ex is unlikely to peacefully follow the rules. They will try to push back and having records of their bad behavior protects you and your child(ren). If they cancel or try to move around visitation, write it down. If they refuse to pay for something or are late with the money, write it down. Using phone calls to manipulate your kid? Let them know you are going to be recording the call. Any communication between you two should be saved, if possible. This evidence lets you hold them accountable.

What You Can Do To Be A Better Parent

By now, you know that your ex will never be a good co-parent. Parenting is all about putting your child's needs before your own and narcissists aren't capable of doing that with anyone. At least, not consistently. This means you have to be both a parent and someone who counters any toxic, negative messaging coming from your ex. You'll feel overwhelmed. How can you accomplish this?

Take care of yourself

Self-care is not selfish. As a parent, this has never been truer. If you let yourself get drained, worn down, and depleted, you'll have nothing to offer your kid. You'll have less patience, less stability, and more irritability. Your kid won't come to you because they'll see how exhausted you are, and they won't want to burden you. Not only will you not have the physical or emotional energy to care for them, but you're modeling unhealthy habits they will imitate. They won't know how to take care of themselves and like you, they'll burn out. For both your sake and the sake of your kids, practice good self-care.

Don't let your ex manipulate you

To be a good parent, one of the best things you can do is not let your ex infect you with toxic thoughts and beliefs. As you know, they will use your child as a weapon. Expect to hear things like, "How could you do this to our family?" They will try to make you guilty for leaving and say that the separation is bad for your children. When they see you aren't budging, they'll move on to the custody agreement, and say, "That's bad, too." Don't believe it. You know what your ex was like. They will be just as critical and selfish in their relationship with their child as they were with you, so leaving and sticking to a certain arrangement is the only healthy thing to do.

Your ex probably won't stay quiet about their frustrations and will trash you on social media and to anyone who will listen. Having people, even friends, believe you are a bad parent can be really hard. Keep standing firm and remembering that this is what's best for your child. The people who really know you will be supportive.

Chapter 15
Steps to Getting Your Life Back After Narcissistic Relationship

Being a victim of abuse in a narcissistic relationship is terrible, and the truth is, the longer you remain in the relationship, the worse it gets. A lot of people spend many years of their lives dwelling in such abusive relationships and hoping that things would get better someday. Sadly, when they finally come to the realization that things will either remain the same, or even get worse, they seek redress, and they do so by either abandoning their partners or terminating the relationships.

When these victims terminate and severe their relationships with their tormentors, most times, they come out worse than how they got into these relationships - it is either they are mentally broken, psychologically damaged or physically handicapped, etc. And there is always the need for them to be rehabilitated and brought back to the level where they are capable of making logical decisions and generally embracing who they are as human beings.

As humans, it is normal for people to hold on to their pasts and make decisions based on their experiences - No wonder victims of abuse find it hard to move away from the pains and agony inflicted on them by their partners.

Although victims of abuse reminisce on their pains and agony from time to time, it is important for them to let go of the past and focus on building a bright future, full of joy, happiness, and laughter.

When victims of narcissistic abuse are interviewed during therapy, their display of shock and disbelief is evident, especially when they look back at their relationships and realize the amount of mental and psychological trauma they had to go through. It is even normal for them to ask questions like; did he love me at all? What did I do to make him treat me that way? I thought he loved me!

However, narcissists are who they are; thus, their actions weren't tied to external factors or conditions. They only exhibited traits that are resident in them, and as hard as this might be for their victims, it is important for them to accept it and move on.

Talking about moving on, below are 7 practices you should indulge in while trying to get your life back after leaving a narcissistic relationship;

Make Sure You Set Boundaries

When you walk out of a narcissistic relationship, it is important to build a shield around yourself, and one of the ways to achieve this is to put some physical distance between yourself and your ex. You should also checkmate the things that remind you of your ex, because such memories will only trigger your pain, and potentially slow down your recovery. To achieve this, you are advised to avoid stalking them, and rather blacklist their emails, social media handles, and phone numbers.

In a situation where you are incapable of physically moving away from them, you can explore the old technique called 'grey rock.' The idea behind this one is, although you interact with your abuser, the truth is, you're not engaged mentally and emotionally, thus, there's really no way he can exploit you.

They may get you extremely upset but you'll keep a straight face, and make it seem like everything is fine. However, when you're alone and in your own space, you can let it all out. It is okay to cry, scream or even cuss! Do whatever bring you relief.

Finally, another effective way of building a boundary around you is by mastering the art of saying no. It is important to say no to certain propositions, especially when they lack substance or any real value. The habit of saying 'No' will definitely help you build self-respect and true confidence. Your boundary can be likened to a cell wall in the body (it takes out toxic elements and keeps nutrients).

Get Rid Of The Toxicity

When victims of narcissistic relationships look back at the times they spent with their partners and consider how they did everything within their power to please and appease them, they realize how painful the process has been and the amount of time they've wasted. The truth is

NARCISSISTIC, CODEPENDENCY AND
GASLIGHTING EFFECT BIBLE

that these people have been exposed to some serious mental disorder, which is generally unhealthy for their mental wellbeing.

When empaths go into relationships with narcissists, they make major sacrifices to keep their partners happy, and most times they go as far as putting their partner's interests first. Sadly, these self-serving and manipulative narcissistic individuals know all about this and rather than appreciate it, they take full advantage – their manipulative ways only result in pain and anguish in their partner's lives and this leads to a lot of toxicity.

However, now that the relationship is over, it is time to get rid of the toxicity by restoring some level of clarity, and the way to go about it is to externalize it.

The process of externalization includes talking to trusted friends, engaging a therapist, writing a journal, and even joining a support group to connect with people that have gone through similar experiences. When you externalize, you'll realize that your chaotic thoughts begin to form meaningful patterns bit by bit. There are several other forms of externalization methods including yoga, dance, massage, sweating, and deep breathing, etc. When you indulge in these practices, your body will naturally metabolize the toxic chemicals that have been generated during the different stages of the failed relationship.

Embrace The Truth And Forgive Yourself

This is a very critical step because it helps in setting your mind straight. During this stage, you will have to embrace the truth by accepting the fact that your ex was not only toxic but was also out to knowingly hurt you. Realize you have been manipulated, abused and tricked! Your high threshold for pain worked in your abuser's advantage and he kept pushing you farther and farther with each round of abuse. The fact that you genuinely loved your partner made it difficult for you to see the warning signs and your best traits were explored and used against you: openness, desire to explore, empathy and positivity, etc.

Finally, you were in a relationship with a sadistic person whose only interest is to hurt others, and the fact that you were ignorant of this fact made it easy for him to outmaneuver you.

When you accept the truth, you'll realize that none of it was actually your fault, thus, you'll have to forgive yourself.

Accept The Fact That Part Of You Knew

You have to accept the fact that a part of you knew but you choose to ignore it. This is an important step because it involves you accepting responsibility (do not confuse it with self-blame) and carrying out a post-mortem analysis of all that happened during the relationship.

It is possible that you must have ignored some weird feelings you had during the early stages of the relationship. Maybe a couple of things he said didn't add up. Go back in your mind and ask yourself why you chose to disregard your basic instincts. Was it predicated on the fact that you wanted your relationship to work? Was it as a result of the initial display of admiration and love that filled that void in your soul?

It is normal for people that weren't loved by their parents as kids to seek fulfillment elsewhere in their adult lives and it is a serious vulnerability. Especially in the hands of these narcissistic predators who can easily detect that urge for love and be attracted to it, just like sharks are attracted by the scent of fresh blood.

In this world, your instinct is your best friend, and the more you listen to it, the more embolden it becomes. However, it may be hard for you to connect with your instincts after such an abusive relationship and the reason is that people become hypersensitive as a result of PTSD.

During this stage, it can be hard to identify a real threat, thus, you need to maintain some level of calmness in other to heal. Finally, during this stage, you need to avoid uncertain situations and stay away from people with questionable characters

Embark On A Soul Searching

The process of surviving and healing from an abusive relationship presents a wonderful opportunity for you to learn and grow, and the reason is that you'll see all your vulnerabilities clearly.

When you ascertain your vulnerabilities, you'll know exactly how to go about fixing issues, however, a lot of people lack this knowledge and that's why most of them are stuck with the same modus operandi for the majority of their lives, even while seeking change.

Real change emanates from deep work and the key to this process is soul searching (or self-inquiry). When you walk out of an abusive narcissistic relationship, you might be physically free but a part of you is still stuck in a mental prison, thus, the only way to be truly free is to reawaken your mind through soul searching.

When you do some proper soul searching, you might come to the realization that some of the vulnerabilities that attract manipulators into your life include;

1. Your desire for security – Sometimes, when children are neglected by their fathers during their childhood, it comes back to haunt them in the future. The presence of a father figure is important in the life of a child because one of his fundamental responsibilities is to instill a sense of self-protection in his children (this is naturally achieved through the father's day to day actions). When children lack this essential element, they grow into adults with an impaired sense of security.

2. Your desire for adoration – When children are raised by insensitive and ignorant parents, they mostly grow into adults who display symptoms of a total lack of confidence and low self-esteem. Thus, making them extremely vulnerable to narcissistic predators, that only need to shower them with praises in other to achieve their aims.

3. Your desire for acknowledgment – A lot of people lack self-confidence and it makes them go about seeking validation and acknowledgment unknowingly. Sometimes, even people that have accomplished a lot in life still have these traits, because lack of confidence doesn't dwell on the surface, it is rooted somewhere in their subconscious. Thus, to really have a go at it, you have to master the art of self-talk, which will ultimately lead you to self-dependence (the greatest key to freedom).

Re-Navigate Your Focus

After you walk out of a narcissistic relationship, you'll be naturally pulled towards the past (it is trauma bond and cognitive dissonance at work). When this occurs, it only shows that you still have to process some emotions and understand some things. However, you have to consciously make sure that your past does not outshine your present.

Moving forward, you should be mindful of your present and at the same time, think about the type of future you intend to create for yourself. You have to resurrect all your dreams, especially the ones you let go during your stint with your ex.

When you have a sense of purpose and things to look forward to in life, you'll always muster the required amount of energy to overcome the effects of trauma in your life. When you incubate positive thoughts only, you will quickly move from being a victim to becoming a hero, in the blink of an eye.

Chapter 16
Developing Emotional Intelligence
After Narcissistic Abuse

Once you survive a narcissistic relationship, nothing is more important than healing. You have to learn how to regain your self-esteem and control. Recovery is not just about getting out of an abusive situation; it is primarily about creating a new emotional safety net for yourself. It is possible that it might take you a while to get over your trauma, but it is not the end of the world. Recovery is a gradual but efficient process. The following are some of the important things that you must keep in mind when working your way back into normalcy:

- Self-soothing and grounding techniques

A narcissist will confuse your concept of abandonment. If you have had issues with abandonment before, they will get worse during your relationship with them. The betrayal and subsequent abandonment make you afraid. You feel you are abandoned because you are not good enough. There are negative emotions that can emanate from this, including panic, depression and sadness. Many victims make the mistake of turning back to their abuser because they have learned to believe they cannot survive without them.

Grounding yourself can help you overcome these problems. It is normal to feel like you lack something in the aftermath of this abuse. However, you do not have to react or respond to it by going back. Your amygdala might attempt to hijack your emotions from time to time, and the only way out is to remind yourself why you are not going back.

- Ask for help

You might not be capable of handling your recovery on your own, so seek professional support. In the wake of a narcissistic relationship, you often feel you cannot trust anyone to understand what you have been through. The rest of the world feels alienated from you. Instead of seeing people as a source of support, you feel they will judge you and you hold back.

At the end of an abusive relationship there are so many things that are left unresolved. You have a lot of unanswered questions, unfulfilled promises, unreciprocated love and affection. All these are things that you might not be able to deal with on your own. It is wise to get professional help so that you can understand yourself better and manage your expectations better too.

The pain you feel at the end of this relationship is two-fold. You are in pain because the one person you invested everything on has turned out to be the worst investment of your life so far. You are also in pain because the relationship that you had so much faith in did not work out. You, therefore, need to heal from these two situations to completely heal and move on with life.

- Stay away from your abuser

Resist the urge to reach out to your abuser. Even if you miss them, stay away from them. Cut them off your contact list and forget about them. The confusion you experience will pass. One of the biggest mistakes that many victims make is that even after they are done with the relationship, they still leave room in their lives just in case their narcissistic partner can come back.

Forget about second chances. A lot of victims who go back to their abusers end up worse, and some end up dead. You don't have to reach out to them. Some narcissists will reach out to you after a long period of silence. They might reach out promising to change, telling you how things have been difficult in their lives since you left them. If you fall for this trick, you will never heal.

Whatever they do with their lives once you walk away is not your concern. They are adults and can make adult choices about their lives. You are an adult too, and your adult choice is to start afresh. The moment your abuser reaches out to you and you allow them a few minutes of your time, you are back to the very beginning. Never forget that narcissists always believe you need them more than they need you. They have a lot of tricks up their sleeve that will manipulate you back into their trap, if you allow them.

- Rebuilding your life

There are a lot of things that you can do to rebuild your life. Rebuilding your life is not just about reengaging people you had cut off; it is also about rebuilding your esteem and confidence. You have a lot of feelings bottled up inside. Don't keep them locked down, release them. Find different avenues where you can release your feelings.

Start writing, painting, gardening; or join a dancing class, an amateur sports team; and schedule social meetings with your close friends and have fun together. These are just a few things you can do to help you feel better again. Try and avoid risky or unhealthy behavior though, because these might end up in disaster.

- Accept your partner

You need to accept your partner for who they are. They are narcissists. They might be suffering from NPD. What acceptance does is to remind you that there is nothing you could have done to make them any different. They believe they are perfect the way they are. Since they cannot accept you as you are, it is best if you walk away and start afresh.

Accepting your partner's narcissism is another step towards forgiving yourself. You did all you could, but they could never change. There was never an intent to change in them. This will also help you overcome the feelings of self-doubt that you might have harbored for a long time.

- Forgiveness

Are you willing to forgive yourself for your role in the relationship? Forgiveness sets the tone for healing. Remember that forgiveness will only come after you have accepted your role in the relationship, and accepted responsibility for it. Everyone makes mistakes. It is normal to find yourself in a hardship situation out of your own doing. This is life, forgive yourself and move on. It is the things that you do and how you respond to these situations that will determine how your life turns out.

- Ease the pressure to recover

With your abuser out of the picture, there is a lot of pressure for you to recover and build a new life. Try to tone down the pressure. There is no time limit within which you must recover and start living a normal life.

Your partner might have stolen your identity from you, but this does not mean you have to hurry to earn it back.

Recovery is a gradual process. Everything around you takes time. You have to readjust to a lot of things in life, and if you rush it, you might be overwhelmed. It is okay to feel sorry for yourself, but don't let it turn into self-pity, or you might turn into a self-loathing individual. There is no race to recovery, it is a process.

Fundamentals Of Recovery From Narcissistic Abuse

There are four important tenets that will define your recovery process, and help you survive a narcissist. Everything else you do throughout your emotional journey revolves around the following:

Self-esteem

Self-esteem is simply you, supporting yourself. You take back control from your partner, control over your emotions, your behavior, actions, your mind and your body. Everything that your partner took from you is back in your hands.

Esteem is not just about yourself; it is also about the way you interact with the environment around you. It is about how you respond to people, institutions and so forth. It is important to get back control over your esteem, because without it, you will continue on the destructive path of self-sabotage that your abusive partner had led you to.

You have to learn to speak positively to yourself. Don't hold back from pursuing things that appeal to you. If you had resorted to substance abuse to numb the pain of your abusive relationship, talk to someone about quitting.

Having lived through a life where you were afraid to try anything, it is time for you to motivate yourself to throw your hat in the ring. You might not be selected, but you challenged for something. Take back control over your life.

Self-love

No one will ever love you more than you love yourself. Loving yourself is about protecting the things that are dear to you. Nurture your feelings and emotions. You have to stop sacrificing your needs so someone else can be happy. Make yourself a priority. Let go of the tendency to abandon your needs for the sake of a superficial connection with someone else. One of the ways you can go about rekindling your self-love is to realize the things that you can control in life and those that you cannot. Remind yourself why you feel it is necessary for you to change something in your life. For most ladies, one of the things they have to deal with is body shaming when they get out of a narcissistic relationship. You have to learn to accept and appreciate your body the way it is. In case you are worried about things that you are unable to change, teach yourself to drown those emotions and sentiments instead. Find things that you are grateful for and enjoy doing them. If possible, do them with people who are close to you so that you remember just how amazing your life should be, and embrace it.

Self-trust

Fear and doubt are common in victims of narcissistic abuse. Your partner made sure the only person who made decisions in your life was them. They took away your ability to decide what you want or how you want things done. They became the ultimate source of power in your life. When you are unable to trust in yourself, you struggle to do things. You cannot make quick decisions because you are afraid you might choose the wrong thing. Your worry is that all the bad things you have experienced might happen to you if you decide for yourself. As a result, you second-guess yourself all the time.

Trust in your gut. Do something because you feel it is right. Don't hold back. To rebuild trust in yourself, you must take action. It is impossible to do this without stepping out and challenging yourself to try.

Self-worth

Why is it important that you rediscover your self-worth after walking away from a narcissistic partner? Self-worth is about realizing what your value is. When you understand your worth, it is difficult for someone to begrudge you what you deserve. Your value system sets you up high, and people who interact with you do so because they understand and appreciate how you treasure yourself. If you can't see your worth, no one else will. Even those who do will never take you seriously.

The challenge with lacking self-worth is that you usually end up compromising where you should not. Lack of self-worth also makes you feel ashamed and unworthy even without anyone provoking a reaction from you. You inherently believe you don't deserve the good things because you are not good enough.

Speak up for your rights. Don't shy away from the spotlight. Someone might use this to take advantage of you. Respect and take care of yourself. To rebuild your self-worth, you must embrace courage. You have to realize that even if things get difficult, you will make it.

Chapter 17
Permit Self-Forgiveness

The Power Of Forgiveness

Forgiveness is an act of power. It is also an effective way to release negative energy. If you carry hatred in your heart, then chances are that you will be filled with negativity. When you forgive, you not only do it for the person who is asking for forgiveness, but you also do it for your own good. In fact, forgiveness is possible even if the offender is not sorry for their wrongs against you. You can always forgive.

The following meditation technique is a good way to extend forgiveness to anyone. The steps are as follows:

- Sit or lie down comfortably. Close your eyes and visualize the person whom you want to forgive standing in front for you. Try to visualize the person as clearly as possible. Now raise your hands in the position of blessing with your hands facing outward. Think about the wrongs that the person has done to you but do not dwell on them. Just recall them into your mind. You do not even have to be attached to the memories. Now, find peace in your heart. Once you find this peace, state the name of the person whom you visualize and say, "(Name of the person), I forgive you."

- Forgiveness is an act of love. The more that you forgive, the more that you turn hatred into positive energy.

-   As an empath, it may be easy for you to be offended. A common problem of being an empath is being overly sensitive. Negative energies may be able to affect you more than most people. If there is any person who seems to affect you negatively, you might want to extend forgiveness to them.

- Forgiveness is free. As such, you can extend forgiveness to everyone, even to those who do not feel sorry for offending you. The more that you forgive, the more that you free yourself from

256

negative energy. If you do not forgive and allow the mistakes of others to fill you with hate, then you might end up just like them, or even worse.

- Forgiveness should be sincere. If you cannot find it in your heart to forgive a person, it helps if you spend some time to think about the situation. What is it that gives you a hard time to forgive someone? Sometimes by making reflections, we get to realize our own imperfections and faults.

- Once you realize the value of forgiveness, you will know just how effective it is in cleansing the soul. The more that you forgive, the more peaceful you will feel.

Another important part of forgiveness is learning how to forgive yourself. Indeed, there are people who carry lots of negative energy simply because they do not let go of it. Sometimes, to do this, you need to forgive yourself. You should learn to be kind to yourself. Unfortunately, in the modern world, it has become common to be hard on one's self. This is also why so many people are stressed out. Remember that you don't need to follow what society tells you. Be in control of your life. If something gives you more stress than you can manage, then you should do something about it. When you are an empath, you're more sensitive to stress. Of course, this doesn't mean that you should not face challenges. Rather, this means that you should be more in control, and you need to manage the level of stress that you are carrying.

Healing is important. Even if you are not an empath, you will find that you need to heal yourself from time to time. Healing is a natural part of life. No matter what you do, no matter how careful you try to be, it is inevitable that you will also face challenges and hardships along the way. It is also inevitable that you will have to deal with negative people from time to time. Hence, you will have to heal yourself when the need arises. Indeed, healing is a natural part of the life of an empath. A good thing about healing is that it transforms even negative energies into something that is much more positive. Indeed, healing and forgiveness can create a substantial positive impact on your life.

Taking Care Of Your Inner Child

If you have subconscious childhood wounds, you probably developed defense mechanisms early on to cope with and adapt to grown up expectations. The behaviors or tendencies that you exhibit as an adult directly reflect this molding.

Where you a relatively happy kid? But have you become a gloomy adult who's lonely or angry? Burdened by a bruised sense of self-worth?

When our parents aren't available to provide us with the proper nurturing, as children we experience anxiety and loss. We later develop accommodations to fill these wounds, which then morph into defense mechanisms for getting on with life, habits in our adulthood. This is what is commonly referred to as the false self. Very many false-self personalities make an arsenal. From the funny ones, such as the class clown, to the angry ones, such as the bully, these personas have the ability to convince us we are what we in truth are not.

As we grow up and develop, we forget that this false-self character, the role we play for others (and sometimes even when alone with just yourself) is not who we really are, but the mind makes such a habit of being the false self that we take it to be all we are, nothing more, nothing else. We become so engrossed by the fantasy that we need our mask to continue being safe, even when it is no longer necessary, and even when it's done so much damage to others and to ourselves.

Some theorists say that we are always looking to reestablish our nurturing state, to find our symbiotic mothers in order to feel safe; much like when we were in the womb and had all our needs met automatically, without struggle, worry or anxiety. Of course, life isn't about regression and never will be, and that's where false selves come into play. Assumed identities enable us to cope in public while we secretly burn with our failure to find a state of natural happiness once again. Most of the time, we find ourselves trying to trick others into filling these gaps. We look for mates who we tell ourselves will meet these needs. And when this fails, when these mates are unable or unwilling to meet our every need, to make us feel loved and safe at all times, it becomes the very root of relationship problems.

Exercise

Start doing body weight resistance exercises at home as well as cardio. If you live in an apartment, there are still things that you can do that shouldn't bother the people downstairs too much. For example, you can start running in order to get your cardio in and build up your strength and tonality. You can also start playing sports like basketball—though they may have never appealed to you before, sports can be a great and somewhat enjoyable way to pick up a hobby and start getting some exercise at the same time. They're also strangely therapeutic and will allow you to shut off your thoughts for a while and just get some positive endorphins flowing. If you can afford it, picking up a gym membership and then going three or four times a week can be a great way to start getting back into shape and improving your self-image.

There's a possibility that you aren't religious. If you aren't, then you can eschew this next bit of advice. However, if you are, you may find that diving into your spirituality and being active in a church community (or a community of whatever religion you're a part of) can lead to you developing vital friendships and getting to know people that you otherwise may not get to know. Also, spirituality can be a source of great solace for many people. It can be especially helpful to a lot of people to believe in something greater than themselves and you, if you're religious, are no exception. Even the act of praying - regardless of if the individual is secular or religious - has been scientifically proven to reduce stress levels and generally improve the disposition of the individual compared to how they were prior to praying at all.

If you have time in your schedule and can afford it, you may want to start going to a community college or going back to school if you don't have a degree. Getting a proper education and getting bigger pay checks, as a result, can lead to feeling like you're worth more than you are otherwise. On that same note, don't be afraid to find something to be passionate about. Don't just go home and watch TV and stagnate. You need something to push yourself forward. Find something you care about and start researching it. Start gardening or learning about something you've always been interested in. If you can do that, then you'll make a ton of extremely important progress.

In the end, the best things that you can do in order to heal are to better yourself and focus on yourself. Don't be afraid to spend a little extra to get a therapist or a gym membership, or even to treat yourself to a nice dinner once or twice per month. These things can be massively important parts of the healing process and can do a whole lot for helping you to feel better in general. You can do this—things will be better someday! Keep a smile on your face and fake it until you make it.

Chapter 18
How to Hurt a Narcissist
(Without Getting Hurt Yourself)

Narcissists are self-absolved, petty, wicked and extremely hard to deal with. Their manipulative ways are so destructive that sometimes, survivors of their abuse go through years of therapy to fully recover. If you have a narcissist as a friend, sibling, boss, parent or spouse, etc., then you must have tasted the bitterness involved in having to deal with them.

Sometimes narcissists hurt people so bad that they begin to explore ways to hurt them back. Mind you, when you decide to play dirty with narcissists, you should understand that there are risks involved, and things could easily spiral out of control for everyone involved.

If I Decide To Hurt A Narcissist, Won't I Be Playing Into His Hands?

Narcissists are petty and always ready to fight dirty, thus, you have to be mentally prepared before you engage them. Keep it at the back of your mind that you're approaching uncharted waters, and chances are they already possess information about you. Even if they lack any real information, they are capable of fabricating lies just to strike a heavy blow and can go further in tearing you apart emotionally. They can use their fabricated lies to defend all sorts of attacks you mount and are skilled at sowing doubts in the minds of third parties – they are capable of manipulating your friends and allies and turning them against you completely.

Narcissists can play the victim and make it look like you're the one with the toxic and hurtful behavior. Furthermore, since they blossom in situations like this, they will enjoy every minute, because it gives them a false send of purpose and direction. They thrive in situations like this because it provides them with the attention they constantly desire.

With that said, you have to really consider your stance on the subject matter, because while you're trying to hurt a narcissist, you may actually be feeding his ego, and providing him with the star treatment he seeks.

If I Try To Hurt A Narcissist, Won't I Be Hurt In The Process?

Before you consider the option of causing emotional hurt to a narcissist, you should reflect on what Confucius said: "Before you embark on a journey of revenge, dig two graves." Basically, it means that in your quest to hurt them, you should also expect some level of hurt too. You may eventually strike by deflating their ego, but they'll never take it with throwing a few punches of their own.

When narcissists feel threatened, they go all out and are at their manipulative best in times like that. They become extremely destructive and petty, so you have to ask yourself whether you're ready to put yourself in such a position. And to be honest, most times, it isn't worth it.

The truth is that narcissists are already down emotionally and are constantly fighting their internal demons (feelings of self-doubt, insecurity, and inferiority, etc.), thus, even if you don't sympathize with them, you should at least let them be.

Being An Abuse Survivor, Isn't It Risky To Engage A Narcissist?

Whether you were married to a narcissist or was involved in an abusive relationship with one, the truth is, re-engaging them for sinister reasons is a terrible idea, to say the least.

The fact is, you might still be mentally and emotionally fragile, and there is every possibility that you maybe be reintroduced to the sufferings you initially escaped from by ending the relationship.

You may anticipate an easy scenario, where you snap in out with your pound of flesh, however, the narcissist might just suck you back into his life permanently.

Narcissists embrace conflicts; they live their best lives in times of conflicts and disagreements; thus, they'll never fold their hands and take insults from people they consider inferior.

You have to sit down and consider your options carefully. Ideally, as an abuse survivor, it is best to get professional help and pursue your case in court.

Even If I End Up Hurting The Narcissist, Will I Feel Any Better?

The prospect of hurting a narcissist that made your life a living hell may be extremely enticing, to say the least, but the truth is, it won't give you the peace you seek.

When you hurt a narcissist, you may derive some level of satisfaction, but it'll never be what you must have hoped for, and it surely won't last long. Revenge might be sweet, but it can also end with a bitter taste. Some of the reasons why you should consider your actions are; it is possible that your actions are being controlled by the narcissist, and your urge for revenge is triggered by the severe pains you suffered in their hands – which ultimately means that they still control you indirectly.

Keep in mind that you can only begin to truly heal when you let go of the feelings of hate and resentment you harbor towards your abuser. Thus, when you desire to seek revenge, you indirectly fan the flames of your own ill feelings, which directly stall your recovery process.

How Do I Hurt A Narcissist Without Getting Hurt?

There are people who believe it is impossible to hurt narcissists but that isn't true, the problem is that most people in their quest to hurt narcissists, unknowingly fuel their anger, rather than hurt them. To hurt a narcissist, you have to play him in his own game, and although it's not easy, it is very possible.

Below are some of the ways to hurt narcissists without possibly hurting yourself in the process;

First Of All, Take Some Time To Consider It

To exert revenge against anyone involves a lot of time and effort, and in the case of a narcissist, it's even a little bit more complicated. For someone to seek revenge, it is obvious that the person is hurt, emotional and pained; however, you cannot achieve anything sensible while you're a hot mess. Thus, before you act, you have to calm yourself down, that way you can avoid silly mistakes that might backfire in the long run.

Set Aside Your Feelings

The importance of setting your emotions and feelings aside cannot be overemphasized. Whoever the person is or whatever he/she means to you, it is necessary to dig deep into your head and convince yourself that they don't genuinely love you. This is not the time to be weak, you have to believe you've been used for too long and it's time to make things right. Remember that narcissists are manipulative and may try to make you believe that you have the upper hand, resist their advances and stick to your plan.

Reciprocate Their Actions Towards You

Narcissists are extremely egoistical; they hurt others but expect to be given special treatments. Thus, one nasty way to hurt them is to give them a taste of their own medicine, and this involves messing with their heads (reciprocate all their actions). When they ignore you, ignore them. If they distance themselves from you, distance yourself from them also. When they decide to be hot and cold to you, be hot and cold to them too. When you do this, you deflate their ego, and narcissists are all about their ego.

Focus On Their Weaknesses

The fact that narcissists are obsessed with themselves means they are well aware of their strengths and weaknesses. They know all about their insecurities and vulnerabilities, but they mask it with overconfidence, in other to put others down and stay in control.

Narcissists love to receive praises and compliments because it inflates their ego and self-importance. Thus, if you want to hurt them, rather than praises, politely discuss their numerous flaws and weaknesses with them. Do this and watch them crumble before your very own eyes.

Don't Give Them The Amount Of Attention They Need

Narcissists believe everything they do is right, and most things other people do makes zero sense. They are attention seekers and that is why this strategy is effective. In your quest to hurt a narcissist, you should limit the amount of attention you give to him – you don't have to be completely cold. Pay minimal attention to them, just enough to keep them around, and when they seek any sort of validation from you, disregard them.

Narcissists are who they are, and as such, will never change. This is only a way of making them feel bad.

Make Them Question Your Feelings Towards Them

In their minds, narcissists believe they have everyone figured out, they see themselves to be perfect and everybody loves them. They go into relationships with people for self-gratification and validation. To hurt them, you have to make them doubt your love and dedication. From time to time, they'll seek to ascertain your level of commitment, but you shouldn't give in, keep doing your thing and continue living your life.

Criticize Them In Public

Narcissists require constant approvals and praises to keep their egos inflated. Thus, one of the most effective ways of humiliating them is to do the exact opposite, which is criticizing them, especially in front of people. When you do this, make sure you are constructive enough, and desist from insulting them.

Be Selfish Too

Narcissists are extremely petty, and it is evident in their manipulative attitudes. Nothing makes them happier than believing others are obsessed with them, which leaves them badly hurt when they discover otherwise. Thus, to hurt them, you just need to focus on your own life – when they see you happy, enjoying your life, laughing and hanging out with other people, they get jealous and feel bad.

Narcissists do not like strong and independent partners; they prefer to deal with weak and dependent people. Thus, when they realize you're strong, independent and happy without them, they become depressed.

Swap Them With Other Friends

If you've decided to hurt your narcissistic friend or spouse, then you have to consider replacing them with other people. The depressing behavior of narcissists must have made them lose close friends in the past, so when you cut them off and replace them with new people, it brings back painful memories.

Depress Them With Your Success

Narcissists are extremely loud and vocal when it comes to their achievements in life. Thus, to make them jealous and unhappy, consciously work towards achieving more success in your life. They may act like they're happy with your growth and success, but deep down they're dying of jealousy and anger. When you surpass all the achievements that they would normally brag about, they begin to feel useless and uncomfortable.

Mock Them

It is normal to poke fun at your friends, make them temporarily uncomfortable and laugh over it at the end (These are some of the things friends do to each other). However, with a narcissist, it is a different ball game entirely. Narcissists are sensitive to jokes, and this presents an opportunity for you to strike a blow. You don't have to be abusive, just play pranks on them, tease them, and make fun of them. Trust me; you'll get them humiliated, especially in front of people.

The prospect of hurting someone that put you through so much hurt might be enticing, but revenge won't make you feel any better. It might temporarily lessen the amount of frustration that has steadily built up over time, but that is all to it. The best way to hurt a narcissist without hurting yourself in the process is to completely ignore him. In other words, terminate whatever is left of the relationship, walk away and never look back. When you walk away and maintain a healthy distance from your abuser, you'll realize that in no time, your life will pick up, and you'll be surprised at how peaceful and happy your life can be.

Chapter 19
Differences Between Self-Love and Narcissism

In order to develop a sound mind, it is critical that we as humans figure out how to love and understand ourselves. However, if self-love becomes a sort of fixation, it has morphed into a type of narcissism. In the present world, it is viewed as unthinkable to love yourself completely, and so this is often confused with narcissism. Truthfully, this is only a display of high self-esteem and confidence in one's self. What then is the distinction? When do high esteem and love for oneself go too far and become narcissism?

Self-love is simply the unashamed demonstration of putting yourself first and genuine confidence in one's abilities. This is a sound mindset, in contrast to narcissism.

Narcissism is a personality disorder where the person has a swelled feeling of self-significance and an absolute absence of empathy. They believe they are better than most people and can only be understood by individuals who are likewise similarly as unique. This feeling of prestige comes with some major disadvantages and is inconceivably sensitive. Those with narcissistic disorders need consistent consolation from their companions because their self-esteem is very delicate.

Self-Love Versus Narcissism

Self-love: Those who have high self-esteem and practice self-love aren't concerned with acknowledgement or praise for their accomplishments. They are very much aware of their endeavors and their achievements, and that information is all they need to be content and satisfied.

Narcissism: If a tree falls in the wood and nobody is around to hear it, does it make a sound? If a narcissist achieves anything in their life and nobody is around to observe it, will they consider it one? The answer is NO. Without receiving acknowledgement and applause, they have not achieved anything by any stretch of the imagination. It makes their success feel vacant because they only get fulfillment from the reverence of others.

Recognizing One's Own Flaws

Self-love: Everyone has flaws and qualities that make them unique. The individuals who love themselves acknowledge their flaws and work to improve them if need be. They comprehend that those shortcomings or weaknesses are what makes them who they are.

Narcissism: They go about as though they don't have any flaws. They want to be, and like to prove that they are, better in every way than every other person. If somebody observes a flaw or catches them making a mistake, it must be a misguided judgment, because it's impossible that any part of them could be anything short of great.

Knowing What Your Identity Is And Being Ok With It

Self-love: These people are happy with acting naturally and acknowledge what their identity is and what they have to offer. They don't feel like they have to undergo any tremendous improvements to themselves or their lives to achieve happiness since they already are.

Narcissism: They are forever discontent with what their identity is and what they have. They frequently wind up fantasizing about a more perfect way of life, employment, or appearance. They never genuinely feel happy with any part of their life. They feel that they merit better yet put no effort toward accomplishing their desires.

Humility Is A Virtue

Self-love: They have a solid feeling of empathy and humility. They encourage and urge others to improve and celebrate other people's achievements with them.

Narcissism: They cannot deal with seeing others progressing in life. They feel envious and will find ways to undermine their achievements so as to feel that they have the upper hand. The expression "misery loves company" is very accurate.

View Of Others' Feelings

Self-love: These people are responsive to others' feelings and can level with their battles and pain. They will offer encouragement and help if and when they can, and truly care about their friend, colleague or family's situation.

Narcissism: Although they may show concern, they really could not care less about any other person's issues. Truth be told, they benefit from it. It's one less individual who is doing great, which makes them feel better about themselves.

Impression Of Others As People

Self-love: Appreciation for others is a solid characteristic of individuals who have high self-esteem. They consider others as valuable. These individuals can be like old buddies since they are unimaginably strong and comprehend that it takes a wide range of individuals to make the world go 'round.

Narcissism: They don't see others as valuable. The main worth they find in others is a chance to utilize them for their advantage. Narcissists usually surround themselves with other narcissists: the "uncommon" individuals, the "world-class." No one else is deserving of their time.

Competition With Peers

Self-love: With high self-esteem, it is not difficult to see others as your equivalents. Every individual is only that, someone else attempting to make it, not trying to steal your spotlight.

Narcissism: Narcissists consistently need to show superiority over their friends, or if nothing else, radiate the illusion that they are. They feed off of dominance and manipulation. They are not really cheerful except if they feel that they are in complete control. The motive behind their endeavors is to be commended and venerated. Generally, narcissists are drawn towards careers and hobbies that put them in the spotlight. Narcissists spend the vast majority of their time alone because most people can distinguish their toxic behavior.

Indications of narcissistic behavior will in general pop up in the early years of adulthood, and more often in men. Fifty to seventy percent of the individuals who develop Narcissistic Personality Disorder are male. The reason for this is unknown. Perhaps it is a mix of genetics, childhood experience, and encounters during adolescence. As children, young men are often trained to believe that they are extraordinary and superior. While this may appear as encouraging feedback, if the commendation isn't directed fittingly, these young men may grow up to be men who believe that they are better than every other person.

Narcissism is inconceivably toxic behavior and will repulse anybody who can distinguish these traits. That is the reason individuals with this disorder often have few companions and spend most of their time alone. They turn this rejection back around on others, figuring that since they are better than everyone else, nobody is deserving of their valuable time.

The solution to this is to find a fair compromise. It's good to love yourself, but don't let it become an obsession. With the evolution of the internet and social media, it is easier to spot narcissists since they feature themselves day by day. Do you notice any young ladies or fellows who post numerous selfies a day and are continually changing their profile pictures? They are doing this for the attention. They need individuals to see them and to acknowledge their beauty. The likes and comments they receive feed their intrinsic need for veneration. Social media has made it alarmingly common to continually get such acknowledgements from friends and strangers alike.

Unless the individuals who experience the ill effects of NPD look for therapy, it is unlikely that their behavior will change since they are ignorant of having this disorder. That sort of reflection would demonstrate that they are blemished, something that doesn't register in the brain of a narcissist.

How To Encourage Self-Love Without Developing Narcissism?

How You See Yourself Matters Most

Try not to put such great importance and value on your material or immaterial attributes. Narcissism is inconceivably superficial. Try not to stress over what impression you give and how others perceive you. Rather, concern yourself with how you perceive yourself and which characteristics can be enhanced on a realistic level.

Don't Compare Yourself

Try not to compare yourself with others and their achievements. Be happy with your own hard-earned achievements and make individual goals to work at. Be grateful for what you already have and be willing to put the work in to achieve your goals.

Look For Ways To Improve Yourself

You cannot improve your self-confidence by telling yourself that you are better than every other person is, since in all actuality, you don't have a lot to offer other than your arrogance. Rather, improve your skills or learn new ones. Mastering a skill or becoming an expert or specialist in a given area will improve your feeling of self-love tremendously. You will be commended for your accomplishments and will gain confidence from realizing that you are valuable and skilled.

Chapter 20
10 Tips How To Deal With Manipulative People

I f you don't give education to people, it is easy to manipulate them"
- Pele

Being a manipulation expert is as much about spotting
manipulation and deception in others as it is about leading others to do
what you want them to.

Do you want to safeguard yourself from manipulation on a daily basis?

Do you want to prevent people from taking advantage of you for
fulfilling their own selfish goals?

Do you want to be able to sniff manipulation from miles away?

Here are 6 brilliant strategies to protect yourself from manipulation.

1. Ignore Their Words And Actions

Manipulators almost always go after shaking people's confidence and
making them insecure to get them to do what they (the manipulators)
want. They will do their best to plant seeds of apprehension and self-
doubt. There is a tendency to make the victim believe that the
manipulator's opinion is actually the truth or fact. Rather than wanting
to help you, they are more interested in trying to control you.

The best strategy to deal with these negative manipulators is to ignore
them rather than trying to argue with them or correct them. This allows
them to set an even deeper trap for you. Do not fall for their conflict or
confrontation bet. Simply bypass them, without revealing your
emotions. Do not let them see the emotions that make you tick. Once
they gain a good understanding of your emotional triggers, they will
sneakily use it for influencing your thoughts, behavior, and decisions.

Some people are difficult to delete from our life immediately. Think –
boss, neighbor, family member, etc. Just pretend to listen to what they
are saying, agree with it and eventually do exactly what you want.

2. Do Not Compromise

Guilt is one of the most insidious tools used by manipulators to get their victims to do what they want. Of course, it can be used positively to influence a person too, but in negative manipulation, its usage can spell disaster for the victim.

Manipulators induce a feeling of guilt in their victims for their past mistakes, choices, and failures. They will make you guilt about being self-assured and self-confident. Each time you experience happiness, they will make you feel bad about it. Their objective is to never make you feel good about yourself or happy.

They'll sow seeds of self-doubt about your true worth, persona, and abilities. Do not get knocked off balance or feel guilty they start blaming you. Do not doubt your self-worth or abilities. Never believe that you do not deserve happiness or to feel wonderful about yourself. Take pride in who you are and your accomplishments. Build a strong sense of self-esteem and confidence. Do not compromise on your happiness or your feelings about yourself.

3. Do Not Fit In, Stand Out

It isn't funny how many people make them susceptible to manipulation by trying hard to fit in. Manipulative people count of your desire to want to fit in to push their agenda. They lead you to believe that everyone does what they want you to do and that those who do not conform are abnormal. That is the only way to control your decisions and behavior.

Give up the notion of trying to fit in and encourage the idea of standing out among the rest. Be different from other folks. Focus on reinventing yourself, laying your own rules (for what is good for you and others) and avoid cowing down to peer pressure.

4. Stop Seeking Permission

We've been conditioned to ask for permission since childhood, right from when we wanted to be fed as a baby to when we wanted to visit the bathroom in school to waiting for our turn to talk in the boardroom. The result of this conditioning is that people seldom do anything without seeking permission.

There is an excessive focus on being polite and making things comfortable for others. Manipulative people want their victims to live by their own self-drafted, imaginary rules or values. The underlying idea is you are not free to take any decision without consultation. Be brave and give up this sense of confinement. You have the power to change your life without the need to live by someone else's self-fulfilling rules.

5. Do Not Be A Baby

If you are tricked once, it isn't your fault. However, if you are tricked 15 times, there's something wrong with you. Do not let people take advantage of your by being everyone's favorite punching bag. Have the courage to stand up to manipulators and say a firm no when you know they are taking advantage of you. Stop whining about other people are taking advantage of you and take complete control of your life.

Victims of manipulation almost always complain about how people use them. No one can take advantage or you without your consent. You are indeed responsible for your own actions and their outcome. If someone has used sneaky tricks to outwit you, it is your fault. Learn from past blunders and stop trusting slippery people again and again. Move away from them. Focus on surrounding yourself with positive, constructive, inspiring and like-minded folks who make you feel good about yourself.

6. Have A Clear Sense Of Purpose

When you do not know what you want, you'll be more prone to do whatever everyone else wants. You'll be easily tricked into doing what other people want you to do without a firm goal or objective in life. People who lack a clear purpose or aim tend to function or go through life more mechanically. There is little logic in their actions or decisions. They will be more prone to experiencing a growing sense of emptiness in them that will craftily be filled by a manipulator.

This lack of objective or constructive activities makes the manipulator feel empowered enough to easily distract you or draw you to their agenda.

Have a higher purpose in life. It can be anything from taking up a cause for the betterment of the community to traveling around the world to rising in your professional life. Do not allow manipulators an opportunity to prey on your sense of purposelessness. When you are absolutely clear about where you are headed, it is difficult to stop you or get you to change tracks.

Chapter 21
Toxic Relationships and What to Do About them

How To Recognize A Toxic Relationship

Some of the signs may be too subtle to tell. But if you consistently feel bad, in any way, then you may have to take a closer look at your relationship. Perhaps things aren't so bad on the surface, but beneath the visible surface, there may lie a deep pattern of abuse.

Let's Consider Your Workplace.

If you find yourself working with colleagues who drag you down rather than spurring you to be your best, then you are most likely in a toxic workplace environment. If you add to that a boss who is demanding, overbearing and domineering, then you might as well get a new job.

Think About It In This Manner.

If you get home absolutely spent at the end of your workday; if you feel like you have run a marathon; if you feel that you are emotionally drained, every single day, then you might very well be the victim of toxic relationships. Now, it's one thing to have a tough job which is demanding and requires a high degree of physical and emotional conditioning. You can tell the difference because you feel that your job gives you a sense of purpose beyond the paycheck. But if you would rather go through a root canal rather than go to work, then it's a safe bet that you are not in an ideal environment.

Another telltale sign that you are in a toxic relationship is when you feel that you are giving more than you are getting. While this may be the manifestation of unfulfilled wishes (for instance, a narcissist may feel that they are not getting what they want in a relationship), an honest assessment of both your actions and those of the other parties may reveal that you are in a toxic relationship. It could very well be that others are simply taking advantage of you.

Furthermore, toxic relationships are manifest when there is a clear benefit for one party as compared to other parties. For example, parents clearly derive a benefit from their children while the children themselves don't receive the love and attention they need. This is generally seen in child stars. The parents reap the benefits of their child's success while the child is neglected and forced to work.

On the whole, toxic relationships are fairly obvious once you begin to peel back the onion. This assessment begins when you see that you are hurt in some manner, or you are not receiving any kind of benefit in the relationship. Moreover, if there is any kind of physical harm in a relationship, then it's time to end it.

Types Of Toxic Relationships

- Toxic Romantic Relationships

This type of toxic relationship can take on any number of facets. It is the only one we are going to explore in isolation as it is the one which is the most vulnerable to degenerating into a toxic, abusive interaction among both parties.

In general terms, toxic romantic relationships tend to be broken from the beginning. As such, the foundations of the relationship are set up in such a way that there is hardly any semblance of what a normal romantic relationship would like.

In theory, romantic relationships involve two individuals who profess affection and fondness for one another. This means that there is an affinity between both of them in such a way that they commit their time and energy to caring for each other.

If a relationship is set up under those pretenses, then the chance of it surviving over time is far greater than if they are set up under any other type of pretenses. The situation now shifts dramatically when one of the parties in the relationship enters it with a hidden agenda. When this occurs, the relationship may be broken from the beginning. Then, there is the case in which a relationship deteriorates over time thereby leading to its toxicity.

Roughly speaking, one, or both, parties in the relationship are somehow hurt by the dynamic that ensues. When this happens, resentment brews leading to potential animosity between the parties. At this point, the relationship may be beyond repair. In fact, the only solution may be to break up and move on. The situation gets further compounded when there is some type of physical harm involved. Natural, physical harm is extremely difficult to deal with as it could lead to serious injury or even death.

That's why it's important to note that abuse in a romantic relationship can range from verbal aggression to physical harm. Everything that happens in between can be a sign that the victimizer, whether acting consciously or unconsciously, is looking to extract as much benefit for themselves as possible. As a result, the manifestation of blackmail, gaslighting, guilt or blame can be evident. As the abuse deepens, one or several of these phenomena may emerge. The victim may be left broken with their self-esteem shattered in a million pieces. The victimizer may end up resenting themselves though unable to break the pattern that they have become accustomed to.

- Dependence

Dependence is especially toxic when the victim is the party who sustains the dependency of the victimizer.

To clearly exemplify this, think about a drug addict or alcoholic. The addict becomes dependent on their spouse, parents, siblings or friends especially when they are under the influence. When addiction takes over a person's life, they may be unable to function in a traditional social context. For instance, they may depend on financial support as they are unable to work. If we assume an adult child who is financially dependent on their parents, the addiction may perpetuate this dependency on the parents. The relationship then becomes toxic for the parents especially if they are older and no longer able to work. In addition, the emotional toll that such a relationship can take on a person is truly exhausting.

Dependence can also be seen at an emotional level. For instance, a person is completely dependent on their partner's attention and validation. In this case, the dependent individual may be unable to function properly without having the full attention of their partner. This can be seen in jealous types (regardless of whether they are male or female). The jealous types will strive to control their partner's every move so that they can feel safe and secure. Naturally, the relationship becomes toxic for the victim as they tend to feel suffocated and smothered by the relentless desire for attention from their partner.

- Narcissism

This is one of the most toxic relationships you can be in. A narcissist will generally stop at nothing when looking to take full control over their partner's life, or in the case of narcissistic parents, their children's lives.

Let's explore narcissistic parents a bit further.

Narcissistic parents are the kind that seek to control everything about their children's lives. They will be eternally vigilant and overprotective. This attitude is not the product of genuine concern for their children's wellbeing. Rather, it is a manifestation of their own insecurities. As a result, they need to be in full control of their children's lives so that they can feel more at ease. Furthermore, narcissistic parents have a tendency to live vicariously through their children. This means that these types of parents will push their children into activities and areas in which they, the parents, failed in their own lives. As such, the parents are looking to realize their own dreams through their children. Hence, the support that these types of parents put into their children's development is done more out of the desire to realize their own dreams rather than pursuing their children's wishes and desires.

Lastly, dealing with a narcissistic boss can be a terrible experience. A narcissistic boss is generally a micromanager and very slow to delegate any kind of responsibility or decision-making power to anyone else. Thus, they are totally committed to supervising everything that is done while centralizing all decisions. Needless to say, this can be extremely frustrating while leaving employees with a profound sense of powerlessness. In the end, these types of bosses manage to alienate their employees to the point where they may no longer care about the work they are doing. The boss, on their end, may end up feeling completely exhausted, both physically and emotionally, as all of their energy is spent on trying to maintain control of everything around them. This type of relationship is completely toxic for all of those involved.

- Manipulation

Manipulation in relationships can be subtle or quite overt. In some cases, manipulation occurs when the manipulator has a hidden agenda that they act upon. In other cases, the manipulator simply acts out instinctively without really being aware of what they are going to their victim.

Regardless of the case, the manipulator uses their victim for whatever purpose suits them. In some of the most sordid cases, the manipulator may choose their victim out of sheer pleasure and enjoyment, that is, they take sadistic satisfaction in victimizing a vulnerable person.

Manipulation can occur through blackmail, guilt, lying or even mind control techniques. The level of sophistication on the part of the manipulator may end up determining how well these techniques can work on their victim.

Furthermore, when the victimizer gets bored or fulfills their purpose, the victim may very well be discarded. This is the type of attitude that manipulators with psychopathic tendencies might take. They may not have the slightest amount of compassion for their victim. As such, they will see their victims are disposable.

One other thing about manipulation: when a victim becomes aware of the manipulation but does nothing to stop, they become complicit. In a manner of speaking, they become an enabler as they do not attempt to put an end to it.

When this occurs, the victim may take pleasure in being victimized. This is a masochistic response that may evolve as a result of prolonged periods of exposure to the abuse and even torture. So, don't be surprised if you happen to find people who actually enjoy being subjected to painful experiences.

How To Avoid Toxic Relationships

There are two ways of going about this: first, what to do when you are already in a toxic relationship, and second, how to avoid getting one in the first place.

If you are in a toxic relationship, you need to assess how toxic the relationship really is. If you believe that it may be repaired, then it would be wise to talk with the other party to see if there is a possible resolution. However, if you feel that the relationship is seriously compromised, then you may need professional help in order to restore a healthy balance.

On the other hand, if you believe that the relationship is beyond repair, then there may be no other way but out. Often, professional help may be of benefit, but repairing a toxic relationship requires the commitment of all parties involved. If any one of the partners is reluctant to work on the relationship, then there may be no solution to it.

In addition, it is important to spot the red flags as they emerge. Here is a list of red flags to look out for:

- Excessive control

- Jealousy

- Insecurity

- Emotional dependence

- Physical violence

- Guilt

- Hurtful comments

- Passive-aggressive attacks

- Name-calling

- Constant blaming

- Constant reminder of past mistakes

Any of these red flags, should you spot them, ought to give you an indication that you might be in a toxic relationship. The sooner you spot them, the sooner you may be able to get out, or in the best of cases, repair the relationship. If you realize that you are, in fact, the manipulator, then you might be able to make amends and restore balance to your relationship.

Chapter 22
Developing Mental Strength

As philosophy developed in the West, we became obsessed with separating the mind and body. The indecent philosophers of greatness like Aristotle and Plato have provided the foundation for thousands of years of philosophy that sought to state that we had been prisoners of the body and that the mind was the holy part of the human.

This attitude basically makes it seem like the mind is the godly part of the human and the body is the animal type part of the human. This is a classically Christian view, as the Christian view states that man was made in God's image. If we are made in God's image but as humans, we must have some part of both, and to the ancient thinkers, the mind seemed more god-like. Of course, the body has to deal with waste and food and sights and smells that seem quite unsavory. The mind, in contrast, deals with matters of cognitive ability and feelings and reason and science. This was the classical attitude toward the mind-body split, and it was a good thing because the mind is godly, and the body isn't.

What these ancient philosophers forgot, though, is that our most human part is not the brain or the mind or the hands, but actually the big toe. Not just any of our toes, but particularly the big toe. The big toe is what separates us from the other animals physically. It is what lets us stand up, and not be all wobbly, and lets us develop incredible athletic feats like running and sports.

Mindfulness is interwoven into almost every subject, and it is definitely interwoven into the mind-body connection. Most of us these days grow up with a relationship far too focused on the mind. We must remain positive and working for capital gains constantly to be able to have our lives go on. We are subjected to modern media, which is all-pervasive, and this affects our cognitive structure as well. We are mostly told to ignore our bodies in order to work eight-hour shifts standing or sitting. When you do this kind of work, you have to do extra to keep up with the demands of the body, because the body is not designed to be happy when it is inactive for most of the time. The body craves engagement and interaction in the world. The body needs to be a part of the world and to do that, it must interact with the world in a physical manner. This can be accomplished in many ways but the easiest is directed exercise, whether just running or walking or some other form.

For most of us, the transition that needs to happen is to be more toward the body from the mind. This is because we are slanted too far in one direction. Therefore, we need to make up for this disconnection and find a way to be more oriented toward the experience of the body in different moments to take information in.

The mind/body connection is important because you can't be integrated without it. An integrated person is not only one who has experiences and knowledge but also has the ability to synthesize different ideas and concepts to build beliefs and success through behaviors. This is the difference between knowledge and wisdom. Knowledge is a knowing of some information and data. Wisdom is the ability to really know what the information means, for them and for others and the ability to employ information in different ways.

The mind-body connection is an illustration of the ultimate integration that a human could hope to achieve. By achieving high levels of awareness and mindfulness, a person can develop their personality beyond their current state of development towards self-realization.

Self-realization is the concept that a person can be so integrated and truly act in their authentic self, rather than keeping it rewrapped in layers of repression and denial. It is when a person is no longer concerned with what the world thinks about them, and they act totally honestly. It is a state where you do not doubt yourself because you are confident and ready to engage with whatever comes along. It is a state of being yourself. Most people are far from this, and they have things that stand in the way. One thing that stands in a lot of people's way is youth. When we are young, we don't have experiences in the world to look back on and draw information from. This makes us so confused about where to go and dealing with our problems.

Self-realization, then, is something that probably comes well ahead in life than adolescence and young adulthood. It is usually someone somewhat advanced in their years, who has do a lot of soul-searching, tried a lot of things out, and done a lot with their lives. These are people who are usually good candidates for this type of transformative experience.

Part of getting there, besides experience, however, is awareness of the body. Awareness of the body has been so demonized in our culture that we are only rewarded for what is visible in our cognitive accomplishments and we are torn desperately away from things that will keep us healthy being connected to our self and earth.

The mind-body connection is extremely important because, in order to read body language, a person must have a balance between their cognitive mind and their emotional mind. The emotional mind is more focused on the unconscious, which is giving us information as to our animal selves. This is really where the rich analytical body language stuff comes into play, but it has to be tempered by the cognitive state of mind, the thinking mind. The thinking mind is able to take the information from the emotional mind and really interpret it into something that actually means something for us. We can't be working in either of these minds exclusively, and that's why you need to foster a balance in the mind-body connection. A person who is too much in the mind will over-process things, and a person who is too much in the emotional mind and the body will not be processing enough. They will be taken over by the impulses of the animalistic side of our minds, and they will not be able to process body language information, but rather be overtaken by the information and too involved to have a sense of self around it.

You see the first one all the time: people too much up in their heads. These are people who worry a lot and can't be in the present moment. You may know someone like this. They might come off as whiny or complaining or too self-oriented. This is because they are a slave to their mental habits, and their mental habits just happen to be thinking negative thoughts about themselves and others. This is fine, and they are not bad people for it, but it isn't the healthiest way to live and if you search deeper and connect with the body, you can change his fate and be a balanced individual. There are some who are too in the body and they never process in a cognitive manner that they are experiencing. This may include addicts or people who have trouble with eating or sex addiction. The addict is not concerned with the future when they are taking a drug; they are only thinking about the present. This is obviously not good for them, but it doesn't line up with the idea of being present. Why? Because we are not doing things in the present moment with enough intentionality. Intentionality is the difference between an addict's mind and a well person's mind. The well person is able to act with intentionality because they know that if they partake in a certain experience, they will know that it will affect their day. They have that knowledge and they use it. An addict does not have the knowledge, and when they do, they are not able to use the knowledge.

An addict is not only exclusively in the body and emotional mind, however, and sometimes, they are skewed too far towards the head; they are always up in their thoughts. This is the type of addict who is good at rationalizing and hiding things. This is the addict who is functional and smart and capable but never changes. If this type of addict chooses to get more in touch with the body and address the mind-body connection, they will start to come out of their heads, and they will start to realize that we all have a common experience in our bodies. Once the addict realizes that we all have a common experience and we are all trapped in our bodies, they start to realize that they no longer have to suffer from their condition like they used to. They can learn new ways to deal with their condition.

Chapter 23
Use of NLP in Improving your Health and Overall Well Being

Stress Reduction Using NLP

The body will allow you to experience just enough stress in order to stay healthy but once too much stress is experienced, it causes chemicals in the body and interferes with the functioning of the brain. NLP techniques will help you to manage a certain amount of stress and to let go of the excess stress that is damaging to your health and wellbeing.

Below are some effective NLP exercises that you can use for stress reduction:

Reframe The Stress

This technique will require you to find out the underlying reason behind the stress. In most cases, we are aware of our stressors, so this should be very easy for you once the cause of stress is determined. You will be required to come up with possible solutions to fix the problem without involving stress.

If for instance you do not have enough money to run a certain project, this is a good stressor. What you need to do is to analyze the problem and come up with possible solutions that do not involve stress in any way. You can for instance decide to go for loans, borrow money from friends, or deal with only the amount of money that you have.

Use Of Meta Mantras

In this technique, you use some words to reassure yourself and make yourself feel better about the situation. If you messed up at work for instance and you do not know what will happen once your boss finds out what you did, repeat such phrases like 'so what?' If you hear yourself ask 'what if' questions, it is time to repeat the mantras over and over again so as to make the situation better in your mind. This will help reduce so much stress.

Meditation Or Relaxation

You only need a few minutes in a day to relax. During this time, close your eyes and allow your mind to wander. Think of how great things would be if the situation was different and enjoy the feeling. Make your imaginations as clear as possible and fantasize with no limitations at all. Your main focus at this instance is relaxation and not the solutions to the problems that you are facing. Once you are fully relaxed, the stress will be gone and y0u will be ready to face another day.

Staying In The Present

Take some minutes off your busy schedule to just live in the moment. Enjoy the sounds, the sights you see, and the feelings you experience and try to relax at that moment. This is a sure way to drive out the stress. This can take only 5 minutes, but it can help you reduce your stress to a manageable state. During this time, try not to think of anything else but what you are feeling and what is happening around you. Forget about your worries and stressors and just enjoy the present.

Finish Tasks

Always have a list of things that you ought to do the following day in the place where you work or at home by the time you leave. You need a diary for this since you want these things back in your mind as well. This can be a great way to avoid stressors and reduce stress.

Change Your Mental Pictures

The images you create in your mind when you are stressed are very different from the ones you create in normal circumstances. Take note of the images you create when you are stressed and come up with some images that could replace those. You can try to eliminate those images created when you are stressed by trying as much as possible to make them small, move them away in your mind, and eliminate them completely. The images you will choose for the replacement should be more relaxing, big, colorful, exciting and so many other good things you can imagine will bring a relief to your mind.

Changing The Tone Of Your Inner Voice

There is always an inner voice that speaks to us in different circumstances of our lives. When you are stressed, your inner voice will sound stressed as well and it can keep you in a stressed mood for some time. You have to change it to a better sounding voice, maybe a funny voice that will make you feel much better. The changed inner voice is capable of taking your stress and worries away and the kinds of things it will communicate to you are much different from what is stressing you, therefore choose a better voice.

Close Things Off At The End Of The Day

A major stressor is the thought that you have not finished all the tasks you had planned for the day. At work, finish the day by checking out your to-do list for that day once again, opening and closing all the drawers just to be sure that everything is in its place and shutting down the computer. Ensure that you are aware of all the things you do as you close things off so as to register to your mind that everything for that day has been done. You may take that time to create a list of things that have to be done the following day.

The Worry Pads

You need a worry pad and ensure that you bring it with you all the time just in case something worries you out there. As soon as you encounter something that is worrying you, write it down and come up with solutions there and then. If it is something that can be dealt with at that moment, do not push it aside as it may stress you. If there are things you have not been able to take care of, just take a few minutes in the evening, go through the worry pad list and worry for only those few minutes. This will prevent you from stressing over anything.

Use Of Laughter Filter

This is a technique that you can employ in order to view every stressful situation you encounter in your life in a humorous way. This will definitely reduce the stress and make you feel better as you figure out a way to fix the stressor.

Generating Brainwaves For Healing Through NLP

The human brain experiences 5 frequencies, which are beta, alpha, theta, delta and gamma. All these are important in the day to day functioning of the brain. Of all these frequencies, theta is the one that is associated with the body's natural self-healing.

NLP exercises are meant to ignite theta brainwaves so as to promote self-healing and ensure that the person is feeling much better in the end. This is done during meditation, deep relaxation, dreaming and also during hypnosis.

During NLP exercises, you are required to induce the theta brainwaves through certain mental practices. Once this is achieved, your stress levels are lowered as well as your anxiety levels and this helps to facilitate healing as well as personal growth.

As theta brain activity goes on, the body experiences rejuvenation, enhanced growth as well as healing. Theta brainwaves promote deep relaxation, which in turns restores the mind and the body during an illness and also after the illness. This can be done even during physical exertion or when you are experiencing burnout.

An increase in your theta brainwaves helps to boost your immune system. This is because these brainwaves are associated with stress reduction as well as boosting vitality. When you are stressed, the body releases chemicals that interfere with the immune system but after the activation of theta brainwaves, the stress and anxiety are reduced so much in order to optimize your immune system. Theta brainwaves do this by releasing pleasant chemicals and neurotransmitters which boost your immune system above the effect of stressors.

Theta brainwaves are also associated with increased creativity, an advanced level of problem-solving skills, increasing levels of learning abilities, an improvement in your memory, and an increase in intuition levels among so many other benefits. That is why you should always use NLP exercises whenever you feel unwell, anxious stressed, down, less motivated and any other negative feeling you might have. Once you stimulate theta brainwaves, you will receive your healing and restoration in no time at all.

Anxiety Reduction Through NLP Techniques And Exercises

Anxiety is a very serious emotional state. It has been reported to be the leading reason why many people seek psychiatric treatments all over the world, meaning that it can get serious. Serious anxiety may lead to depression, which is why you need to take measures before it gets out of hand. NLP has been used for so many years to help reduce anxiety by so many people therefore if you are the kind of person who struggles with anxiety, you can try out a few exercises and NLP techniques to help reduce anxiety and bring yourself to a state of relaxation.

This is an exercise that you might find helpful whenever you are feeling anxious, overwhelmed or in a panicky state. It is a visualization exercise, therefore if you find it hard to follow through with the exercise alone, you can ask someone to take you through it:

☐ Sit comfortably in a quiet place, with eyes closed, take three deep breaths as you inhale deeply and exhale slowly.

☐ Think about the anxiety; where is it in your body? What is its shape? Does it have any color? Find out if it has a texture, its temperature. Is it big or small, light or heavy, moving or it is still, is it flexible or it is still?

☐ Find out the exact part of your body that is feeling anxious. Is it your face, throat, stomach, chest, shoulders? You have to guide your conscious self to the exact place where the anxiety feels. Find out if the anxiety is in one part of the body or in many places and take yourself there.

☐ Determine the surroundings of the part of the body with anxiety. What color is the surrounding? How does it feel? What does it look like? How exactly is the surrounding, still or moving? Stiff or flexible? Dark or clear? All these are imaginations you should create in your mind.

☐ Alter the way the place surrounding the anxiety looks like in order to fade it away if it seems angry and stressed.

If for instance it is colored, try to pour water on it in your imaginations just to fade it away. Try to dilute it as much as possible. If it feels hot, pour water on it just to cool it down. Alter the image in your mind about that surrounding until your mind's eyes see something better than what was there before.

☐   If nothing changes and the surrounding is resistance to anything that you are doing to it, try moving it about, changing its location, shape, loosening it up; just anything that will make it feel different and better. Take time to do all this as you breathe deeply. Ensure you are relaxed all this time.

☐   Now watch as the anxiety is taken over by the better surrounding; watch as the surrounding dissolves the anxiety, pushes it away, makes it smaller and weaker, fades out its color and anything else that will make the anxiety disappear completely from your mental image.

☐   Once the anxiety is gone, fill the empty space with new energy. Take deep breaths. Imagine something pleasant, with bright colors, big enough coming to fill the empty spaces that anxiety occupied. You should be feeling better at this stage and more energized. This should take away your anxiety and promote healing to your inner self.

Chapter 24
Practicing Mindfulness

You have heard the word mindfulness before; it's featured on magazine covers, mentioned in fitness classes, and touted by top business leaders across industries as a tool to enhance productivity. But as mindfulness practice has become more mainstream, the meaning of the word has become clouded. People may encourage mindfulness, or "being present," but what exactly does this entail?

Mindfulness is often described as the practice of simply "being in the present moment." But this is only one aspect of the practice. Resting in the present moment is an important piece—it's the first step in bringing your attention to whatever is happening here and now, whether it's a thought, a difficult emotion, a task at work, or the breath—but it's just the beginning. When you limit your definition of mindfulness to the practice of just being present, you overlook several other important aspects.

The idea of sitting silently in meditation can be scary if you've never done it before. It is helpful to understand that the word meditation refers to anytime you are putting dedicated effort forth to be mindful. This may be in a sitting practice or while you are washing dishes. Remember that mindfulness is practiced not just on a meditation cushion; you can introduce mindfulness into any daily activity.

Mindfulness may be more completely understood as being present with clarity, wisdom, and kindness. If you bring your awareness to the present moment with judgment and anger, is that really useful? In order to build a healthy, beneficial mindfulness practice, it's necessary to cultivate several different behaviors, attitudes, and skills.

As you dive into mindfulness practice, you will likely discover a deep well of personal strengths—and a few places where you have room to grow. I call these places the growing edges. Try not to be discouraged by these edges—we all have them. Acknowledging and exploring them is how you work toward growth. Every one of your growing edges offers an opportunity for you to decrease stress and discomfort in your life.

Nine Aspects Of Mindfulness Practice

You are here because you have made the decision to begin investigating mindfulness. It is a powerful step and one that should be recognized and appreciated. Take a minute to pat yourself on the back.

To begin your journey of understanding mindfulness practice, let's look at the different abilities you will be cultivating.

›BEING FULLY PRESENT. This is the most well-known and basic piece of mindfulness meditation, but it takes time to cultivate. You may have to coax the mind back to the present moment repeatedly as you practice. As you continue to train the mind to be present, you'll find yourself more naturally able to rest in present-time awareness.

›SEEING CLEARLY. This aspect of mindfulness may also be understood as a recognition of the experience you are having. When pain arises, you are able to identify it as pain. When anxiety is present, you recognize it as anxiety. You are cultivating the wisdom to clearly see what you are experiencing in the present moment.

›LETTING GO OF JUDGMENT. You may notice your mind labeling something (a feeling, a thought, etc.) as good or bad, right or wrong, positive or negative. In mindfulness practice, you can let go of such value judgments. When a judgment does arise, you can remind yourself that you do not need to believe it. Accept what is present in the mind, including any feelings of "liking" or "disliking" what you find.

›BEING EQUANIMOUS. Equanimity is the quality of remaining balanced, especially when presented with difficult or uncomfortable circumstances. Whether the experience you are having is easy or difficult, the energy and effort you bring to it can remain unchanged. In this way, you build inner resilience, learning to move through difficult situations with balance and stability.

›ALLOWING EVERYTHING TO BELONG. Life contains a variety of experiences, and you may find yourself inviting some in while pushing others away. The English monk Ajahn Sumedho often tells his students, "Everything belongs." With mindfulness, you do not need to exclude any thought, emotion, or experience. Pay attention to whatever arises and make space for the uncomfortable moments.

›CULTIVATING BEGINNER'S MIND. When you learn something new, approach it with curiosity and eagerness to understand. As you grow in your understanding of the world around you, you can fall into "autopilot," believing that you know exactly how things work and what you're doing. To support a healthy mindfulness practice, work to cultivate beginner's mind, observing experiences and situations as if it's your first time. Remain open to new possibilities and watch out for the times when your mind begins closing.

›BEING PATIENT. Most people come to mindfulness and meditation practice with a goal in mind. They want to relieve some anxiety, deal with daily stressors, or learn to work through anger. It's okay to have an intention but remember to be patient; clinging to a specific outcome can hinder your progress. Patience requires a little bit of trust in the practice, in your teacher, and in yourself. Keep your intention in mind and remember that growth takes time.

›MAKING A FRIEND. Mindfulness is not about beating yourself up. Kindness is an essential part of practice—and that starts by being kind to yourself. Without kindness, you can be reactive and unable to see clearly. When practicing, respond to your experience with gentleness. Act as if your mind is your friend, not an enemy.

›HONORING YOURSELF. You don't need to clear the mind, be perfectly calm, or be a master of kindness to start practicing mindfulness. Start wherever you are and honor yourself for being here in the first place. This is a practice—not a race. You're not being graded, and if you struggle, it doesn't mean there's something wrong with you or your mind. Be true to yourself and allow space for growth.

The exercises contained in the following pages offer practical ways to build these qualities. You can return to these nine factors throughout your practice, recognizing where you have room to grow.

When I sat my first silent meditation retreat, I was struck by one thing that continued to arise in my mind: judgment. I knew from my training that I should seek to understand the judgment, not judge myself for judging. My retreat teacher suggested that I practice some kindness and forgiveness toward my mind. I really struggled with this—forgiving oneself can be a lifelong challenge—but I committed to an intention to do just that. Years later, this gentleness and kindness toward the thinking mind is an essential piece of my mindfulness practice.

You, too, will experience difficult moments in practice (and in life). You may need to try a few different approaches before figuring out what works best. Do your best to remain open and remember to forgive yourself for not always having the answer immediately. As you continue to practice, you will deepen your understanding of what it is you need. You will know intuitively when to return to beginner's mind, when to practice gentleness, and when you are getting knocked off balance.

Chapter 25
Meditation for Mental Health

Taking care of your brain is crucial if you want to live a long, happy life. Your brain controls the rest of your body, so if your mind is neglected and left to decay, it will have a negative effect on the entire body. Taking care of and improving your mind now may also help you prevent mental problems in the future.

Simply practicing meditation is already a great step forward when it comes to taking care of your mental health, but there are some meditation techniques designed specifically to help you improve your mind.

Mantras can be a great way to help you meditate, and it's easy to find a mantra that works for you. If you want to use a Sanskrit mantra, it would be a good idea to use the OM mantra, which is very simple and powerful. Another great Sanskrit to use is OM NAMAH SHIVAYA. Many who have used these mantras in regular meditations have claimed to have noticed an improvement in their long-term memory.

If you want to use a mudra, or specialized hand position, a good one to use is the mudra of knowledge. Press your fingers together and straighten them. Making sure to keep your other fingers straight, bend down your ring finger at the first joint. Place your thumb over your ring finger, as if holding it down.

Brain Building Meditation

This is a simple form of mindfulness meditation that's especially effective in strengthening the brain and improving your ability to focus. It's also good for keeping your brain healthy and active. This meditation should last roughly five minutes:

1. Start by sitting on the floor or in a chair and implement the right type of breathing that we've covered - slow, and focused.
2. Spend the first minute of your meditation focusing only on your breathing. Then, try to gradually begin to focus on the rest of

your body as well. Try to feel or sense your heartbeat, take in all the sensations in your body, and focus on those as well.

3. When time is up, give yourself a chance to exit the meditative state.

This meditation is a little more difficult than it seems, since people tend to forget to focus on their breathing as soon as they try to broaden their concentration, and it's difficult to focus on your entire body without paying more attention to one element at the cost of the rest. To start, try focusing on only one additional element, rather than all of them. Take the time to gradually incorporate your entire body into your meditation.

Guided Imagery Meditation

This is a form of meditation that has many benefits for your mental health and is used by many trained psychologists and medical practitioners. This technique can be used to support the treatment protocols for depression, addiction, PTSD, and anxiety. It can also help you deal with grief, and temporarily ease acute pain and symptoms of chronic illnesses.

For this practice, you will have a guide who, after gathering enough information on you, will guide you through a visualization meditation, telling you to visualize images they know you will find pleasing. The guide will ask you questions that will push you to involve all five senses in your visualization. The guide will monitor changes in your posture and facial expression to see how you react to the mental image and how to guide you through the next visualization.

For example, those suffering from chronic illnesses like cancer, the guide will tell the patient to visualize healthy cells growing inside their body, or the source of their illness growing smaller and weaker. This is not to say that cancer can be treated via guided imagery. However, it can help alleviate symptoms, and reduce the stress response in the body, while the cancer is being treated.

For this meditation, you will need a trained professional to act as guide, but there is a way to simplify this technique so that you can practice something similar on your own at home.

1. Before beginning this meditation, choose one or two scenes you will be visualizing. Make sure you choose something that will relax you, like a secluded beach on a tropical island if you like the ocean, or sitting in a library on a rainy day, reading your favorite book if you're a bookworm.

2. Once you've chosen a position and managed to control your breathing, begin to visualize the scene. Once you've created a clear image in your mind, include your other senses in the visualization. Add the sound of the waves crashing and the birds singing in the distance, or the patter of rain against the library window. Visualize the smell of the salty sea breeze and feel it on your face, and feel the warm sand beneath you, or the smell and feel of the pages of your book. Imagine the taste of your frozen mojito made with fresh lime juice or your steaming cocoa.

3. Once you've completely immersed yourself in the image, enjoy it for a moment and let it gently fade away. You can end your meditation there for a short session or move on to the next scene.

As you can see, the different styles of medication can help heal different aspects of your life. For instance, Metta meditation is great for your mental health in general, and especially well-suited for helping the treatment of depression, as it teaches you to love others and yourself. Movement- based meditations are great for connecting your mind and body, which helps you maintain a healthy balance, physically and emotionally, and can also have many benefits for your mental health.

When To Meditate For Mental Health

There are no set rules to when you should meditate if you want to improve your mental health, although you should try to follow a regular schedule. If you're using meditation to treat anxiety, PTSD, depression, or similar problems, try to practice a quick meditation session whenever your symptoms are acting up, like when you feel a panic attack starting, or if you're feeling exceptionally low. While this may not always work, and it can be difficult to quiet your mind in these situations, a successful meditation session can do wonders for your condition at that moment.

Chapter 26
Tips For Prevention

Don't Hope To Change Them

It is the number one rule when dealing with narcissists. They are convinced that they are always right, they have no self-critical capacity and they just can't put themselves in others' shoes. They tend to manipulate you by giving you feelings of guilt, anger, fear and insecurity. Establish a relationship of psychological subjection. The change in them will never occur. Therefore, it is useless for you to try to argue with them and waste energy unnecessarily. To live with a narcissist, you must act on yourself. And change your attitude towards them to put up with them. The hard reality here is that it's impossible to change someone else and trying will only hurt you. What you can start with is changing the way you see the situation. For example, you can view your interactions with the narcissistic person as a way to train your mind in areas of self-control, patience, and general focus. Since listening to a narcissist at work can be so draining, this is a great chance to improve yourself.

Choose Freedom

Hyper-controlling narcissists use different techniques to keep you at their mercy. They leverage a sense of duty or gratitude; they make you feel guilty. Anything to force you to agree with them. Instead, learn to react independently of them, accepting their disapproval or anger. If you get dominated by another person, you betray yourself. Then choose the freedom that, besides being a right, is also a responsibility. By sacrificing it, you would lose your own identity. No one can live a satisfying life by following the tenets of another person. Choosing freedom helps you live a life without stress. A narcissist does not like losing an argument and therefore, it is impossible to keep on arguing with them even when you are right. This way, you are good to go.

Keep Your Expectations Low

Passive-aggressive narcissists are elusive and evasive, they tend to postpone commitments and not keep promises. They show friendly, but don't act like friends. They do not openly discuss problems. They assert their will by behaving passively, that is, without ever cooperating with others. They are very frustrating. How to react? You must keep your expectations low. The less you rely on them, the less disappointed you will be. In this way you will not authorize their behavior irresponsible, but you will deal with reality. You must learn to accept them as they are. Remember the first rule: they will never change! When you are dealing with someone like this, having high expectations of them is only setting yourself up for disappointment. Part of realistically assessing the situation is realizing that they are going to care about themselves first and foremost, and others second. They'll always think of themselves first and you should therefore have little, if any, expectations from them.

Don't Pay Attention To Their Justifications

It is never their fault. If you try to criticize them, know that you will only get a boomerang effect. The remarks you will make to them will fall on you. Narcissists have little capacity for introspection and have a strong need to feel special, so they will not recognize that they were wrong. You will never be able to prove them the opposite. So, don't listen to their "reasons", continue on your way. Get used to doing without their blessing. Being wrong is never a thing for them and they will spend a lot of time trying to justify how they are right.

Don't Protect Them

It can often happen that they ask you not to talk about your problems to others. They must maintain an irreproachable image at all costs. Being silent, they think they can continue to treat you with arrogance. It occurs particularly in couple relationships. It is not up to them to decide how much of your life you will want to share with another person. By continuing to protect the narcissists by following their rules instead of yours, you will do nothing but prolong your unhappiness. Do you want to always be unhappy? I guess not. If you protect them, you will continue suffering alone.

Be Resolute In Your Decisions

Narcissists often try to manipulate you using your guilt. They take advantage of their capacity for empathy and compassion, feelings that are foreign to them. To defend yourself, you must then balance this empathic tendency of yours with firm determination. The complaints of narcissists must not take over your decisions. Give priority to your common sense and your legitimate self-defense instinct. Stick with what you decide as they can easily try to manipulate you and make you feel guilty.

Use Assertive Anger

Narcissists inevitably provoke anger. It is wrong to let oneself be overcome by anger, but also to repress it because it is deposited in a fold of the personality and damages it is causing depression, anxiety, resentment, cynicism, self-confidence ... A positive way to express anger is assertiveness instead. This is how we defend our beliefs and show respect for others. Set aside aggression, speak firmly and remain consistent with the decision taken. In this way, anger will be used constructively to make you feel better, without expecting anything in return from narcissists.

Stop Justifying Your Choices

Once you have made your decision showing that you are adamant, avoid justifying your choices. Faced with the stubbornness of narcissists, who would like to continue to manipulate you, the dispute could never end. Moreover, those who give themselves too much to rationalize their choices suggest the idea of not being so sure and of being able to change decision in case of insistence. A narcissist will never let you win, so your justification does not matter to them. Don't fall into this trap!

Be Humble, Don't Become Like Them. Egoism Generates Selfishness.

If you are dealing with narcissists, be careful not to let yourself be conditioned to the point of becoming like them. We all have an innate selfish tendency and the risk is to start treating the narcissist in a disrespectful way. At this point the instinct of self-defense becomes self-centered. To avoid this, we need to focus on humility. Indeed, those who are authentically humble are psychologically confident and do not need to take others to their side. He does not want to be overbearing towards others, but at the same time does not allow others to be against him. Egoism may slowly turn you int a narcissist! When you are humble you are able to control yourself and avoid becoming like them.

Forgive

The positive aspects of forgiveness are manifold. It makes you free to focus on more important priorities than anger. It encourages you not to get obsessed by those who wronged you anymore. It allows you to look to the future. You cannot control the behaviors and choices of another person, but with forgiveness you can learn to accept and tolerate narcissists for what they are. More so, forgiveness gives you a peace of mind which is very important

Chapter 27
FAQs

What's the Difference Between Healthy And Extreme Narcissism?

Healthy narcissism is all the good points of narcissism, such as a whole bundle of self-confidence and the positive energy to use that to drive you towards success, without any of the negative side effects of it. Someone who has this isn't cut off from the emotional side of life and doesn't put others down to make them feel better. This won't come from anything in childhood and is actually a desired trait. A bit of self-love can help us all.

Extreme narcissism is the opposite end of the scale. Its narcissism taken as far as it can, to sociopathy and psychopathy. People who suffer from Narcissistic Personality Disorder cannot be helped by someone who isn't medically trained in this area, and it's much better to escape the situation before you get caught up in it yourself.

What's An Abusive Cycle?

An abusive cycle is a continual pattern of negative behavior that doesn't stop no matter what happens. It can be hard to recognize this is what you're in until you take a step back and examine your current situation. It's thought to start with a tension building, then there will be an incident of yelling or maybe violence, then there will be a reconciliation followed by a calm. But the calm never lasts, and the victim is always acutely aware of that.

If this is something you think you might be involved in, then you need to get some emotional support right away. Check out the local abuse resources in your area, because they will be able to point you in the right direction.

How Can You Identify A Narcissist?

Working out who is a narcissist early in is a very useful tool because it means you'll be able to identify what's going on before you become consumed by it. Usually, people don't realize what's happening until they are much too embroiled in the situation and cannot extract themselves easily. presented five early signs to look out for:

- Bragging about having a perfect life – no one has that!

- Generosity is a show for others to see, then they are cold at home.

- Imagining rejection and criticism that isn't really happening.

- Experiencing manic emotions, shifting wildly high and low, especially if they don't get what they want.

- Insulting others frequently, especially people they consider beneath themselves.

If all of these sounds all too familiar, then it might be time to think about what you want your next move to be before you get stuck yourself.

Why Was I Targeted?

There are many reasons why a narcissist might choose you, but the simplest answer is that you had something that they want. That might be power or beauty, it might be information, or even a vulnerable side that they know they can manipulate. You might even have been chosen because you are a challenge, someone who they know they will struggle to manipulate, making it all about the game. It isn't a bad thing that you were targeted, and it doesn't make you weak. Unluckier.

What Are The Signs I Need To Look Out For?

If you believe that you might already be in a relationship with, or are very close to, someone who suffers from narcissism, you might notice the following things:

- Wanting to control everything about you; who you see, what you wear, how you act – nothing belongs to you anymore.

- Obsession with how they come across. A constant need to impress everyone else.

- A fragile ego that's easily damaged, often by perceived things rather than something that's actually happened.

- Devaluation of others. The narcissist might quickly become enamored with someone with power, but the slightest provocation can cause them to drop them and despise them.

- No regard for others, especially those seen as below them.

- A history of volatile relationships. If when you first meet them you hear of hundreds of 'crazy exes,' it might be time to worry a little. That isn't good news at all. Don't believe everything you're being told.

How Do I Overcome The Narcissistic Abuse?

You can overcome the abuse you have suffered, but you might not be able to do it alone. The person you really need to work on is yourself. You need to understand the other person but work on you and regain your own strength to help you move past it. A medical professional or therapist will have services to assist you with this. Asking for help is a big, but essential, step to getting control of your own life once more.

Where Can I Get Help For A Narcissist?

Not every case of narcissism is as clean cut and as easy to walk away from. If the way the other person behaves isn't abuse, then what you might wish to do is help them. Narcissism Cured is an excellent online resource filled with real life stories of people who have suffered from narcissism and recovered. This can help you to see how other people who have been through similar situations have recovered from it. Medicine Net also can help you to find a relevant support group and medical professional in your area.

What Causes Narcissism?

Narcissism is widely thought, by medical professionals who have studied it, to be caused by a difficult childhood. Either neglectful parents or ones who piled on the pressure too much. Something has caused the sufferer to disassociate and deal with their emotions differently. Because of this, there are ways to recover from it, it just takes a lot of willingness and hard work.

Conclusion

It's interesting how it all comes full circle. Here are the stages of self healing journey:

In Stage One of the self-healing journey, there is a necessary strengthening of the ego and sense of self. It's imperative during the first stage of healing to recognize that the problem is the manipulative person with the disorder and not you, reminding yourself that the abuse wasn't your fault. It's necessary to put a label on the manipulator and make ego judgments about who they are in order to gain clarity and dissolve the cognitive dissonance. It's important to strengthen your boundaries and say NO more often to protect your peace.

It's helpful and often necessary to isolate for a period of time during the restructuring of the ego and redefining of the self, the intense research on the topic of narcissistic abuse, as well as the making sense of what happened and the deep self-care work that takes place in Stages One and Two.

By Stage Three you've released your ego attachments to the fears, wounds and experiences so you can move beyond those patterns. You're reintegrating with others socially and putting into practice what you've learned along the way. Your boundaries are now healthy and clear. You now know you're worthy. Your self-trust is solid, and you no longer ignore your inner guidance. Your choices are in integrity with yourself. You're living at new levels of purpose.

The three stages of the journey are like three different realities. When you're in Stage Two or Three, you can forget how you felt in Stage One, which is great for you. However, remember to have empathy for others who are still in Stage One as they're not going to "just get over it" or "just let it go" because they are not ready yet.

Recovery is a natural process revealing itself, much like the journey of life.

The journey of growth and personal development is never really over until we die. When one cycle ends, another begins. We learn and transform one pattern, then we move onto another. Layer by layer we cleanse ourselves and grow. We often revisit earlier patterns and work on them at another level down the road.

There is the macro (Big Picture) transformations and then there are the micro (smaller scale) transformations taking place. In some areas of your life you might feel more like the victim and in other areas you're in the survivor stage, while in another area of your life you may be in the thrive stage. The nature of the healing journey is abstract. As you observe your own transformations, I encourage you to look upon them as if you were looking at abstract art rather than figurative art.

You might notice that you go through the Rite of Passage for every life transformation that you make. Maybe first you go through a spiritual awakening process, then you go through a career transformation, and then you go through the self-healing after narcissistic abuse transformation or in any other order. Perhaps you live to old age and one day you're facing the end of your own life, so you go through a transformational process of acceptance around that.

Through relationships we grow the most. All of your unconscious stuff comes up in the mirror of another person and so you work through more transformational cycles. Maybe you work your way through the self-healing after narcissistic abuse from your ex and/or original abuser, and then you find a new and wonderful life partner, so you enter a new cycle of transformation. Then maybe one day you have a child and suddenly new memories and feelings come up from your childhood, so you enter another transformation. Maybe you enter a new cycle of transformation due to the death of someone dear to you.

Protect your Inner Circle of people like your life depends on it.

Don't hang out with people who don't support your success and wellbeing or those who don't want to grow because they will tempt you to stop growing yourself.

There's always the next level that you can grow toward.

If you want to keep growing, continually check in to see where you currently are and aim toward the next level. Remember that the nature of life is change. Everything is in a constant state of change. Don't get complacent in your growth or you will lose your inspiration and ambition. When that happens, the universe will often challenge you to spark your sense of passion and purpose again.

Jackson MacKenzie, author of Psychopath Free1 (which is a must-read in Stage One), says the recovery takes about one to two years. Looking at my own journey and the hundreds of people I've worked with personally in coaching sessions, one to two years sounds about right. Don't beat yourself up or give up if you feel like you're not getting there fast enough. Keep working at it consistently and you will see steady progress.

Everything in your life shifts when you have a healthy relationship with yourself. The journey is both internal and external so as you shift the way you relate to yourself, that changes how you interact in the world and how the world responds to you.

The massive shifts out of the trauma take place during spontaneous breakthrough moments. The work you do on your self-healing with structure and consistent, dedicated practice is your preparation for when the one of these sacred moments presents itself to you.

Psychology addresses the dangers of magical thinking. In the case of the rescue fantasy that most victims have, it's true that the magical thinking can be dangerous because it takes away the tenet of self-responsibility and the ability to take action to change your own life. However, as a person who feels deeply connected to the universe, I have also seen how magical moments of life can be. I can't deny the powerful impact of synchronicity, those seeming coincidences when everything aligns to reveal the connectedness of all things the amazing shifts that can result from the right connection at the right time.

For some people, life is randomness and that might be true, but that doesn't make those synchronistic moments any less magical. It's precisely in those spontaneous moments of connection when the biggest breakthroughs from the trauma are possible. This is because the trauma is not managed by the intellectual, logical understanding parts of the brain. We have to go beyond that level of awareness to shift the trauma in massive ways. All the work of consistency and dedication that you do leading up to those moments is your preparation for the opportunity.

It's the fear that's the most toxic part of the aftermath of abuse.

The fear is the chronic sickness caused by abuse. In psychology they say it's the shame and loneliness at the core and those definitely exist too, but at the very epicenter affecting everything else and holding together the house of cards, is the fear. The fear cannot be resolved at the intellectual level either.

In shamanism, fear and disconnection are seen as the common ailments that humans suffer. Everything negative and toxic originates from there. The fear after childhood abuse is often wrapped up in the absence of a healthy emotional attachment to the primary caregiver/s. The fear of separation from the source of love and nurturing (caused by the rejection, cruelty, abandonment or neglect of a parent or caregiver) leads to the toxic shame and pathological loneliness that a child carries over a lifetime until maybe one day s/he discovers keywords like "narcissistic abuse" after an adult relationship and starts to wake up.

The fear is how we end up hurting ourselves even after we cut off contact with manipulative, abusive people. We try to run from our fears. We wrap ourselves in a blanket of false security to protect ourselves from those fears and in the process we don't allow ourselves to live freely. Eventually the false security falls apart and we get hurt again. Because of our fears, we end up getting in our own way and holding ourselves back. When the fear dissolves in a spontaneous breakthrough moment, the shame dies too.

Until I crossed the Second Threshold, my ego was so attached to those fears holding my reality paradigm in place with the false sense of security that I had built around myself to stay safe from the toxicity of others… but in the moment of breakthrough I discovered that the cosmic joke was the fear was already inside the gates.

If you grew up with a narcissistic parent, you were disconnected from a source of love and nourishment and instead you absorbed a lot of fear. Fear was used as the currency of power in the household. Fear is used for control in adult abusive relationships. Fear is also the tool used by the powers that be in the world to keep the human race enslaved and reacting as they want us to.

When your baseline feeling is fear, that's reflected in your self-talk, which creates your perspective. Your fearful perspective then creates your negative reality paradigm. That then attracts a negative vibrational resonance in the world around you so "bad" things, feelings and thoughts keep repeating ad nauseam.

You can break the cycle.

You and only you have the power to do so for yourself.

It is never too late to start.

We are in this life to learn and grow. No one is perfect. No one is without problems or entirely healed. Anyone who tells you they are done growing and they have nothing more to heal is probably not someone to trust. At best they're not self-aware of their problems. At worst, they're unwilling to admit that they need to change some things about themselves and they're purposely deceiving you into worshipping them like a guru.

You are your own guru. You are the hero/heroine of your story. You are the writer and protagonist of your story. You also need to be able to ask for help when you need it. You need allies, teachers, and helpers who give you faith and nudge you back to yourself through their living example and your interactions with them. Yet you've still got to do the hard work yourself. You've got to rescue yourself.

This journey of self-healing after narcissistic abuse is about creating an entirely new relationship with yourself. It isn't easy but it's totally worth it.

You got this!

NO MORE CODEPENDENCY AND GASLIGHTING

HEALING & CURE: THE NARCISSISM RECOVERY GUIDE.

HOW TO ESCAPE FROM A CODEPENDENT RELATIONSHIP EFFECT WITH A NARCISSIST & RECOGNIZE MANIPULATIVE PEOPLE

PART I

Introduction

C odependent" is one of these oft-utilized popular expressions that imply different degrees of poverty in a relationship, or connections tinged with a dash of urgency. Be that as it may, just, the term originates from something a touch more prominent explicit to dependency and recuperating.

Codependence is an imbalanced relationship test where one friend accepts an extreme cost 'supplier rescuer' job and the option the 'taker-unfortunate casualty' job."

Codependence implies that the friends and family of addicts, in view of their fundamental, every now and again intuitive early life issue commonly tend to, as grown-ups, give excessively and love an unreasonable measure of. Therefore, they tempt, empower and entangle with dependent accomplices.

Those expecting those jobs, deliberately or unknowingly, propagate the taker's enslavement pushed bad conduct. The codependent taker is commonly a couple of blends of penniless, underneath working, juvenile, dependent, entitled or stricken. they rely upon the provider to take care of them, envision or mellow the poor outcomes for their moves, and to make up for lost time with their under-working. Meanwhile, the codependent supplier is commonly an empathic, pardoning, prepared and benevolent person. They assume the job of unnecessary guardian, rescuer, supporter or associate. They show love and being worried by methods for making penances for the taker that usually license rather than enable them.

This diverse trendy expression "empowering agent" signifies, reliable with the Merriam-Webster word reference: "one which empowers some other to harvest a stop; extraordinarily one who empowers each other to endure in self-antagonistic conduct (counting substance misuse) through providing reasons or by means of making it suitable to avoid the aftereffects of such conduct."

Healthy connections as the years progressed, have an equivalent parity of giving and ingest expressions of fulfilling wishes, rather than favoring the desires of one friend. Codependent connections are worked cycle an irregularity of intensity that needs the requirements of the taker, leaving the provider to protect on giving. Codependent connections disregard some of the basic elements of solid cozy connections since they are enmeshed in inclination to reliant, and imbalanced in inclination to impartial.

While individuals are marked as codependent, they are informed that they are looking to both empower or deal with the individual who is addicted. They put an excessive amount of spotlight on another person's lead and now not adequate all alone.

Why Codependent Connections Exist

What reasons us to be us searching for out these types of connections? To the extent suppliers pass, accessible examinations show that psychological mistreatment and overlook set us at risk for codependence. on the off chance that you discovered that the best method to interface with a troublesome decide changed into to subordinate your own one of a kind wants and take into account theirs, at that point, you will be the establishment for comparative connections over an amazing span.

The timespan codependence comes from something is known as "injury idea," which proposes a requesting event, sometimes happening eventually by way of immaturity, most likely coming about because of brutality or some unique state of infringement.

You can moreover have standards or character qualities that make it simpler to fall into a codependent pursuing. You can over-disguise otherworldly or social qualities that recommend generosity for other people. Being the provider in a codependent relationship can likewise fulfill needs that incorporate the need to depend on somebody, they need to encounter skilled, the need to detect close to somebody. To the extent takers go, they are once in a while narrow-minded and manipulative, flighty and entitled. Anyway, a couple is simply pained, dependent, or ailing in presence abilities.

In accordance with a more established examination inside the diary of substance misuse, the two ladies and men in codependent connections will, in general, be reliable to their friends regardless of the unpleasant strain. In any case, clearly adequate, codependent ladies demonstrated 5 of the attributes foreseen in codependency: control, overstated duty, extremely worth reliance, salvage direction, and exchange direction, even as codependent men handiest affirmed two: control and misrepresented obligation. Their feeling of fearlessness was not as identified with their accomplices as ladies.

Regardless of your sexual orientation, on the off chance that you experience you are likely in a codependent relationship, it has justified, despite all the trouble to attempt to harm the cycle. a Mexican inspect from innovation and aggregate wellbeing says codependent connections don't least complex influence the strength of the provider and taker, anyway, also impacts the wellbeing in their family units. They, for the most part, will in general experience the ill effects of more weight that is prominent (and medical problems from weight), their children have a superior danger of getting to be addicts themselves, and highlight a "less fortunate top-notch of ways of life inside the psychological and physical area names" than the general populace.

Indications you will be in a codependent relationship

You are most likely in a codependent relationship if:

•You are in a caretaking or potentially protecting dating with an individual who uses you to evade age-fitting obligations or the troublesome artistic creations of private exchange.

•You are in an imbalanced pursuing with appropriately intentioned, anyway over the long haul inefficient steady practices, comprising of permitting your partner, sitting above abused understandings and tolerating counterfeit clarifications.

•Your endeavors to reclamation a distressed, dependent or underneath working individual has cultivated reliance on you, instead of on their ways of life progress.

•Takers interface on the other side of the above practices, the utilization of or actualizing upon their connections (or the blame of them) to maintain a strategic distance from obligation, stay away from their real progress and private change. On the off chance that you believe you are likely in a genuine codependent situation, you first need to recognize the practices you have to exchange and acknowledge what codependence costs you, your accessory and your connections.Advising and self-improvement substances help you to comprehend the underlying foundations of your lead since one of kind exchange systems can be pertinent depending on the reason. You besides may likewise need to comprehend that picking up learning to set obstructions may be the quality viewpoint you could accomplish for yourself. There are a lot of things that make putting restrictions intense, together with the contrary individual's obstruction and your blame, and your commitment, which can be great estimated in the event that you have committed bounty time, power and assets to the association.

In case you are thinking of seeking help, connect with an approved specialist for the necessary assistance.

Chapter 1
What Is and What Isn't Codependency?

What is Codependency?

The word 'codependency' sounds like it stands for something positive–something mutually beneficial. If you had thought it was something good when you first heard the word, you are not alone. Of course, codependency refers to something 'mutual,' but the 'beneficial' part is completely off.

There is nothing beneficial in a codependent relationship, neither is there anything beneficial for a codependent person. Indeed, a codependent person is someone whose relationship with himself or herself is in a state of deep-seated self-doubt, whereby they no longer trust themselves. When a codependent relationship ends, one of the partners is likely to indulge in self-abuse, self-blame, self-shaming, and an inability to handle even the slightest form of criticism. This is usually a precursor to self-sabotaging or even suicidal behaviors.

Codependency, in its basic form, is excessive psychological or emotional reliance on another person who needs support because of an addiction or ill health. A codependent person is someone who allows the behavior of another person to influence them significantly to the point of taking full responsibility for controlling the other person's behavior. The dependent person in the relationship is enabled by the codependent person. That is to say, the codependent partner behaves in ways that encourage the other partner to continue in their irresponsibility, immaturity, addiction, and illness.

Codependency goes beyond mere clinginess. A codependent person typically lives their life for their partner–their world revolves around the partner's world. They go to extreme lengths to please their partner. A codependent relationship is one in which one partner believes that their sense of purpose depends on the support given to the other person, and the other person believes that they need to be needed. The codependent partner usually engages in self-sacrificing behavior for the sake of their partner who, incidentally, expects nothing less. The neediness by one partner and the need to feel needed by the other partner is known as the cycle of codependency.

Codependency is not restricted to romantic partners alone. It can happen between friends, family, and even colleagues at work too. In many cases, the relationship can degenerate into a physically and emotionally abusive one. Often, other people outside the relationship can easily see that something is off, but the codependent partner usually doesn't realize it.

Codependency is not...

Codependency is not caregiving.

A lot of people can confuse the two because the word has been so overused in our lexicon that nearly all examples of kindness and caregiving are looked at as codependent when in fact there is a huge difference. When someone is giving of their heart and for example taking care of a sick parent or child.

There is a big difference because they are giving of themselves to that person because they love them, and they want to see them get better.

These are specific situations.

This is not a pattern of relationships and dysfunction that they are getting into and seeking out even if they don't know they are seeking it out on a consistent basis. You can look at it almost as if one is chronic and one is acute.

Even if the acute situation turns into long-term caring. It is not because the caregiver is codependent. They are doing it out of love for a child, a parent or whoever.

It is important not to mistake kindness and love for codependency.

They are two different things.

Some people are thrust into situations where they have to give of themselves, such as the examples mentioned above, they are not seeking them out but they approach them with love and compassion, kindness, and a genuine giving of themselves to get that person back the way they were.

Look at it this way, codependency is something that a codependent person will seek out because that is all they know.

It is a compulsion to become involved with somebody in that type of relationship where you're going to give everything you have in order to please that person or take care of that person or control that person.

It is not coming from a place of love.

It is coming from a place of need, because in a way the codependent person is satisfying their own need for acceptance and validation by being involved with this person.

On the other hand, the person that is caregiving is doing is out of genuine love and concern and kindness. They are doing it because they feel compelled to help a loved one, it is not a compulsion.

It is really important to differentiate the two and understand the difference.   It signifies a healthy response to a loved one in need and not to satisfy their own needs or compulsions.

It is to help, and care give to the one that they love.

The codependence arises from shame. They will deny their own needs and feelings. They have a perfectionist attitude towards helping this person that they are involved with. It is their low self-esteem keeping them around and they have this insatiable need to people-please and feel guilt if they do not act perfect. This is codependency.

The boundaries are just completely out of whack.

The healthy individual, on the other hand, is looking to care for the person. They are doing it out of love. They are doing it out of genuine caring and concern and kindness.

Codependency is a fake proximity of what true love is. It's an obsessive all-consuming need to please, win approval, and validation from others.

Just because you have the feelings of wanting to help others and to be there for your loved ones, that does not make you codependent.

To summarize, codependency is not caring and giving everything, we have to people that we love to see them happy or get them through a difficult time. Also, it is not when you are briefly hurt because someone betrayed you, or that we want to see somebody improve and get better because they are acting in a destructive manner.

These are normal reactions.

This is just part of being human.

Codependency, Dependency, and Interdependency

It is not uncommon for people to confuse interdependent relationships with codependent ones. This confusion stems from the idea that the individuals in an ideal relationship should depend on each other. While that idea is correct to an extent, extreme dependence on someone else can be detrimental in many cases. Children and pets may not have any choice than to depend completely on their parents and owners. But for adults, relying totally on a partner, friend, or boss may not be a sensible thing to do.

Perhaps a brief explanation of the related terms (as it concerns relationships) is necessary to provide more clarity.

- Dependence: This refers to extreme reliance and trust in someone else. It can lead to emotional clinginess and falling victim to a controlling person. A dependent person is abnormally tolerant to someone else because of an expected benefit.

- Independence: An independent person is self-directed. He or she is not subject to external control or influenced by others. A relationship where the partners are strictly independent of each other might experience insurmountable challenges. Partners who depend on each other irrespective of their ability to be independent stand greater chances of thriving together.

- Interdependence: This is being mutually dependent. It is a state of equilibrium that maturely weaves dependence and independence. In other words, interdependence in relationships is a healthy dependence on each other.

- Codependency: This refers to psychological or emotional over-reliance on someone else. A codependent person gets their sense of self by approval-seeking behaviors.

Codependency versus Interdependency: What's the Difference?

As adults, we depend on others to experience sexual intimacy, friendship, love, communication, touch, and appreciation. We give up our true identity when we allow ourselves to be abused by others to have these needs fulfilled. But instead of fulfilling the social, emotional, and sexual needs, their insecurities prevent them from enjoying these experiences. One or both partners in a codependent relationship live in constant fear of losing the other person because they think they are not capable of functioning without them. They feel trapped and resentful but can do nothing about it, or so they think. Fear also keeps them from being emotionally intimate (even if they are physically intimate). It is usually challenging for them to relax and let their guards down to become vulnerable to each other.

On the other hand, an interdependent relationship is a healthy one. The paradox in interdependent relationships is that it takes place between people who are capable of autonomy. The individuals are free to be themselves even though they understand that they need each other to make the relationship work. Couples in a healthy interdependent relationship respect each other's sense of self. There is no pressure to make the other person in the relationship forfeit his or her value system.

A healthy interdependent relationship is born when individuals or couples in a relationship strike a balance between extreme dependence and excessive independence. They understand that their human need for interconnection can only be met in a healthy atmosphere of interdependency. They approach their relationships like a collaboration or partnership. Just as a partnership has interdependent parts that are vital for its survival, couples in a healthy relationship also understand the importance of having mutual respect for their partnership to function optimally.

The feeling of deep love can make couples desire closeness and even appear as if they can't do without each other, but this is not the same as being codependent. Two of the major differences between a codependent and an interdependent relationship are responsibility and power.

Codependent couples assume responsibility for the other partner. They feel responsible for their partner's moods, feelings, and behavior. There are usually power tussles in their relationship—either partner trying to control or enable the other person's behavior.

Interdependent couples, on the other hand, only assume responsibility for their behaviors, moods, and feelings. And because they share power equally, there is hardly any room for controls and emotional manipulation. They don't have to cajole the other person to know their sense of self-worth. Their happiness does not depend on making the other person behave as they want. They share mutual respect and support for their individual and collective goals. Since they have positive self-esteem, they are open and honest with each other. This makes it easier for them to hear each other out without being defensive or feeling guilty. Also, it is quite easy to have their social, emotional, and sexual needs fulfilled because they have no fear of being intimate with each other.

Codependency versus Dependency: Any Difference?

The codependent enables the dependent by 'fixing' them through care and support. In some instances, the dependent can be incapacitated due to ill health. In other cases, the helpless behavior is formed over a long period of enablement.

Here is why it is called codependency: The first person depends on the other to be fixed, and the other depends on fixing the first person to feel good about himself or herself. The codependent partner's sense of self-esteem and self-worth is then linked to how well he or she can help others, sacrifice his or her happiness, and please others in the guise of being proactive. Over time, such a person loses their sense of self since they cannot embrace their honest feelings and make their own decisions. A codependent person can strongly dislike something, but because they can't own their feelings, they would tolerate it if their dependent partner likes it. For example, a typical codependent person would say something like, "I don't like a melancholic person, but since my partner is that way, I guess I can find ways to cope. Who knows, I might change them."

Chapter 2
Causes, Symptoms and Effect

Causes of Codependency

Codependency is not a character or personality flaw; it is not a genetic trait either. It is a learned habit that usually starts early in an individual's life. The following factors are associated with the development of codependent behaviors.

Living with a Mentally or Physically Ill Family Member

People who lived a significant part of their lives with and giving care to a constantly ill family member are prone to becoming codependent. They learn to put the sick person's needs ahead of their own and make huge personal sacrifices for them. Over time, such caregivers may begin to disregard their personal needs to fulfill the needs of their ill family member. Eventually, they can unconsciously reprogram their minds to hinge their sense of self-worth on the care they can give. Taking full responsibility for the sick person's wellbeing becomes an obsession – a form of control.

Growing up with Dysfunctional Parents

Children who were raised in families where one or both parents abused drugs or misused some other substances are likely to develop codependent traits as adults. Growing up in such families and experiencing how their parent's irresponsible and behavior put the children in a position to take on caregiving responsibilities early on in life. Also, through constant harsh criticisms, harassments, mistreatments, and neglect, the children learn to put their parents' needs ahead of theirs. They grow up to believe that it is more important to give care to others than to oneself. These types of influences shape the child's psychological development and can lead to seeking codependent and dysfunctional relationships as adults.

Growing up in an Abusive Family

Exposure to physical, emotional, and sexual abuse can cause severe traumatic experiences for young children. Children who grow in such abusive families where these experiences are a frequent occurrence are likely to live with these traumas throughout their lifetime. It is not uncommon for such children to enter into lopsided and abusive relationships as adults because that is their subconscious idea of what a relationship looks like.

Children who grow up in abusive families are likely to learn how to disregard or mute their feelings of anger and frustration to cope with the pain of abusive experiences. If carried into their adult years, they are likely to become codependents.

Signs of Codependency

The following can help you to determine if you have codependent behaviors or are in a codependent relationship.

Low Self-esteem

Typically, a person with codependent behavior thinks of themselves as not good enough. They live with a strong sense of their inadequacies and always feel shame and guilt. These are all signs of low self-esteem. To overcome this feeling of unworthiness, codependents go to great lengths to prove themselves worthy to be loved and needed. This attitude can lead them into unhealthy focus on other people's needs, problems, and feelings.

If you find yourself overly worried about being unfit, less qualified, or not worthy enough for your partner, you are likely codependent on them for your sense of self-worth.

Taking Things Too Personally and Being Highly Sensitive to Criticism

Codependents are generally defensive and are quick to feel threatened by opposing views or disagreements. Since they have a hard time creating and maintaining strong personal boundaries, they easily take things personally and live mostly from a reactionary place.

They are also very sensitive to criticism. For most of their lives, codependents have endured blame, hurt, and criticism. They become quick to soak up other people's opinions and believe that views are a true reflection of who they are. To avoid criticisms, codependents do their best to avoid conflicts, please others (even when it is not convenient) and try to remain unnoticeable to avoid unnecessary attention and possible criticism.

Continuous Renunciation of Personal Interests and Feelings

Codependents seem to think that if they ignore their true feelings, they will go away. But all that leads to is resentment. Because they value other people's feelings and interests above their own, they live in continuous self-denial and repression of their feelings.

In the same vein, they don't acknowledge that they have problems. Instead, they see their dependent as the one with the problem and they try to fix them. Even when codependents enter into new relationships, their problems remain unresolved until they recognize that the problem is with themselves and not others.

If you or someone you know seems to be in the habit of putting other people's feelings and interests above theirs, it could be a sign of codependency.

Inability to Ask for What They Need and Want

For many codependents, saying exactly what they want, and need is usually not possible because they are careful not to hurt other people. Manipulation seems to be their preferred method of communicating their desires to those they care for. But in many cases, they will suppress their desires and pretend to be okay – a precursor to frustration.

If you tend to tiptoe around certain people, you may be having a codependent relationship with them. If you live in constant worry that being honest will upset your significant other, you are likely having a codependent relationship with them. If the communication in your relationship is not open and is controlled by fear, it is an indicator of codependency.

Seeking Approval Through People-Pleasing Behavior

Partners in healthy relationships please each other within reason and it is okay to do so. However, a codependent partner believes that they have no choice but to please their partner. They do this for two reasons: to gain approval from their partner, and to feel good about themselves. It is only by making others happy (through people-pleasing behavior) that codependents feel worthy.

Another way codependent people-please is by saying "yes" to every request by their significant other. A person who feels anxious about turning down a request from their partner or someone they love is showing signs of codependency. They are giving away their power and losing themselves in the process because they value connection with others more than they value their personal power.

A typical example of people-pleasing is when someone is afraid to turn down sexual advances from their partner even when they don't want to have sex. Since codependents have difficulty in communicating effectively, they may agree to just about any request from those they care about to avoid conflict. It is not uncommon for codependents to feel repulsed by their partner but still go on to have sex with them just to please them.

Chapter 3
Types of Co-dependency: Passive Active and Flavors

Passive and Active

Primarily, a co-dependent is dissected into two categories of emotional manipulation. They are,

a.   Egoistic

b.   Addicts

c.   Selflessness

These three phases of co-dependency together explain the factor of the cofactor of co-dependency meaning that the subject always hunts for a partner who is not mutually reciprocating. The subject is passive or active about their response.

Briefly put, they look out for partners who are passive or active about the subject's overlying attachment, dedication, surprises and care, to be active or passive themselves!

I. Passive Co-dependents

Mainly living in the fear of avoiding any a conflict with their partners, passive co-dependents try to choose partners whom they can abuse, subtly seduce and manipulate into being in a relationship, intimacy or exploit. They are passive about their blaring power over the dependent but remain passively attached to the partner who is not reciprocal.

II. Active co-dependents

III. These co-dependents and direct, frank and loud about their necessities from their partners. They demand their respect, care and love through varied emotional ways of manipulation, even though the partner remains un-reciprocating.

Some of the various types of Co-dependent virtues of characters in each of us or in our vicinities are elaborately listed below. This is not to cause panic but is a clear idea of how co-dependency exists in person, in each of us or amongst us!

1)	Caretakers: This person feels motherly towards their partner and tries to take maximum care of their u-reciprocating partners. These co-dependents find contentment in meeting their partner's demands and orders to provide all satisfaction through the pleasure of being servile or as a masochist. They are addicted to giving love and needs to love, in order to live. They find peace in life only through the various ways of being a nurturer, caregiver, mother/father or helper, in what-so-ever-a-way!

2)	Romantics: These co-dependents choose their partners through an elaborate fashion of finding the never—ending love, romance and fun of life. These categories of co-dependents are focused on being in a relationship that nurtures their romantic life or relationship and intimacy addiction/issues. They find peace with the self only by possessing another being's love for them or approval or even acceptance of friend's love. This involves the nymphomaniac who is centered to have relationship that sex can be a cause and effect of. He might keep on being the rolling stone with you gathering any marriage rings!

3)	Saviors: This category of co-dependents are based on realizing their satisfaction to their life through choosing their partners as helpless addicts, jobless, homeless or the disabled. They find peace only by being the saviors. They feel productive, happy and content only by being the constant messiah, hence they help and live for realizing other's dreams, and move on constantly to help others realize their dreams, to realize their own!

4)	Narcissist: When the boundaries vanish and disintegrate, a vehement co-dependent realizes others as for or against their own use. This is a sign of anti-social behavior as well as disinterest in society or public to follow one's own whims and fancies, which is a true Narcissist.

5) Victim Mentality: Another type of a co-dependent personality is the feeling of being a victim. As mentioned above, victim-mentality makes the person feel like a victim who constantly needs a partner who abuses and de-motivates the subject, in order to find contentment with the own self. The feel abandoned and disinterested due to victimization, almost all the time.

6) Linguistic dysfunction: Another vital co-dependent factor is the linguistic dysfunction. Simply put, this defines that bad communication skills are. If the communication dwindles between two people, this can give rise to an assumed sense of relationship, which in turn induces a dysfunction in the relationship that the subject seems to find comfort and convenience in.

7) Perfectionists: Yet another category of co-dependents are a kind of people who are terrible perfectionists. This category of characters finds peace in arranging things, things, people and their thoughts in one certain way. They need to constantly arrange people and set their motion through one type of way that they believe the perfection is in. Perfectionist co-dependents try to choose partners who adore and admire their narcissism to create a bond that involves the other's adoration and love to bring about a setting that is in accordance with the subject's plan of perfection.

8) Low-Self Esteem: These categories of co-dependents are people of terribly low-self esteem. This is one way a character of victim mentality as well as hopelessness, despair and fear. These co-dependents are attracted to partners that make them feel ungrateful, inadequate, worried and other's perspectives towards the self. This is the cause and effect of poor communication skills in a relationship that which becomes co-dependency and then, low-self-esteem and absolute dysfunction.

9) Poor Response, Reaction and Reflexes: This factor of co-dependency relies on the aspect of poor response and reflexes of reaction in the aspects of setting poor boundaries with others and the self. Parameters of weak, marred, blurred, too hard, abusive and bad intimacy can result in bad co-dependency that can result in a personality that is always poorly reacting and responding to things, people and situations.

334

10)   Poor Dependency or Addiction: Another aspect of co-dependency is the factor of the afraid one or the paranoid one. This personality is terribly scared of being out of any a relationship or to be alone. This is also dependent on the fact that they constantly feel as if they are caged, trapped or confined due to their addictions. Bad boundaries of dependency and other undue addictions can give rise to many insurmountable issues with being independent ever or being paranoid in isolation to find the self-peace.

Chapter 4
Advantages and Disadvantages of Codependency

When we look closely at the co-dependent we are often quick to judge and only see that dysfunction in their relationship. However, it is quickly forgotten that while this dysfunction is visible to us at its worst was most often rooted in the very foundation of one's love for their spouse, parent, or child. The question then becomes, when does one's love for their partner, parent or child turn from something wonderful to be cherished and becomes something dysfunctional?

Love for another and feelings of charity towards them are not often viewed as a disorder. However, the truth is that when the attachment towards another surpasses the norm to the point that we deny our own needs in order to provide for the selfish needs of our loved one, our feelings of self-worth and self-esteem are greatly diminished as a result. At times like these, it is right to conclude that there is something missing in our lives, am emptiness that we are looking to fill either one that we have had since childhood or one that has developed as a result of our past relationships. Either way once an individual has taken a turn down this path the emotional toll is vast.

Advantages of Co-dependency

Certain uneven traits displayed towards the partner, like

1) Love

2) Responsibility

3) Caring

4) Peace

5) Assurance

6) Faith

7) Safety

8) Security

9) Support

10) Finance

11) Stability

12) Happiness

13) False Contentment

The advantages of co-dependent relationships are often momentary, the results of certain events which give rise to a favorable set of circumstances. These advantages can be achieved even in a co-dependent relationship if there is at some point a healthy attachment to each other, one in which the needs of both partners in a relationship participate. However, this does not stand to say that love alone is a valid reason to become obsessively possessive of one another. Certain experiences together such as intimacy are capable of creating the illusion of everything in our lives becoming magical, miraculous or eternal. But in reality, the danger in not being able to recognize when the attachment has crossed from normalcy, to dysfunction! If you find a virus in your computer and it fails to function properly you do not continue to operate that machine hoping that it will fix itself, instead your backup your computer and take it in for repair before more damage a can be done. Just like repairing your computer, it is possible to seek out help and repair the "virus" that is a co-dependent relationship in order to attain a healthy relationship. There are so many forms of help available to those who wish to find it, therapists, support groups, 12 step programs, counselors, treatment centers and self-help books. There is a tool to fit everyone's life and personal needs. All you need to do is take the first step and admit that you need help.

Disadvantages of Co-dependency

Now to come to the obvious side of the issue, co-dependency is evidently a high dosage of negativity that can mentally damage or impair not only you but all of those around you. If you're the co-dependent or not, it is undeniable at least one addiction or negative emotional force has become the center of your world. This is not only an unhealthy relationship but has the potential to cause further disruption to your emotional state with feelings of depression, distress or hopelessness. The first disadvantage of co-dependency is that if you are incapable of tolerating any disapproval, then you're setting yourself up to be exposed to manipulation. We are all individuals, no matter who else is in our life, parents, children, spouses, significant others, our failures and our successes are purely ours and not the result of what we can do for others. Each of us has a different perspective on life and a different perception of life than every other person alive. Once we are gone, no one else will ever have this same perception again, because it was purely ours alone. If people are unable to be content as an individual, their life is going to be one rough ride. It also means that at the advent of any a relationship, good or bad, the intensity and the toxicity of the bond shared has a chance of being misunderstood by the co-dependent. It is to everyone's benefit to be aware of the signs that you are slipping into these negative trends and prevent them from harming you and your relationships.

Some of the most toxic disadvantages of co-dependency are:

1) Anger

2) Ownership

3) Commanding

4) Intolerance

5) Blame-game

6) Worthlessness

7) Strong Nihilism

8) Loneliness/ Abandonment

9) Undue pressure of responsibilities

10) Fear of everything

11) Recurrent panic attacks

12) Laziness

13) Exhaustion

14) Lethargy

15) Poverty

16) Contempt

17) Hatred towards people

18) Social awkwardness

19) Possessiveness

20) Confusion

21) Paranoia

22) Low-self-esteem

23) Pessimism

24) Instability

25) Indecisiveness

26) Guilt

27) Rigidity

28) Chronic lying

29) Poor communication skills

30) Poor personal space/ boundaries

31) Abnormal dependency

32) Obsession

33) Repression

34) Lack of faith

35) Intimacy issues   36) Control-freak

37) Perfectionism   38) Drug/Sex/ Substance abuse

39) Critically sensitive to personal criticism   40) Suicidal tendencies

Chapter 5
The Key Differences: Codependency VS Intense Love

When You Love Too Much, Maybe You Don't Love

Some tolerate and justify the abusive or toxic behavior of another, saying that they do it because they love them too much. What lies deep down is a codependent stance, born of deep insecurity and fear of abandonment.

Some people are willing to do anything or endure any humiliation in the name of love. They start from the premise that when one loves too much, there must be, above all, self-denial. That is, provide affection without conditions and forgive a thousand and one times if necessary. All in order not to lose or dislike the loved one.

Within that group of people are, for example, mothers who pay again and again the debts that their children contract. They know that this is not correct, but they end up justifying it in the name of love. There are also those people who embrace the same partner who mistreats them. They never leave them or leave them alone to return a short time later. They argue that when you love too much, no offense can break that bond.

The truth is that in cases like this, we are not facing a great love, but rather a dependency. This leads a person to experience a kind of affection that is overflowing and unmanageable. They feel they cannot live without the other. That is why they are willing to do anything except break that link. In these cases, you don't love yourself too much, but you lack love for yourself.

"The victim depends on the aggressor; there is emotional dependence. But it is that the aggressor also depends on the victim because he bases his self-esteem on domination."

-Ana Isabel Gutiérrez Saralegui-

Do you love too much, or do you need too much?

This is accompanied by a perspective in which the other person does not matter. Their needs and desires should always be in the background. The only thing that matters is the needs and desires of the codependent. They are willing to sacrifice for them. They explain this unfair situation by merely saying that when you love too much, the limits on delivery disappear.

However, this situation causes them suffering and anxiety, mainly. When you love too much, likely, you will also have difficulty sleeping or experience a state of constant restlessness, eating disorders, or problems in other areas. They say that they love the other, but sooner rather than later, they turn their care and dedication into control behaviors, oriented in the background to keep that person tied.

I need you to need me

The distinctive feature of codependency is that on the one hand, there is someone who wishes to feel intensely useful or, rather, needed. This cannot be achieved with someone autonomous and mature. It requires a fragile person with many problems. Then a bond is formed when, on one end, there is someone with deficiencies and difficulties who does not want to take responsibility for himself. And on the other end, there is a codependent, who, in one way or another, assumes that responsibility belongs to him.

What emerges from this is an insane symbiosis—a type of relationship in which there is an abuse of side and side. In the end, there is a tacit agreement: the one "commits" not to solve his problems and the other to prevent him from doing so, in exchange for an unconditional "love." It is a neurotic entanglement that is challenging to recognize and analyze for those involved.

Therefore, the codependent feeds the abusive behaviors of the dependent—their excesses of consumption, anger, passivity, or whatever. Also, their excessive demands. What terrifies the codependent most is if the other stops needing him. In his imagination, if this were to happen, that person would probably depart from his side, for they would no longer need his protective mantle.

When you love yourself too much, perhaps what is in the background is a deep fear of abandonment. In this type of "love," suffering prevails, not happiness. They are common in people who have unprocessed childhood abuses. It results in such a situation when it is recognized that much of what is felt and done is not the fruit of love, but fear. Also, when those involved decide to cultivate self-esteem instead of projecting the lack in another.

Loving too much destroys us

When we talk about love, it seems that "more" is always synonymous with "better," and to believe this lie is to take a poisonous pill disguised as caramel. If we analyze the moments lived with the person we want and the moments of suffering abound, we have become victims of what they call "love. "

To love is not to suffer; it is not to continually sacrifice and always bet on black. To love is not to be blind, it is not to justify the unmentionable or forgive any act for mercy. To love is not to depend; it is not to develop an umbilical cord that chains you to your partner.

Loving is not just a matter of quantity but quality. To love is not to overprotect, it is not to go back solving all the problems that the other sows nor to protect among children a child trapped in an adult body. And, of course, to love is not to end up physically or mentally torn; if our relationship impairs our emotional balance and even, perhaps, our health and physical integrity, we undoubtedly love excessively.

"That the love of a couple expects nothing in return is an invention of the submissive: if you give, you want to receive. It's healthy, reciprocal.

-Walter Riso-

The masks in the couple

It seems that a vast chasm between men and women separates the way of understanding and facing relationships. Cultural ideals, the education received, the family environment in which you grew up, and even the biology itself are actively involved.

Children's experiences with their reference figures and especially with their parents, play a fundamental role in how they interact with others throughout their lives. Painful and challenging situations, emotional deficiencies, absence of essential figures, or lack of limits are just some of the factors that mark the way we seek and care.

On the one hand, some women tend to handle love by developing a strong dependence or obsession for the other person. The torrent of emotions is lived very intensely, expressed through the need for care and understanding towards the other, and adopting the role of "savior" on many occasions. Thus, it is quite ironic that women can respond with such compassion to others and remain with a blindfold in the face of the pain of their own lives.

On the other hand, many men escape their emotions through externalizing forms, that is, obsessing with their work, using drugs, or turning their free time into hobbies that leave little time to think. They are usually emotional blocking strategies due to their inability to manage and understand them. They do not cope with discomfort or problems because they pose an unmanageable, overwhelming, shameful, or blaming burden, which is best avoided.

This type of behavior can occur in both men and women, but it is generally women who develop patterns of care and sacrifice as a way of seeking and offering affection, while men try to protect themselves and avoid pain through more external than internal objectives, more impersonal than personal.

When is it too much?

Many times, we are not satisfied with a partner, but we deny reality by saying that it is only a bad time. We justify the experience thinking that this is how relationships are, passionate in the beginning, and tortuous to the end.

We forgive each other's actions by convincing ourselves that it will change. Or maybe we don't dare to break the relationship "for fear of hurting." Actually, behind all this is our fear of suffering, we are afraid of being alone or of not finding another person who can stand us.

Have you ever fallen in love, and the feeling was not reciprocal? Or maybe you had excellent, heady sex that made no sense, but the rest of the relationship was an ordeal. Perhaps you have discovered yourself acting like a mother with your partner, or you think that without a person by your side, nothing makes sense.

The situations that we have been able to live with when we interact with other people are very diverse, and therefore there are also many mistakes we make and forms of self-deception that we invent to soften the pain.

"Guilt, shame, and fear are the immediate motives of deception."

-Daniel Goleman-

There comes the point where we are immersed in a vicious circle, which only repeats itself. We are unable to leave and do not even know how we got there. Again, the same dramatic melody, the same bitter chords, and although the orchestra is different, the conductor is still you. Although the person is different, although the vital moment you are in is different, although you promised not to go through the same thing again, there you are again, loving too much, and also severely.

The traces of the past

Why does this happen to us? The patterns we learn at an early age to relate to others are very fixed. We have been practicing them for a lifetime and trying to abandon or change them is threatening and a terrible challenge. But it is more challenging to realize and be aware of the reality of the situation, to be able to see from within everything that is happening.

The key is to begin to understand each other, to ask ourselves why we continuously look for someone to care for or protect, why our voice is cut off when we try to explain what we feel and end up abandoning the task. Why do I need to know what the other person is doing and control them when they are not next to me or why, despite the suffering, do we continue to maintain a relationship that is dead?

If our way of relating hurts us and hurts the person next to us, but we do nothing to understand and change it, life will not be a way to grow but a struggle to survive. If loving is painful, it is time to love yourself to stop the pain.

"Loving oneself is the beginning of a story of eternal love."

-Oscar Wilde-

Chapter 6
Stages of Codependency

STAGE ONE:

Stage one may last for five to six months for some, or it can take up to a year to get through this first stage.

Begin with a zero-step, in which you acknowledge that you have a problem. It may be hard to admit, but you need to realize and accept that you have a problem and there is an actual name for the problem. This leads you to seek help. This gets us to stage one.

The first stage is setting boundaries. In therapy, this stage is when the client decides they are ready. It's time for them to change the psychological landscape of their life. Their therapist has gone over all the risks of getting into the program.

The first stage is spread over a zero to three months range. It is the most difficult and challenging stage of all. It is analogous to be an alcoholic and quitting alcohol. It could be like any addictive drug that has a difficult withdrawal syndrome. It is extremely anxiety-provoking.

Codependents are reflexively and magnetically attracted to narcissists. One is a caregiver and the other is a caretaker. They both fit perfectly in this functional relationship that requires their opposite personality to keep them together.

But when you break free from this dance and you challenge the person by disagreeing with them, the narcissist tends not to have the ability to accept fault in the problems. They tend to get very angry and feel betrayed, and they move toward blaming the person who is blaming them. They fail to see what's wrong with themselves but can always see what's wrong with others.

In stage one, when you are setting boundaries for the first time, this is the first time that you stand up to the narcissist. It is the time to insist that he or she do something that they would normally do to you, such as saying to your partner, "I am going out with the girls today," or ask them to take the children to the swimming classes.

The narcissist is always going to be very angry with this reversal. They can be threatening, whether overt or covert, and they may use anger or emotional manipulation. This can be very scary for the codependent because they have never really experienced safety in speaking their truth. The aggression or passive aggression of the narcissist is something they have avoided standing up to their whole life.

Another important thing to keep in mind in this stage is the possibility of immediate loss of friendships and relationships. Both the people who love you and people who don't love you are all going to be angry. Even though this sounds silly, it is a fact. You won't be able to tell the difference. There will, however, be a separation of two in the latter stages.

Your children may be enraged. You will tell them to leave their phones and laptops and come to the table to have dinner for the very first time. You have set a boundary. They will treat you like you are a stranger. They may look at you with hatred. You will very quickly learn what happens when a codependent sets boundaries and reasonable expectations. It immediately seems like the world is going to explode.

You are going to feel isolated. You will deal with criticism and condemnation. You are going to be told paradoxically and unfairly that you are being selfish. Even though it is a very sad accusation to the codependent who has always been selflessly connected to their loved ones. They have done everything for everybody.

The moment they set boundaries; they are called selfish. The reason why the emotional manipulators say these things is because it has always worked on the codependent before. Dating back to their childhood, if someone told them that they are going to become a person who is either a codependent or selfish, it has always enticed the codependent to back down and meet the needs of the emotional manipulator.

STAGE TWO:

This is where the intensity of the conflict comes down a few notches. It is still a very difficult stage. Stage two is about maintaining boundaries in a hostile environment. You have already set boundaries for the things you will or will not do anymore. You have spent two or three months with people being very angry, threatening, and trying to be manipulative to get you back to your codependent ways. But you have been strong, and you believe that you deserve to be loved and cared for in an equal proportion that you do for others.

In this stage, those who don't love you, whether they are your spouse, best friends, or people you have known your whole life—even family members, they start to go away. This process is like separating the wheat from the chaff. This is when the narcissist can't tolerate a relationship that is balanced to some degree of mutuality and reciprocity. They decide that they can't be in a relationship like that and leave. The recovering codependent moving beyond stage one starts to hold fast to their boundaries and the relationship ends.

It is a very difficult stage because relationships that you thought were loving and caring just break down. It becomes a daunting experience when the people whom you nurtured were only good as long as you were taking care of them, and as soon as your codependency stopped, the relationship fails to persevere. The narcissist goes away. This is when the codependent may need to begin grief work. The indignant unreasonableness of breaking off the relationship by the narcissist hurts the codependent, and this is what this stage brings about.

The questions that arise are, "What is fair?", "What level of reciprocal mutuality is acceptable?" and, "How much empathy am I willing to give up?" The codependent needs to acclimate to the narcissist's slung injuries, guilt trips, shaming, and allegations of being selfish.

Once they get accustomed to it, they can start to predict it. They start to feel more confident, have fewer negative thoughts and fears, and over time, they become more and more confident. They set their boundaries without the fear of someone not wanting to be in a relationship with them.

Before their recovery, the codependent would not set boundaries because of the fear of being alone. In stage two, the boundaries are set because they know that having a healthy relationship is far more important than the anxiety, fear, and grief in these stages.

STAGE THREE:

This stage lasts for over 6 months. It's longer than the previous stages. The first stage includes everyone being angry. You doubt whether this is the right decision, and you struggle with finding whether it's worth it.

Stage two is separating the wheat from the chaff, where you start to experience people disappearing. You maintain your boundaries and hostile environment but eventually, over time, the smoke clears. In the time of building relationships and experimenting, this is the stage of dissolution for the codependent and narcissistic relationship experience.

The codependent no longer feels codependent. They no longer accept others unfairly, like expecting more from a person than what they are willing to give. Their anxiety and fear of being lonely start to lessen. They start to experiment and reach to those who are around. They start to build upon new relationships or reconfirm some older relationships. Family members may get over what they unfairly perceived as selfishness.

It is usually very satisfying to clients in stage three, when they find out how people come back to them, who once promised and threatened never to see them again. This new relationship brings more mutuality and sharing. The recovering codependent experiences the support and respect that they may have never experienced in their whole life.

This can be termed as reconfiguring human magnetism. We, as humans, are magnetically drawn to others... such as a codependent to a narcissist, and the same as a healthy person to another healthy person. A healthy person who is loving and caring may find themselves attracted to someone who is bold and a little bit self-centered. This is the reconfiguration of attraction patterns. You may find that you are no longer attracted to narcissists.

In this stage, you talk about what it's like to date someone who listens. The excitement of some of my clients who start experiencing conversations and associations with people who really listen to them and reciprocate with kind and polite things is surreal. If things don't go right and the narcissist resurfaces, the codependent can detach themselves easily. They are not pulled into the drama that the emotional manipulators subject them to. They spot it and they set a boundary.

When it doesn't work out, they remove themselves, because they have had a practice of about six months to a year.

Their painful episodes of loneliness are less frequent. Loneliness is key with withdrawal symptoms of codependency recovery. In the first stage, the codependent faces deep bouts of loneliness that are painful. Those bouts are now gone. Sometimes being lonely even feels good.

STAGE FOUR:

This is the last stage, which lasts for more than a year. At this stage, your relationship orientation has taken roots, and you are essentially focusing on reinforcing and strengthening the relationship. It is an exciting time, especially for the therapist, to see that their client is finally finding a happy place and are in love with people who share and love as much as they do.

There is a complete cessation of pathological caretaking. The relationships that they have are mutually loving, respecting, and caring. It doesn't mean that it's equal all of the time. No one has ever experienced any relationship equally. You just have to find a balance.

The new relationships will be defined by a fair distribution of love, and healthy boundaries that are open and go both ways. There is going to be interdependence. Interdependence means they are separate but connected. It means to have your own individuality, but also be connected in a relationship. Interdependence and reciprocity in any healthy relationship are of the utmost importance.

In this stage, your loved ones will admire and affirm your growth and change, unlike stage one where everyone is angry. All of a sudden, you find that people are admiring you. The people who criticized the recovering codependent in stage one and two for being selfish, start to say how much healthier and stronger you seem. The critics have forgotten their complaints and feel closer to you.

Relationships are balanced, and cravings and withdrawal symptoms have dwindled or stopped. Now the codependent is repelled by a narcissist. There is almost a reflexive reaction when they are in a situation with a narcissist. They are immediately turned off by narcissists and turned on by healthy perspective partners.

Chapter 7
Do You Have a Codependent Personality?

Are You Codependent?

This question seems like what we are supposed to address, but there can be a twist to it. Emotional and behavioral tendencies of codependency affect people of all kinds. But if you are the kind that avoids personal strong or uncomfortable emotions and instead switches to focus on your counterpart's needs, then you could be codependent.

Are you normally concerned about your partner's needs and welfare while you ignore yourself? If this is the case, you are codependent, and that is not good for your relationship.

Do Codependent Behaviors Exhibit in You?

Codependents have certain behaviors that can be pointed out in isolation. Throughout your life till now, have you exhibited any of the following behaviors?

-     Do you avoid conflict or extreme emotions, or control your genuine emotions with passive aggression such as anger or humor?

-     Do you like owning your partner's actions or sometimes offering excessive favors in return for their actions?

-     Do you confuse love for working to rescue your partner and focusing all your thoughts and energies on their needs?

-     Do you play the most part of giving than sharing in your relationship?

-     Do you keep sticking to relationships for too long in the manifestation of loyalty feelings to your partner even when they harm you because you fear being abandoned?

-     Do you oftentimes agree to what you would have preferably declined?

- Do you concern yourself with other people's opinions about you than your own?

- Do you find it difficult to identify your needs, deciding over simple personal things, and communicating your thoughts to your partner?

- Are you easily resented when your partner does not notice or appreciate your efforts, and sometimes feel guilty for not satisfying them?

These questions show how you try to act in a way that could please your partner in your hope that they will affirm your self-worth in return. You want to prove yourself to them so they can keep having you.

Have You Questioned Your Codependent Behaviors?

If you think your behaviors alone are not enough to tell of your codependence tendencies, then you need to question your behaviors further for sensible justification or revelation. Consider the following:

- Has your counterpart abused you – physically, emotionally, or mentally?

- Do you always find it hard withholding or limiting your help to your partner and other people?

- Do you find it hard asking for help even when you get overwhelmed?

- Do you doubt what you want to become in life, or are uncertain of your needs and wants?

- Do you always find ways to avoid an argument?

- Do you the other people's thoughts about you cause you anxiety?

- Do you find your opinions less relevant compared to those of other people?

- Do you live with an addict or underperformer and are okay with it despite your concerns about them?

- Do you like sticking in familiar environments and routines and resist voluntary change?

- Do you feel neglected or secluded when your partner communes or converses with others?

- Do you find it perplexing receiving compliments or gifts from your partner or other people?

In considering the above questions, evaluate your answers and see if they are logical or reasonable enough for you to keep manifesting your behaviors. Are you being reasonable behaving the way you are behaving? Are your mannerisms rational, sound, and beneficial?

Are Your Feelings Caused by Codependency?

Codependents continually suppress their genuine original feelings and emotions and only display those that relieve their partner's anxiety or excite their partners and over time, lose touch with themselves and their identity. Ask yourself the following questions.

- Do you sense a feeling of emptiness inside?

- Do you have low self-esteem or feel inferior to your counterpart, falsely think highly of yourself?

- Do you sense uncertainty about your personal needs, objectives, and feelings?

These three questions genuinely answered speak of one who has disregard for themselves and whose situation in life is deteriorating because they have lost control over their lives.

Is Your Relationship Susceptible to Codependency?

Codependency does not just commence in adulthood. It can originate from your upbringing in school or at home or from the previous relationships you found yourself in prior years.

- Do you hail from a family whose historical background at one point existed in a codependent state, that is, all the needs of the family were suspended or put aside for the well-being of a certain member then?

- Did any of your caregivers in school or previous childhood lover make you begin adopting codependency behaviors?

If you can trace happenstances of codependency in the people around you in your prior years, then you are likely to exhibit their influences on you in your adulthood relationships.

Does Your Partner Fit the Role of a Taker in Your Relationship?

Codependent relationships have two individual roles. You, the codependent individual, are the caretaker – taking care, and your counterpart, the dependent is the taker – receiving care or being cared for. Therefore, find out whether your counterpart is a taker.

- Is your partner always trying to control attention, love, sex, and affirmations they can get or give?

- Do they exhibit violence, finger-pointing, criticism, righteousness, irritation, neediness, invasive touching, incessant talking, or emotional drama just to get show you or get you to give them what they need at any time?

If your partner displays such behaviors, then they are likely to affect you in such a way that you automatically take on the role of a caretaker, perpetuating codependence in your relationship.

Do You Recognize Your Child Is a Codependent Too?

Do you observe codependent tendencies and behaviors in your children? If yes, then you could be a codependent yourself. The children's displays of codependence may be subtle as they are actually still on their learning curve. But ask yourself the following questions about them:

- Do they seem unable to make their own decisions, however simple?

- Do they feel extreme worry, anxiety, or stress?

- Do they have low self-esteem?

- Do they try so hard to please others over themselves?

- Do they fear being alone?

- Do they become angry every so often?

- Do they communicate passively than with assertion?

Children who are mostly unable to be by themselves or on their own to speak for themselves are likely to become codependents, and that might tell of you as the parent possibly being codependent.

Is There a History of Codependency in Your Family?

Do you recall in your past witnessing or participating in codependent relationships? Might you have been taught that you could express your needs and emotions only in specific ways? Do you remember being asked to serve others first and yourself later in your familial upbringing?

It is likely that even after you left that family environment, you persisted acting in a similar manner into your subsequent relationships, and you this tendency might be passed on to your children.

Did You a History of Abuse Growing Up?

Did you begin to take on codependence tendencies in attempts to deal with traumatic situations earlier in life? Might you have begun suppressing your needs and emotions in favor of others to keep your well-being and peace for yourself and them? Abuse in early life, if not intervened and stopped in time might make you adapt to it and rationalize other people's hostile behaviors toward you because you feel defenseless and powerless to stand up against it. Abuse is also possible to occur in codependent familial relationships.

If you have any unresolved historical emotional, physical, or sexual abuses, then you might be enduring the current situation as before – which is unhelpful.

Do You Recognize Your Prevalent Causative Situations for Codependence in Relationships?

In what ways or circumstances do you behave in ways likely to encourage your codependence tendencies in relationships? You probably go seeking people who exhibit signs of weakness and who need being taken care of or looking after. Think about the following:

- Are you naturally drawn toward the suffering or addicts?

- Do you consider yourself a passionate toward the mentally impaired persons?

- Do you have a heart for those living with chronic diseases?

Being drawn toward such individualities, most of your interactions is likely to lead you into codependence with them.

Might There Have Happened a Divorce in Your Past?

Divorce can be a causative factor for codependency. If you witnessed your parents go separate ways and you stepped up to fill the gap of the missing parent for your siblings, then you might grow up with tendencies for codependency.

- Did you avoid discussing the difficulties with the remaining parent because you did not want to upset them more?

If yes, then you began suppressing your emotions then, setting yourself up for codependent behaviors.

Have You Considered the Symptomatic Details?

Codependents manifest a myriad of symptoms that might hint toward their codependency motives. Do you often act with motives of controlling others, avoiding trust for others, attaining perfection, avoiding certain feelings, avoiding intimacy, caregiving, monitoring others, denying some realities, neglecting signs of stress-related illness, etc.?

- How would you consider the family environment or structure or system that nurtured you during upbringing?

- What kind of rules did you adhere to?

- Did they slow down overall development or hinder flexibility and spontaneity in your thoughts and actions?

See if some of these rules applied:

- It is generally not good to discuss your problems

- Avoid trusting your instincts and other people

- Do not express negative or extreme feelings openly

- Keep and have your feelings contained within yourself

- Avoid direct communications

- Do not always approach some members directly or by yourself

- Always be in your strong, right, good, and perfect form whatever the circumstances

- Work hard the best you can and makes up exceedingly happy

- Always be generous and share what you have, however little

- Follow my instruction, not my actions

- Playfulness is childishness and lack of seriousness

- Avoid the limelight and do your things without expecting to be noticed or appreciated

- Avoid extremes, either is bad and loss of grip or control on issues

- Always be careful whatever you do; mistakes like spilled milk are forever regrettable

- Do not share family secrets out there with other people

- Do no ever decline responsibility

- Learn to live with problems as if they were not there

- The nice people most of the times boring

- Disagreement is bad, at all cost avoid it because it is personal in nature

- Bully or sympathize and you will easily gain control over others

- Speak loudly with exaggerated signals to get attention

- Other people's feelings are your too – if one is not well everyone is not well

- Take full control things and people around you to be assured of your safety today and tomorrow

Think of the following:

- Is your family system rigid? Everyone has their roles, and they do not need to be helped to do their chores. No one gets involved in the welfare of the other hence everyone acts out in ways unfamiliar to the rest. There lacks versatility in what one can do.

- Is there inconsistency in the way of doing things? Does the incapacitation of one party cause the things to be done in ways that are interconnected?

- Is the system becoming unpredictable for the future? Are there signs of uncertainty where resources are likely to dwindle and render the family into crisis living, for instance?

- Is the system impulsive? Are decisions being arrived at out of anxiety and in a reactionary manner rather than logically?

- Is the system closed? If one acts in a manner contradictory to what is the norm in the family, they are reprimanded.

Chapter 8
The Common Origins of Codependency and Narcissism

The origin of codependency; Trigger and inherent tendencies

It is not everybody that is an abusive relationship that ends up being codependent, though. In fact, in almost all codependents, the seeds are sown long before they are mature enough to make personal decisions for themselves. Childhood experiences can form a latent tendency towards codependency that is carried to adulthood. Therefore, most times, the toxic or imbalanced relationship that you have now is acting as a trigger for dormant codependent tendencies that have been laid in your mind since childhood.

What are the potential causes of these tendencies in childhood?

Megan Shawn Burn, a professor of psychology accurately summarized them when she said, "If you learned that the only way to connect with a difficult parent was to subordinate your own needs and cater to theirs, then you may be set up for similar relationships throughout your life." As the most pivotal influence on our early lives, our families and the kind of relationships that exist within it form a large part of our emotional and mental profiles for the rest of our lives.

Children are naturally expressive, pick up cues subconsciously, and are known to form deeply rooted character features from those around them. So, anything that restricts the expressiveness or teaches you to subjugate your need or the ability to express yourself in favor of other people can be a potential cause of codependency. In our formative years before teenagerhood, it is easy to get impressions of how to act, and these impressions may never go away.

Let me tell you the story of my childhood and how I believe I got my codependent tendencies rooted deeply in me.

I was born into a family where my parents had different views about life. My father, a hardworking clerk for the vast part of his life, had liberal views about the little money he had. He was a staunch devotee of the you-only-live-once creed, and he spent what he had in pursuit of material happiness. That included knocking off some bottles with friends whenever he could weasel out the money. He was a man of high spirits but little conviction. My mother, on the other hand, was the strictest disciplinarian, I know. A high school teacher, she prided herself on the kind of discipline she exuded and tried to install the same ethic in both of her children and husband. She rarely agreed that she might have crossed the line too frequently where privacy and freedom were concerned, but she loved her family all the same.

The polar opposites of my parent's disposition towards life left me swinging between two extremes too quickly. It also generated a tense mood at home most of the time as they often disagreed on what to do with money. The rows were even worse on the days my dad went drinking. By the time I was seven, though, a calm unease seemed to pervade the house. My mum seemed to have won, and there were strict rules for everything, from where to keep my toothbrush to how, and when to complain, if I ever got the chance at all. I got scolded a lot when I flouted any of the rules, and I had to learn to make myself as useful as possible. In fact, I found out that the best way to avoid being scolded was to make myself as small as possible, every time. So, I learned to look after myself, learned not to complain at all, and devised an excellent ability to disappear the few times the storms of a verbal row showed up. The few moments of sunshine I enjoyed at home were down to my elder brother, John, who always had new games to entertain me.

When I was eight, though, tragedy struck my family in a big way – John was hit by a car on his way back from school and was condemned to a wheelchair for the rest of his life. The rows over money started once again, and it became even harder for me to stay unaffected. My parents worked extra hard, and I was left to fend for John's needs most of the time. This was in itself not a bad thing, but I grew to relegate my own needs in favor of everyone else's, even those of my friends. I always felt it was my position to be ready to help and take the short straw of every deal.

So, I bore the brunt of my mother's anger and excessive rules, my father's desperation and frustration, and John's physical needs. Even when I went away to school, I learned to be a people-pleaser because it felt natural and the right thing to do and because I believed it was the only way I could be liked. Yes, people took advantage of me all the time, but I never complained. In fact, I enjoyed helping them out because it made me feel important.

Many years later, when I got married, I was essentially the same little girl who wanted to please everyone. Now that I was married, I simply switched my focus to my husband and marriage. To say I didn't get warnings about my potential husband's narcissism would be a lie. Even before marriage, I found it hard to cope with some of his rapid mood shifts. One moment, he would be nice and gentlemanly; the next, he would say very hurtful things or make abusive comments about me or my work. Instead of complaining, though, I just switched to my default mode – pleasing people. That switch took me a whole decade to reverse.

Now, it's quite possible that even without a troubled childhood, I might still have married a narcissist. It is also possible that despite my childhood experience, I might have met a more considerate partner who allowed us to stay in sync and balance. Still, the combination of my inherent tendencies and a narcissist as the trigger catalyzed my codependency.

That is often the story for most codependents.

Now, take a look at your childhood. What were the rules or circumstances you grew up in? If you are truly codependent, the chances are quite high that your childhood felt restrictive, or you dealt with an emotional weight that was beyond your years.

Children find it hard to thrive emotionally in dysfunctional families because they are unable to make their own decisions about what is right and what is wrong. So, they swallow the family's way of life hook, line, and sinker even when it is unhealthy and unfair to their abilities. What are the marks of a dysfunctional family? A dysfunctional family is often,

- Chaotic, disordered and filled with conflicts

- Built upon rules that promote secrecy and make it hard to express your desires

- Controlling, overbearing and overwhelming for children

- Abusive, repressive and restrictive

- Structured in a way that denies the existence of any problem

- Sets unrealistic expectations for children and compares them unfavorably

- Highly judgmental and quick to mete out unjust punishment to offending members

- Has parents who set rules they don't follow, but they expect others to obey

When a child is thrust into this sort of environment, it is easy to get confused or come to the false conclusion that they are the problem. This sets them up for the low self-esteem that codependents feel later in life. They become used to the idea that even loved ones have the unlimited ability and propensity to hurt them, and they learn to shut out their true feelings while pleasing people. Even if these traits are not pronounced while they are children, it only requires a trigger such as an addicted relative or abusive spouse to send them to the fore in adulthood.

Chapter 9
Codependency and Narcissism: Same Needs, Different Behaviors

Narcissism and Codependency: The Unholy Union

Opposites attract, that is just the way nature works. In most cases, this is a great thing, after all, every yin needs its yang. For instance, if you are neurotic and high strung, a composed and emotionally balanced person will make a perfect partner for you because they will balance you out. If you are introverted and end up in a relationship with an extrovert you will likely find that you start to open up more and more.

Opposites bring out the best in each other by complementing each other's strengths and flaws. This is true in most cases unless of course, we are talking about a narcissist and a codependent. Far from being ideal, the codependent – narcissist union is quite literally a match made in hell. But who exactly is a narcissist?

The simple definition of a narcissist is a self-entitled person who places their desires, needs and feelings above those of others. A narcissist is incapable of empathy because they cannot understand or contemplate needs or feelings beyond their own. Narcissists need to be the center of attention and demand that everything is done their way.

Narcissistic personalities abound in society. Most of us have that one friend who is never happy until things are exactly the way they want. They want you at their beck and call at any time, yet they are rarely there for you if you need them. They ask you to do things for them that they would never do for you if the tables were turned. Narcissists are the reason we find ourselves in toxic friendships, relationships, and even families.

If you interact with a narcissist on a personal level, at work or even as an acquaintance, if you are not codependent, you are likely to survive these toxic relationships largely unscathed. However, for codependents who are unable to take care of their own needs and establish boundaries, their relationships with narcissists are damaging and have long term effects on their emotional and psychological wellbeing.

At their core, narcissists and codependents have more similarities than you may think. Both these personalities are driven by the need for approval, a need to control others and dependency on others for validation. What separates the two is that while the narcissist wants to control others to get what they want and meet their own needs; the codependent wants approval and to feel useful by being overly functional in other people's lives.

Think of it this way, if we go back to our case study, Matt is the classic narcissist. He has no qualms intruding on Jenny's life whenever he needs help or to be saved from some mishap or other. Jenny, on the other hand, is a codependent who thrives on being needed and taking control of other people's life. Essentially these two people are dependent on each, but for two very different reasons. One has selfish goals while the other needs the validation they get from being the rescuer.

This toxic dependence is what makes narcissists and codependents often end up together. They satisfy each other's need for approval and validation but in different ways. When a narcissist finds a codependent, they know that they have found someone who will always be at their beck and call no matter what. On the other hand, codependents find a sense of purpose in being needed by the narcissist.

But what could go wrong in such a union? After all, if they complement each other's needs so well don't they sort of deserve each other? Unfortunately, no, the relationship between the narcissist and a codependent is not only destructive to both parties but doomed to fail from the start. Whether the narcissist in your life is a parent, spouse, child or even friend, for a codependent this is one relationship they need to get out of and avoid all costs.

Of course, if it were that easy, then there wouldn't be a problem. Why do codependents find it so hard to leave toxic relationships with narcissists? This is partly because narcissists are masters of manipulation and have perfected the art of laying traps for codependents.

Traps narcissist lay for codependents

a) Shame

There is probably no other personality as adept at using shame to control others as the narcissist is. Narcissists know that codependents are people pleasers who need the approval of others and this makes them the perfect victims for shaming. Shame is an effective tool for control because it makes the codependent want to make up for their shortcomings by doing whatever the other person wants to keep them happy.

If you have grown up with a narcissistic parent then you are no stranger to being shamed into things you did not want to. In narcissistic family situations, phrases like: look what you made me do…, you are so ungrateful…, what will people think…, look at how you have hurt so and so…, why are you so selfish…, do it for the sake of the family… are the order of the day. A narcissist will use shame to control a codependent and justify their own actions.

Now imagine someone who grew up being shamed consistently and being made to feel sorry for every little action that their parent did not agree with. Chances are this person becomes codependent as an adult and is susceptible to being controlled using shame.

Shame has kept many a codependent in an abusive situation simply because they feel they are getting punished for something they deserve. If you are a codependent person in a relationship with a narcissist, you will often find yourself feeling ashamed and wanting to make up for your shortcomings, real or imaginary, by letting the narcissist control what you do, feel and even think.

"if you hadn't done this then I wouldn't have had to…, am only doing this to protect you…, you would look so much better if you…, you never do anything right…, it's your fault….If you often hear these types of phrases in your relationship, it may be time to re-evaluate whether you are being manipulated.

b) Low self-esteem

It is hard to control someone with healthy self-esteem and a sense of self-worth. Naturally, a narcissist does everything in their power to make you feel worthless. From criticizing how you look, your outfits, your weight, your career choice and everything in between. A narcissist has one goal, to make you feel you are not good enough and that you need them to make your life better.

Ever had a friend who would make cruel jokes about you in front of others and enjoy when people laughed at you? When you told them later how you felt about it, their defense would always be, lighten up it was just a joke. This is one of the classic ploys' narcissists use to break down your self-esteem. They are experts at putting you down both in public and in private.

If you grew up with a narcissistic parent, you were probably always being compared to a "better" sibling or relative. Constantly being told how if only you could be like so and so or why can't you do it the way so and so does it. These criticisms not only undermined your self-esteem but preconditioned you to thinking that other people are better than you in some way.

If you carry this low self-esteem into adulthood then you become the perfect victim for a narcissist. This is because you already think very little of yourself and the narcissist only has a short distance to go to convince you they are better than you.

A narcissist needs you to think there is nothing special about you so you can devote all your attention to them and catering to their needs. Codependents in relationships with a narcissist will often get lost in the relationship and lose all sense of their personality, likes and dislikes because they are constantly being critiqued.

A codependent in a relationship will slowly start changing how they dress, speak and even their friends. This is because they have been told their choices are wrong in some way by the narcissist. As a result, the codependent starts to strip away bits of themselves little by little until they are a completely different person.

You may have a friend who completely changes when they are in a relationship. Or you may be the codependent whose personality changes depending on who you are with. While it is not unusual for people to rub off on you and make you want to be a better person, if you often feel the need to change who you are in order for a relationship to work, you may be a codependent being manipulated by a narcissist.

c) Envy

Have you gone from a completely normal and emotionally balanced person to an obsessive and jealous version of yourself you barely recognize? Narcissists are masters of making you feel jealous and insecure. They want you to make them the center of your universe and devote all your energy to protecting and guarding the relationship.

A narcissist will flirt with other people in your presence just to make you feel envious. Narcissists understand that most codependents need to be in relationships to feel whole. They exploit the codependent's fear of being alone by making them feel envious and insecure. You are more likely to ignore someone's faults if you are scared of losing them and narcissists know this only too well.

If you are in a relationship with a narcissist you will find yourself constantly feeling insecure. You will start doing things you previously thought only crazy people do. Going through your partner's phone, becoming clingy and needy, always suspecting your partner is cheating and emotional outbursts become the order of the day.

Envy breeds insecurity which in turn lowers your self-esteem even more. Of course, there is a certain level of jealousy even in healthy relationships. However, if envy consumes you to the point that all you think about is what your partner is doing, who he is with or whether he might leave you, then you may just have fallen into a narcissist's trap.

Ultimately, narcissists exploit a codependent's weakness to the point where the codependent is helpless and unable to leave. The power of narcissists over codependents is not just in their ability to lay emotional traps, but also the fact that they can easily check out codependent personalities. Once they have established your need for approval, all the narcissist has to do is lay a trap and you are sunk.

Chapter 10
How to Reprogram Your Inner Critic: Building Self-Esteem and Self-love

Practical Steps to Building Self-esteem
Learning to live with your inadequacies

The Perfectionist has inaccessible standards concerning every little thing about you, your conduct, and the people throughout your life. It lives in a universe of fantasy. Perfectionist may concentrate on botches, efficiency, your body, athletic capacity,

or on the other hand work, at its center is the conviction that you're not sufficient here and there — sufficiently appealing, adequate, sufficiently brilliant, sufficient, etc.

Perfectionism is a departure from these excruciating convictions. You may think that it's hard to complete assignments on the grounds that your work is rarely great. The Pundit makes a decision about you for not fulfilling the Perfectionist's ridiculous guidelines. The way that there's no such thing as perfection is pointless to the Perfectionist since it would be out of a vocation.

The remedy for perfectionism is self-acknowledgement. To acknowledge something, you don't need to like it, just to recognize it — as it stands. A few things about yourself you can transform; others you can't. Incomprehensibly, until you acknowledge yourself, it's hard to change at all since you're in strife with the real world.

Make a run-down of your convictions about yourself. In what ways do you feel you're most certainly not enough? How do your convictions influence your activities? Glance in the mirror and state, "I genuinely acknowledge myself similarly as I am." Would you be able to mean it — without gagging? Do you like what you see? What protests ring a bell? Gracious,

I forgot — look in the mirror bare. Possibly you keep away from mirrors by and large. That in itself undermines your confidence. You're attempting to keep away from and deny what you as of now accept about yourself. Unavoidably, there are a few things you don't care for. Possibly you think you look old, or your bosoms are excessively little, your hips are excessively wide, or your legs are excessively short. You don't need to like what you see, just to confront and acknowledge the truth this is you. Rehash out loud, "I accept myself unequivocally, despite the fact that . . .." In the event that you can't, at that point state, "I acknowledge my refusal to acknowledge that I'm (fat)." Do this mirror work out over a few weeks. Compose your feelings in your diary. Notice any progressions in your disposition as you progress.

Start Doing

Putting what you've discovered without hesitation and risking is the most dominant

approach to assemble confidence. Making self-avowing move, for example, communicating yourself, defining limits, and doing what you need, can feel uncomfortable from the start and make nervousness, blame, and self-question. Disgrace and accompanying low confidence, dread, and uneasiness about being judged, committing errors, or flopping all make it hard to go out on a limb. Moreover, having an outside locus of control and having had controlling or disgracing guardians thwart your capacity to recognize needs and wants. Working yourself out of self-confirming action can stagnate your development. These are largely deterrents to building confidence, making choices, and putting yourself first.

Plan to anticipate this obstruction — like irritation subsequent to utilizing frail muscles — what's more, realize that it's an indication that you're making the best choice. Give yourself credit for going out on a limb. Going out on a limb constructs another self-discernment. You become acquainted with yourself, your inclinations, and what you're fit for in another way. You would then be able to expand on that and go out on a limb, all structure your fearlessness.

Sooner or later, such actions feel progressively regular and less tension inciting, until at some point, you end up precipitously doing them — setting limits, inquiring for what you need, taking a stab at something new, communicating a minority supposition, giving yourself credit, and accomplishing progressively pleasant exercises — even alone. You discover you have less feelings of hatred and decisions and that relationships are simpler. You begin to like and love yourself and appreciate the way toward living.

Make a run-down of things you'd prefer to do and do them — don't hang tight for a companion to oblige you. Make a run-down of things you're hesitant to do. Converse with a supportive, urging companion or support to assist you with testing your feelings of trepidation and take more dangers.

Positive Mindset

You're in every case either putting yourself down or lifting yourself up. You can

decide to be for yourself or against yourself. You perceived how the Pundit, Pusher,

what's more, Perfectionist damage you. Presently you should plant seeds of positive self talk. It's dependent upon you to energize yourself, in any event, when you're down or apprehensive. A positive internal exchange is likewise critical to propel you to go out on a limb, make changes, and become progressively autonomous. You can do what you trust you can, and you can't do what you don't trust you can.

To do this, first, you have to recognize your worth. Everybody likes praises, a gesture of congratulations, and acknowledgement for an occupation well done. Why sit tight for the kindness of others? It's dependent upon you to recognize and acclaim yourself. Have you seen how the glow of others' acclaim rapidly blurs? At the point when you offer it to yourself, the radiance waits. Converse with yourself about your victories, as you would commend a companion. You can rehash it and relax in it as frequently as you like. Doing this really changes how you consider yourself and raises your confidence. It isn't equivalent to purge attestations.

It's offering credit to yourself that is sponsored up by understanding — recollections of positive actions that you can review. Keep in mind, positive certifications are supportive, yet they should be upheld up by positive actions. Certainty isn't vanity or pomposity. Certainty is feeling secure in yourself dependent on genuine information on your qualities and restrictions. On the other hand, vanity is unwarranted self-sweet talk or an overstated feeling of self-importance, and haughtiness is a misguided feeling of prevalence over others. Both make up for low confidence.

Make promises to yourself and fulfil them

Codependents who wouldn't consider breaking a date with a companion ordinarily break responsibilities to themselves: "Tomorrow I'll begin an eating regimen"; "Tomorrow I'll go to the rec center." When you do this, you're relinquishing yourself — except if, in certain cases, it might be more wanting to rest as opposed to do what you arranged. There are decisions and results, and you're responsible for your decisions and actions.

Attempt consistently to pick in your most elevated personal circumstance — which may not give you prompt satisfaction yet will bring about long haul benefits and improved self-esteem. This is the manner in which you feed your garden and keep it sound.

The other thing about remaining quiet about responsibilities is meeting your own desires. Be certain your desires are sensible. Would it be reasonable to do a spring cleaning in one day or run a long-distance race before a 5K? Remaining quiet about responsibilities is like rehearsing your values. On the off chance that you anticipate that yourself should document your assessments on schedule however continue putting it off, before long you're going to be tired of yourself, and your Faultfinder will have a field day.

Chapter 11
Exercises, and Self-Tests To Help You Along The Road To Recovering Your Own Life

S tress can make you more vulnerable when you are in a dysfunctional relationship like a codependent relationship.

The emotional burden you carry around can push you into deep depression and destructive behavior. It can suppress all your strong points. To prevent this from happening, you need to take care of your body and mind.

When you realize that it is not others you have to take care of first but your own self, you should find the ways and means to make that happen. And the first step is taking care of your body.

Have you had a health check up recently?

If not, it is high time you got on to that. Even if you do not have any obvious issues, a checkup will help clear any doubts regarding conditions like high blood pressure, diabetes and other systemic conditions. Since you have neglected yourself in your rush to take care of others, now is the time to take the necessary steps.

When you have done a health evaluation and necessary treatment or precautions, consider your diet.

Is your diet a healthy one?

Are you aware of the right foods that are nutritious and healthy for your body?

Take up a diet plan that suits you best. There are plenty of diet programs that are really good in helping you maintain the right balance. Choose a reliable diet program that not only teaches you to consume the right foods but also teaches you how to maintain good nutrition.

And make the changes in small steps instead of diving right in. Set small goals, like adding a vegetable to your daily diet or drinking 3 glasses of water more than what you normally do.

When you succeed in the small goals, you can step it up. It is not necessary to be perfect. You have just to start focusing on the right path.

Exercise daily

If you are not in the habit of exercising daily, make it a habit to do some sort of physical exercise such as walking, cycling, aerobics, Pilates, yoga, etc.

Or, take up a sport that you enjoy. Devote twenty to thirty minutes of a day, three to four times in a week. This will take care of your cardiovascular health.

Just like with the diet start setting aside ten minutes daily in the beginning and increase the time gradually.

With exercise, you not only get to improve your blood circulation, but also keep yourself relaxed and energetic. Further, exercise is something that you have full control over.

To make it a routine, you need to set certain boundaries. As you focus on your diet and exercise you will start feeling better. Try being nice to yourself as you deserve it.

Mind and Body Relaxing Exercises

Relaxing helps in relieving stress. It also eases your depression, sleep issues and anxiety. Relaxing calms body and mind. It makes you feel calm and your muscles feel more fluid and less tense.

Relaxing can be done in a variety of ways. While some focus on mind relaxation, others focus on your body. But in general, most of the relaxation methods work on body and mind. Here are few of them

Mind Relaxing Exercises

1. Take slow and deep breaths. Try breathing exercises as these help in relaxation.

How to do:

Here are steps to help you practice deep breathing:

- Sit in a comfortable position with your back erect. Rest a hand over your stomach and the other over the chest region.

- As you breathe in, the hand placed over your stomach should move outward and the other should remain as such.

- Now breathe out with your mouth pushing maximum air out as you contract the stomach muscles. The hand over your stomach should move inwards when you exhale, but the hand over your chest should remain as such.

- Repeat the above steps either in sitting or lying down position. You can even place a book over your stomach and observe it rising and falling as you inhale and exhale.

The benefit:

The above breathing method is also called belly breathing. It stimulates vagus nerve that extends throughout the body from the head to your colon. It triggers relaxation response and reduces blood pressure, heart rate and lowers your stress.

2. Meditation is another powerful relaxation technique. Body scan meditation helps you concentrate on your body.

How to do:

Begin with your toes and work upward. Instead of relaxing the muscles as in the breathing exercises, here you just focus on each body part and label the sensations you feel as either bad or good.

Here are the steps:

- Lie in a supine position. Keep your legs and arms in relaxed position with eyes closed or open. Concentrate on breathing for a couple of minutes to let yourself relax.

- Now focus on the right foot toes. Observe any sensation that you feel as you concentrate on breathing in and out. Imagine your breath moving to your toes. Focus on each area for about five or more seconds.

- Repeat the same for the sole region of the right foot. Then move to right ankle, calf, knee, thigh, hip and then shift to the left leg. Now move to your torso, lower back, abdomen, upper back, chest and shoulders.

- Once you complete this body scan, be in a relaxed state for a few minutes. Now slowly stretch if needed.

3. Guided imagery is a good way to feel relaxed and calm. Use scripts, audiotapes or get assistance from a teacher to help with the guided imagery.

Here is an example of visualization technique:

Think about a tranquil lake. Include maximum sensory information that you can from this image such as see the calm and blue water, listen to the birds chirping, smell the blossoming flowers, feel the cool water and taste the clean and fresh air.

When you visualize, you will start feeling your worries going away as you explore your visual image. This may make your lose track of your present and you may feel your limbs getting heavy or you may twitch or yawn, which are all normal responses that you need not worry about.

4. Soak in nice warm bath

5. Music is an excellent mind relaxing tool. Listen to music

6. If you like to write about your feelings start keeping a journal.

Body Relaxing Exercises

1. Take up yoga. There are plenty of videos and books that help you practice yoga at home. You can also attend yoga classes.

2. Progressive muscle relaxing process: This technique involves focusing on each muscle group in your body as you tense and relax them. This helps reduce tension in your muscles and anxiety.

This method helps, if you find it difficult falling asleep. As you relax your muscles, signals are sent to your brain that falling asleep is okay.

How to do:

- Begin with your feet. Work upwards until you reach your face.

- Wear loose clothes, remove footwear and sit or lie down in a comfortable position.

- Breathe in and out deeply for a two to three minutes

- Now focus on right foot and how it feels. Tense the muscles tightly and hold for 10 counts

- Relax the foot and focus on the tension easing and on how the foot feels loose and limp

- Relax for a moment and shift to the left foot. Follow the same steps as you did for the right one

- Continue focusing on all parts of the body contracting your muscles and relaxing them

- This may need practice as you have to just tense only the intended muscles at any given time.

- Take up a relaxing activity like walking or other activities that you enjoy and keep you in a good mood.

3. A massage or back rub also relaxes your muscles. The relaxing effects of a massage session at a health club or spa may be known to you. Massage helps relieve pain, reduces stress and tension in the muscles. You can also practice self-massage.

Massage yourself between chores on your couch or bed when you retire for the day. This will help you unwind and sleep better. Use scented lotion, aromatic oil etc. along with deep breathing method.

Use a combination of strokes like tapping with cupped palms or fingers or gentle chops using your hands. For muscle knots, apply fingertip pressure. Use long, gliding and light strokes for kneading the muscles.

Here are steps for head and neck massage:

- Begin by kneading muscles present in the back of your shoulders and neck. Drum quickly upwards and on the sides and back of the neck using a loose fist.

- With your thumbs, do tiny circles near the skull base and massage the entire scalp region using fingertips. Using tapping movement of fingers on your scalp all over.

- For the face use tiny circles with thumbs or your fingertips and focus on forehead, jaws and temples.

- For your nose and eyebrows, use middle finger for the massage.

- End the massage by closing your eyes, covering your face with hands cupping them and breathe in and out for some time.

4. Drink something warm such as herbal tea or milk and avoid adding caffeine or alcohol.

Before You Begin the Relaxation Practice

The above techniques are just a small example of the type of things you can do to relax yourself. Learning them is easy but what you need to remember is that they should be practiced regularly to get the full stress relief benefits they provide. Make sure you spend a minimum of 20 minutes per day for relaxation.

If you have a busy schedule, try to meditate when you are commuting via train or bus or during your lunchbreak. Practice mindful walking when you exercise your dog.

Use your smartphone to view the relaxation guides available online. There are apps that you can use that guide you through the exercises, help you follow a proper routine and track your progress.

There will definitely be some hiccups as you try to stick to a proper schedule. Don't be discouraged. Even if there is a break of a few days or weeks, start again and build the momentum.

Chapter 12
The Human Magnet Syndrome

The experience of falling in love can be indescribable. You cannot tell why; cannot explain how you just feel irresistibly drawn to someone as magnets do. Little do you know when you actually get allured into leaving your goals and wishes, and even your will for what suddenly turns feeling much less like love. People are drawn onto love much more by some invisible forces than what they think, feel, and see. This strange force of attraction seems to work so naturally that the parties tend to flow along and think it is okay and in fact go their way to justify how it happened.

Codependents are naturally passive members who automatically take on the role of the follower in the relationship. On the other hand, narcissists are naturally assumed and the leadership role, deciding how and where to direct the relationship. The narcissist and the codependent, on a conscious level, feel they are matches as soulmates. However, underneath, there lie deeper and darker feelings of anger, frustration, resentment, and pain. These feelings reflect the emerging dysfunctional patterns that eventually show up.

Narcissists and codependents are brought together by psychological forces that function subconsciously, reflexively, and repetitively leading them into a long-term relationship in which they consciously experience each other irresistibly desirably. And these forces get stronger and stronger with time. The attraction is normally overwhelmingly strong for codependents. They become addicted to it. They are compelled to seek closeness with their partner with the view to soothe the intense emotional pain that has been with them since before.

People fall for unmatched romantic partners for certain characteristics of familiarity, which are actually dysfunctional relationship patterns, not so perceived at the start. The relationship we experience with our parents laid certain patterns which form the instinct that we use to judge our romantic relationships. There exists an instinctive sense of calmness, familiarity, and safety that underlines interactions between people who are having a romantic company based on a preformed and matched relationship template.

The two become infatuated or obsessed with each other, and typically involuntarily experience this as a strong desire for reciprocation of feelings, though not necessarily sexual. Lovers express each other depending on their relationship orientation. The others-relationship orientation focuses mainly on giving love, care, and respect, while the self-relationship orientation focuses on receiving care, respect, and love.

Couples often play within such a relationship in a manner that they balance their orientations and subconsciously keep an equilibrium that is autonomous, lacking in health and dysfunction. Things are not good, but they are not bad either. Compatibility in relationships is not fixed. While our personalities may differ greatly, but the human spirit and psyche are capable of achieving compatibility.

It begins with developing understanding. Codependents have a deficit of self-love. They sacrifice themselves for others. Their circumstances from childhood seem to progress from attachment trauma with their caretakers, then core shame when they fail to regard themselves as worth beings, then pathological loneliness as they become withdrawn from the world, and finally addiction to relationship at a stage where they desire to find with themselves by searching for that in their partners hence not loving themselves at all - self-love deficit disorder.

By understanding the human magnet syndrome, codependents embark on their recovery journey towards self-love abundance. They need to focus on understanding and breaking away from their addictive pathological relationships. Mastering the power and control tactics used by narcissists, setting, and observing sound self0boundaries, addressing their mental traumas, and moving from disregarding to embracing their self-love will help to transition into self-love abundant relationships consciously. It is not normally an easy road to travel and may take time, but such is how the biggest payoffs are worked toward.

The Codependence Dilemma

Codependent Men

Only a few men discuss their relationship problems with their friends and family. They internalize their hurts, live in denial, suffer silently, and are addicted to numbness to their needs and feelings. Rather than attract attention, they try doing the right things, being good sons, siblings, husbands, and fathers, to the extent of abandoning their duties of making a living for themselves and their wives and children and meeting their needs as well. Codependent men think that spending time away from their wives is being selfish, and that way sacrifice themselves.

Men are viewed as strong and as not having the need to express their feelings or needs and can be shamed for it. Hence, they turn to addiction to cope, mainly by living in denial of their needs, suppressing their feelings, and losing control.

Men who grow up in dysfunctional families do not find safe to express their feelings and needs. It is easier to ignore criticized feelings and denied or shamed needs. Age-inappropriate duties during a man's growing are evidence of ignored childhood. This could be because the parents lacked control, irresponsible or immature in some way. Growing up amid chaos and conflicts in family forces one to exercise self-control to survive. This very self-control could lead you into an inactive life, avoiding extremes and seeking to live on the lowest edge.

Men who think their wives are codependent, are most likely codependent themselves too. Frequently codependent men embrace needy, demanding, jealous, or critical women. These men end up being dependent on the approval of their wives, whose demands, expectations, and manipulations can be trapping. Abusive, or ever demanding or unappreciative women are kept by codependent husbands. Their men cannot set boundaries and live in fear of emotional vengeance and refutation, including being denied sex.

Paradoxically too, very emotional wives can provide a sense of aliveness that compensates for the coldness that their codependent husbands harbor within. This can cheer up a man in the start showing him as powerful and sensitive to his wife, who needs extra care or attention or gifts. Long after he has conformed to her expectations, assured of her loyalty, he realizes it never gets enough satisfying her. She could simply be desperate or addicted to something and will keep desiring more of it all the time.

Workaholic men try to justify themselves for time alone, but leave their need for nurturing, freedom, respect, appreciation, etc. unmet. There is the caliber of men who stick around their wives physically but withdraw into emotional bubbles then become resented for feeling trapped or controlled. The wives are no cause in this case, but the man's codependence tendencies.

Naturally, a wife who often wants more intimacy from her man brings him to therapy. She wants him to open up and share his feelings freely. While the man is fully capable of communicating his feelings, setting healthy boundaries, and being just assertive, he reacts to criticism and demands by fighting back, withdrawing, or endlessly apologizing for sufficient reasons.

Some codependent men endure abuse from their wives because they know they will not be believed by authorities calling their wives abusive. Occasionally, their wives do or threaten to lie instead, accusing their victim partners of the violence. The man then chooses to keep it secret, silently suffering from the inside.

Addicted Men are codependent. Whether it is alcohol, drug, gambling, food, sex, or work, that is what they turn to for modulation of their attitude and self-esteem.

Codependency in Women

More women than men are codependent. The following are some of the reasons for it.

Biologically, women thrive on relationships. They are more sensitive to feelings, and they bond more easily and deeply. Under stress, they seek to care for children and make friendships. Men prepare for attack when stressed. Women prepare to love and be loved instead.

Women are more emotionally involved with their parents and, therefore, husbands. Losing a relationship is most painful to them. Threats of separation create a lot of anxiety for them, and autonomy is not something they naturally prefer.

Generally, also, women are subordinate to men in terms of handling money, entitlement to rights, and access to power. They have learned to be compliant in these ways. They endure more trauma and abuse than men, hence acquiring lower self-esteem by default.

Men are generally more drawn toward independence and autonomy than women. Women are more restricted and do not have more natural willingness and power to fight for their certain freedoms. Women are also granted less opportunity for independent life progress.

Chapter 13
Establishing Healthy and Happy Relationships

Have you ever made stupid errors that have destroyed major relationships? I have read many things about the psychology of how to have healthy, long-lasting connections–with romantic partners, family, or friends since I have been making my own mistakes in the past.

Below, I want to share some vital information for better relationships:

  1. Be truthful.

Some problems you ignore or do not understand would possibly damage your relationship. It is better to face the facts straight away and fix them, instead of allowing them to undermine your relationship over the long run.

Be deliberate and understand the truth of your relationship. Therefore, think of everything like your feelings and thoughts, the feelings and thoughts of the other person, and their external environment. If you notice a certain aspect of reality is being flung away, it's time for the focus to double and get to the truth.

  2. Avoid failing in their mind

One of the greatest dangers in close relationships is to assume that the other person is just the same as you are in their feelings and emotions. Sometimes, our psychological selves just don't acknowledge the difference between the other person in our relationship and ourselves.

  3. Use the language of Say.

Say Culture is a social tactical approach in which you are honest and open about your emotions, opinions, and what happens to near people in your life. It makes you more honest and real. Tell them things you feel they'd like to hear about yourself. Be Expressive!

If, for example, you want to have a hug, tell someone else you'd like a hug. It is crucial, however, that you don't expect the other person to hug you for the Tell Culture to function. You just have to tell them your needs and wishes, instead. We can then act openly on our demands and desires as we choose.

4. Remove barriers to communication.

To communicate openly and honestly, social barriers must be eliminated. Find your individual preferences for interaction and settle on something that fits best for you both.

5. Using psychological tuning.

As you talk, don't hear just what the other person says, but also the feelings behind the words. Note if the person appears anxious, frazzled, sad, upset, confused, angry, happy, happy, etc.

Note the tone of the voice, the language of the body, and not the sentences, and the meaning of the words. This emotional accentuation will improve the ability to understand and respond in ways that will lead to healthy, long-term relationships.

6. Check your relationships.

This is a magical solution to so many issues with relationships! Schedule regular meetings to address and strengthen the status of your relationship.

For example, every two weeks, my wife and I are checking in. In the last couple of weeks, we first thought about what we enjoyed the most. So, we discuss how our relationship should strengthen and how it can be strengthened. Eventually, we end up being grateful to each other for checking in and have some good chocolate to pay off. This has done great things to strengthen our relationship. It works!

7. Confide in others.

All of these techniques help you build trust that is essential to healthy, lasting relationships. Hold your relationship's confidence level in your mind, still individually assessed. How much trust do you have in another person acting in ways that suit your personal mental model? How much confidence do you have in this person?

8.   Boundaries and confidentiality must be respected.

It is so convenient for us to watch each other and to be in constant communication with technological developments. Moreover, it helps make us happy in relationships, because it increases mutual trust, and it does not force the other person to do something they wouldn't like to do.

9.   Have disputes that are safe.

Surprised? In relationships, disagreements can be good! If your first battle could lead to an end of the relationship, you're entering a relationship that expects never to fight. Instead, learn and talk to another person about strategies for healthy conflict resolution in advance.

Furthermore, when a conflict arises, start by stressing the importance of the other person and the relationship. Say the truth as well as your thoughts about them. Avoid the blame and be as forgiving as possible when understanding the actions of another person. If you find out that you have made a mistake and apologize quickly and thoroughly, be ready to change the mind. Do not dwell on the past and instead focus on improving future behavior. Focus on reconnecting and restoring conflict-stricken emotional links at the end of every conflict. My wife and I found such techniques helpful in resolving our tensions! You can benefit as well.

10. Fulfill your own goals.

Note that for yourself, you are not the other person in the relationship. Therefore, in any relationship, achieve your own goals first. If you judge it in your mind and heart, be patient and remember what you want from the relationship. Don't let others overshadow their needs and desires. Follow the Tell Culture Rules: be honest and open in your needs and wishes with the other person, and expect them to be honest and open with you. Otherwise, you face both anger and dissatisfaction, which reduces the likelihood of a healthy and lasting partnership.

11. Concession

Today's society stresses uniqueness, but we need to get out of the shell and place ourselves in another's shoes to make any relationship to work.

This means that we need to consider their opinions, thoughts, and feelings.

Yet make sure that your interests are matched with the needs of the others. Seek a mutually advantageous solution in any conflict area. My wife and I always compromise— big and small — and this is the way we maintain strong relationships.

12. Don't struggle with transition or diversity.

Persons and interactions constantly change. This cannot be wept; it is only a fact of life, which can be remembered and celebrated. Often, for both partners to be content, a partnership must be more inclusive. Find, therefore, the possibilities for non-traditional interactions like polyamory and others. At other times, people who once were right are no longer compatible. It is necessary to let each other go at this stage in order to ensure mutual happiness. What counts is to be careful in your relationship and to follow your own goals. Unilateral sacrifices don't guarantee a healthy relationship. A healthy relationship secures the mutual interests of both stakeholders.

Chapter 14
Helpful Strategies When a Loved One Has Codependency

B y now, you have had the opportunity, just like the person suffering from this condition, to become familiar with all the aspects that characterize the codependency condition.

What is most important now is to help your loved one. Let's be clear from the beginning. I know that living with a person suffering from this condition is not easy, but you still read because you want to help her. So, here are some useful strategies for you to help your loved one.

What is essential?

When a person manifests one of the psychic symptoms, no matter what the problem is, their loved ones tend to deny it as the first reaction. By denying, refusing to recognize a symptom, it provides an escape from reality that is painful. Culturally, the first reaction will also depend on the attitudes of the dominant culture and the culture fostered by the family within its system. Thus, in some families, mental health care is an integral part of caring for oneself and loved ones, while in others, it is a topic that is not discoursed because mental health problems are equated with weakness. Families who normalize the existence of mental health problems will sooner accept the existence of the problem and seek professional help. In other families, the period that elapses to seek professional help is usually longer, and the person who has the problem often copes with the problem itself and fears that it will be labeled weak, inadequate. To each person, the support, understanding, caring, and loving networks give hope that recovery is possible, that life will be functional again. In the absence of the above, recovery is significantly impeded.

What are the steps in supporting a loved one?

Sometimes a close person will run the story of the difficulties he or she is experiencing. Although the situation is significantly easier than, very often, family members respond by denying the severity of the problem. Unlike the aforementioned denials, the severity of the symptoms is reduced here; the person is sent the message, "You can do this, it is not so terrible, you have succeeded so much, look how it has worked ...". In fact, such conversations are not very helpful because the person feels even less competent and the problem before him even bigger and less solvable. The truth is that no one, not even a professional person, can feel the same as a person with anxiety, depression, obsessive thoughts, anorexia, and especially codependency. They can still help, though. Not only based on the knowledge they have but also by listening carefully to what the person is saying about the problem. So, the first step, if one exposes the problem, is to hear it in the intensity and size in which it is present. It's also more useful to say, "I don't understand because I've never felt anything like that, but it seems like a very difficult experience for you."

Sometimes it is the responsibility of recognizing the symptoms on loved ones. The situation is a little more complicated then, but one should always keep in mind that a person may just be ashamed and afraid to share what is bothering him. Many mental illnesses (addiction, anorexia, psychosis) alter the experience of reality and prevent a person from perceiving that he or she is in trouble. A timely response can sometimes significantly determine the course of recovery. It also shows the moral responsibility of loved ones to seek professional help, despite resisting and denying the person having the problem. It is useful to approach through expressing feelings of concern about perceived symptoms or behavior, giving hope that recovery is possible, giving clear information that the person is not alone, loved and accepted. Tolerating certain behaviors (e.g., drinking, gambling, avoiding eating or cleansing the body, acting uncharacteristically and not engaging in daily activities) with the belief that it is harmless is tantamount to fostering disease. It is sometimes reassuring for family members to think this way, making the right decision that they do not want to participate in the development of the disease.

The second step is to seek professional help

In this quest, loved ones can be there for support when it comes to minor problems (by supporting a close person to schedule a medical examination or talking to a psychotherapist), while for more serious problems, treatment can be supported by scheduling a consultation with a professional. If there is a refusal of professional assistance, or by scheduling a joint meeting with an expert. Further role in the treatment is evaluated by an expert (care of taking medication, agreed activities, check-ups, etc.).

The third step is to provide ongoing support

Most loved ones want to support but do not know-how. Seeking answers from both the expert and the person who has the problem gives you the clearest guidance. There is no need for anyone to be alone and ignorant because there is certainly a different path. Openly listen and ask questions about feelings and thoughts, talk openly about how significant a person is with all their roles in life, that the problem is the problem, not the whole personality. She is still a good person with many qualities and potentials, beloved mother/father, daughter/son, friend, and she still exists with everything that makes her a person as she is and that she still has roles that are very important to others. Even when there is no backlash, loyalty and support have an irreplaceable and invaluable place. Sometimes close people are meaning a lot that they hear from an expert person what is happening, that they are not the only ones who go through it with their loved ones. This experience of talking by an expert, in the presence of a person with a problem, often knows that it can be easier for everyone. For a person who has a problem, support is for someone to understand what is being said and what is happening to them, in front of the support person, while providing others with information that is neutral and helps to dismiss misconceptions and prejudices. Often, people with anxiety or depressive disorders, despite the physical support they receive (joint visits with physicians/psychotherapists), at the same time get misunderstandings, labeling themselves as cowards, lazy, irresponsible, to make up. As noted above, each of these messages is a stumbling block to recovery.

Control

The fourth step, which occurs after getting acquainted with the problem in detail, is the control of relapse (recurrence of symptoms). As they are already familiar with the problem and the symptoms, loved ones will know that they are recognized if they reappear. Although relapse is known to be discouraging, it is important not to give up and seek professional help as soon as possible. Taking the first step towards treatment is always harder than dealing with the symptoms later. Whether it is parents or children, husband or wife, friend or friend, regardless of gender, gender roles, roles in family and society, social expectations, successes achieved, psychological difficulties are not a measure of a person's strengths or weaknesses. The person is still the same person you know, except that they have a problem. The problem is no bigger than it and it is not useful to identify it with a complete personality. Each person will soon come to stabilization or recovery with love, support, care, freedom to communicate what is bothering him.

So, the basic message here is simple. Be as much supportive as you can and learn to stand up your position according to this condition. Don't take any actions that may activate the triggers you read about and convince your loved one to start with the therapy. Coherently do that and have a lot of patience for your loved one.

Remember that your loved one is a victim of this condition. Your loved one suffers the most. Now, I know that you might not believe in that, but unfortunately, that is the truth. That person is difficult for you in some sense, but you still love that person. That person is dealing with an enormous amount of guilt, shame, and depression. The effects of the traumatic experience are very big inside that person. You can salvage your loved one only in you are willing to overcome your inner ego and put away the past. Be supportive, be compassionate and throw away the past. Do not be judgmental because that will only backfire at you. If you don't accept your loved one and forgive everything wrong you will lose that person forever. Don't make that mistake. Suppress the anger and resentment you might feel and do things the right way. If you do that the person you love will get better mentally and both of you will have a whole new life.

Chapter 15
Getting to Know the True You:
Being Your Authentic Self

The struggle of the codependent individual is that they have never felt safe and comfortable enough and allowed to be their natural true self. Due to the fact that they have always had to mold themselves and adapt themselves to a frightening and unstable home environment and have sacrificed themselves for others. They have lost touch with what they want, and who they are, what their dreams are and what they want to do with their lives. On the journey to recovery, the fun really begins when you begin to learn how to be your authentic self and express it in the world.

Identifying your values

If you are a codependent individual than likely your whole life you have not had your own values, but have adopted those of your family and friends, and those around you. You have learned to suppress and hide your own feelings desires and wishes to such a degree that you aren't even sure what they are anymore. Therefore, an important aspect of being your authentic self is identifying your values.

One way that you can do this is to make a list of the things you care about, and the things that are important to you. Perhaps you care about taking care of the planet, or maybe you value financial success. You may place high emphasis on building strong friendships and close ties with your family, or perhaps you highly value artistic and creative expression and wish to dedicate your life towards being a musician or an artist. This can be a very useful practice and can help you define what is important to you in your life.

You can brainstorm and make a list of everything that comes to mind, that are things you care about, and wish to experience in your life. It is important that you do your best not to allow the values that have been instilled into you from your environment, your parents, and your family to interfere in this brainstorming process.

This is your time to assert your desires your needs. Your dreams, the values that you inherited from your family and society may or may not align with your own. You must learn that it is perfectly acceptable to have your own opinions, your own values, your own perspective on the world,

Learning to trust yourself

If you have been raised in a home with people who struggled with addiction and therefore have codependent traits, you have learned not to trust yourself. You have learned that your own feelings and desires are not right. You have been taught that you are wrong. This is completely false.

Perhaps you have learned from a very young age that your opinions are wrong and because of your early childhood experiences, you were not supported in speaking your true voice. Your parents may have told you that you are stupid, or they made you feel in some way that your opinion doesn't matter from a very young age. You have been told explicitly or implicitly that your natural impulses and true desires are not acceptable. The process of learning to trust yourself means that you find a place within you that knows what is true for you. This again requires taking time to be alone. And to reflect on your truth.

Living your passion

It is a sad truth that many people in our world today are taught from a very young age that the thing they love most, their greatest passion, is not able to support them and that they should not do what they love but rather do something that will make them money and provide them with security.

Codependent individuals have experienced many ways in which those they loved and depended on for support and validation have made it difficult for them to follow their passion. Perhaps when they were young, their home life was too unstable, and they never had the space and feeling of security to be able to allow their creativity to express itself and for them to explore what they were interested in. Or maybe they had passions in music or art, but their parents were unable to support them in this because they were too focused on their own addiction and dominated by their own depression. Therefore, the child who wished to play guitar never had the opportunity because their parents would never obtain one for them to practice. The child has learned from a very young age that the thing they really love to do, is not practical or is not important. They may go the rest of their life and be very successful in some job, but they will always be disappointed and have resentment towards the fact that they were never allowed to do what they love to do.

A key aspect of breaking free of dependency is beginning to live your passion in your daily life fully. This doesn't mean that you have to quit your job or make any major changes to your life right away. You can begin doing simple and small things that are what you want to do and what excites you, rather than doing what you feel you must do in order to please others. You can begin writing that book you've always wanted to write. You can take up playing an instrument you always wish to play. You can start drawing and painting. You can start a garden; you can study a subject you always wanted to study.

The possibilities are endless, but the key point is to begin, living your passion. This is just the simple following of whatever is the most exciting thing you can do in the moment. By living your passion, you begin honoring your true desires and letting the universe know that you are willing to be who you were created to be. This will set up a cycle of creativity and flow, and you will feel more and more empowered to see to your own needs and do what brings you joy. This life is your life and you are born here to do what is most exciting for you. You are not here to make others happy or fulfill their desires. It is okay to be selfish to a certain extent, and you're your true life in the pursuit of your dreams.

Authenticity

At the core of all of these ways that one can follow to be their true self is this idea of authenticity. As we already said, many people have gotten lost and forgotten their true self to such an extent that they don't even know what their true, authentic self is. It is a paradox that's something that is so close to us and so naturally becomes so difficult, but this just shows the insanity and dysfunction of much of our modern world.

Only you can define what is authentic and true for you. This is the core of the issue - that you cannot look outside of yourself to anyone, not to any authority. No matter how wise or smart they may seem, only you know what is true for you, what is real for you, what makes you happy, and what is your deep need.

As you begin to live an authentic life, you will find that you don't need to go against your natural impulses. You do not need to lie; you don't need to change yourself in order to make others happy. There are few joys in life, greater than feeling that you are living your true authentic life. You will discover that as you follow your passion, your destiny and the universe will seemingly magically provide for you exactly what you need, exactly when you need it. This is because you are on the track of your true self. It is when we become inauthentic and do things that we do not wish to do that we find all of our actions having some sort of failure and feeling like we are pushing against the current. When you go with the current you float easily downstream, and do not cause any pain to yourself or others. Your task is to reverse many years of conditionings and patterns which have taught you that you cannot be your true authentic self. You have an image of what you must be, what others wish you to be, and what others need you to be. This process of rediscovering, and recreating your authentic self is one that may be difficult at first, but as you go on, you will find more excitement and joy in the process.

Chapter 16
The Psychological Theories That Explain Codependency

Codependency may be a relatively new construct, but it has been in existence since the 1940s even though it wasn't termed "codependency" from the start. Research on codependency was first conducted on the wives and families of alcoholics who were formerly referred to as co-alcoholics. However, the first identification of codependency as a psychological construct can be said to be rooted in the theories of Karen Horney, a German psychoanalyst. In 1941, Horney proposed a theory about how some people adopt what she referred to as 'Moving Toward" personality style to get rid of their anxiety. According to Horney, people with this 'moving toward' personality tend to move towards others in order to gain their affections and approval. By doing this, they subconsciously try to control them by acting dependent. They are the type to turn the other cheek when slapped on one cheek. They would rather gain approval and acceptance from others than to respect or love themselves. Initially, the term 'codependency' was used to describe families of alcoholics who were believed to interfere with addicts' recovery in a bid to 'help' them.

To really understand codependency, psychologist have referred to two important psychoanalysis theories, "Family systems theory," and "Attachment style theory." So, let's take a deeper look at each of these theories and understand how they explain codependency.

Family Systems Theory

A family is the most basic emotional unit in a society; it is probably where humans learn to develop feelings, bonds, and important human emotions. Although family relationships can be complex and no two family can be completely alike, the family systems theory suggests that all family have a similar emotional model or system. That is, emotions are learned in all families almost the same way.

The family systems theory aims to look at the family as a primary and unified emotional unit. Proposed by Dr. Murray Bowen, a psychiatrist, the family systems theory proposed that every member of a family is emotionally connected to each other in an intense way. Bowen proposed that the family is a system where each member plays a specific role and follows certain rules. Each member of a family interacts and responds to one another based on the role assigned to them. This leads to the development of a pattern in the family system; a pattern where the actions and behaviors of one member impacts the rest of the family in certain ways. Depending on the system, these behavioral patterns that have been developed, result in either a balance, imbalance/dysfunction, or both in the family.

What the family systems theory is saying is that the family has a massive impact on the actions and emotions of any individual and these could be negative or positive. It is also saying that when a certain member of the family system behaves in certain ways, it is bound to affect the behaviors of every other person in the system. When a person in the system experiences certain changes, it affects the family as a unit and the members in terms of actions and emotions. For instance, if a member of a normal family system where everybody plays their role and everything functions like it should, experience a change such as a sudden addiction to alcohol, this sudden change will affect every other person in the family and how they act/play out their role in the system. Bowen further said that maintaining a certain behavioral pattern within the family system can lead to a balance in the system, but also cause dysfunction. Although the level of interdependence among families vary, every family has some degree of interdependency and that is how a normal functioning family should be.

Attachment Style Theory

In the simplest terms, attachment can be defined as emotional connection and bond with another person. However, in the words of British psychologist, John Bowlby, who is the first developer of the attachment style theory, "attachment is a lasting psychological connectedness between human beings." The origin of the attachment theory was to understand the distress felt by children when they are separated from their caregiver. This theory can be used to explain and understand codependency and why it is rooted in individual childhood and upbringing.

With the attachment theory, Bowlby tries to understand the relevance of attachment in tandem to an individual's personal development. Particularly, this theory proposes that an individual's ability to form a physical and emotional attachment to other people, produces a sense of security in self which is required for growing and developing the right personality. Bowlby argues that the earliest connection formed by children with their primary caregivers has a massive impact on the child's development of self and personality.

Children who were raised in proximity (emotional and physical) to their primary caregivers are likely to have a recognition of their inherent self and be able to protect themselves from any sort of problem or abuse. The main point here is that when there is a primary caregiver available in a child's life to protect all the basic needs from food to shelter, such child is very likely to develop a sense of security in him or herself. On the other hand, children who didn't receive support and care while growing up, whether emotional or physical, tend to experience more anxiety in their relationship with their parent and also future relationships.

How does this attachment theory relate to codependency? Researchers and psychologists who supported the attachment theory, as relating to child development, believe that the type of attachment style a child develops from childhood is the same one the child engages in his relationships as an adult. In other words, how we act and manage our intimate and romantic relationships as adults is usually dependent on the type of attachment style we developed as children and how we were treated by our caregiver as children. Psychoanalyst Bowlby believes that family experiences have a strong impact on a child's behavioral and emotional wellbeing.

Children who form an insecure attachment style with their caregiver are more likely to show codependent traits than children who develop a secure attachment style with their caregiver. For a child to develop a strong, secure and independent personality, he or she must have had a strong relationship with at least one primary caregiver which could be the mother, the father, or a guardian. For a child to have a strong relationship with a caregiver, the family must be a functional and normal one where the child is being provided with all of the basic needs and he is able to express himself without a fear of repression. In a dysfunctional family where either of the caregiver is probably an addict or an irresponsible parent, it is highly unlikely for the child to have a strong, dependent relationship. Therefore, a child raised in this kind of family will develop a lack of security in himself or the caregiver, thereby causing him to recoil from seeking new experiences, and sometimes relationships, that require intimacy. Based on the research conducted, there are four attachment styles children are likely to develop based on the sort of relationship they have with their caregiver but people with codependent personalities usually have the avoidant attachment style.

Chapter 17
Resisting the Temptation to Go Back

At this stage in your progression path, you have identified the codependent relationship(s) (hopefully, there is only one) in your life, you may or may not have decided to give that person a chance to remedy the issue, and you have either begun a path of healing with that person or you have separated yourself from them completely. In this part we will go over fighting temptations to return to your abuser, how to deal with abusers who have initially committed to change but are not actually holding up their end of the bargain, and we will cover how to deal with the people you have distanced yourself from but who refuse to respect your decision of separation.

Chances are that even if you miss the person, the negative aspects of the relationship with them will weigh heavier in your mind than the fond memories. But in the instances where you feel tempted to go back to them, it will be useful for you to have created a list. Make a list of all of the demeaning, hurtful, or otherwise negative things that you did, or the person made you do while you were around them. Add to the list ways in which the other person's actions directly or indirectly harmed you. Make headings of these types of incidences and then write the details underneath. The headings should trigger the details in your mind allowing you to remember the reason you left the person in the first place. If not, read your more detailed notes to help you recall how the person truly made you feel. Take care to only use these notes when you are tempted to go back to your abuser. Recalling traumatic events can be taxing on your mental health so you want to keep this type of activity to a minimum.

False Promises

Most manipulators are very well-versed in their trade. When you initially confront them, they may commit to changing just to get you to stick around. Even if they are initially defensive, they will eventually admit responsibility only to lull you into a false sense of security. Since most people in codependent relationships tend to suffer from low self-esteem, the abuser knows that they can take advantage of your weaknesses and ultimately have the dynamic revert back to one that favors them. Therefore, even if you are able to put on a brave face and initially confront your abuser, that person is counting on you to lose your resolve sooner or later. And in this way, the abuser will have gotten their cake and eaten it too. Not only will they get to keep you in their lives, they know that they do not have to do much to go back to the codependent behavior that they are so familiar with and the behavior they depend on.

Therefore, if you agree to allow your abuser to make amends, be very vigilant, especially in the first year of their commitment. Make sure that they are actually making efforts to change, whether it be attending counseling sessions, couple's therapy, doing their fair share around the house, not trying to guilt you into doing things you are not comfortable with or that you know is their job, and so on. It is essential that you not fall back into the same rut that you just worked so hard to climb out of. This can be quite taxing on you, and may even seem impossible at times, but as long as you stay vigilant, the rewards will pay off in the long run. Now, this is not to say that there cannot be relapses on the part of the abuser. Once again, as long as the abuse is not physical or sexual, which is something you should never tolerate under any circumstances, it is likely that the abuser may fall off the wagon, so to speak, even if they are truly committed to changing. Although, how much you are willing to let this recidivism slide, is entirely up to you. Remember, that you do not owe them anything, you have already given them enough.

Stalkers

If you are in a situation where you have decided to end things with the abusive person and you have created distance, but this person refuses to respect your wishes, you will have a much more difficult time holding onto your resolve. As mentioned earlier, manipulators are masters at preying on your weaknesses and they know how to entice or coerce you into allowing them back into your life. The temptation to give this person a second chance can be great, and that is why you need to be prepared when it comes along.

Remember those notes you made with the headings earlier? Well, the chances are that when this person tries to come back into your life, you will not have your notes with you, nor will it always be convenient for you to get to them, but the headings you created will be a good way to jog your memory even without your notes. This way, even if the person is sweet and charming when they are attempting to get back into your life, you will be triggering yourself with the worst memories of your time together. This should give you the strength to fight them off.

When you have mastered this strength and you are able to tell them to leave, they will likely become angry. Since manipulators are so used to getting their way, they rarely lack the maturity or the tools to deal with rejection and hearing the word 'no'. Therefore, make sure that you are in a public place when you decline their advances. If they corner you at your home do not answer the door and ask them to make an appointment or to leave altogether. It may sound a bit clinical, but this will actually help set boundaries, something manipulators really do not like. Chances are that they will not call you and will leave you alone altogether. The most important thing to remember, no matter what the situation, is that you want to stay in control over your own faculties and you want to make clear to the manipulator that your resolve will not diminish. In both cases, those who make false promises and those who do not take 'no' for an answer, they will grow tired of the extra 'work' they have to do and move on.

Chapter 18
Establishing Healthy Boundaries

As you back away from being your partner's caretaker, it is normal to feel lost and confused. After all, you have been enmeshed in this codependent relationship for some time, possibly for years. It is quite understandable if you no longer know how to act around your partner or other people in your life.

While you lived the codependent life, you probably did not think much about boundaries. Most likely, you felt that every problem was yours to solve and every pain was yours to feel. Now that you know better, take some time to work out what your boundaries are and how you can claim them in your thoughts and actions.

Identify Your Boundaries

If you ever purchased a property such as a residence or a vacation lot, you probably had a surveyor come out and locate the boundaries of the property. You needed to know where your land stopped, and the other person's land started so you would know what land you had control over. For instance, you wouldn't want to put a fence on someone else's land, but you might want to put one on yours.

As you work through identifying your boundaries, think of yourself as the surveyor. Your business is simply to find what you own and mark off the property line, so you and others know when it is being crossed.

Personal boundaries, of course, are not as easy to identify as property boundaries. Only you can decide where your boundaries are and no one else will know what they are unless you tell them.

Feelings

You need to have emotional boundaries to be a healthy, strong adult. When someone feels sad, angry or depressed, do you feel the same way right along with them? Or do you have your own feelings about the situation?

Think about how you feel right now. What contributed to that feeling? Was it something someone said or did to you? Or was it something that was done to your partner or someone else?

Your feelings are your own, but to understand what your true feelings are, you need to separate your partner's feelings from your own. You can be sad when he is on a high. And, believe it or not, you can be happy when he is angry or depressed. It does not mean you care any less about him. It just means that you have your own feelings.

Possessions

Your boundaries can extend to your personal possessions. Many addicts and alcoholics take over the possessions of their significant other. An addict who wants to feed his addiction may feel perfectly welcome to go through your purse or wallet for money to buy alcohol or drugs. Is this right? That depends on whether you have given him permission to do it. You have every right as an individual to say, "No. My wallet is mine. You need to ask me if you want money rather than going through my things to find it."

A desperate addict may also take over other possessions as well. If he goes through your wallet and finds nothing, he might go through your jewelry to find something to pawn.

In fact, alcoholics, drug addicts and compulsive gamblers commonly go through the house looking for items that are worth something to a pawn shop. They put the item in hock and rarely go back to make the payments. Instead, you lose your most valuable personal possessions one by one.

Physical Boundaries

You own every part of your body. You can see your physical boundaries when you look in a full-length mirror. There is an important reason to think about physical boundaries when you are in a codependent relationship. Addicts and domineering partners often invade physical boundaries. They may hit, kick or punch their partner, or they might force sex when the partner does not want it. Addicts seem to lose their sense of what is theirs and what is not.

The first step toward claiming your physical boundaries is to realize that you own your body, and no one else can touch you if you do not approve.

If your partner is simply being disrespectful, you can try working it out by explaining your position. However, if he is physically abusing you, you need to get out of the situation immediately. No matter how your partner is violating your physical boundaries, your emotional and possibly physical well-being can be at stake.

Personal Space

Imagine a cushion of air around you that keeps others at a comfortable distance. This is your personal space. Everyone needs a certain amount of personal space. Some need more than others. One thing is for sure – if someone is yelling at you with their face just inches from yours, they are invading your personal space.

People in close relationships often feel less need for a lot of personal space. However, even if the person you are in a codependent relationship with is your spouse, you still have the right to back away if you feel you are being crowded.

Privacy

Privacy boundaries are difficult to maintain in any close relationship. They can completely disappear in a codependent one. If you write in a journal, your words need to remain private as long as you choose. If you like to do your grooming tasks in private, you need to protect that boundary to feel comfortable. Some people like to talk to their family members and friends in private. As long as you let your partner know it is a private conversation, you have the right to hold onto that privacy boundary.

Consideration

You also have the right to common courtesy and consideration. To explore these boundaries, think about what is okay with you. Is it okay for people to ask you about your weight? Do you feel comfortable when people quiz you about your finances? Consideration boundaries often involve sensitive and touchy subjects. Show consideration for your partner and insist on getting consideration from him.

Respecting the Boundaries of Others

Just as you have personal boundaries, remember that others have boundaries too. A part of codependency is taking on the roles, responsibilities and emotions of the other person. You have put your life into taking care of your partner, and now you probably have trouble letting his or someone else's problems be theirs.

Personal possessions can become a battleground in a codependent relationship. Your partner buys a carton of cigarettes even though he has promised to quit. As a codependent partner, your first reaction is likely to take the carton away and dispose of it.

However, if you do this, you are asking for trouble. Your partner very rightly feels that you have crossed his personal boundaries by taking control of his possessions. Like it or not, he has to be the one to make that decision.

Another issue codependents face is that they have lost a sense of the personal space of others. If you see that someone is backing away from you, you might be standing too close. Since you are trying to make positive changes, the best thing to do is to ask the person if you are too close simply. As you continue to do this, you get a feel for how much space people need to feel comfortable.

Claiming Your Own Boundaries

Once you identify your boundaries, it is time to let people know what they are. If you have been in a codependent relationship for a long time, you might have problems informing your partner about this. Next time your partner invades any of the boundaries you have identified as your own, stand up to him and tell him the way it is. Use assertive communication to get your point across without crossing his personal boundaries.

Chapter 19
Maintaining Your Relationships with Family, Lovers, and Friends

C hanging your behavior can be confusing to your loved ones. They will definitely react to this, and the reaction may be positive or negative. The ones closest to you will be affected the most. Given enough time, they may finally come around or at least make their peace with the new you. You have to stand your ground. Be affirmative and consistent, even when they badger you with the same issue over and over. When they ignore or pressure you, you are going to need support from elsewhere. That's one of the benefits of support groups. Support groups will provide you with confidence until your loved ones stop complaining about your changed attitude and selfishness. Remember they have enjoyed your caregiving at a detriment to yourself. Now you are taking care of you; the change is for your own good. It doesn't mean you will stop caring for them. It just means you won't let their struggles control your life.

Dealing with an addict

Coping with an addict is difficult and confusing. They probably have two personalities. The one you love and the one managed and controlled by their addiction. Consider it as a "Jekyll and Hyde" situation. Dr Jekyll is the good guy, who you can talk to. He is nice to you and always reminds you of the good times. Mr. Hyde, on the other hand, is the monster, who may be under the influence of alcohol, drugs or not. The main similarity between under the influence Mr. Hyde and not under the influence Mr. Hyde is their meanness and the pain they cause.

You can reason with Dr Jekyll. Reactions like blaming and criticizing are unproductive. Be calm and assertive, speak in a friendly and loving manner.

Trying to reason with Mr. Hyde is a waste of your time and energy. Still, ignoring and suppressing your feelings won't help either.

An addict's disease is their cross to bear. When you realize this, you become more free, independent and happier.

After sobriety

You hope your addicted loved ones will try to heal themselves, and sometimes it happens. After the brief feel-good moments, fear of the past may hunt the relationship. The partner of an addict remembers the bad times and may want to talk about it, but the addict may not remember, or he/she may be ashamed of the past. This can cause problems in the relationship.

Apart from that, the recovering addict's partner may start to feel neglected because of the time the addict spends attending therapy sessions or support groups. Remember the issue with attachment, you have to let the other person grow because that is how you also grow. A better partner will make your life easier.

Dealing with family

Families have the most influence on us; our parents, especially are the most influential. No matter our age, we are still our parent's children. Codependents usually come from families with boundary issues. As an adult, you may live away from your family. Whether you are in proximity or there is a great distance between you, you have to set and remember your boundaries, when they ate around you. Don't stay away from family, family is important.

They may be supportive, or they may push your button and challenge your progress. When they challenge, you expect them to complain about letting other people influence you or that you are being selfish. Expect these but stand you to them.

Recovery is also the ideal time to fix the issues you have with your family. Even if your parents are no longer alive. Childhood issues are responsible for dependency; targeting them allows you to challenge the matter from the source.

Dealing with friends

Friendships may not be as intimate as family and love, but codependency can infect it too. Your friends will notice the change in you, and you will notice the changes in the dynamics of the friendship.

Times where you have played the submissive soles or let others take advantage of you. Your self-esteem and confidence will grow. Friends may feel their position of power threatened by nobody needs a one-sided friendship. If you have to limit your time with or stay away altogether from dysfunctional friends.

Your friends may change with you and begin to understand you better. They may also look for help with their issues when they see the positive effect of the changes on you.

Dealing with lovers

Dating

Sexual relationships start from casuals encounters to marriage. Frequent interactions gradually increase the intimacy of a relationship from casual to acquaintances, and maybe marriage, at the end of the spectrum. It is healthy to want an intimate relationship. Recovery improves your mental health and self-esteem, so you tend to become more attracted to healthier people, which improves the quality of your relationships. Old habits will try to raise their heads, don't let them.

You may not understand what you want from the relationship or be scared because of your prior experience. Add it to your recovery journey and try to fix these before starting a new relationship. Your confusion and fear will likely attract someone that is unhealthy for you.

Love

Codependents go all in for every one of their relationships. Love is not excluded. They either lose themselves in the relationship, or they are totally indifferent to it. There is no middle ground. In the early stages of a relationship, we tell the person about our interests, story, feelings and secrets. It increases as the relationship grows until boundaries merge and we begin to see a part of the other person in ourselves. We start to prioritize them and make sacrifices on their behalf. It is the same for everyone. The problem with codependents is the extremity of their actions.

As a codependent, you may have unrealistic expectations of the relationship. When your expectations are not met, you start to manipulate the person with kindness. Reality stars to chip away and you begin to rationalize and make excuses for the situation. You hide your feelings as needs because you are afraid of losing the person.

Sex

Codependents sometimes substitute sex for intimacy. Sex itself is an intimate act, but it loses the intimacy when there is a lack of emotions in the act. Good sex involves both lovers receiving and giving pleasure. You need the cooperation of your sexual partner to enjoy sex. And your partner must understand your sexual needs and desires before they can pleasure you sometimes. They can't read your mind, so you have to tell them. Here is why the codependent's problem starts. You shame, and anxiety prevents you from having a productive conversation about sex.

Codependent's sexual problems can be pretty complex. They are not only liable to substitute sex for affection and intimacy or struggle to communicate their sexual needs which can derail their sex lives. They can also express repressed emotions in sex. Remember that un-expressed feelings, always find a way to get out. Sex can be one of those ways. Repressed anger or sadness can reflect in your sex life. They can make you lose passion for sex or develop unhealthy and harmful kinks.

Building and maintaining relationships

Majority of relationships are unhealthy. We romanticize dysfunction relationships and cling unto them. It may be because of our fear of loneliness. A healthy relationship should be supportive, non-controlling and non-manipulating.

There are two parts to every relationship.

1. The self- which symbolizes uniqueness and autonomy.

2. The group- which symbolizes intimacy.

A healthy relationship is about finding the balance. Nobody can truly love another person unless they know who they are deep down, but people can't truly know you unless you have a clearly defined "self." This seems like a paradox. You need to be autonomous before you can be intimate. I hope you can now see the paradox clear.

I mentioned a balance in the first line of the last paragraph. You need to balance your individual needs with your needs for emotional and physical closeness. Here are some tips to help you strike that balance.

- Be assertive in your communication

- Be accepting of each other's differences.

- Be cooperative and make the decisions together.

- Have compatible views

- Spend quality time both together and apart from each other

- Have a common goal

- Be realistic about your expectations.

Chapter 20
Codependency in The Workplace

Have you ever felt put upon in the workplace? Yet you still volunteer to help out when there is something that needs doing in a hurry. The problem may be codependency, but it may not be adding to your career prospects. No matter how hard you work and how much work you produce, if you are codependent upon a boss who uses you, the chances are that you also play a part in the situation. People who lack confidence and who seek approval for the work that they do are often codependent without realizing it. When they don't receive praise of any kind, they go out of their way to seek it. This doesn't make you a valuable member of staff, even though you may see yourself as being indispensable. You may even find that you are taken for granted so much that even when you take a vacation, you come back to all the work piled up ready for you.

In a situation such as this, you are being used because you allow yourself to be used. You may not see it that way and may crave the approval that you have. However, it's unlikely that you will be considered for promotion, because your needy nature means that you don't have what it takes to be management material. It may sound like a bit of a downer to you that you have worked so hard for little return, but you are placing yourself in a very vicious circle and need to break free of it. Not only that, you may also be someone who prefers to work alone and are not a particularly good team member. You don't know how to delegate and would rather be weighed down with work and feel needed than share what you have with others.

This is a situation that will eventually lead to burn out and although people may have warned you about that, your nature won't make you believe it. You do what you do because perhaps you don't get praise in any other area of your life.

You need to appraise your life and decide upon the following:

- Do you have a good work life/home life balance?

- Do you enjoy the work that you do?

- Would you enjoy it as much without the praise that you seek?

To get out of the vicious circle that you have put yourself in for some reason or other, you need to look back into your past and find out at what stage of your life you first felt that you were not given recognition for something that you did, because often this type of codependence stems from childhood.

Linda knew that she had problems, but she didn't know how serious they were. Every day she dutifully went to work and slaved although no one had ever expected that amount of devotion from an employee in a relatively junior position. The problem arose when she suddenly realized during the absence of her boss that no one else seemed to give her the kind of feedback she craved. She was lost. Then, looking through her past with a therapist, what she found was that during her childhood, her mother never recognized anything that she did as being worthwhile. Her mother would even leave the room rather than acknowledge that Linda could do something that her mother was incapable of. All the years of childhood, she had tried her best to impress her mother – not because she needed to – but because she felt displaced and even had doubts about whether her mother was really her mother. She couldn't understand why her mother could not acknowledge her. This followed her into adulthood and in her first job, she was surprised that people actually thought what she was doing was a worthwhile job. Then she questioned their sincerity in her own mind, believing herself not really to be worthy of the praise that she was getting. Thus, the cycle began, and she craved that feedback that only her boss could give her.

The problem with this type of behavior is that she didn't actually need that acknowledgement and was quite capable of doing a good day's work but had slipped into the need for it feeling that it was the only thing that validated her. If you feel that you are falling into this trap at work, you need to find a new way forward because it is neither healthy nor productive to be so dependent upon someone else to validate who you are. A boss who wants more and more out of you may actually encourage weak people to do more and more work because usually people with low self-esteem don't ask much in return for their work. Often feeling validated is every bit as important as getting a fair pay for a good day's work.

Exercises related to work-based codependency

While it may not be the healthiest thing for you to give up your job, especially if you count on it to pay your bills, you need to take a different approach. Observe people around you and see how they cope with the workload that they have. If you don't ask for validation, the only validation you really need is from yourself. If you know that you did a great day's work, learn not to ask for validation. Instead of that, treat yourself to something and congratulate yourself for what you have done. In Linda's case, she learned to do things to please herself. You must do the same. Inside of you, you have something called motivation. Don't let it be controlled by someone else. Control it yourself and you become motivated without needing insincerity and wasting the time seeking it. Most of the time, abusive bosses pile on more work when you seek this kind of validation and you end up feeling overwhelmed instead of pleased that you were able to manage your workload.

Don't do it for him or her. Do it for you. Set small goals for yourself that no one else knows about. People who always try come out as winners. Believe me, it takes a while for this to sink in but it really does work. For example, if you have a dozen tasks to do in a day, work out which ones take priority and set yourself little targets that are doable. Gain your confidence within yourself by keeping to your own timetable. Of course, priority jobs get done first, but you need to switch the motivation. It's not for the boss. It's for you. Make the competition inside yourself sufficiently motivating that when you succeed at something, only you know about it. What other people know about your skills and your goals is inconsequential at the end of the day.

By doing this, you build up confidence in yourself and don't need validation from anyone. In Linda's case, she was a brilliant artist, but because her mother had never acknowledged it, she had put away her paintbrushes and had given up on her passion in life. No one should ever let someone else dictate their success. When she finally built up her reputation as a brilliant painter, she did so on her own terms and people were quick to ask her to do drawings for them. In fact, she had no trouble making her passion into something quite substantial, although she also learned that she didn't have to please someone else as long as she was happy with the results. She also learned to say "no" which is a very hard lesson for someone who has self-esteem and codependency issues.

Exercise 2 – Setting yourself free

Give yourself some personal goals as well as work related goals and make them manageable. The reason you start simple is so that you can attain those goals. Then, little by little, as you gain confidence, you can make the goals a little harder. Remember that you are only creating them for yourself and for no one else. You are the only one that you are out to please. When you have made your goals for at home and you have kept them, look at your face in the mirror and see yourself as the success that you are. At the end of the day, the only person's opinion of you that matters is your own. When you can acknowledge your own successes, you don't need to be dependent upon your boss to validate you and you can go forward in your career because you are no longer a drain on people.

Chapter 21
Subtle Codependences

The Controlling Codependent

These CD people are both controlling of others and feel controlled by others. They do not know how to take control of their own lives due to their afflictive emotions and thought patterns, therefore they express this in a negative and unhelpful way. This manifests in many ways such as getting frustrated, angry or over-reacting, attempting to provoke another's frustration or anger, attempting to control external events and others through a range of manipulative tactics, not dealing with their loss of control efficiently, practically or helpfully, and becoming fearful to let others be who they are and allow situations to happen naturally. These types of codependents have often lived through life experiences with people that were out of control or overly controlling, therefore deep sorrow and disappointment have accumulated over time as a result.

The Distrusting Codependent

Distrusting codependents simply don't trust themselves or others. Feelings, decisions, life choices, thoughts and beliefs are all things which come into question daily. This extreme uncertainty with their self leads to an uncertainty and distrust of others and this lack of trust in its extreme eventually creates a highly codependent personality. Life is balanced and any negative polarity will eventually lead to the manifestation of its opposite.

The Angry Codependent

Angry codependents have most likely suffered as a child and bring unconscious traumas into adult life (the same can be said for all codependent personality types). They often feel sad, hurt and angry, and live with people who are sad, hurt and angry as a norm. They are afraid of their own anger and frightened of another people's anger. Repression of emotions and authentic and healthy communication is common, and they may actively shame, punish, or abuse others for feeling real and genuine emotions. This stems from a place of inner shame and guilt and is projected outwards. Angry codependents often feel safer and more secure within their own anger, and around other's, than consciously working through their emotions and painful feelings. Codependency therefore arises from attaching to this feeling and making it a daily reality.

The Ungrounded Codependent

This form of codependency is due to being ungrounded. There are simply no boundaries and little sense of awareness as to their own right to self-love, self-respect and a healthy, happy and peaceful life. Weak boundaries can be the result of many things including saying they won't tolerate certain behavior or treatment but then allowing it regardless, increasing their tolerance to such behavior, and actively allowing others to hurt them. This subsequently leads to all the different types of codependent manifestations present in relationships such as anger, fear, blame, hurt, repression, suppression, controlling tendencies, and addictions. Eventually this self-detrimental tolerance to other peoples' 'stuff' can lead to an ingrained intolerance which leads to the need always to control, criticize, judge and abuse.

The Self-denial and Repressing Codependent

These people repress, deny and suppress everything. Every thought, feeling, emotion and self-acceptance which could eventually lead to healing and wholeness becomes denied and repressed, further leading to vicious and unhealthy cycles. Problems are ignored, bad circumstances are 'pretended' out of existence, and frequent business is a norm. They often get confused, depressed or sick, become workaholics, suffer from frequent anxiety, stress and nervous tension, and tell themselves daily that things will get better tomorrow. Health problems such as overeating or undereating are common as is a turn towards substance and intoxicants. Codependency therefore arises from a constant shift to the external world of distractions instead of looking within and getting to the root.

The Obsessive Codependent

This personality is symbolized by perpetual worry, fear, anxiousness, tension, stress and inner turmoil. The mind is attuned to a reality of fear and concern for other people, or extreme interest in others' lives. Obsessive personality disorders can manifest in many ways however, the main point is that the obsessive codependent continuously keeps their focus on another person, place or thing which take the spotlight off of themselves and any real problems or issues that may be manifesting. Their focus on 'another' therefore becomes an obsession.

The Caretaking and Giving Codependent

These people take on a caretaker or caregiver role. They think they are responsible for other people's choices, actions, wants, needs, emotions, wellbeing and holistic state of health. They often feel pain, anxiety, pity and guilt, and suffer when other people have problems or issues in daily life. The highly caring codependent often feels compelled to solve everyone else's problems and gives advice when it is not wanted or needed, in addition to attempting to 'fix feelings.' This excessive caregiving ultimately affects others in that they are disallowed to be independent and have a healthy sense of self-autonomy. This, of course, has a profound effect on the codependent person as by preventing others from looking after themselves and developing their own independence, they themselves unconsciously adopt an extremely CD personality. Furthermore, these codependents often over-commit, make false promises, and neglect their own wants and needs. Eventually resentment builds up which manifests as anger and all other sorts of CD expressions and they can feel victimized, unappreciated, harassed and neglected; as a result, they also tend to project their personal unresolved issues into others, further energizing their own unhealthy characteristics.

The Low Self-esteem and Self-worthy Codependent

Social Networking

With the average user being on some sort of social media platform on average an hour a day those numbers are telling. It can lead to a whole host of issues and problems.

We will just touch on some of them here.

We all know the person who shares too much of their life on social media. The one who updates everyone on how their boyfriend is cheating on them or they are having a fight with their mom.

Like a window into someone's soul, social media can reveal great insights into the codependent's outlooks, insecurities, and validation seeking behavior. It can also contribute to codependency because it can give an instant response if someone is seeking attention or wants sympathy for something.

They are likely to get it too because the cost for the person giving it is not high. It doesn't take much to like a photo or make a sympathetic comment as a response to someone.

Another way to look at social media is as a giant enabler. How many times have you seen someone 'take up a cause' be it political or otherwise on Facebook or Twitter? What is the ultimate result besides hurt feelings, bruised egos, and damaged real-life friendships?

Nothing.

Except that it gives the codependent something else to focus on. To be the caped crusader for justice and to feel really good about themselves at least for a little while. There is no end to the number of causes a codependent can take up either. They can literally go from one pet crisis to the next within a matter of seconds if they are so inclined.

This isn't to say that all social media is bad or anything like that. Simply, that it is another vehicle for people who exhibit codependent traits to tread very lightly around especially if they are in recovery. This platform can easily take the place of a relationship and give the codependent a way to get validation on a continuous basis.

How to deal with social media if you are codependent?

Like anything, the first thing you need to do is recognize that it's a potential problem. Simply acknowledging the fact that social media can impact your life in harmful ways is the first step.

Second, once you recognize the issue you need to control it. For some this will entail cutting it out of their lives completely. For others it will mean severely curtailing its use. You need to see where you fall on the spectrum and be brutally honest with yourself about where you are at.

The following are steps you can take to control your social media and not let it control you: (bustle article -7 ways to stop your social media addiction)

1. Turn off notifications on your phone.

Getting that little icon telling you someone liked your post or made a comment on your soliloquy about our current president gives a little dopamine rush that is very addictive and feeds into the codependent's need for validation.

2. Limit the amount of time you spend in total.

Using a timer or getting a blocking app on your desktop or phone can work wonders. Eventually the need to go on will decrease the less time you spend.

3. . Try something new.

A new hobby is a great way to fill the extra time you have now that you are no longer posting or checking social media compulsively. It also creates a 'producer' mindset rather than a 'consumer' mindset. The former is when you are creating something which works in a different area of your brain than when you are simply consuming information.

4. Spend more time with your loved ones.

Nothing replaces in person contact. Sometimes it can be easy to forget that and assume because we see someone everyday on social media that it replaces talking to them in real life. The other thing it does is reduce being distracted and distant from loved ones because you are constantly checking your phone or tablet.

5. Make it something you earn.

In other words, look at social media breaks as something you get to do after you are finished with your work. It makes it special for you. You do not take it for granted, you earned your social media time. Also, by only checking it occasionally like after you have accomplished something, you will spend less time on it making its lure less powerful.

6. Meet people.

Meeting friends for coffee instead of texting or messaging on Facebook is so much better for your social life. Communication is so much more than verbal or written. Non-verbal cues such as body language can be missed if you are not in front of the person.

7. Just stop.

Delete your accounts, go through the very real withdrawal you will experience and get out there and see what your life is like. I think in time you will see that you will notice the bigger world outside of your screen and automatically find yourself interacting more with those around you.

Chapter 22
A Step-by-Step Program to Recover through Mindfulness

Mindfulness Techniques For Everyday Use
MINDFUL SHOWERING

The first exercise to take up is mindful showering. You have to remain focused on your activity and not be distracted. Don't be in a hurry to finish everything. You should first start by standing under a shower and then pick up the bar of soap in your hand. Now rub it over your body, lather up and then shower yourself again. This sounds too basic, but it is important for you to remain focused and not start thinking about the next activity. Once you have the temperature set, enjoy the water pouring all over your body. Feel it massaging your body and turn around, so that you can feel the water flowing over the other side of your body. Once done, you can take five minutes to relax. When you do this, you need to make sure that the temperature is controllable and at a comfortable level.

While you are showering, think of nothing else at all. Concentrate on the sensations, using all of your senses. Use your sense of smell to take in the aroma of the soap or the shower gel. Use your sense of touch to feel the soap touching the body and caressing it. Your sense of sight may be closed off, but blind people often feel more with their other senses so use them to the maximum. Listen to the water splashing against the floor of the shower. Use all of your nerve endings all over your body to feel the water tingling against the skin.

What you don't realize most of the time is that you are presented with so many possibilities in your life and you don't maximize them. In fact, you may even shower without noticing much at all. By concentrating on the experience and thinking of nothing else, you are preparing yourself for your day or for your night of sleep in a way that is able to relax your mind and clear all of your thoughts so that your body is ready for the next phase of your day or night. Relaxation is taking in every sensation that the shower offers you. When you wash your hair in the shower, feel the water running down your hair onto your body. The more you experience when you are having your shower, the more mindfulness you are introducing to this otherwise mundane task and that allows your mind to drop all negativity so that is really going to help you to move forward in a positive manner.

MINDFUL EATING

Mindful eating is the next activity to take up. Sit down at the table and lay all the food in front of you. Now set a timer of 30 minutes and try to spend all that time slowly chewing and enjoying the food. Don't give into the practice of grabbing food on the go and eating. That is a silly practice and will not help you remain mindful. You should also mindfully cook the food first, enjoying all of the aromas of the food that you are producing. Mindfulness during eating is something that is vital for several reasons. The digestive system of a human being can dictate the state of health that someone is in. There is a saying that "dying starts in the gut" and it is very accurate. There are so many processes happening as a result of what you eat and drink. If you do not chew your food properly, you open up a can of worms because you can make yourself ill. The digestion becomes sluggish, you also get this horrid feeling of indigestion, acid reflux, the potential of constipation and leaky gut. These are all because you didn't choose the right kinds of foods and you didn't stop to eat them for the required amount of time.

You can actually make this very enjoyable indeed. Choose foods that have different textures because the experience of eating them will be a delight. Soft foods should not simply be swallowed. Let them linger on your tongue for a while so that your taste buds can take in all of the taste. Tease yourself with things such as dark chocolate which has a lot of magnesium in it which is good in reasonable quantities. Let it melt in your mouth. You could even take a mouthful of hot coffee and let it melt the chocolate and feel the wonderful sensation that happens in your mouth. If you have never tried it, there is also a candy which will make you laugh a lot which is called Space Dust. This creates a popping noise in the mouth, and you leave it there on your tongue until the crackling has stopped.

Eating shouldn't be a really rushed experience. Those who take time with eating and who concentrate on every facet of the meal really do enjoy their food and feel satisfied with their state of health. Encourage the family to experience it too. When you have a cup of coffee in front of you, don't just drink it without noticing anything. First take the cup into your hand and feel the warmth of the cup going into your hands. Then, the next thing to do is to smell the aroma of the coffee. If your coffee doesn't have a particularly good aroma, try more aromatic varieties to make the experience more complete. Then take the coffee onto your tongue and allow it to caress your tongue to get the full enjoyment from it. While you are doing this, you are stopping the temptation to be distracted. Put your cell phone away during eating times. Make your eating time a serious venture that concentrates only on the enjoyment of the food, the flavors, the aromas and the textures.

MINDFUL EXERCISING

Mindful exercising is the next mindful activity that you must adopt. Exercising is extremely important for the body. You should pick an appropriate time and then start with the practice. Whether you are walking, jogging or cycling, place your mind over the activity and don't let it wander. One exercise that can be great for beginners is Zumba but not in a class setting. Do this in the privacy of your own home with a video from YouTube and make sure that you have comfortable clothing on. From the moment that the music starts, enjoy moving in time to the music. There are no rules about how you dance. Let your hair down and enjoy it. If you cannot be that energetic, how about going for a regular walk in the park? It's a great experience to be up close and personal with nature, but it's also important from another perspective. Concentrate on your movement, on your breathing and you will help your body to feel better. Whenever you get involved in any kind of exercise be totally mindful of what you are doing rather than letting thoughts of other things enter your mind.

MINDFUL CLEANING

You must also get rid of unwanted clutter from your house. For this, you have to engage in mindful cleaning. You should not have the television playing in the house and keep the house as silent as possible. Your mind should be fully focused on the task and this alone. You will see that it is serving a dual purpose. On the one hand, it is helping you get rid of clutter and on the other; it is working as therapy. If you don't feel that you can get through the whole house in one sweep, try one room at a time. Look at what you have that is getting in the way of everyday life. If it does not give you joy, get rid of it. This is the kind of philosophy that is employed by an interior design helper in China who goes into people's houses and helps them to find order in their lives. If you concentrate totally on making your home streamlined and easy to live in, you get the added advantage at the end of it that your home will be more relaxing, and you won't have to live in such chaos.

Unfortunately, in this day and age, people collect so many things. They place such importance on the trivial. By doing this and doing it mindfully, you get to see where your priorities are and can begin to see a new you are emerging from the chaos. This is helpful in so many ways. As well as teaching you an appreciation for the good things in your life, you will get to recognize habits and be able to avoid them in the future. As with all of these exercises, no interruption should be encountered, and you need to keep your mind totally on the job at hand. It is best to do this alone. If you go into the room in question with three plastic bin bags, you can decide whether an item is to stay or whether you can give it away to those who are needy, whether to throw it away or whether to gather up the unwanted possessions and sell them so that you can use the money for something that you really do need instead.

MINDFUL WORKING

Mindful working refers to remaining focused on your work at the office. You should avoid getting distracted and must fully focus on the task at hand. Try to set yourself reasonable timelines to finish your work and that will help you better concentrate on the tasks. The way that you do this really depends upon the way that your workplace operates. If you have things that you need to give a lot of concentration to, try to have lock down times when you do not answer the telephone or speak to others. These are periods of total concentration to get rid of those items which are the most difficult. The rest of the day can be divided into singular tasks such as bulk work that is relatively simple and to getting your email box empty.

If you are mindful of the task you are doing, bear in mind that if someone tries to interrupt you, you must be single minded. Tell them to hold on for a moment, finish the task at hand and then move into the next moment when you can give yourself a certain amount of time to talk to them. If you allow yourself to be interrupted, what you do is waste all of the energy you have already put into the task at hand and have to restart that task when the interruption is over. You will have your flow of thoughts interrupted and that should be something you should avoid entirely. If you work in this way, you will find that you are more organized and that you can get more done. Put all of your concentration into each task that you take on.

MINDFUL DREAMING

It is believed that dreams tell us a lot about our subconscious. By mindfully dreaming, you will be able to get an insight into what your subconscious mind is thinking. You must make it a point to dream lucidly. Then, maintain a book in which you can write down the dreams. That will help you have an insight into your subconscious. Did you know that you can invent dreams? When you go to bed, lie in bed and think about the dream that you want to be in. Create the scene in your mind and concentrate totally on that scene. Be there, see the people who are in that dream and use this dream time to allow your mind to feel free. This may even give you the incentive that you need actually to feel refreshed the next morning. The dream stages that you go through in REM sleep are wonderful and it is these that you may remember when you wake up.

Chapter 23
Six Stages of the Codependency Treatment

I ntroducing Hope: hope is essential for those who have hit rock bottom and are finding it hard to get on their feet. People that fall into this category feel that life is totally out of control. With this thought, losses and consequences build, causing them unbearable pain. They even think undefeated, worn out, tired of life, as they have gotten to their breaking point. I know it sometimes feels like giving up feels like an option. You feel like you would prefer being in that relationship than out of it to suffer. The losses that have been accumulated would then pile up and lead to depression.

You feel us these things, but you are still alive, surviving. I am very happy for you. How do you get yourself up from the pit you are standing in? First, you have to speak up, break the silence after deciding to end the relationship, transition slowly from desperation, and fear to hope. Muster courage till a glimmer of hope presents itself. Reach out for help, attend support groups if you are up to it, or better still consult a trusted friend, seek mental health advice, and their services.

1. Detachment: 70% of codependents are attached to people and the problems within their environments. They tend to be overly involved and sometimes hopelessly entangled. Such attachments can come in different forms, some of which are;

- Codependents tend to become too worried about a person or problem. Everyone is turned into charity cases.

- All their energy is directed at objects they become obsessed with. These objects are majorly humans. They tend to give their all to humans they take a liking to. They behave like they cannot do without the person. They feel like if they have to stay with the person every second of every day, and this might be quite irritating.

If I were the person being clung to, I would flare up and tell the person away. Most people would use such character to their advantage. They would use the codependent to their advantage.

- They do not act according to their own volition. They listen to others before they react to whatever thing they are facing.

- They become emotionally dependent on people in their external world.

- They become caretakers to the people in their external world at the same time, attaching themselves to the needs of the people.

Now when this happens, they detach from themselves. Codependents forfeit their ability to think and the feelings they were supposed to have had. They also forget how to take care of themselves, allowing them to lose control. Their involvement in other people's lives can keep them in chaos, but not just them, everyone connected to them. Before you can work on yourself, you have to learn to detach yourself from the main object of obsession. Detachment does not mean you should withdraw with hostility. It is merely a base on the fact that everyone is responsible for himself and that no one can solve problems that are not personal. Also, worrying about who will and who will not solve your problems does not help. Detachment is an art and an act. It is a gift and also can be given to anyone who would want to seek it and use it appropriately. How does detachment work? It works using the HOW method or formula as it is usually called;

H means Honesty,

O means Openness, and

W means Willingness to try.

- Honesty: for you to be out of the codependence lane, you should become honest with yourself and accept the fact that we humans have our expectations and limitations. Know this, and no one can be perfect in solving other people's problems. Do not spoil your life at the expense of others.

- Openness: Being open means you can welcome people's thoughts and opinions and also be able to express your true feelings and thoughts about them. Expressing yourself would allow you to lose the object of your obsessions steadily.

- Willingness to try this is where you would have to accept that everyone, especially you, has strengths and weaknesses. All you have to do not is to find your potentials instead of trying to find happiness in the lives of others.

3. Courage and Commitment: this can be done in therapy. It is a more difficult and challenging stage. Here, you must remove every filter for pure, undiluted perception and emotions. In this stage, change is perceived as a high-level threat. Mobilize forces to help neutralize the difference because if it proceeds, equilibrium is lost, and without it, there would be severe problems.

4. Secure boundaries: learn to set boundaries, create boundaries, practice the limits established. Know the difference between a healthy and dysfunctional relationship. Stay in therapy, practice some prevention work, then practice self-time and self-activities. You can set boundaries in very hostile environments; try addressing all forms of addiction; concurrent addiction (drugs, behavior addictions), alcohol cross and comorbid health (mental) disorders. Choose a hobby, get busy, exercise, and work on getting your social life back together.

5. Resolving trauma: fall in love with yourself. Let the relationship go. You do not have to forgive because it is not necessary; besides, you were not at fault. You were killing yourself in the relationship. It is a decision and not a path. Though achieving and maintaining self-love takes a lot of work and makes it difficult. Self-love

requires a lot of things of patience, practice, humility, self-empathy, and also learning from mistakes.

6. Practice self-love driven relationships: create enough time to allow someone into your heart again. You would have enough time to experiment with relationships to find the right now; but you must be sure to be getting into the one(s) that is different from the last one, if you notice any sign of codependency, pack up your bags and leave.

Here is a take-home quote; if you like someone, set them free. If they come back, it means nobody wanted them, and then set them free again.

What does a recovered codependent life look like?

A recovered codependent life;

- Identifies personal need;

- Learns to make plans to meet the needs of others;

- Takes excellent care of him or herself;

- loves unconditionally;

- shows respect to others;

- sets rules and boundaries and abides by them;

- stays connected with people;

- learns to create a network of healthy relationships; and

- Teaches others to show respect.

STEPS TO RECOVERY

Recovery takes a while to be completed, but as you go on with it, you will feel a sense of fulfillment. There are four necessary steps to recovery. They are as follows;

1. Abstinence or Forbearance: Abstinence is essential to recuperate from codependency. The objective is to take your consideration back to yourself, to have an inward, as opposed to outer, "locus of control." It implies your activities are persuaded by your values, needs, and sentiments, not somebody else's. You figure out how to address those issues in substantial ways. Perfect forbearance or restraint isn't fundamental for progress, and it's unimaginable regarding codependency with individuals. You need to rely on others, and this way give and bargain with relationships. Rather than abstinence, you figure out how to isolate and not control or are obsessive. You become increasingly self-coordinated and self-governing.

In case you're engaged with an abuser or grew up as the offspring of one, you might be reluctant to disappoint your partner, and it can require extraordinary fearlessness to break that example of surrendering your capacity to another person.

2. Show of awareness: It is said that denial is the sign of compulsion. It is genuine whether you're a heavy drinker or in love with someone of that class. In addition to the fact that codependents deny their very own dependence or addiction – regardless of whether to a medication, individual, or activity – they reject their sentiments, and particularly their needs, especially passionate requirements for supporting and genuine intimacy. You may have experienced childhood in a family where you were not well-nurtured, your emotions and opinions were not regarded at all, and your enthusiastic needs were not met as they were supposed to. After some time, as opposed to criticism and rejection, you figured out how to overlook your needs and emotions and accepted that you were not

right. Some codependents chose to end up independent or discover comfort in sex, nourishment, medications, or work.

It prompts low confidence. To turn around these damaging propensities, you initially should be mindful of them. The most harming snag to self-esteem is negative self-talk. A great many people aren't conscious of the inward voices that push and reprimand them.

3. Acceptance: Mending includes self-acknowledgment. It is not just a stage, yet a long-lasting adventure. Individuals come to treatment to change themselves, not understanding that the work is tied in with tolerating themselves. Amusingly, before you can change yourself, you need to acknowledge the circumstance. As is commonly said, "What you oppose persists. "In recovery, a whole lot of things about yourself is uncovered that requires acknowledgment, and life itself presents restrictions and misfortunes to acknowledge. It is growth and development. Tolerating reality opens the entryways of plausibility. Change at that point occurs. New thoughts arise that recently stagnated from self-blame and battling reality. For instance, when you feel tragic, or desolate, rather than feeling worse, you have self-sympathy, calm yourself, and find a way to feel good.

Self-acknowledgment implies that you don't need to satisfy everybody for dread that they won't care for you. You respect your needs and undesirable emotions and are pardoning of yourself as well as other people. This altruism toward yourself enables you to act naturally intelligent without acting naturally basic. Your confidence and certainty develop, and you don't allow others to mishandle you or instruct you. Rather than controlling, you become increasingly self-assured and are fit for more prominent intimacy.

4. Take inventory: This advances self-duty and coordinates familiarity with the shadow consistently to keep the record clean involved with others. Blame feelings must be managed by changing them into reasonable obligation, by advancing the

acknowledgment that a law of circumstances and logical results is working. At the point when somebody feels he isn't right or something is wrong, he has something to do with it, and it is his very own duty to act and to control himself – even to change himself.

5. Take Action: To develop, mindfulness and self-acknowledgment must be joined by new conduct. It includes going out on a limb and wandering outside your comfort zone. It might consist of making some noise, taking a stab at something new, heading off to someplace alone, or defining a limit. It likewise means setting inside limits by remaining quiet about responsibilities or saying "no" to your critic or other old propensities you need to change. Rather than anticipating that others should meet every one of your issues and satisfy you, you figure out how to take the right actions to meet them and accomplish things that give you satisfaction and fulfillment in your life. Each time you evaluate new conduct or risk, you gain some new useful knowledge about yourself and your sentiments and necessities. You are making a more grounded feeling of yourself, just as courage and confidence. This expands upon itself in a positive criticism circle versus the descending winding of codependency, in which fear is created, discouragement, and low confidence also.

Words are simple actions. They have control and mirror your confidence. Getting to be confident is a learning procedure and is maybe the most incredible asset in recuperation. Assertiveness necessitates that you know yourself and making that open at your own risk. It involves setting limits. This is honoring and respecting you. You get the opportunity to be a mind-blowing creator – what you'll do and not do and how individuals will treat you.

Chapter 24
When the Relationship Got Abusive – How to Recover from The Trauma of the Codependent Relationship

The trauma bonds

One topic that we need to take a look at is a process known as trauma bonding. This is going to be a condition that is similar to Stockholm Syndrome. Basically, a person who is held captive, in this case in a relationship, is going to develop feelings of trust eventually and sometimes affection to the people who were able to capture them, and to the ones holding them against their will. It is a survival like strategy that allows them to still hold onto some sense of normalcy in a situation that is out of their control.

This kind of survival strategy is sometimes going to show up in a relationship. Instead of being known as Stockholm Syndrome though, it is going to be known as trauma bonding. We are usually going to see this one occurs when the target enters into a relationship with a narcissist. The individual, who is often going to suffer from some codependency issues, first will feels loved and like the other person cares for them. But over time, this is going to begin to erode, and the physical, mental, and emotional abuse is going to start becoming the normal in the relationship.

The codependent is able to understand that the change has happened, but they may be confused as to why this kind of change is occurring. They will see that they themselves need to shift their understanding to know what they are doing wrong, and once they do this, they will be able to reach that loving and caring part of the relationship again. Of course, they don't have that kind of control. Only the narcissist does, and the narcissist will be able to decide if there is love or only abuse in that relationship.

If the target seems to break free from the relationship, the narcissist is able to just go back to that courtship phase in order to win their target back. The more that the target works to get to the narcissist for approval, recognition, and love, the trauma bond is going to be strengthened. This means that the codependent will stay with this bad relationship, even when the abuse starts to escalate, and this can create a very destructive cycle for the target.

The abuse

There are times when a codependent relationship is going to turn abusive. This happens when you end up in a relationship like this with a narcissist. The narcissist is going to keep the control power over their target and may use abuse and other intimidation techniques in order to keep the control over that person. And the abuse can get quite bad. The narcissist and others in the codependent relationship are not going to have a lot of empathy or understanding of the other person at all, so they will continue on with the abuse, without worrying about regret or any kind of emotion for their actions.

Depending on how long the person stays in the relationship, the abuse can go on for a long time, and usually will get worse over time. This can definitely include things like physical abuse but may include options like emotional and mental abuse in some cases. This can make it hard for the target in this codependent relationship to get what they want, or even to break free, and the situation just gets worse.

As the physical, emotional, and mental abuse will continue getting worse. The narcissist has no idea that they are causing harm, and they honestly don't care as long as they are able to get what they want out of their target. The target though, is going to feel that their self-esteem goes down, their confidence, and they will continue walking around with the bruises and more because they think this is all they are worth for. Getting out of this situation and realizing the negatives that come with the codependent relationship is key to ensuring that you see the results that you want and that you are able to get away from the abuse to live your own life.

Breaking free

Now it is possible that the target can break free from the codependency and from all of the abuse, but it is going to be tough and the other person in the relationship is not going to be very happy when this starts to happen. Breaking free from the trauma bond is going to usually need some form of professional help in the form of life coaching or psychotherapy and it is always best to have someone who is safe, and whom you trust, to talk to and get to making effective coping and escape strategies with.

There are a few steps that you are able to do along with the support of your therapist to ensure that you can get away from the abuse of a codependent relationship and ensure that you are able to gain some of the freedom that you want. The first step is to separate out from the narcissistic person, and the abuser. This means that you need to separate out emotionally and physically. Often getting away physically is easier, but the narcissist is going to keep pulling on the target, trying to get them back and doing what they want, making it hard for the target to let go. The target has to be willing to separate on all fronts to see the results.

The next think that the target needs to be able to do is acknowledge their choice. Exploring the past relationship with the narcissist, and what happened, through therapy can help you to see some of the bad things that were showing up in that relationship. With the help of your therapist, you will be able to see some of the addictive, control, criticism, emotional abuse, and gaslighting aspects of that relationship and the toll they were having on you.

During this process, it is a good idea for you to develop a good support network around you. These are going to be people who are there for you, who understand the struggle that you went through, and can help you to get over the codependent relationship in a healthier manner. Without this support group, it is going to be so much easier for your partner to get back in and start the abuse on you again. But with a good support group that can be with you, who can help you to raise your confidence and self-esteem, and to talk things out with, you are going to find that it is so much easier to break free.

Just as you are working hard to reach the emotional freedom that you want from abuse and trauma bonding, the narcissist is also working to regain their control over you like they used to have. To avoid letting this happen, it is important that we are able to develop a network of friends, family, and professionals who will be able to help you stick with your goals, and who can support you through every step of your journey towards being free.

Breaking free from the abuse is going to be so important. It will ensure that you are able to get away from all of the pain and the hurt that has been going on in your life for so long. Many people who are in an abusive codependent relationship are not going to see the problems that are going on, and they will stick with that relationship, despite all of the pain and the suffering that they are going through, thanks to the trauma bond that develops.

Remember to spend time with your friends and loved ones

It is likely that due to the narcissistic abuse, you spent a lot of time isolating yourself away. You were worried that having anything to do with other people outside the relationship would make the narcissist really mad. And often the behaviors that the narcissist showed to others would make it likely that your friends and family would stay away. There are many ways that a narcissist is going to try and keep you away from others, in order to make sure that the only person you can "trust" and rely on is them.

Now that the relationship is over, it is time to get back some of those relationships. Depending on how long the abuse went on and how bad the situation got, you may find that some of your friends and some of your family members are still hurt about the experience, and they will not want to have anything to do with you now. You have to accept that. Maybe at some other point, when they see that you are really done with the situation and ready to move on, they will come back. But you have to realize that they were harmed in this too and they may not be willing to forgive.

Many times, though, once you are really done with that toxic relationship, you will be able to find lots of friends and family who are willing to come out and spend time with you. Take advantage of this as much as you can. They are going to be the ones who helped to form your identity before you ended up in that relationship. Now you need to work with them in order to help form this new identity now that the relationship is over.

It may seem weird in the beginning. You were isolated for so long that you aren't sure how to make this work. You may feel like it is strange to be around others and that it is outside of your own comfort zone. Give it some time. the more that you do with your family and friends, to socialize, to catch up, and to do even some other things with them, you will find that your old sense of self is going to come back, and the interactions that you have with people, outside of the narcissist, will become stronger.

This support group is going to be so important to you when it is time to heal and feel your best again. It is hard to find people who are going to be supportive sometimes and depending on the rules that you set and the kind of boundaries that you want in place, it may take some time to really work to find that group. But when you stick to your rules and work on yourself, and add in some more positivity to the whole thing, you will find that over time, it is easier to get this group built up, and this will do wonders for your self-esteem and how good you feel about yourself.

If you are in this kind of relationship, it is important to learn how to get free. Things are not going to get better, the abuse is not going to stop, and this is not a happy or productive relationship for you to be in. Finding the professional help that you need and sticking with a support group you know and trust can be so important to your overall health. At the time, it may feel like you are giving up on someone you love, and a relationship you have worked so hard on over the years. But just think about all of the things that you are able to gain when you give up this bad relationship, and you are able to focus on yourself and developing a healthy and happy relationship later on.

Chapter 25
Reflection Exercises

MEME AND ME

My late paternal grandmother, Meme, was the glue that kept the family together. She had a significant impact on my life. My family always reminds me that I am just like Meme. My mother is my biggest role model. As I shared earlier she is a woman who has endured a lot of hardship in her life, but she kept going in order to improve her life and the life of her children and others. I believe I possess the strength they both exhibited. But there were other areas of their lives which I witnessed and mimicked, which carried into my adult life as an enabler.

When Meme met my grandfather, he was fifteen years her senior. She was fifteen, pregnant, and married, in that order. My grandparents had an emotionally distant marriage, and as a result, Meme suffered from attachment issues and lack of connectedness (two of the characteristics of a codependent). This emotional deficit resulted in my grandmother overcompensating in the lives of her children, grandchildren, and anyone else whom she believed needed her. My father was my grandmother's most challenging project. Even in my father's adult years, Meme felt the need to provide for him and picked him up every time he fell.

MY DAD DISAPPOINTED

My father was the last child between my grandparents. My grandfather and his mother did not hide the fact that my dad was not wanted. He was called ugly by his grandmother and his father never talked to him. (No wonder he suffered from low self-esteem.) Meme immediately began to shelter my dad in an attempt to make him feel loved, but the love that he needed was from my grandfather. Meme was hurt that Pop rejected my dad, so she overcompensated when it came to the needs of my dad. Dad enlisted in the Army and returned home with an addiction to drugs. He had found something to ease his pain of rejection and low self-esteem. When my mother and father met, she did not know that he was addicted to drugs. He kept it a secret. When she realized that his long stays in the bathroom were because he was shooting drugs, she was devastated, and after many years of hiding the fact out of embarrassment and shame, eventually, mom put him out. After my parents separated, my father went to live with my grandmother, who had thus far done a good job of enabling him.

MIMIC

As children, we look to our parents and grandparents as role models. We want to be like them. We watch how they respond to various tasks and issues and usually carry that information with us. We use it to help us make decisions in our own lives. It was a sad thing to watch my father exist as a drug addict, and I was certain that I did not want any part of that in my life. So, instead, I watched and learned from my grandmother, whose actions were mostly good and always from a place of love. She always encouraged me to be better and to reach high in my accomplishments. As I matured, I watched Meme take care of my father as if he were still her little boy. She cooked for him, washed his clothes, cleaned his room, and opened the door if he forgot his key. Although she never mentioned the fact, Meme knew that my father was a drug addict, but I think she blocked it out because she thought if she helped him, by showing him love, he would change.

LEARNING TO ENABLE

I continued to learn from Meme what it meant to care for people; everyone could depend on her. She could make you cry when she was angry and laugh when she was happy. Over the years, I watched as Meme opened her doors to many people who were down on their luck: alcoholics, people who had legal issues, people she allowed to move in and rent a room in the family house. There were several people who could not pay the rent, and she let them stay anyway, hiding this fact from Pop. On many occasions, she would use her own money to supplement the tenants' rent. She loved the company, the attention, and being loved by everyone. It filled a void and made her feel like she really mattered, (she did really matter because the entire family loved her beyond measure). It was evident by her actions and her words that she

447

was not complete unless she was giving to others, even to her detriment. The very depths of her soul reeked sadness. She lived with the spirit of an enabler.

I watched and learned as Meme continued to care for people who were undeserving and inconsiderate. She constantly made excuses for bad behavior. One of my cousins was a drug addict and thief with violent tendencies. Meme slept with her pocketbook under her pillow because he had stolen from her in the past, yet on the occasions that he asked for money, she gave it to him never turning her back on my cousin. He always had a place to stay. In my adult years, I began to mimic Meme. She was the matriarch and I was like her, so I needed to operate like she did— learned behavior.

I don't believe that children are born bigots, or drug addicts, or killers, I think that there is something that they see or have experienced in their life that shifts their thinking and causes them to react to situations differently. This is not to say that all people who have negative experiences turn into bad people - quite the contrary. I think our experiences help shape us, but we make the final choice in which way we will go. However, some things are learned. Kids do not know prejudice unless they hear it in their home, on television, or with people they associate with. I don't think it is a stretch to see that becoming an enabler has something to do with what you saw in your family.

THE LOVE OF A SON

Mommy's struggles continued with my brother, Shawn, who was a year older than me. Shawn (whom my son is named after) really had no male role model; our father certainly wasn't one. At an early age, my brother cried out for attention. He started acting out, stealing his first car at age fourteen. Mommy did everything she could - getting him counseling, enrolling him in a military academy, even sending him to live with Meme, with no concept of what enabling involved. When my brother was in the youth detention center, Mommy would pack us up to visit him. When Shawn returned home, he would come back to our house or Meme's house. Money was repeatedly spent on lawyers and bail for Shawn mainly by Meme but sometimes by Mommy.

CANDY BABY

Candace is the baby, and you already know that she and I were in jail together for a short time. I believe that the relationship between my mother and sister has been the biggest example of enabling between family members. Candy was always quiet and observed things. She never had to accept any real responsibility in the home and never was disciplined by my mother or father. In her young adult years, she grew more dependent, even while living on her own. Candy made poor choices in men and usually ended up with someone who would not work. So she took care of her man and her children.

When her money was short, which was often, Candy would call Mommy or Meme and eventually, me. We all came to her rescue at different times. Eventually when her relationships failed, Candy moved in with Meme, into the very room on the third floor which my now deceased dad had existed. I say existed because he wasn't really living or thriving. Drugs had taken over his life and he merely existed for many years. Candy lived rent-free with Meme and handled her finances poorly. Candy eventually moved to North Carolina to escape the pressures she had placed on herself. She thought by moving away that everything would change, but she forgot that she took herself with her. In her later adult years Candy tried to keep her issues secret, but that was impossible because every time she needed money she called my mother, who in turn bailed Candy out. That's what enablers do - they constantly come to the rescue of others, never addressing their real problems, just patching up what is broken. Eventually, the patch wears out, and the enabler has to return to mend what has come apart.

FAMILY DYNAMICS

It is safe to say that the existence of codependent behavior involves an excessive preoccupation with the lives of others. Family dysfunction is the best teacher of this behavior.

As painful as it has been to share my family struggles I want you to see how a combination of family dynamics can propel you to act before you think, sending you on a downward spiral without you even realizing that is what is happening. My grandmother suffered from low self-esteem and attachment issues because of her relationship with my grandfather.

Consequently, she enabled my father and whoever else she could manage to get her hands on. My mother, who never experimented with drugs, suffered from embarrassment, guilt, and shame because she had challenges in her childhood and married a drug addict. As a result, she enabled my sister and brother. I suffered from anger about my life, feeling inadequate, and needing to control all situations pertaining to family, so I enabled everyone. Helping not only hurt the ones I love, but it hurt me, too. I stopped caring about myself and only cared about fixing others. The women I spent ten months in prison with were victims of the family tree, too. I heard countless stories about abuse and drug addicted mothers, fathers, sisters, and brothers. I also witnessed Grandma, Auntie, a sister, a cousin – who would visit the women in jail, raise their kids while they were in jail, and allow them to return home to continue on the same course of negative conduct most of the time which involved repeat incarceration. Enablers are repeat offenders just as much as the enabled is a repeat offender, a term used in the criminal justice system which means a person who habitually commits offenses, causing them to return to jail. The enabler habitually rescues the drug addict, alcoholic, and emotionally troubled, makes excuses for them, and picks the enabled up when they fall.

REFLECTION EXERCISES:

You can look at your family dynamics by drawing your family tree. Start at the top of the tree with the oldest person that is deceased on your mother's and father's side – great grandparents, grandparents, parents, etc., List the names on each branch. Think about each family member's story and try only to focus on their strengths and weaknesses.

IS THERE A HISTORY IN YOUR FAMILY OF?

    □ DRUG ADDICTION ABUSE

    □ MENTAL ILLNESS

    □ PERSONALITY DISORDER

    □ ANXIETY

    □ THIEVERY OR MISCHIEF

    □ HABITUAL LIAR

Who is the person everyone turns to for help – mother, father, grandmother, grandfather, sister, brother? Who is the person who always comes to the rescue of those who behave badly-mother, father, sister, brother, aunt, uncle?

List yourself on the family tree and decide what your role has been in the family dynamics.

Try to find a connection between the strengths of family members and the weaknesses of family members.

What did you learn from the behavior you saw in your family?

Do you mimic the unhealthy behavior as much as you do the healthy behavior?

Chapter 26
When It Doesn't Work

Unfortunately, not everyone is committed to take the steps of recovery from codependence. Anna Sheri was someone who loved her children, who are now adults. Her son, Mark, was continuously getting in trouble for drunk driving, damaging people's property, instigating arguments and showing outbursts of anger. As his mother, Anna Sheri "protected" him from the consequences.

She paid for bail to get out him out of jail more than once. She paid for damaged property and apologized on behalf of her son, even though he never apologized himself. She made excuses to people about her son's aggressive and impolite behavior. She told lies in order to protect her son – or at least delay the inevitable.

When she finally had become exhausted, she came to me. After extensive conversations about her issues and her relationship with her son, I walked her through the steps of recovering from codependency. However, she refused. She was in denial. She did not think she had an issue. She just wanted to know how she could better control her son.

When I told her that she needed to overcome her own issues, she became angry and left my office. I never saw her again. My point is that denial will prevent the steps of recovery from working because they are not even given a chance.

Another person, Mason, started the process, separating from a toxic relationship and starting to practice self-acceptance after doing extensive journaling to increase her self-awareness. However, when it came to action, she experienced a huge flood of emotions that became a roadblock for her to move forward. She had an anxiety attack and needed to seek more extensive treatment.

I really liked Mason, and I believe she will have her breakthrough in recovery someday. She was dealing with childhood memories of abuse, and the trauma was something beyond what she was ready to deal with. It's okay.

If your experience is like Mason, I want to cover you with love. I want to tell you that you are a good person and you are going to be okay. It will just take more time, and you can get help from a therapist. You don't have to do it alone, especially if you are dealing with the effects of abuse.

You can still practice self-compassion and self-acceptance but take the action at your own pace. The idea is to focus on yourself. It is okay to go off and have a mini retreat by yourself. Get alone. You may even need to connect with your higher power. Whatever will give you spiritual nourishment and solace for your soul.

Any activity that brings you joy is considered self-care. If you don't care for yourself, you will burnout, but by doing things for you, you renew yourself. It may sound simple, but it's part of recovery from codependence.

But if doing your own self-care is not enough, you can get professional help or join a support group, which I highly encourage. There is absolutely no shame in it.

Beatrice was experiencing depression, and she blamed her partner for her emotional distress. She said that her partner was being abusive emotionally. Interesting, she blamed herself. She started to go to Al-Anon, a support group. She learned to express her feelings and her needs. She discovered through group discussion that she had distorted beliefs about herself and her relationship. This awareness was her breakthrough.

She had been trying to solve her relationship issues for many years and she knew about codependence, but it wasn't until she became aware of her own belief systems – and how distorted they were – that she was able to heal.

Furthermore, through therapy, she examined the codependent behavior that she learned as a child. She began to believe that her partner is responsible for his own behavior. She did not have to 'save" him anymore. There was a radical change in her belief system, and she cultivated this change.

Her recovery did not lead to her relationship improving, however. Her partner became worse, but through recovery she gained the strength to leave the emotionally abusive relationship. Although her relationship did not work out in the end, she gained a new freedom to be true to her authentic self and be compassionate toward her own needs.

Rejection & Fear

When you feel rejected, the key to recovery is to identify the situation accurately, as well as look at yourself and the other person. This is where your belief system changes: you choose to believe that you are not responsible for the way other people choose to see you. Instead, you stand firmly in who you are.

When I counsel people on the issue of rejection, I usually ask a series of questions to prompt forward movement:

- What is the rejection really about?

- Is the rejection more about your feelings?

- Have you done anything that may have contributed to the rejection?

- Is the other person projecting their own issues on you?

- What are ways to deal with this rejection?

Fear of rejection provokes negative feelings. When you fear being rejected, it has not happened yet, unlike rejection which is a reality that has happened. Part of the recovery process is to do an inventory of your fears. Write them down.

Once you have done your inventory, you can choose to establish a new belief system in your mind: all fears are illegitimate. Yes, you can choose to live with confidence.

I helped walk a man named Ralph who worked overtime all the time because he secretly feared that, if he didn't work hard enough and perform beyond expectations, he would be replaced by someone younger. He also didn't have a social life, choosing to be alone on the weekends. He was angry that he didn't have a social life, but it was because he feared rejection. He was shy, so he drank alcohol in the few times he approached women for dates in the past, but he was rejected; he stopped asking women out on dates.

I helped Ralph through a recovery process of doing an inventory of all his fears and then challenging him to admit the lies he had been believing, calling out his fears as illegitimate, and replacing his beliefs with the new belief that he is worthy of love and is secure within himself.

Overcoming Painful Emotions

When someone says to you, "Just get over it," what do you feel? It's not so easy to just get over emotions. Dealing with emotions is a real challenge, especially with people struggling with codependency. Let's gain some perspective on emotions.

Emotions are not facts. They are basically a response to something; they may not even be the real problem. The byproduct of grieving a broken relationship is sadness. You don't want to deny or suppress your emotions because it would lead to other problems. However, as we go through the grieving process and learn to accept reality, you accept it and move on.

Unfortunately, sometimes some people stay in the grieving stage and it becomes paralyzing for them, emotionally. They don't try to move past it. Despair envelopes them, but It doesn't have to.

You are to identify the belief system that drove the emotion. You need to identify the origin.

Caroline was a person who said she felt that she could not live with her husband, who was a drug addict. As her marriage collapsed, she believed a lie – the lie that life is not worth it if her husband and her divorce.

The reality was that her marriage did indeed break down. She experienced a loss. This should not be diminished. But the truth is that she can move on with her life.

Caroline came to realize that her husband was not responsible for how she felt. By "owning" her own emotions, she found the inner strength to deflect the negative messages that her husband (soon-to—be ex-husband) was spewing at her. Her husband called her "ignorant" and "naïve," but she did not need to receive those negative words. She told herself in her inner dialogue (or self-talk) that she is smart and wise.

Another person who battled courageously to overcome her painful emotions, which led her down a path of attempted suicide, was Madison. A sweet young lady, Madison was abused as a child and struggled with severely damaged emotions as a teenager. After falling into drugs and alcohol abuse, she attempted to take her own life multiple times. While her situation is more than just codependency – obviously the drugs and alcohol abuse, as well as suicide attempts – codependency was part of it because she was looking for approval from other people, especially men.

She went through a program that helped her become aware of the root of her emotions and he behavior. She unearthed her belief systems. She accepted what had happened to her in the past, but chose to accept herself, accept the situation and move on with her life.

She struggled with self-hatred and guilt. At the root were shame and a lack of love. She felt like no one could ever love her. She felt, as she put it, "damaged." She covered up her pain with drugs, alcohol and sex. She wanted to numb her emotions. Her codependency accompanied the substance abuse and the sexual addiction, but all of it was rooted back to shame.

For any woman to admit a sex addition publicly is a courageous act. She felt that she needed to be open about it within the safe environment of a support group (as part of a 12-step program) to help her to face it and start to heal. As she healed, her codependent behavior patterns started to change. She started to love herself in a healthy way. She replaced the lies of self-hatred with the truth about her worthiness of love. She said that she felt "so relieved" and "really felt unconditional love."

I want to dig deeper into the role of love itself in the recovery from codependency. When there is true love – starting with healthy love for oneself – it is unconditional love, and it breaks the unhealthy patterns.

Chapter 27
Mirror Neurons and Codependency

B rain science sheds a whole new light on relationships and the role they play in our life. Only within the last 20ish years has science discovered the marvelous reactions of mirror neurons. They are essentially the mind's mirror. Scientists once believed that people used logical thinking processes to figure out how other people behave. However, mirror neurons reveal that we actually predict and interpret other people's behaviors by feelings.

Up until the 1990s, scientist understood that neurons fire off when a person performs a particular action. However, research is now revealing that mirror neurons fire off when a person simply *observes* another person making the same action. This ability allows us to empathize with other human beings. It means that our brain replicates other people's emotions and intentions behind an action without us actually performing that action.

Using the example of smiling, brain scientists observed the same neurons light up in the brain of the person smiling as the person who witnessed the other person smiling. The effects of smiling that the smiling person would feel are also felt by the person not doing the smiling. This powerful information means that we are way more connected than we ever realized…even in ways that we aren't consciously aware of.

So how does this relate to codependency? Codependency typically has a negative spin to it – it is undesirable to be codependent with another person. Our modern North American culture prizes independency. This value is characteristic of individualistic parenting where a parent trains a child to grow up to care for themselves. However, mirror neurons contradict this belief.

Mirror neurons teach us that we are greatly influenced by the people around us, particularly the ones closest to us. Without our awareness, our brains are continuously incorporating the other people's actions, goals and beliefs. What mirror neurons mean for codependency is that our intimate partners are having a profound influence on our brain without us even knowing it. This is insightful information that explains the reasons why people can be more susceptible to codependency.

In actual reality, humans are hard wired to be in relationship. Over thousands of years, human beings have evolved to fit in, not to stand out. We are genetically built to follow along rather than be individual and separated from others. This is contrary to our North American ideals.

Along with mirror neurons comes another component that influences our brain: complex contagion or social contagion. The counterpart of social contagion is simple contagion. Simple contagion occurs when a disease is spread from one person to another, similar to passing a cold to another person. It's logical to think that when we are in contact with a contagious person, we are at higher risk of contracting that same illness.

Social Contagion

Complex or social contagion is different in the sense that we can pass on "social viruses" by simply being in the presence of another individual. Social viruses can include smoking, drinking, drugs, obesity, depression, loneliness, and happiness. However, do not fear about contracting social viruses. The process doesn't happen that easily. Social contagion isn't as simplistic as merely standing next to a person and contracting their social "disease." Social contagion research is more intricate.

In the Annals of Internal Medicine 152 (2010), J. Niels Rosenquist, MD, PhD, et al, conducted a study to discover the likelihood an individual had of drinking heavily based on their degree of separation to their social network. The study showed that a person was 50% more likely to drink heavily if their best friend drank heavily (1 degree). This likelihood was 36% if a friend of a friend drank heavily (2 degrees). Furthermore, a person had a 16% chance of drinking heavily if a friend of a friend of a friend drank heavily (3 degrees). Lastly, there was a 0% chance with the 4th degree of separation. This research demonstrates that social viruses can be passed along within a social network up to 3 degrees of separation. Can you imagine what this means for people who are codependent?

It's no wonder why people wrestle so much with codependency. We are hard wired to be influenced by the feelings and actions of the ones closest to us: our parents, our partners, our close friends, our coworkers. The information about mirror neurons and social contagion almost seems to set us up for failure. But we can use this information to our advantage. We can start to take control of the people we choose to surround ourselves with.

We can purposely choose to be around people who own the very traits and characteristics we desire. You want to be confident? Hang around confident people. Simply being in their presence means that your brain will begin to adopt their tendencies. The same goes for any other quality you desire: success, joy, self control, weight loss, happiness, etc.

Knowing what we know about mirror neurons and social contagion means that we have to be that much more careful hanging around the people who are closest to us. This doesn't translate to you leaving your partner because they are a negative influence. However, it does add a challenging dimension to your recovery from codependency. What it does translate to is the fact that you can be more compassionate towards yourself when you fall into codependent habits. Remember, we are built to fit in, not stand out. We are meant to be more intertwined than our North American culture allows. Perhaps, in the end, a little bit of dependency isn't such a bad thing when it's in balance with a healthy respect for you.

Chapter 28
Ending Co-dependency in A healthy way

One should understand that the change and transformation of unbinding oneself from co-dependency and its negativity does not start until a person begins to do something constructive with the knowledge of their situation.

Every time that we judge or label ourselves as anything, the subconscious takes note of both positivity and negativity arising. Labeling anything enforces and emphasizes all of the effects experienced both desired and undesired.

The following elaborates some of the steps to analyze, dissect and resolve co-dependency in a healthy way inclusive of ending it properly.

Determine if you are Co-dependent:

There is co-existing, and there is co-dependence, while one is a healthy and loving relationship the other is damaging to yourself and your partner. It is important to examine all aspects of your relationship for signs of co-dependency in order to curb any destructive patterns before they become full on dysfunction. The easiest signal to determine co-dependency is by stepping away from the relationship. This means, take a minor break away from the routine, to determine if they are indispensable to you. This helps in understanding what things you are addicted to or dependent upon, inclusive of your partner.

Filter out your honest emotions:

The complete understanding of co-dependency is determined when one understands the roots of their own behavioral issues as well as their inner feelings and emotions. When you become capable of filtering your own emotions, the ability to understand what is good for you and what is not becomes much more fluid. This is applicable to anyone who has become accustomed the same routine over and extended amount of time. It is necessary to filter out what is functional, dysfunctional, healthy and unhealthy for each situation that happens in your life.

Mindfulness:

One of the most complicating and even misunderstood a topic of society is mindfulness. Mindfulness is defined as concentrating on every aspect of an action. Simply put, it is to be aware or conscious of how your actions impact others. Today, mindfulness is debated as one of the most necessary things that a person needs to attain happiness, contentment and satisfaction. It is the basic acceptance and acknowledgement of everything that we do, think or plan. Briefly said, one should start living in the present, comprehending and heeding to one's inner voice, needs, hopes and aspirations overcome failures and hurdles to attain personal success. This helps in determining the right way, towards what is good and what is not.

Connect with your anger:

It is true that your gut feelings can help a person get over certain aspects of pain, discontent, anger and fear. Only when a person connects to their own anger can they successfully understand the toxicity of the situation. When a person is intimately acquainted with their anger the energy to overcome and reclaim the self becomes a reality. In the case of co-dependency, the damage arises due to one person's lack of boundaries physically or mentally. The belief in dysfunctional behavior and relying on that dysfunctional behavior arises from the dissatisfactions one has learned. When this crosses the limit and creates the toxic environment which propagates co-dependence in a relationship anger may be all that keeps you from seeking the tools to acquire a healthy change in your relationship. When one connects to the anger, manages it in a healthy manner as well as recognizing the damage it does to the body and mind, he is successfully armed to repair his self-worth.

End things healthy way:

Ending co-dependency in an unhealthy way might result in a faster separation from the individual who has caused the toxicity to seep into your life however it could very well be ineffectual and cause more damage down the road. The improper handling of co-dependency can result in an individual spending their entire life jumping from one co-dependent relationship to another without ever coming to the point where they are able to fully recover and move on in a healthy and happy way. Hence, it is imperative to take care to resolve all issues and to heal your wounds properly.

The core of ending co-dependent relationships in the best healthy way is to seek out professional assistance for yourself as well as your partner. After you have successfully made yourself aware of your co-dependent situation, how it has impacted yourself and your relationship you have made the first step to resolve the dysfunction of your relationship.

Co-dependency is a term frequently used alongside co-addiction, ending both requires proper knowledge, qualification and experience. Co-dependency can be directed towards a healthy end, when both the partners start to analyze their relationship and hope to recover together. The transformation starts with finding the root of toxicity that has worked its way into your relationship. When a person starts to work out the reason for their anger and discontent, their mind starts to analyze everything, with a priority being self-recovery.

The ultimate motive for healing co-dependency is learning to be a happy healthy member of society. In order to do this, it is important to understand how you have come to be in this position, identify the toxicity and seek to remove it from your life. When tolerance is exceeded and the pain is felt deeply, self-realization will drive the person to improvise and resolve their co-dependent relationships in order to heal themselves.

Hence, putting an end to the co-dependent relationship should be handled with great care and concern. Analyze the situation, dissect the root cause, and seek out the guidance to heal in a healthy way.

Chapter 29
How to End a Codependent Relationship

Recognize the decision is yours

When it comes to ending a relationship perhaps the most important thing to remember is that the decision is yours. You alone have chosen to remain in the relationship, and you alone are now deciding to bring it to an end. While this may seem to add a significant burden of guilt on your shoulders, especially in the case where the other person appears devastated from the decision, it also adds an element of control that is critically important. More often than not the other person in the relationship will fight to maintain the relationship, thereby maintaining control over you. However, by recognizing that the decision to leave is yours you can prevent them from taking the decision away from you. Once you allow the other person to talk you out of your decision you fall back into the codependency that you are striving to escape. Therefore, it is vital that once you make the decision to end a relationship you stick with it no matter what.

Needless to say, such an act should never be taken lightly, therefore it is important to take the time to weigh all factors involved when reaching this final choice carefully. However, once you have made up your mind to end a relationship the important thing is to trust the decision you are making. If you allow yourself to second guess things, especially in light of any arguments that the other person might have, or of any sympathy you might feel toward them, your resolve will begin to waiver, creating doubt, confusion and even guilt in your heart and mind. These are the tools that a codependent person will use to gain control over another person, therefore you need to protect yourself from them at all costs.

Subsequently, once you make the decision to end a relationship you need to trust that you are making the right choice and you need to see the process through to the end.

Have the conversation

Once you have decided to end a relationship the next step is to have the conversation. Some people choose to end relationships through notes or letters, and while that may be easier and less painful for the person ending the relationship it isn't necessarily the better option. For one thing, it suggests that the other person doesn't deserve a face-to-face conversation in which they can speak their piece. After all, a letter is essentially a one-sided conversation, thus it forces one person's opinion on the other. Therefore, in order to be fair, it is best to have a conversation where both sides can have their say.

Choosing the right location for such a conversation is absolutely critical, as this detail alone can significantly affect the nature of the conversation itself. If you have it in a place where the other person feels in control they will try to take over the conversation, thereby changing the course of events in their favor. Alternatively, if you place them in a strange environment where they feel out of control it can cause them to become overly defensive, closing off to you in every way. While this may not be the worst thing, especially in the case of ending a relationship, it can still add pain and suffering that can be avoided. The best option is to choose a place that is familiar to both parties but that doesn't give an advantage to either. A place that is both public yet somewhat private, such as a quiet corner in a park or on a beach, may be the perfect choice. Here you can have a private conversation without feeling intimidated, trapped or on display.

The next thing you will want to do is write down the things you want to say. This is important since the emotional nature of the event will be so strong that it can easily scramble anyone's mind. The last thing you want to do is stumble over the points you want to make, or even worse, forget many of them altogether. Therefore, it is vital that you write down those points so that you can refer to them in the event that your mind begins to cloud over. That said, you don't have to write a speech as such, reading word for word as if you were holding a press conference. Instead, list the topics you want to cover as though you were writing a grocery list. You can even check off each item as you cover it in order to keep track of the progress of the conversation. In addition to ensuring you stay on point with the things you want to discuss, having this list will also eliminate the stress that trying to remember everything can cause. Now, instead of having to memorize your lines for a performance you can have a flexible conversation, one that allows for heartfelt discussion from all sides and that still ensures you get your points across.

Avoid placing blame or guilt

No one ever ends a relationship for good reasons. You wouldn't end a marriage because you were having too much fun, or you felt too loved. Nor would you end a friendship because your friend was too nice to you. Instead, you choose to end relationships with people who bring pain, suffering and misery into your life. As a result, it can be all too tempting to fill the relationship ending conversation with accusations, blame and guilt, thereby attacking the other person as though they are on trial. While this may seem like a good way to bring closure by releasing all of your anger and frustration it can actually backfire, causing you to feel guilty long after the relationship is ended.

Therefore, in order to avoid causing more pain than necessary, both for yourself as well as the other person, it is vital that you avoid placing blame or guilt on the other person in the course of your conversation with them.

A good way to achieve this goal is to avoid from focusing on the past. While it may seem logical to focus on the reasons for ending a relationship, such as the actions and behaviors of the other person that caused you pain and suffering, this will only come across as accusatory in the end. A better approach is to focus on the future. After all, you aren't ending the relationship just to get away from the codependent behaviors that are causing you harm, you are ending the relationship in order to start a fresh, healthy and happy life for yourself. Thus, rather than focusing on the dark past that you are breaking free from you should focus on your future hopes and dreams, those things you are moving toward. This will put a positive spin on the conversation, avoiding the negative aspects of anger, blame and guilt.

You can treat it like you would if you were putting in your notice at work. Anytime you quit a job it's usually because you are unhappy with the job you have. When you put in your notice you can rant and rave about how badly you have been treated, or you can choose to tell your boss that you are ready for new challenges, or that a job you have always wanted has become available. In the end, it is always best to live and let live. Once you end the relationship you will be free from the codependent behaviors and influences that caused you pain, and that is all that counts. Therefore, focus on the positive future rather than the negative past. While the process of ending a relationship will be painful, it doesn't have to be traumatic. By staying as positive as possible you will ensure that the pain and suffering experienced by everyone involved remain as minimal as possible.

Remain calm and compassionate

As already mentioned, ending a relationship is a highly emotional event, therefore it can be all too easy to allow your emotions to get the best of you. This can be especially true in the event that the other person becomes argumentative or overly emotional in any way. While ranting and raving may serve to blow off steam it will usually cause you to feel regret later on. After all, you should never forget that the person you are leaving is someone you once loved. In fact, you may still love them, even though you are choosing to end your relationship with them. Therefore, rather than treating them like an enemy or a monster it is best to treat them with the love and respect that you owe yourself, if not them. Thus, always remain calm and compassionate in your conversation.

Again, this may not be an easy thing to do, especially if the other person reacts in a highly emotional way. And since they are codependent in nature, this is probably a very safe bet. Fortunately, there are a couple of tricks that can help you to keep your calm even in the worst-case scenario. One is to treat the conversation as a done deal. In other words, this isn't a negotiation in which one side or the other will come out the winner. This is a decision that you have already made, therefore you have already won. The outcome is already decided. The future is already written. Therefore, you don't have anything to worry about. You can't be roped back into the relationship, nor can you be forced to do anything you don't want to do. Those days are in the past. In the here and now you are in control of your life, your destiny, and even your emotions. You don't have to get drawn into an argument as there is nothing to prove or gain as a result. Instead, you just have to deliver the message that you are moving on with your life.

Another trick to help you remain calm and compassionate is to recognize that aggressive behavior is usually a sign of pain. Therefore, if the other person flies off on a tangent, ranting and raving about all of the things you have done or how bad you are as a person, rather than arguing back simply recognize that they are crying out in pain. If you react in an emotionally charged way you will only increase that pain and suffering, making you a monster in the process. You aren't a monster, which is why you want to end your codependent relationships. Therefore, act as the decent, loving person you are and be ever-compassionate no matter what. See this act of love and compassion as the first step toward your newfound happy and healthy life.

Be firm

Finally, when it comes to ending a relationship it is absolutely vital that you be firm. Stand by your decision, no matter how much the other person argues, begs or even threatens. You have decided to move on with your life, and nothing should undermine your conviction to do so. Therefore, be strong, be confident, and most importantly, be firm in your decision to end the relationship.

Being firm doesn't mean that you have to be mean or aggressive, it simply means that you have made up your mind and you need to stick to the choice that you have made. If you allow yourself to be dissuaded from your decision you can find yourself sliding down the slippery slope that leads back to codependency. The fact of the matter is that you have reached the conclusion that in order to be healthy, happy and strong you need to be out of this particular relationship.

While staying in it may benefit the other person it won't benefit you, and you need to start putting yourself first in order to create the life you deserve.

Conclusion

B y now, you should have a strong understanding of what codependency is, how it impacts people, how you may be exhibiting signs of it, and what you can do to begin curing your codependency so that you can healthily detach from people in your life and experience higher quality relationships. If you have made it this far, I sincerely want to congratulate you on your commitment to yourself and your willingness to change.

I hope that this book was successful in helping you understand what codependency is and how it has impacted your life until now. Through gaining information from experts and psychologists who are trained in supporting codependent individuals, I hope that you were able to feel confident in the information you received and its ability to support you in healing.

This is no easy feat, and it can take quite a significant amount of time to break codependency behaviors and begin experiencing total freedom from your dependency on others. I know that this time may feel challenging as you focus on overcoming codependency and nurturing your sense of individuality. However, trust that the more you stay devoted to your healing journey, the greater your chances of healing from codependency and moving forward in a healthy manner.

You can heal from this and you deserve to. The relationships that you stand to gain in your life following your healing will nurture you in a way that you cannot possibly comprehend from a codependent perspective. More importantly, you will experience a greater relationship with yourself that will nurture you in ways that you may not even realize are possible at this time.

After you have read this book, it is imperative that you continue on your path of healing so that you can fully recover from your codependent experience. Regardless of what stage you are in, whether you are seeking to avoid entering a future codependent relationship, fix your current codependent relationship, or heal from a recent codependent relationship, I hope that you found access to supportive insights in this book. As long as you continue following these steps and implementing them in your life, you can feel confident that you are going to experience freedom from codependency in your future.

In addition to following the steps outlined in this book, it is a good idea to continue educating yourself on codependency and how it may be impacting you in your life. By keeping this book available for future reference, you can easily look back and pay attention to the next relevant stages in your life. The more you educate yourself on this pattern of codependency and understand where it comes from and why, the easier it will be for you to build your self-awareness around these tendencies and prevent them in the future. This also means that you can not only heal from codependency itself but also whatever experience may have led to you being codependent in the first place, such as a childhood trauma or an abusive past relationship.

As a next step, you may find it important that you consider working with a trained therapist when it comes to overcoming codependency or the past experiences that led you to it. Having the support of someone who is educated on the impact of codependency and who can help you understand yourself and support you in healing can be extremely helpful. The right therapist can support you in growing more aware of who you are and what your needs are, in feeling confident in yourself and your abilities, and increasing your sense of self-worth and self-esteem.

I wish you all the best in curing your codependency, so that you can go on to experience a healthy, happy life filled with high-quality relationships, starting with the relationship with yourself.

PART II

Introduction

G as lighting is a form of mental abuse, and it is commonly used by narcissists. The term itself was pegged in 1938 because of a play. The play portrays a man attempting to make his wife insane by messing with the lights inside of their home. The wife in this play tries to point it out to her husband, and he completely denies that the lighting within the household is changing at all. She starts to question herself, and he gains control. He is gas lighting her, and this is a brilliant example.

Many people deal with narcissists daily; however, it is surprising how many don't understand what gas lighting is. Gas lighting is one of the narcissist's favorite tactics to get complete control and power within their relationship. It abuses their partner and makes them second guess every thought and idea that crosses their minds.

Sometimes you are dealing with a narcissist, and you have no choice about it.

For instance, if they are a parent or family member, it is likely you can't rid yourself of the burden that is them. Narcissism can also be experienced in romantic relationships, as well as ones of a friendlier nature. Realistically, any relationship in your life could involve a narcissist, and each one is going to be a challenge to deal with. It is not only hard to deal with. It is frequently hard to recognize.

Narcissists have huge egos, and they only know how to love themselves. They will go to great lengths to have people perceive them in a certain way. They often tell stories of grandeur and think that there is no one better than them. Most narcissists are charismatic and can draw the attention of a crowd very easily. This can make it easy to fall for them and for them to gain control of you and your life. Recognizing a narcissist early on is the best defense against them.

If your partner ever repeatedly tells you that you are making things up or that you are remembering something incorrectly, they are likely trying to gaslight you. This happens slowly over the relationship until the victim can't understand reality as it is. If you are being affected by gas lighting, it is common to find yourself questioning reality, your relationship, or possibly your level of sanity. These are all signs of gas lighting.

This tactic is not only a form of mental abuse, but it is also a form of emotional abuse. When a person suffers from emotional abuse, it will take a toll on every aspect of their life. They will likely have very low self-esteem. It is also common for those who suffer from emotional abuse to have problems with anxiety and depression. They often feel a sense of helplessness. In a gas lighting situation, they will become dependent on their narcissistic partner in every way. They start to accept the abuse as something normal and acceptable.

As noted, emotional abuse causes a lot of damage throughout their entire life. They will likely question or not understand their feelings. Additionally, likely, they will not trust their instincts, and they may even question their sanity. When these types of behaviors become an everyday occurrence, it puts all of the power and control into the hands of the narcissist. Once someone is no longer able to trust their thoughts and ideas, it is much more likely that they will stay in an abusive relationship regardless of how terrible it is for them and their wellbeing.

The victim of gas lighting will suffer, but so will the people that care about them.

Victims of this type of manipulation withdraw from the people they love, and that love them. They no longer trust what their most trusted assets have to say or what they think. Frequently, their relationships with anyone other than the narcissist will dissolve completely. This is painful and harms everyone that cares about the victim. Trying to make the victim understand that what is happening is not right is almost impossible. This is especially true in terms of narcissistic relationships that have been going on for some time.

Besides, gas lighting is exceptionally effective in keeping a person under the narcissist's thumb. Mental and emotional abuse are ways for the narcissist to gain power within the relationship. They will gain control by any means necessary, even at the expense of their partner's happiness and wellbeing. Gas lighting is only one of the many forms of manipulation that the narcissist will use to maintain the life that they find suitable.

The effects of gas lighting do not happen overnight. It takes quite a bit of time and is typically quite gradual. In the beginning, their tactic may just look like simple misunderstandings. However, with time, the abusive behavior will become continuous.

People on the outside of the relationship may be able to see the pattern of it, but it is unlikely that the partner being affected by it will be able to see this perception.

There are several reasons that the abused party will not be able to understand it when their friends, families, or loved ones try to tell them what is actually happening. Most narcissists will do their best to isolate their partner, which can lead to breakdowns of important relationships in the inability to hear what the people that truly care about them have to say. Victims of this type of use can also become extremely anxious or confused. This can make talking to them extremely difficult.

Depression is another element that comes along with gas lighting. People tend to disassociate with what is actually going on around them. Additionally, they may experience a lack of trust with people that care about them the most.

One of the saddest things about being in a relationship with a narcissist that uses gas lighting tactics is that eventually, the partner that is being abused will feel as if they absolutely need the narcissist to survive. Due to the fact that they cannot define true reality, they feel that they need their narcissistic partner to define it for them.

This makes the situation insanely difficult to get out of. It takes a lot of time and effort to help somebody open their eyes and realize that the person they love the most is actually abusing them and taking advantage of them.

Gas lighting not only manipulates people, it, realistically, is also a form of brainwashing. It lays seeds of doubt in the victim in every area. They won't be able to perceive the world as an individual, they may lose their identity completely, and it is likely that they feel very little self-worth. The thoughts, statements, and accusations of the gas lighter are consistently falsifications that are deliberate.

Their intention is thought out to make the person they are dealing with feel crazy, and thus, the narcissistic gas lighter holds all of the power and control within the confines of the relationship.

It does not matter how intelligent you are when it comes to gas lighting. If you do not see the signs and take action quickly, it is very likely that you will succumb to the wishes of the narcissist in your life. This is due to the fact that it can be hard to recognize. There are misunderstandings in every relationship due to poor communication or simple human errors of memory, so it can be easy to brush off the signs of gas lighting, especially in the beginning.

There are a variety of different signs that you are dealing with a narcissist that is using gas lighting tactics.

For now, simply know that if you notice constant miscommunications where you are the one in the wrong, it is possible that you are dealing with someone that actually means you mental and emotional harm. You must remember that this form of manipulation is a slow process. When you are aware of the experiences you face, by being present in the moment, it can offer you the protection you need to not proceed in a relationship with someone who utilizes gas lighting.

The narcissist loves the tactic of gas lighting because it is so hard to perceive. Tools like accusations, denial, lying, and misdirection are all used to throw the person they are focused on off the trail of truth. It often leaves them feeling as if the issues they bring forth are simply part of their imagination. Additionally, they end up feeling like everything is their fault because of the things that the narcissist says and does. Gas lighting truly can make a person feel insane.

SECTION I

Chapter 1
How The Human Mind Control Works

Before you do anything, you need to know you are in control of yourself. You need to know that you won't be emotionally affected by anything the subject does.

You might be surprised at how hard this is to do. Once you actually get ready for your first attempt at getting into someone's mind, there is a good chance you will run into a wall. This wall is the way the subject is affecting you emotionally, verbally, behaviorally, and more.

If the subject is having an impact on you, you won't be able to get into their minds. They are the ones getting into your mind if this happens. The reason for this is now understood by scientists who study the brain or neuroscientists.

It comes down to a special kind of neuron in our brains called mirror neurons. Mirror neurons were found on accident while neuroscientists were studying chimps. Despite how many implications mirror neurons have, the way they work is actually quite simple.

The neuroscientists were scanning the brains of two different chimps. The first chimp was holding a banana when this special neuron (the mirror neuron) started to fire in their brain.

The fascinating part is how the other chimp fits into the picture. The other chimp wasn't holding a banana themselves: they simply watched the other chimp holding the banana—yet despite this, the exact same special neuron fired.

This led the neuroscientists to accidentally find mirror neurons. Mirror neurons are now understood as the neurons that help our brains envision actions, whether they are actions we are actually doing or just actions we are imagining. What makes mirror neurons so incredible is that we don't have to actually do anything in order to get the same response from our mirror neurons. They will fire either way.

You can apply this to a countless number of things: when we read a story, and the character eats chips, our mirror neurons go off as though we are reading chips. Mirror neurons are the way our brains understand the meanings of things. Scientists postulate we adapted to have mirror neurons so we can prepare for the future. We might not be doing an action right now, but when we observe an action, our brains prepare for potentially doing it in the future. This is the purpose of mirror neurons.

Now, you have probably figured out how this applies to mind control and manipulation already—because when you watch the subject be emotional, it can tend to affect you as well. It feels like a social force that makes us want to get emotional along with them. While social factors certainly play into it, because of neuroscience, we now know the science happening in the brain that leads to this.

Not only do we feel pressured socially to express emotion in response to the people in our lives, but our mirror neurons are firing in response to the person's behavior. Our mirror neurons are firing just like theirs are, even though they are the ones doing the behavior, and you are just witnessing it.

That's what makes it so hard to control ourselves in the way that is necessary to become skilled in mind reading, mind control, and manipulation. There is a biological and neuroscientific mechanism that leads us to be influenced by them.

Mind Control Tactics to Be Aware Of

• Peer pressure and social proof. Those people who try to influence a large crowd of people will often use peer pressure and social proof to brainwash their targets. Social proof is a psychological aspect where others assume that the beliefs and actions of other people are right, and because every person does that, then it must be justified. This technique works specifically well when the person is not very sure what to think, what to do, or how to behave. Many people will look at what other people do and copy what they are doing.

• Repetition. Constant repetition is also a persuasion tool. Though this seems useful and straightforward, repeating a similar message over and over again makes it easier and familiar to recall. If repetition is used together with social proof, it can deliver the message with no failure.

• Fear of alienation. People who are new to manipulation will often receive a warm welcome and create new friendships that seem too deep and very meaningful than anything they've ever experienced.

• Isolation. When it comes to physical separation, it can be compelling, but when it is not possible or impractical, manipulators will often try to isolate you mentally, thus limiting any other influence by regulating flow, which is the ultimate goal.

• Criticism. It may be applied as an isolation technique. Manipulators will often speak in "us against them" terms; they will criticize the outside world and claim their superiority.

• Fatigue. Sleep deprivation and fatigue result in mental tiredness and physical tiredness. If you are physically exhausted and less alert, you will be very susceptible to persuasion.

• You are forming a new identity. The main goal of a manipulator is to redefine your personality. Manipulators want you to stop being yourself and become someone who is mindless and follows orders, like a robot. Using all techniques and mind control tactics listed above, they will try to extract a confession from you—some form of acknowledgment that you believe that they're friendly people doing good deeds.

Once you have accepted one little thing, you may be ready to agree to another one and another. Before you realize it, out of the desire to be consistent with what you say and do, you begin to identify yourself as one of the members of the group. It is individually powerful if you know that the confessions are being filmed or recorded for reference in a situation where you forget.

Overcoming Mind Control

• Acknowledge your multiplicity. Mind control is all about splitting the mind infancy.

• The internal parts of the manipulator placed in control of the personality system require to work together toward healing, along with the self-created durable parts. If the person is strong enough, he/she may also be involved.

• All programming is based on a big lie. Allow the entire system to know that the big lie is a lie. The manipulator only knows what you say, do, or think if you tell the manipulator. Though manipulators do kill or torture, most of the threats are lies.

• Ensure that you choose a safe therapist if you can afford one.

• You may choose to either work through everything or achieve stability. What you choose will depend on your health and age and present-day responsibilities. 'Closed down' and 'stable' are not the same as healed; people who are closed down have hidden hurt nursing inside. Know that full healing takes time and works best with a skilled therapist.

• Co-consciousness and integration come naturally as an outcome of memory work; do not focus on them.

• Once you feel that you are safe, you can start the memory work, which thoroughly undoes the programming. There's no shortcut in undoing programming.

• When you decide to work through the memories, keep records of what you do, and ensure that you include every inside part which has a single piece of each memory you work through. Memory piece consists of drugs, emotions, and pain, not just storytelling. Programming itself is often in spoken words.

Chapter 2
The Cognitive Faculties of the Brain

Consciousness is perhaps the most challenging area of the human mind to understand. It enables us to be aware of, process, and understand both internal and external stimuli.

Our conscious mind identifies wakefulness. It is always in a state of "current awareness" and challenges us to think and respond to stimuli such as sensations, memories, feelings as well as fantasies, and all that we perceive through our senses.

For example, if you inadvertently touch a hot object, your brain registers pain and your mind immediately reciprocate by cataloging the sensation and how you responded to it. The memory is cataloged and stored for future reference, and you will remain wary of hot objects for the rest of your life.

Imagination

Our imagination is that part of our mind linked to our memory and that reproduces mental images either from past experiences or manufactures new ones through the use of your personal creative imaging skills.

Being afraid of the dark when you were young may have become a serious cause for fear. Your imagination may have run wild and led you to believe the worst possible scary "creatures" lay in wait to ambush you as soon as the lights went out.

Our imagination has the power to create fear and anxiety as well as pleasure and excitement from simple scenarios that it either fabricates from the evidence we already have stored in our mind or to recreate new scenarios.

Perception

Perception is the ability you have to identify, interpret, and organize the information received through your senses. Our sensory channels are the gateways via which information such as sound, visual images, smells, taste, and touch experiences enter our mind, bringing valuable learning opportunities about the environment around us.

For example, you are able to discern a variety of sounds around you and identify these and learn their specific purpose, as in the school bell from the church bell, your cell phone ring from the ringing of the doorbell.

Thinking

Thought processes are still an enigma to scientists as these are challenging to monitor and are highly personal and individualistic in nature.

Thinking involves our ability to allow our minds to consider many different possibilities on any number of subjects and scenarios. It gives us the opportunity to seek potential answers to specific questions and to resolve problems on a mental level.

For example, when faced with the dilemma of having to choose a suitable gift for your significant other, you will weigh up the available options against his or her likes, personality, interests, and the usefulness of the gift.

Judgment

Your judgment skills assist you in weighing up evidence and being able to reach a conclusion to make a decision that will impact positively on your safety, security, a long-term investment, or a special relationship.

For example, if you decide to invest in a well-known, successful company listed on the stock market, you may have made a sound judgment call with regard to earning a good return on your investment.

Language

Language is the complex system used for communication and is made up of verbal and non-verbal symbols and clues that we use to convey our ideas and thoughts in a constructive, organized manner, either verbally or in writing.

For example, when you want to demonstrate displeasure, your non-verbal communication clue might take the form of a scowl or a frown, while your verbal dissatisfaction will be encoded in words.

Memory

Your memory is that area in your brain that encodes and stores information in order for you to retrieve this when needed.

For example, as a child, you may have learned about road safety. Later in life, your automatic retrieval of that information will remind you of the rules of the road when you, for example, drive for the first time.

The human psychology behind decision-making is one that is often rooted in an emotional foundation as well as one based on assumption, rather than a logical one. Although we have infinite supplies of information and research available to us at any given minute, most humans are not interested in researching this information and coming up with a rational answer that reflects their research. In fact, in many cases, even when an individual has conducted research on a specific topic, they will still choose in favor of what they prefer emotionally or based on our assumptions versus what they prefer rationally. The reason behind this is interesting, and we are going to explore it deeper, now.

Emotional Choosing

One of the biggest reasons people make decisions rooted in emotion versus in rational logic and reasoning is because we are very emotional driven people. Yes, it truly is that simple. Often, our decisions are made based off of experiences we have had in the past, and whether we associate them with a positive emotion or a negative one. This type of choice is typically based on the fact that, as humans and creatures of both comfort and survival, we do not want to choose decisions that have previously put us in danger or made us feel unhappy on some level. By avoiding these types of decisions once more, we avoid having an unhappy or negative experience again in the future. For example, say you once went to a specific park and while there someone broke into your car. Even though that park is a generally safe place and the number of break-ins that have actually happened there may be much lower than other parks, the fact that you had a bad experience there would leave you likely hesitant or unwilling to return. Here, you would be choosing based on emotions drawn from past experiences versus logic based on evidence that the likelihood of it happening in the first place was low. Therefore, the likelihood of it happening again is almost impossible.

Assumptive Choosing

The other way that humans tend to choose is through assumption. Assumptions allow us to make decisions quickly, without relying on the act of doing research. Because we are faced with many decisions on a daily basis, we often feel as though the idea of research would simply be too much. Instead, we prefer to make decisions quickly based off of assumptions from past experiences and knowledge we have carried from what we have heard from others. Assumptions are often made based on perceptions, which is why big brand names have such an effortless time selling things. Since they are perceived to be higher quality and to have better selections that are generally preferred, a person would quickly choose brand name over anything else. This is also why you get many knock-off brands with names that are very close to brand names that already exist and are already popular. They are essentially tricking the human mind into believing they are high quality because they sound like a high-quality brand.

Influencing Behaviors

The greatest part about humans being driven by emotions and assumptions when it comes to how they make decisions is that it makes it extremely easy to influence people to do anything you want them to do based off of these two basic decision-making practices. If you can influence their emotional state to create a positive association with whatever it is that you want them to do and create the assumption that this choice would be the best one to make, you ultimately make it significantly easier for them to choose in your favor. For example, if you wanted to create a company that was going to be extremely successful in a short period of time, using a name that sounded similar to an already-successful companies name and designing it to have a similar luxurious or otherwise high-quality feel to it would result in you rapidly rising to success. This model would generate the assumption that you were high quality or high class early on, and the "feel" would inspire emotions that help the person feel positive when shopping with you, therefore creating the perfect situation for them to choose your company over many others. The same goes for virtually any decision you want someone to make in your favor: if you make yours sound good and feel good, the person will be more likely to choose in your favor.

Chapter 3
What Is Emotional Manipulation

E motional manipulation is the ability to monitor our and other people's feelings, differentiating between various emotions, naming feelings and leveraging this invaluable emotion-based information for directing our actions, thoughts, behavior patterns and decisions. This illustrates emotional manipulation using broader or more general terms, though there is a lot of debate within the socio-psycho scientific community about emotional manipulation exactly is, and what it includes. One component of emotional manipulation that everyone agrees with is that it is an ability to recognize, understanding and to manage our and other people's feelings.

The psychology of attachment mentions that our present emotional experiences can be tracked to our early encounters with emotions. It can be overpowering emotions or feelings we experienced in our childhood or adolescent years that left a profound impact on us. Our present-day ability to deal with a variety of feelings such as unhappiness, joy, fear, anger, nervousness and more in closely linked to the nature of our early emotional experiences. If your emotions were identified, acknowledged and valued in during the early stages of psychological growth and development, they can become value assets. Likewise, if the experiences were more negative and painful, you may be conditioned to detach yourself from these feelings and emotions.

Emotional manipulation facilitates our connection with our emotions and helps us identify changing feelings whenever they occur. This is critical to regulating our thoughts, emotions, and actions.

Identifying and understanding our emotions is the key to controlling them. When we can predict how you are likely to feel in a particular situation, doesn't it become easier to manage your reaction beforehand? This allows us to think logically about a feeling before responding or reacting it impulsively or involuntarily. We are no longer servants of our impulses and have higher control over our actions owing to greater awareness of our feelings and emotions. This prevents us from taking irrational, regretful and destructive steps that we can harm our relationships in hindsight.

We also master the art of placing ourselves in other people's shoes by developing more empathy. This can be a huge asset in our personal and professional life. For example, if a worker is not putting his best effort, an emotionally manipulative manager will not simply assume the worker is being lazy or is not interested in working.

They will attempt to reach out to the individual and understand his/her reasons for not performing to the best of his/her abilities. The person may be afraid of making mistakes, or her/she may be low on confidence about his/her abilities. Resolving people related issues becomes easier when you can place yourself in someone else's shoes and think and feel things from their point of view.

The concept of emotional manipulation can be more complex than it appears because naming emotions and feelings is no mean feat. Emotions registered in the subconscious and unconscious are often nameless, marked by an inability to comprehend their experience or understand them. There are far more emotions than words created in any language to express them. Also, emotions are often entwined into one another or overpowered by another mental state. For instance, fear may be an overpowering desire to escape and can be fully experienced only in retrospect. Another aspect is that certain emotions are too painful to dwell upon, creating more complex emotions.

Emotional manipulation can be tricky because all emotions do not possess a convenient uniformity. Though our emotions are largely reflective of our values and refinement of those values, we can also feel emotions about an existing emotion. Sounds complicated? Ever felt guilty or shameful about envying someone? Yes, that is an emotion about feeling an emotion. While some emotions are transparent, others are hazier and more equivocal. For example, our love for higher virtues such as truth is experienced as intensely profound, while our resentment for an individual of accomplishments higher than ours leaves us feeling uncomfortable.

So, what it is about emotional manipulation that makes it the single largest predictive index for success at work? Goldman pointed out that emotional manipulation includes 67% of all abilities required for higher performance among leaders. It matters more than (twice as much to be precise) technical expertise or the conventional IQ. Other research points to the fact that general intelligence and ability is closely associated with leadership. As emotional manipulation is becoming more and more coveted by personality and behavior analysts, new markers of emotional manipulation and techniques of developing EQ are rapidly gaining popularity.

There are various emotional manipulation models such as the specific ability model that has noted ways through which emotions can facilitate better thoughts, behavior, and understanding. For instance, an individual who is more emotionally reactive to important issues will focus on those specific crucial facets of his life. Emotional facilitation factors also include knowing when to encompass or remove emotions from one's thought according to the context and circumstances. The model correlates to heightened emotional reasoning, and responsive understanding of people, situations and the environment in everyday life.

Emotional manipulation filled a significant gap in a rather strange finding which concluded that individuals possessing average IQ outperformed those with high IQ in about 70% of all instances. This created a huge wrench into the existing belief people held of intelligence quotient being the single largest measure of a person's success. In 1995, research began to quickly identify emotional manipulation as a critical component for setting superstar performers apart from the average Joe pack.

Emotional manipulation consists of both, personal and social competence. It affects our ability to manage behavior, negotiate social complexities and exercise personal decisions which help us achieve greater positive results.

Personal competence consists of self-management and self-awareness that emphasizes more on your ability to interact with others. It is a person's competency in staying aware of their own emotions and managing their behavior and behavioral tendencies for optimal results. Self-awareness is one's ability to correctly perceive your own emotions and gain a better awareness of them when they happen, while self-management is the ability to use this awareness to manage your behavior for more positive results.

Social competence comprises of greater social awareness and social relationship management skills. An individual can gain an intuitive understanding of other's moods, motives, and behavior for forging better relationships. Social awareness, under social competence, is all about correctly identifying emotions in others and trying to perceive what is happening inside them. Relationship management, on the other hand, is the ability to utilize self-emotional awareness and understanding of other's emotions to manage social interactions successfully.

We can utilize our emotions to increase self-control and safeguard ourselves emotionally. It can also often be misused to gain complete control over others by manipulating their emotions to create feelings of fear, despair, and self-control. Psychologists and behavior experts who emphasize the importance of emotional skills to enhance people's lives do not sometimes take into consideration the ethical dimensions of having access to an individual's emotional make-up.

Emotional manipulation has a large impact on several sectors, including the corporate world. Several firms use emotional manipulation assessments as part of their recruitment process. Studies have consistently pointed to the fact that people with evolved leadership skills tend to display higher emotional manipulation, revealing that well developed EQ is a crucial characteristic for business leaders, supervisors leading big teams into performance and future managers.

Politicians and advertisers harness the power of emotional quotient brilliantly to influence masses to make purchases or vote in their favor. Advertising agencies quite successfully manipulate emotions such as fear and aspirations to accomplish their client's objectives by using information about their target audience's emotions and how these emotions function for influencing voting or buyer behavior.

Emotional manipulation is distinct from one's intellect in the sense that it taps into the fundamental elements of human behavioral patterns. Also, there is no established connection between intelligence quotient and emotional quotient. You cannot predict an individual's EQ based on their smartness. Also, your IQ will be the same at age 15 as it will be at age 60. Emotional manipulation, on that hand, will most likely evolve other the years according to practice and experiences. It is a more flexible set.

Types of Manipulators That We Find In Our Daily Lives

There is nothing to be false, we all want to achieve ours and satisfy our own needs and desires, but there are people who are most shamelessly able to manipulate others to achieve what they want. Very often these manipulations are hidden behind smiles and are masked as nice and friendly gestures. But if you learn to recognize the basic methods of manipulators, you will never fall into their trap.

Today I present to you types of manipulators and manipulations, which we come across quite often and which we must guard against.

1. The helpless

Such people pretend to be helpless to pass on their responsibilities to other people. Mostly women are the ones who resort to this manipulation. They make themselves weak and helpless and while the rest of them do their jobs, they happily climb the career ladder.

2. Those who are tickling

Everyone happens to misinterpret someone's words or actions, but these types of manipulators say things in such a way that you can't later hold them accountable for their actions. Then, when they see your reaction, they turn things around, so you are guilty. They also claim they never promised anything, you just didn't understand it.

3. Unfulfilled Promises

How often do you make fulfilling live promises? Maybe the problem is not in you. The manipulators force you to respond immediately and use your guilt to make you accept their wishes. It is also very difficult to deny a friend who asks you for a favor. The next time someone asks for your help, do not rush to promise but think about whether you can help.

4. Parents manipulators

Sometimes it's hard to accept the truth that our parents manipulate us, but it's a fact - they often try to impose their opinions and understandings on us, try to control our actions, and interfere with our lives. That is why it is important to stand up for yourself and not allow your parents to dictate your life, yet it is your life and your parents want nothing more than to be happy.

5. The parents of your half

Not only your parents are trying to interfere in your life, but your parents are half your life. The mother-in-law often teaches the daughter-in-law or speaks against her son, thus creating tension that has destroyed more than one marriage. The mother-in-law also doesn't have a very good reputation ... In order to protect yourself from such manipulations, you must clearly state that your family consists of you, as spouses, and your children, you do not need the others to be confused in your affairs. Be kind but firm.

6. The eternal innocent

Unfortunately, many people cannot take responsibility for their actions and try to blame others. You will notice this behavior, especially from the immature men who make their half guilty of everything, and she feels crushed for what has happened and tries to make up for it. This vicious circle is typical of toxic bonds. If this happens to you, do not be afraid to point out the real reasons for the situation and stand up for yourself. If you continuously take the blame, you will be manipulated even more.

7. The price of forgiveness

Disputes and quarrels arise in every connection. Unfortunately, sometimes disputes go out of control and then it's hard to regain confidence in the other. Therefore, many manipulators try to buy forgiveness from their half. Such gifts are not kind gestures of love, but ordinary bribery. If the transgression is really great (for example, cheating or grievous grievances), do not accept the gift and stand up for yourself.

Neuro Linguistic Programming (NPL)

NLP refers to neuro-linguistic programming, and it is a simple concept that allows a person to control their mind, and those of others, while influencing thoughts and behaviors to gain more out of life.

NLP stands for neuro linguistic programming. It is a concept that has existed for quite some time now and has gained prominence in the last decade or so, owing to a large number of people taking it up, and using it to their benefit.

The main aim of NLP is to help a person exploit their complete brainpower. It is to push them to the brink of excellence and do things that they were not aware of being capable.

Richard Brandler and John Grinder first described NLP in 1970. The former was a self-help author and the latter, a linguistic expert and together, they worked on previous concepts that were laid by experts in the field of neurology and linguistics.

They laid heavy emphasis on human beings using both sides of their brains and also uniting the conscious and the subconscious minds. As you know, all of us have an active mind that is consciously awake and helping us think and an unconscious or subconscious mind that is dormant.

From then on, the concept grew in leaps and bounds. More and more linguists and neurologists started researching it and presented their individual views. Although much progress has been made, NLP is not yet recognized as a bona fide scientific concept. A lot more work needs to be done on it for the scientific community to accept it with open arms. However, for those that have used NLP, the results are apparent and there are several testimonials available on the Internet that speaks of the concept's actual uses.

Despite being dormant, it will constantly be thinking things and storing them for the long haul. If a person successfully taps into this mindset then he can make the most of his brainpower.

One quality of NLP is that, it helps in drawing from a person's existing thinking and teaches the person to make the most of it. All human beings will have a lot of mental potential that they will not be able to tap into fully. But with the use of NLP, not only will it be easy to tap into the subconscious mindset but also think out of the box.

It is a theory that teaches you to cut down on the wrongs that exist in your life and promote the rights. This will ensure that you do right by yourself and have the chance to focus on things that are important.

You can think of NLP as a framework that is provided to you to base your mind power's principles upon. It will assist in helping you think clearer and in a better way.

Now it is standard for people to assume that NLP will only find its application in the work field given its description of helping people increase their brainpower. But that is not true. NLP is applicable in all walks of life encompassing personal and social as well. You can make use of NLP to increase your communication skills, attain more professionally etc. All of this will allow you to do more in life and attain your goals.

But the primary focus of NLP will be to help you sharpen your mind and make full use of your brain. So right from polishing your memory to easily recalling something, NLP will help you do a plethora of things with equal ease. In fact, NLP is a tool that many psychologists use to get over certain mental conditions such as anxiety and Dementia.

The uses of NLP are hard to measure as research has shown how it can go beyond mental impact and also has several physical benefits as well. It's seen that NLP helps certain people combat physical ailments as well as they will have a great control over their mind. They can literally ask their bodies to heal faster as the body responds to the mind's calls.

How does NPL works

NLP is designed to suit everybody. Anybody interested in increasing their mind's capacity and willing to put in the effort is welcome to take up NLP. It is a person's personal choice to do so and once they make up their mind, they will not regret their decision. There is no age restriction as such and anybody above the age of 15 can take it up. School children will find it useful, as it will help them in their studies. It is also for old people who are trying to fend off illnesses such as Alzheimer's and Dementia.

Working professionals can take it up to do more in their work field. They can use NLP to work faster, be more productive and be done with work early. All of this will go a long way in helping them realize their life's goals.

Apart from these, there are many other uses of NLP, which you will only realize once you take it up. For you to take up NLP there are two choices. One if to undergo training at a professional course and the other is to practice the concepts of NLP by yourself.

Both can be equally useful and it is up to you to choose either. For the former, the place might charge you a certain amount for their services and the latter will mostly be free of cost. But the firmer might teach you things that will help you understand the concept better and faster as compared to the latter.

Once you learn the concept of NLP and successfully implement it in your life, you will not want to go back and will constantly and consistently use it to your advantage.

In fact, you can also have a relative; a friend or a colleague join in and the two of you can reap joint benefits of taking up NLP.

1. NLP Concepts

For any subject, its concepts are what make it unique. NLP too, has its own set of concepts that you need to learn in order to successfully implement in your life. Let us look at them here.

NLP, as we know, stands for neuro linguistic programming. So, let us look at these concepts separately.

2. Neuro

The first concept that we will look at is known as Neuro. Neuro stands for anything related to the brain. A concept known as neurology is pertinent with neuro. Neurology refers to making use of your senses to pick up data from your surroundings. This is done through sight, sound, taste, smell and tough. So, by looking at something, you understand what it is, by hearing something, you know what made that sound, by touching and feeling, you know exactly what you are touching and by smelling you know what is emitting the odor. All of these are basic human reactions and occur naturally to everyone.

Through the years, you would have experienced just so much that your mind would go into an auto pilot mode. You will look at a parrot and know that it is a parrot. You will hear the sound of a train and know that it is a train. All these are supplied by your conscious mind and you don't really have to put in too much thought into it.

However, this will not extend to everything that you do and you will put in extra making an effort to think things through. This will waste your time and you will not be able to do more in less time. So, if you come in conduct with a new situation that you haven't seen before then you will spend a lot of time trying to understand and analyze it. This is a waste of your time and effort.

But there is a solution to this problem. As you know, the human brain is made of two components namely the conscious and the subconscious. If you learn to tap into the latter, then your problem of thinking automatically can be remedied.

Once you learn NLP, your mind will learn to associate. This means that you will start associating a previously seen situation with the current situation and know what to do next. This will not take up any of your time and you can quickly move from one task to the next.

3. Linguistics

Linguistics refers to language. It deals with the language that you use to communicate with others. All human beings need to communicate with each other and also with ourselves. We need to speak with our inner selves to connect better.

While communicating with others, we need to be as clear as possible. The other person must understand whatever we are trying to convey to them and there should be no scope for discrepancies.

We are generally used to speaking with others in a way that we have developed and used for years. We don't really think it through. So, it is important that people think before speaking, to drive the point across better.

Apart from speaking with others, you must also learn to communicate with yourself internally. Your mind should give your body instructions and there should be a clear line of communication.

NLP will help you go about that process. It will teach you to communicate in an easy way.

4. Programming

Programming refers to batching up information. Everybody knows how the human mind is capable of organizing information in their brains. It's a habit that people develop right from a young age.

This information can be emotions, feelings, thoughts, analysis etc. All of it is batched into groups and stored in the mind like storing files in a cabinet.

Although it will be extremely efficient during the early years, as time passes, the brain will not work as fast. It will take some time for the person's brain to organize the data efficiently. This time tends to increase with age and will start deteriorating.

But this issue can be remedied by making use of NLP. The programming aspect of your brain can be increased, and you will be able to have everything sorted and organized in no time.

Not just that, you will also be able to recall the information with ease and use it to your capacity.

These form the different concepts of NLP. It is important that you understand all this carefully as it will aid you in your process.

5. Important Steps Of NLP

NLP has three important steps that you must understand if you wish to implement it in your life. In this segment we will look at those steps.

Step 1 End result

One of the main steps of taking up NLP is setting yourself a goal. This goal should be whatever that you wish to have achieved at the end of the journey.

Whatever that you choose to have as your result, it is important that it remains gettable and feasible. This means that you choose something that will satisfy you.

Say for example you are a salesman. Your end goal is to be the best and sell a lot of the products. For this, you have to make use of NLP to communicate better, learn more and also program information faster.

But don't limit yourself to just a simple goal, keep it as diverse as possible.

If you go about it having such a plan, then you will be able to achieve your goals faster.

Step 2 Change

The next important aspect of NLP is to make positive changes. This means that the person changes the way they think, perceive and other such things.

NLP helps a person to spring into action. It aids in a person acting instead of simply thinking of it.

This action-oriented approach is what makes this technique extremely easy to adopt and exploit.

Chapter 4
Principal Components and Core Concepts of NLP

The core concept of NLP

According to Bandler, one of the developers of this technique, NLP is a model of communication at the interpersonal level, and it brings out the relationship between patterns of behavior and experiences that are subjective, especially to the mode of thought. In NLP, the higher the level, the more your state of mind or body (neurology) is involved.

NLP is made up of several concepts and techniques that ensure you improve your life. Some of the ideas are related to one another in one way or another. Some of the concepts in NLP are deliberated below.

A. Anchors and neuro-linguistic programming

An anchor is a situation where two events are related such that when one of the events happens in the next event, the mind automatically recalls and connects the two events.

How to develop an anchor
The anchor is developed when you do the two events at the same time on a regular basis for somehow an extended period. This can be clearer by use of an example; for instance, when you are used to watching television while eating, after some time, you will realize every time you watch your TV set, you feel hungry.

People who are overly sensitive develop an anchor much faster than any other people. For example, when two field engineers are working in a mining company, the one who is overly sensitive may quit the job, as the overwhelming work experience may be anchored to this engineer's mind, while the other engineer, who is not that sensitive to external conditions, may find the work tolerable.

The anchor can be used in shunning off bad habits. For example, when you are a smoker and you want to quit, you can develop an anchor that brings bad feelings whenever you smoke.

How to remove an anchor

Some anchors can lead to bad habits, and you might want to get rid of them. The question arises, how?

As a human being, when you do two events at the same time repeatedly, they become connected and become embedded in your subconscious mind. When you want to get rid of a particular anchor, all you have to do is stop doing one of the events for some time. Your mind will separate both events, and the anchor will be removed.

B. Rapport building and neuro-linguistic programming

This is one of the NPL techniques that make other people have similar feelings toward you. For instance, when you are in a foreign country where everyone speaks a different language from yours then suddenly you bump into someone who speaks your language, how will you feel about them? Most probably you will feel more secure and comfortable when you are around them, right? The reason you feel comfortable when you're around that person is, a rapport has been developed. Developing a rapport involves making sure the other person gets to know there is a common thing between you and that person.

For you to develop a rapport, you have to convince your subconscious mind that there is something common between you two. That thing that is familiar can be a simple thing, like body the tone, and your mind now is capable of developing a rapport between you.

C. Reframing and neuro-linguistic programming

Reframing is a technique that involves taking everything positively rather than taking them negatively no matter the situation you are in. To understand this, let's look at this example: You have bought a new novel, but at the same time, there is something you want to do on your personal computer. After some time, while using your laptop, the power goes off. Most likely, you will start cursing. But using the reframing technique, you can use the time before the power returns to read your novel. Reframing is not a technique that helps push you away from reality, but it helps you in overcoming difficulties by discovering the opportunities that are there.

D. Eye accessing cues and neuro-linguistic programming

It is normal for human beings to move their eyes in different directions whenever they are asked a question. Researchers have proven that there is a connection between the direction of eye movement and the thoughts crossing the mind of that person. We all know our eyes can be moved in six different directions and each direction passes different information perceived by what is going through the mind.

Eye accessing cues and liar detection

This concept is crucial in determining if someone is telling the truth. For example, when you ask someone the color of his car, but the eyes move to the upper left, it means that person is trying to construct an image of a car, and this implies he does not have a car at all.

Although you can use this concept in determining liars, some people tend to focus and refocus without necessarily moving their eyes, and thus you won't be able to determine whether they are lying or not. But the good thing is that these people are rare.

E. Perceptual position and neuro-linguistic programming

Everyone has a different perspective of events; some may be different from yours. You should try to look at those events at an angle that is different from your own. NPL groups these perspectives into three perceptual positions:

1. First position. This is the common perspective that you usually use, taking events from your angle and understanding.

2. Second position. This involves using the perspective of the other person. You are stuck in the same situation. In this position, you place yourself in the shoes of the other person, forgetting about yourself and concentrating on the feelings and what the other person wants.

3. Third position. This is the position of a third person who is not involved in your situation. To understand this, let's say you were fighting

with your friend. The third person is the person watching like a bystander, but he or she is not directly involved.

It helps you to have an understanding of the feelings concerning other people, improving your knowledge and making it easier for you to interact with people from different backgrounds.

Perception differs from one person to another. When the same situation is encountered by other people, they perceive it differently and come up with different solutions to their problems.

F. Metaphors and neuro-linguistic programming

The metaphor is a style that is mostly used when people are talking with one another or giving out stories. Using metaphors will help you to access some values in your brain based on your belief, religion, and background. It also happens to the other person who uses part of his mind when a metaphor is used.

• Do words affect people?

Research shows that words affect how people behave. A study was conducted where people were divided into three groups and each group was given a set of words. The first group was given words like anger, rage, etc. The next group was subjected to words like kindness. The last group was subjected to neutral words. After some time, one person interrupted all the groups, and the results were that the first group responded aggressively toward him, the second was less aggressive, but the last group was neutral in the way they responded.

• Metaphors can manipulate other's people mind

When you use a metaphor, you bypass the conscious mind, and it goes directly to the subconscious mind, making it a suitable method in suggesting to a hypnotized guy. Even without hypnotizing people, metaphors can be used to reprogram people to a certain extent. The best way to make someone feel better or to motivate someone, you should try to use a metaphor.

G. Meta model and neuro-linguistic programming

This is an important tool that can be used in communication, as it counteracts the effects of distortion, generalization, and deletions that people make while communicating.

While communicating, some people filter their message by generalizing their experience, deleting some crucial part, and also distorting the message itself. People usually filter to justify their prejudgment to be true. For example, when a guy does not have self-confidence, he will try to delete all the compliments people give him, distort the reality to justify his belief that people hate him, and finally generalize that no one loves him.

• Hot to Use the Meta Model

The main use of this concept is that it helps one to overcome his or her core beliefs. To overcome your beliefs, which may not be based on any fact, you can challenge them using the meta model, and this will help you to build self-confidence and be optimistic, thus living a better life.

H. The Milton model and neuro-linguistic programming

This involves talking about situations without getting into details, making the mind go into a state of trance. In this state, people can be programmed directly due to the lack of filters to their conscious mind. While hypnosis involves silencing conscious filters by allowing them to relax, the Milton model involves inducing a state of trance by talking in a certain way.

Components of NPL

• Subjectivity

People experience the world subjectively and hence create a subjective representation of their experiences. These personal representations of experience are grouped into five senses and language. This is to say that people's personal conscious experience is termed according to their traditional senses of gustation, olfaction, vision, audition, and traction. An example can well illustrate this; when someone thinks of an event in his or her mind, recalls an event, or anticipates about the future, that person will see images, taste flavors, hear sounds, feel tactile sensations, smell scents, and think in a natural language.

• Consciousness

Neuro-linguistic programming is predicated on the belief that consciousness is separated into unconscious and conscious components. These subjective characterizations that occur outside of an individual awareness are what is known as the unconsciousness mind.

• Learning

Neuro-linguistic programming employs an imitative method of learning termed as modeling. It is said to be able to systemize and reproduce an epitome's expertise in any domain of activity. An essential part of the systemizing process is an illustration of the sequence of the sensory linguistic representation of the personal experience of the epitome during execution of expertise.

Chapter 5
NLP – Higher Level of Thinking

There are different ways in which you can describe NLP, and this is one of the reasons why it is difficult to find a clear definition of NLP. Also, the name seems pretty vague, doesn't it? Richard Bandler, in one of his workshops, recalled an anecdote on how he came up with the name. The police stopped him for speeding. As justification, he tried to explain to the policeman that he was speeding because he was late for a conference. The policeman found this reason dubious and asked him what the conference was about. So, Bandler being the quick thinker that he was, looked over at the passenger seat and replied that the conference was about neuro-linguistic programming. Apparently, this is how he came up with the name of NLP. Well, this story might or might not be accurate.

Even though NLP includes various techniques to change the way you think, the most important concept in NLP is about the mindset.

So, how can you define the term mindset? The best way to describe mindset is as NLP presuppositions. Mindset refers to the assumptions or the principles that a person chooses to adopt in daily life. It is a person's way of looking at the world. The mindset is much more powerful than the simple NLP techniques. You can use NLP to influence your mindset so that you feel powerful and in control of your life.

The Map isn't the Territory

It means that our perception of reality is merely a perception and not reality. The difficulty crops up because we seem to react to such events as if they are true. There is a presupposition in NLP that, often, people respond to an experience and not to reality. So, this presupposition reminds you that you need to question what you believe and see if you might have unknowingly distorted it. For instance, if you have an argument with your loved one, in the course of the argument certain heated words are bound to be exchanged. After such an argument, do you start to believe the harsh words your loved one said? You might even hold onto those words and start feeling terrible about yourself. The reality is that your loved one probably didn't mean what was said and you have probably taken it out of context. So, your memory of the reality you think happened, and the reality itself, are quite different.

There is No Failure

Will you feel different if every time you don't achieve your goal, you see that as an opportunity to learn and not a failure? The general conditioning in society is such that if a person doesn't achieve a goal, he or she is deemed to be a failure. Will you start beating yourself about it and start to judge yourself harshly for failing? How about you try to replace this negative thinking with something more neutral and positive? What if every time you don't achieve something, you merely think of it as an opportunity to learn and to do better? A little positive communication with yourself can change the way you view yourself and the world around you.

Communication and its Response

The meaning of communication is the response or the reaction you receive. This one might sound quite tricky. Most of the time, we think that we are being quite clear in the way we communicate, and it seems like our intention isn't being understood or that the message isn't coming across as we intended. It is certainly easier to blame the receiver for the miscommunication; however, it will do you some good if you accept some responsibility in all this. Yes, you were probably clear in what you said, and the other person didn't understand you, but does it matter? If the message doesn't get through, it doesn't matter who is at fault! Isn't it simpler to focus on the best means to get the communication going? This is where NLP comes into the picture. NLP suggests that, the more flexible the communication, the higher the rate of success. There is a presupposition in NLP that, in any system, the element that has the most flexibility will exert the most influence. Therefore, if you are a little flexible in the way you communicate, the chances of you being misunderstood are quite low.

You Cannot Fail to Communicate

Regardless of what you do or don't say, or what you do or don't do, you are still communicating. Even when you are silent and don't express your opinion, you are communicating. Verbal communication isn't the only way to communicate, and nonverbal communication is as important as verbal communication. Your body language, expressions, the tone of your voice, and such are important aspects of communication.

You need to learn to establish some positive communication with yourself. If you can influence your mind to think positive thoughts, then your perception of yourself and your life will be positive. You need to let go of any negative beliefs you have and replace them with all things positive.

There are five ways in which you can use NLP to transform yourself for the better.

Dissociate Yourself

Emotional stress can consume you. If you leave it unaddressed, then all the negative emotions can prevent you from evolving and succeeding in life. NLP can help neutralize such feelings and will help you view a situation rationally. When you can view something rationally, or when you can rationalize something, the way you react and respond to it will differ. Instead of letting your anger, worries, or stress get the better of you, you need to learn to dissociate yourself from all that negativity.

Reframe

There will always be situations that will make you feel powerless and when you will be overcome by emotions. In such situations, you need to reframe the content so that you can focus on the things that are important and reduce your stress. You need to remember that there are positive and negative aspects of any situation. If you can merely change the way you view something, then you can shift your focus from all the things that don't matter and can instead concentrate on the things that do matter.

Anchor Yourself

If you want to work on positive emotional responses, even in stressful situations, then anchoring will help you. By consciously channeling a positive state of mind, you will be able to alter the way you feel in any given situation.

Build Rapport

Life is all about establishing communication and building relationships. With the help of NLP, you can build rapport with anyone in your personal and professional life. You will learn to connect with a person through their body language and their communication as well as their breathing patterns. Once you learn to pay attention to the other person, you can easily mirror the way they behave, and it will help you build a rapport.

Limiting Beliefs

The only thing that stops a person from being successful is his or her limiting beliefs. You need to learn to identify limiting beliefs that you might have, and you need to correct them. You cannot simply ignore your limiting beliefs because they can have a crippling effect on your psyche. You are the only one that can change the way you think about yourself.

Use NLP on Others

People want different things out of NLP, but one common theme among the various expectations people have from NLP is the ability to be able to persuade people better.

The Antipodean Lilt

First things first, let's talk about the antipodean lilt for a bit. You may have heard of it already, as it is a very popular concept. It's not very potent. It can help you deal better with children, but it doesn't work great for persuasion.

If you don't know what it is, let me explain it in brief. It happens when you let your voice rise in pitch at the end of a sentence. For example, if you say, "I'm going back to Sydney" in a way that the last bit rises up and sounds like a question, it makes you seem unsure. On the other hand, if you say the same part with a lower voice, it sounds more confident and commanding. As a result, the listener feels more confident in what you're about to do, too.

This is a very basic technique that probably won't work on a lot of people, but it still helps to know it.

Embedded Commands

So let's talk about embedded commands. This is one of the simpler yet more powerful techniques. In this technique, you make use of an embedded command in your sentence without being impolite. This makes it difficult for the other person to say no.

Let me give you an example. If you go out often to drink with your friends, think back to one of the times when you were sitting together having drinks and one of your friends said, "Let's have another one." Now, this comes off more like a command, and even though it is fairly polite, it is hard to resist. So, you will most probably oblige unless you really don't want to drink anymore. On the other hand, if your friend asks you, "Do you want another drink?" the power instantly shifts to you, and then it is in your control to decide whether you really want one or not.

The waitstaff at high-end restaurants is often well versed with this technique. They know what to say to get you to buy more. So, for example, when you order something like steak and fries, they will often ask you, "What would you like as a starter?" And this makes you instantly look at the menu to find a good starter. Even if you decide not to have one, they at least made you think about it, and that's really their goal. Saying something like, "Would you like a starter?" doesn't work half as well because it just doesn't have that persuasive pull.

Restricting the Choice

This is another one of those really simple yet really powerful techniques. It works by restricting the choice of the listener while giving them an illusion of choice and making them think that they're really in control. I'll give you an example from the hospitality industry.

When you dine in a fine restaurant, the trained waiter will very politely ask you at some point, "What kind of wine would you like to have?", or

"Red or white wine?" These questions are meant to give you an illusion of choice, but really all they're doing is limiting your choice of drinks to the types of wine they have.

If the waiter asks you, "Would you like something to drink?" or something to that effect, it might not have been anywhere near as effective. Nobody is forced to accept the offer, but the way the question is posed in the former example sure makes it a lot more difficult for the patrons to resist.

Various fast-food joints like McDonald's and Subway use this technique. While you're ordering a burger, they will very politely ask you something like, "Single or double cheese?" This makes you feel that you are being offered a choice, but what they are actually doing is making sure you don't choose the "no cheese" option.

Something similar is often used when dealing with kids when they're being stubborn. In fact, some smarter parents use it from the get-go, so they don't have to deal with stubbornness at all. If you are a parent, you must be familiar with it in some way already.

For instance, when your child doesn't want to go to sleep, instead of trying to scold them or asserting control in a traditional way.

Chapter 6
Body Language

Nonverbal communication is very tricky to understand. What we put into words is very clear to understand, but our facial expressions, gestures, and eye speak the loudest. Understanding nonverbal communication is a powerful tool that can help a person understand others better and build interpersonal and professional relationships. It can also help you to express yourself better and make connections.

Understanding Nonverbal Cues

While having a conversation with someone, you give away a lot by the way you sit, listen, move, look, and react. The other person can tell whether you are really interested in what they are saying or not, or if you are just pretending to care. When your body language is on par with your words, there is an increase in trust and clarity. When your words don't match with your body language it leads to mistrust, misunderstandings, and tension. For better communication, you need to become more conscious and receptive to the nonverbal cues of others as well as yourself.

Nonverbal cues include the following:

Eye

Eye is another nonverbal communication cue which can give away a lot. When you look into someone's eyes while talking it is a sign of genuine interest and understanding. When the other person fails to make eye contact, is blinking too much, or looks away from you it can mean they are distracted, uncomfortable, nervous, or concealing their feelings.

Posture

Postures say a lot about your state of mind. If you are leaning towards someone while talking it means you are interested in the conversation and attentive. An open indicates friendliness and willingness. A closed like folded hands or crossed legs indicates unfriendliness and hostility.

The way you sit also says a lot; if you are sitting straight, that indicates attentiveness and focus. Sitting with the body hunched forward can mean that a person is tired or bored.

Touch

Communicating through touch is very effective. A firm handshake, a warm hug, a pat on the back, and a reassuring arm pat all convey various messages. Touch cues are very subtle and simple to understand. In order to understand and send these nonverbal cues, you need to be emotionally aware during a conversation and be sensitive towards the other person. You need to acknowledge the emotions of others and accurately analyze the cues that are being sent to you. It will help you create and build trust and be responsive to the other person by showing you care and understand.

Tone

The tone of your voice, which means the loudness or the pitch, is also considered a nonverbal cue. The tone of one's voice can have a strong impression on what is being said, when someone talks in a powerful voice.

Nonverbal cues reassure you of what is being said. Make a note of all the cues you are receiving and note whether they are consistent with what is being said. Trust your gut; if you think the cues are not matching up to what is being said then you might be right because nonverbal cues say much more than verbal ones. Learn to understand with your eyes and you won't miss these nonverbal cues.

Understanding Context

While having a conversation with someone, make sure that you observe the body language of the person who you are talking to so you can use your words wisely. Body language can inform you about the comfort level of a person, but that is about it. This is where context comes into play. Understanding context means being mindful of the following things:

The Conversation

You must pay close attention to when the body language of the person changes. What was it that made the person uncomfortable? Was it a question you asked or the topic you were speaking about? Maybe something you said made the other person feel uncomfortable.

The Surrounding Area during the Conversation:

Unless you are in a closed room, all conversations are affected by the environment. Look around you to see the reason why your partner or colleague is uncomfortable. Is there some bothersome noise that is affecting the conversation? Maybe there is an argument going on at the neighboring table, too much of a crowd, or someone your partner knows might've walked in. All these things affect someone's body language and you need to understand that not every person reacts the same way.

Recent Experiences:

During a conversation, you have to keep in mind that your colleague or partner might have had some experiences during the day that might have made them uncomfortable and which may have affected their body language in a negative way. For example, an argument with someone, a rough day at work, health issues, financial troubles, and personal problems may reflect on the body language of a person. If they are still thinking about the stressful situations in their lives, they might appear sad, uncomfortable, distracted, and disinterested.

Take time to determine the reason for your partner's discomfort. Suggest moving to another room or changing the topic and see if that makes a difference. If there is no improvement in their body language, then you can politely ask them if anything is wrong. You might think you are the problem, but there might be something else that is bothering the other person. Offer them some food and beverages and talk about something fun and interesting instead of the same mundane topics. Analyzing and understanding context may seem like an impossible task but with practice, you will get better, and it will become your most valuable skill.

The next time you are having a meeting with your boss, colleagues, or even when you're on a date or out with a friend, watch out for these cues to effectively read people.

Smile

Know a fake smile from a real smile. A real smile will light up the person's looks and cause crinkles near the eyes. Your eyes cannot lie, so next time you want to know if someone's smile is genuine, be sure to watch the crinkles near the eyes.

Eye

Eye is another important aspect when you want to read someone. Eyes are very expressive and are considered a window to the soul. If the person is looking into your eyes and talking, then it means they are comfortable with you. When you are having a conflict with someone and they cannot look you in the eye, it means they are hiding something from you.

Jittery Movements

When someone repeatedly touches their looks hair, and neck, it means they are nervous and are scared of disapproval. Fidgeting with an object while talking also signifies restlessness and distraction. Clenching the jaw, tightening the neck, or furrowing the brows are all signs of stress and anxiety.

When someone copies your body language, it is a sign of agreement and comfort. This is especially a good sign during negotiations as it shows you what the other person is thinking.

Body sigh

Slouching while sitting, and droopy shoulders, are signs of low self-esteem and confidence. Such people have trouble expressing their feelings. Sitting upright shows confidence and enthusiasm. You cannot feign interest, as your body language will not match your words.

Placement of Legs

When someone is shaking their leg while talking to you, it means that they are nervous or uneasy. This is a common habit especially during interviews and creates an impression on the interviewer. This is a sign of insecurity and shakiness, which is not very well appreciated.

Placement of Hands

The placement of hands also says a lot about a person's state of mind. When a person has his or her hands on the hips while standing, it means they are enthusiastic, interested, and energetic. Hand gestures while talking means that the person is trying to explain and express feelings and ideas.

Be aware of the surroundings and context when you are reading someone, as body language is just going to give you a hint at what the person is thinking and feeling. For in-depth analysis, you have to take into account the context and apply it accurately.

Eyes

Eyes are considered to be the windows to the soul. Eyes are capable of revealing a lot about a person's thoughts and feelings. When you engage in a conversation with someone, observe their eye movements. This must be a general part of your communication process. A couple of things that you must look out for are whether the person is maintaining eye contact, is averting his or her gaze, has dilated pupils, and is blinking either normally or rapidly.

Gazing

When a person maintains contact while conversing, it shows interest and implies that the person is paying attention; however, prolonged eye can be perceived to be threatening and intimidating. Breaking contact frequently or looking away indicates that the person is distracted, is uncomfortable, or is trying to hide something.

Blinking

Blinking is quite natural; however, blinking too much or too little can signify different things. If a person seems to be distressed or uncomfortable, the person will blink a lot and quite rapidly. Blinking signifies that the person is trying to control what they are truly feeling. For instance, a poker player might blink deliberately and less frequently to hide his or her excitement about the hand he or she has been dealt.

Size of the Pupil

The dilation of the pupil is a very subtle nonverbal gesture. The level of light in the surroundings often causes the pupil to dilate. Even different emotions lead to the dilation of people. When a person is attracted to someone else, their pupils dilate. This shows attraction and arousal and gives rise to the popular phrase "bedroom eyes."

Pursed Lips

While conversing, if someone purses their lips, it shows disapproval, distaste, or even distrust.

Biting of the Lip

Shows anxiety, worry, or stress.

Covering of the teeth

This is often done for hiding an emotional reaction, like trying to hide a smirk!

A slight change in the teeth is a subtle indicator of what the person is truly feeling. If the corners of the teeth are turned upwards, the person might be feeling optimistic or happy, and if they are turned down, it shows disapproval or sadness.

Gestures

These are perhaps the most obvious signals used. Waving of arms, pointing towards something, or using the fingers for indicating numbers are amongst the most commonly used and easy to interpret gestures. Here are a few gestures that can help you in getting a better understanding of what a person is saying. A clenched fist shows that a person is angry. The thumbs up and thumbs down gestures signify approval and disapproval respectively. The "v" sign made by just lifting the index and middle fingers to form the letter "v" signifies victory or peace.

Arms and Legs

The crossing of arms shows defensiveness, and the crossing of legs indicates discomfort or dislike. When a person has a smile pasted on their look but is standing with their arms crossed, their body language certainly doesn't back up that smile. There are certain subtle gestures that are made by the widening of arms to assume a commanding position or for minimizing the attention of others. When someone is standing with their arms placed on their hips, it shows that a person is ready, in control, or it can also suggest aggressiveness. Tapping of fingers or fidgeting with them shows impatience, boredom, and restlessness. The crossing of legs shows the desire for privacy, and clasping of hands behind the back indicates anger, anxiousness, or utter boredom.

Postures

The way a person holds his or her body is an important part for analyzing body language. This refers to the overall physical form of the individual and the manner in which they carry themselves. A lot can be inferred about a person's characteristics from their sign like whether the person is confident, open, dominating, or submissive.

SECTION II

Chapter 7
What Exactly is Gas Lighting?

Gas lighting is a type of relentless control and mentally programming that makes the casualty question her or himself, and to eventually lose one's own feeling of discernment, character, and self-esteem. Gas lighting articulations and allegations are typically founded on explicit untruths, or embellishment of reality. The term gas lighting is gotten from the 1944 film "Gaslight", where a spouse attempts to persuade his better half that she's crazy by making her inquiry herself and her existence.

Gas lighting is a sort of psychological mistreatment. Somebody who is gas lighting will attempt to make a focused on individual uncertainty their view of the real world. The gas lighter may persuade the objective that their recollections aren't right or that they are going overboard to an occasion. The abuser may then present their own considerations and emotions as "the genuine truth."

The term begins with a 1938 play called "Gas Light." In the play, a lady's significant other attempts to persuade her that she is intellectually precarious. He rolls out little improvements in her condition, for example, diminishing the gaslights in their home. He at that point persuades his better half she is basically envisioning these changes. His definitive objective is to have her focused on a refuge so he can take her legacy.

Individuals encountering gas lighting may profit by finding an advisor.

The Origin of "Gas lighting"

The term "gas lighting" became accepted lingo thanks to the 1944 movie entitled "Gaslight." That's not to say that narcissists and gas lighting never existed until after the film, of course. In the movie, a man brainwashes his wife into thinking she is losing her mind. Whenever he used the gas lights in the flat above, his wife would notice that the lights in their own home would go dim. However, he would continually make her believe she only imagined things.

One of the saddest things about being a victim of gas lighting is that it can lead to Stockholm syndrome, in which the victim begins to look to the narcissist to tell him/her what to think and how to feel, as well as what reality is. You even become sympathetic to the narcissist, because you start to think such false thoughts like, "How incredibly frustrating it must be for them to have to put up with my messed-up memories!"

If you're a victim of gas lighting, you may find it hard to see the abuser for who they really are. It's not because you're stupid; it's more likely that the narcissist can charm you out of your mind. They're so charming that you start to feel rotten forever second-guessing them or doubting them. They lay that charm on so thick that you stop trusting your gut and start trusting them. You don't realize it, but you've been expertly maneuvered into an unhealthy and abusive relationship.

Now, let's look at some of the ways that the narcissist messes with your gas lights without you knowing.

Classic Gas lighting Tactics and Effects

Reframing. This is when the gas lighter reframes or twists whatever happened so that it sounds like they were the good guy, or that they were the victim in the whole thing - and you're the villain. This makes you wonder if you're wrong about what you thought their intentions were. They will often reframe along with insincere compassion, which just adds to the feelings of irrationality and instability that you already feel. For instance, if the abuser hit you and you know for a fact that they meant you harm, they can say, "Oh come on, I didn't hit you that hard! It was only a bit of fun roughhousing. Stop making a big deal out of this."

Switching subjects. The narcissistic gas lighter will choose to change the topic rather than address the questions you're asking them, or the point you're making. They'll often say, "No, you imagine that just like you imagined the other thing. Did that friend of yours fill your head with her silly ideas again?" Now, they've made it about the friend they don't like, rather than focusing on the issue at hand.

Downplaying. The gas lighter will make your feelings and thoughts seem inconsequential, to the point where you start asking yourself why you're always so touchy about things. The more they can make you feel inconsequential, the more power they will have over you.

Denial. I once overheard a conversation between two teenagers at the mall. One of them had been in trouble at home and was telling the other about it. She said when her mother found out, she did the only thing she knew she could do to get out of trouble. In her words, she said, "Deny, deny, deny, until you die." It sounded like a mantra the way she said it, and I've been unable to get it out of my head ever since.

Denial is a classic gas lighting tactic that the narcissist uses. You know that they said something or did something; you bore witness to it with your own eyes and ears. Despite this, they deny it. Sometimes, it's not even because they didn't realize you saw them; they know you saw them do what they did. However, they will blatantly deny it. It is this denial that confuses you. It's only natural to wonder if your mind is working right because normal people would not bother pushing a lie when they know they've been caught in it.

Not the gas lighter. They have no problems going as far as asking you to prove what you're saying is true. This is a classic example of gas lighting, because in certain situations, all you have is your recollection of events. As such, you may start to wonder if they're right and you're wrong. Maybe you're the crazy one, you assume.

Outright Lies. It isn't just that the narcissist tells bald-faced lies that leave you in shock, it's also the ease with which they lie that is disturbing. They're very comfortable with it. These lies promote "crazy-making," presented so smoothly that you begin to wonder if you're not a bit nuts for not believing them.

Killing you softly. A good narcissist has the intention of making you into a shell of who you are. You may not notice as that more they gaslight you, the more you give in and become someone you don't recognize anymore. They kill you - ever so softly - ever so slowly, erasing the person you really are and leaving behind a puppet that they can play with however they like.

Using your Treasures against You. Do you love your job? Your children? Your pet? The abuser has no problem using whatever you hold near and dear as a weapon in their gas lighting techniques. They are adept at making you come to the assumption that you do not deserve the nice people or things in your life. You find yourself questioning why you have it good, and if they've done their job right, you will sabotage all the relationships and accomplishments you hold dear.

Love Bombing. The reason gas lighting works so well as a manipulative technique is that the narcissist conditions you into being okay with abuse by using the carrot and stick method. When they sense they've laid on the lies, denial, and unjust punishment too thickly, they will follow that up with a whole lot of love and flattery. A perfect example is a man who beats his wife only to buy her diamonds or the woman who cuts down her man only to make him his favorite meal, or generously entertain his friends only because she senses she's pushed him a bit too far and just might lose him. The narcissist will use love and flattery to keep you around for more abuse. The sad thing is that you get used to constantly being sad and abused. When they're loving and flattering you, you think to yourself, "Well, they must not be as bad as I thought. I don't know why I got mad. I'm staying."

Are You Being Gas lighted?

It can be difficult to tell if this is the case, on account of how badly the abuser may have messed with your psyche at this point. I have compiled a list of questions you need to ask yourself so that you can figure out whether you are the victim of gas lighting:

1. Do you often ask yourself, "Why am I so sensitive?" all through your day?

2. Do you find yourself constantly making apologies?

3. Do you feel like you're a bit nuts, continually confused in your relationship with this person?

4. Do you have a constant, nagging sensation that there's something wrong with your relationship, even if you can't put your finger on it?

5. Do you keep wondering why you're not as happy as you know you can be?

6. Do you find it challenging to make even the simplest of decisions?

7. Do you find yourself making an excuse after excuse for the way your partner treats you?

8. Do you find yourself constantly feeling like you'll never measure up or be good enough for your partner?

If you answered yes to these questions - and you're not dealing with low self-esteem, depression, or anxiety disorders - then you're most likely being gas lighted by this person or the specific people who make you feel this way in your life. Observe your interactions with the people in your life and notice the ones with whom you constantly feel these things. If you only ever feel that way with a person or group of people, it's likely that you are a gaslight victim.

Chapter 8
Effects of Gas Lighting

Remember that you can get away from the abuse, but there are things that can happen if you're not careful, if you continue to stay in the presence of someone who gaslights you, and who abuses you.

What can happen though/ let's talk about what can happen if you continue to suffer at the hands of a gas lighter?

Memory Loss

This is what's so scary about gas lighting. When you experience gas lighting after a while, sometimes you'll start to feel so guilty and have a lot of self-doubts that you'll tend to forget things that happened. You may not know why it happened, and not remember things that happened between those time periods. Some people will even experience the abuser accusing them of something that happened, but they're unable to actually remember what happened.

Sometimes, what's scary about gas lighting is when you experience that, over a long period of time, you'll begin to realize that you can't remember the exact situations, because your mind and reality is completely skewered. You'll start to realize that you can't remember things that the abuser would accuse you of.

Sometimes, the abuser would accuse you of things that you're doing, but you don't remember doing them, and this, in turn, will lead you to wonder whether or not you did something. You'll definitely start to realize this as well when you get away.

Sometimes, they'll claim you're abusive, and how you hurt them, but you literally can't remember why. You oftentimes will try very hard to remember the abuse and trauma, but you can't.

Another type of way you can lose your memory with this is blanking on various things. When you're gaslight, you start to feel your reality starts to change, and you start to become an effect of the abuser that's there. However, sometimes after gas lighting happens, you can't remember all of the trauma you went through.

Perhaps it's a defensive mechanism, or maybe it's just your brain trying to blackout everything terrible that happened to you. But, you won't remember things. Your memory starts to become less and less, to the point where it becomes a struggle to remember it all.

You may walk around with really bad brain fog too. Abusers love to skewer your sense of reality, so when they do this, you can't remember things and your brain becomes a foggy mess as a result of this.

You Feel Constantly Guilty

One-way narcissistic abusers take you down is making you feel guilty constantly. It isn't a pity party "oh woe is me" concept, it's more of they will make you feel bad for even existing. That's the problem with narcissistic abusers. They will make sure that you feel guilty, constantly terrible, and you're the one at fault.

Narcissistic abusers will throw jabs at you, telling you how you're nothing. They will also say that you're just worthless, a piece of trash, and you're constantly not allowed to be anything more. That's the problem with many abusers. They will oftentimes make you feel guilty, to the point where depression, even suicidal tendencies start to come up.

You wonder if you're the one to blame for everything. You start to feel like you're the one at fault, when you may not be. Even when you're out of the situation and away from it, even years down the road, it can haunt you, like a ghost that hasn't been exorcised yet.

You feel bad for even being alive and that's because your narcissistic abuser has taken you to such a lower level that you don't know what to do with yourself other than to think that hey, you are the one to blame, and you are worthless.

But of course, that isn't the case.

Isolation from Help

This is what's scary about narcissistic abusers. Remember, they will claim that you're the one who is crazy, that others are lying, that you're not the one who is right here. They will tell you that you should only believe them, and never anyone else.

Over time, when you're with an abuser like this, you can develop a Stockholm syndrome, where you know that you need to get away, but you can't. You isolate yourself from help, and oftentimes, even after you get UT, you can't really get the help that you need.

That's because you don't trust other people. They are all liars, remember? Your abuser would tell you that, and even if you've managed to leave, that can hang around in your head.

That's why, when people who have been gas lighted leave their abusers, they sometimes can't trust other people. They don't know if they ever can and are scared to do so because of what their abuser did in the past.

Self-Doubt

Self-doubt stems from how you were treated by your gas lighters. The goal of those who gaslight is to make the other person feel worthless like their own thoughts and reality don't matter. Sometimes, those who have been gas lighted will hallucinate, and sometimes they'll see things that aren't there in order to make the gas lighted happy.

But, the self-doubt extends past that. When someone how has been gas lighted all their lives finally leaves, they are often scared of what's next. They've been living with the reality of their abuser for so long that they don't know how to wrench themselves away.

This causes self-doubt. It's the doubt of oneself, the doubt of what's really out there and the doubt of their own reality.

And boy is it terrible for you.

Self-doubt makes you second-guess everything that you do from here on out. After all, when you've been told you're worthless all your life, you probably will think that everything you do is worthless. But it isn't, that's just the gas lighted talking in your head.

Gas lighters love to do this because they know that, if you are continually taken down, if you ever do leave, you'll never really be yourself again, because you're scared to be. You'll be scared of expressing yourself, of being who you are, and you'll realize that, if you continue with this mindset, it will only make things worse from here on out, and for many, it can be a deadly action that can help erase who you really are.

This type of self-doubt can stifle creativity too and dreams as well, so remember that. You may feel like you should do something, but then, because you've been gas lighted in the past, you shy away from doing so. Oftentimes, this type of abuse will stunt your own creativity, and there is a reason why many people encourage those who have been gaslight to escape while they can.

Social Life Issues

Sometimes, gas lighting does affect your social life. The abuser will try their very hardest to keep the one who is gas lighted away from their friends, or even family too. The constant lying and saying they are bad people will happen. Lots of times, those who have suffered from gas lighting might end up never seeing their family until years down the road. This is something that can happen for a very long time.

What's scary as well, is that the person might end up completely isolating themselves from anyone, only relying on the abuser and nothing else. It can make the person feel like they're not capable of being loved, and also make the person feel like they're not stable, which is the scariest part about it.

For many people who have suffered the effects of gas lighting, they oftentimes will feel their confidence tank as well, since nobody seems to care about them or make an effort to go see them when in reality they're oftentimes being forced away from those relationships.

And what's scary, is that this can last a long time, even after you've left the relationship. Many who have been gas lighted in the past will not go back to their former friends and family right away, due to the effects of it. There is a reason why people will make sure that they seek out the help that they need, so they can reconnect with the person that they missed right away.

Difficulty Making Decisions

Decision Making was done all from the abuser, and not very much from the person who was gas lighted. So, if you've experienced a bit of hesitation in decisions and have a history of abuse, you can probably thank gas lighting for that.

Decisions were left to the other person, and whenever you did make decisions, it was oftentimes seen as wrong, or incorrect to do. So why make decisions then?

That's why many, who have suffered from gas lighting in the past, can doubt the decisions that they make, from there, May not believe what they're doing is right.

This can lead to anxiety disorders in many cases. You're afraid of making decisions because whenever you did, you were always told that they were wrong. You were abused so much that you don't know what to do about anything anymore, so decision making is very hard for those who've suffered from narcissistic abuse. Sometimes, this might seem like a couple of things are hard to decide, and other times, some people will just have trouble making any decision period.

Gas lighting can also make someone feel like their feelings and emotions don't matter, so they oftentimes have to choose what to do from a distanced viewpoint. So, instead of deciding from the heart, and in a way that'll validate and help you, they're swimming in a pool of anxiety and stress, that isn't fun for anyone who suffers from this.

The Mental Health Side

There is also the mental health side of the effects of gas lighting. We did go over anxiety, but that's due to the confusion that the person makes the one who is being gaslight feel. The one who is being gaslight oftentimes doesn't know what's right and wrong, and they fear to do things. This can be a small occurrence, or this can be a major issue in their life that does need to be discussed.

The one who is suffering from being gaslight may also feel a lot of hopelessness, along with self-esteem issues. This can also lead to depression, and oftentimes, people who are survivors of this oftentimes still feel like life is hopeless, that their feelings don't matter, and that they should never talk about it.

Depression is another major issue, since many times, being taken down so low for so long can make the person feel like it's not worth the energy as well.

PTSD is another one. After all, you were in a traumatic and abusive situation. The shock and stress from that person's actions still linger there, and it commonly develops from this.

Finally, codependency is something that can develop from this too. That's because you've been living a life where you had that type of relationship, and it can make you feel like you have to rely on others.

A Refusal to Show Emotions

This is a big one. This is due to the fact that survivors will always be on guard, always looking for the manipulation that's in any situation. Oftentimes, this can lead to people not trusting themselves, or trusting others either, or people do describe those who have suffered from this as always on guard.

They refuse to be vulnerable, for a good reason. They don't want to be hurt like that again. However, the problem with that, while it's a notable reason, it can be a problem for some people, since they'll refuse to show manipulation to the point where future relationships are stained, and they may have trouble holding a relationship because of this.

It does happen. Lots who suffer from this may even refuse to show emotions to others, staying single for a long time because they'd rather not be hurt, and would rather not experience what they did again.

Chapter 9
How Gas Lighting Narcissist Operate

Manipulation is not a good thing, no matter what form it takes. Mental manipulation is some of the worst out there. Oftentimes, mental manipulation is referred to as psychological manipulation. Many people have experienced mental manipulation in their life; however, not everyone recognizes it. If you have not recognized it, it is likely that there have been very negative impacts on you because of it. Even if you do recognize it, depending on how long it has gone on for, the effects can be devastating.

Mental manipulation has the aim of changing the view of other people through deceptive or underhanded practices.

The manipulator will find advancement through these tactics, and more often than not, it is at the expense of another person.

This type of manipulation tends to emotionally exploit people so that the narcissist can gain power. Mental or psychological manipulation can be seen all over the world. From families to the workplace, it is unfortunate how often manipulation of this nature can be spotted.

It is important to understand that there is a difference between social influences that are healthy in nature and psychological manipulation. Most of us are influenced by people that we are in contact with. It is the compromise that we make in many of our relationships. These compromises are not manipulative but well thought out and understood in reality by both parties involved. Mental manipulation is quite different. It will solely benefit the manipulator regardless of the negative impact it causes for the other party. The imbalance of power is intentional. The manipulator's agenda is made possible by exploiting their victims.

There are a variety of different tricks that are commonly used by the person trying to mentally manipulate someone else. Knowing their tricks can better prepare you for how to deal with someone who is trying to exploit you for their own gain.

We are going to look over a variety of different tactics that mental manipulators may use to try and control you or get their own way.

The first thing a manipulator may do to try and gain power over you requires you to meet with them in a space that is theirs. Interaction in spaces that are considered to be theirs gives them more dominance. This could be their car, home, or even their office. These are spaces where they are dominant and have some sort of control. The feeling of ownership over the space gives them power, and they know that you will not feel a sense of ownership or familiarity, which makes it easier for them to stay in control during any discussions that are taking place.

The second thing a mental manipulator may do is always allow you to talk first. This may seem endearing in the beginning; however, it is absolutely a tactic that allows them to take control. They will let you speak so they can search for weaknesses and so they can understand your base pattern of thought. Salespeople use this trick frequently when they are trying to figure out if you will bite on what they have to offer. They will, in general, ask a lot of generic and probing type questions. These questions help them to figure out your thinking pattern and your behaviors. From there, they can figure out what your strengths and weaknesses are, allowing them to make an offer you simply can't refuse. This tactic of asking questions to attain a certain outcome can be done in personal relationships and within your workplace. You can really see it pretty much everywhere.

The next thing that the mental manipulator may do to take control of you or a situation is to falsify facts. They may lie or make excuses to throw you off guard. Mental manipulators tend to be very two-faced. They frequently like to make the victim believe that they are causing the problems themselves. They do this by altering the truth. It is also very likely that if you're dealing with a mental manipulator, they will withhold or change key pieces of information by exaggerating them or understating them.

The 4th sign of mental manipulation is overwhelming people with statistics or with facts. Narcissists tend to present themselves as experts in a variety of different areas. They try and take advantage of people by presenting them with statistics and empirical data to back up what they're saying. Typically, they will talk about topics that the person they're speaking with knows little about so that rebuttals cannot occur.

We see this 4th sign happen in a variety of different areas. It is common in financial situations, sales, negotiations, and even discussions between professionals. Additionally, it can be seen in social or relationship arguments.

Due to the fact that this tactic makes the person look like an expert, it gives them a sense of power over you.

It makes it easier for the manipulator to convince you to agree with their agenda. Sometimes there is no end game; it is simply to allow the manipulator to feel intellectually superior.

Next, mental manipulation can come in the form of extreme bureaucracy. Mental manipulators will try and use procedures, paperwork, laws, and committees to attain or keep their powerful position. This makes your life much more difficult, and the technique can be used to keep you from looking for the truth. It helps the manipulator to hide their weaknesses, flaws, and downfalls. It also allows them to evade judgments from other people.

Many mental manipulators will also use the tone of their voice and the emotion behind it to try and gain control. They believe that raising their voices will make people submit to them. This is a pretty aggressive form of manipulation, but it is surprising how often it works. An aggressive voice, paired with strong body language, certainly makes an impact. Many people will submit because these types of expressions are intimidating, and it is simpler to just lie down and follow what they are saying.

Negativity is frequently utilized by manipulators. They even go as far as to surprise people with negativity.

This allows them to throw you off balance and gain an advantage psychologically. This can be done in a variety of ways. A good example is someone letting you know at the last minute that they will not be able to hold up their end of a deal. The fact that they do it last minute is a clue, this coming at you with no warning does not give you time to prepare a counterattack. You may even find yourself making concessions so that the manipulator will keep working on the task they have agreed to do.

A lack of warning gives a person very little time to make an informed decision. This is a common tactic of salesmen, negotiators, and manipulators. When you put pressure on someone to make a decision by stating that something is a limited time offer or that there are consequences in not answering right now, it gives power to the person doing the persuading. Their demands are more likely to be met because of the tension that is caused by a lack of time.

Manipulators also like to hide behind sarcasm and humor. They will make remarks that are critical and try to pass them off as a joke. They understand that these types of digs will make you feel inferior, and your sense of security in yourself will be weakened.

They may make sarcastic comments on a variety of different things, including your looks, the age of your electronics, your credentials, or even your background. By trying to make you feel bad or look bad to your peers, they believe they will find superiority.

Alongside sarcasm and humor, manipulators are infamous for judging and criticizing others so that they feel inadequate. It is not as low key as negative humor. We say this because when a manipulator decides to go this route, they will ridicule, marginalized, or dismiss you openly. They do this to maintain superiority and keep you feeling off-balance. If they can grow the impression that you have something wrong regardless of how hard you are trying, you will likely start to feel inadequate or as if you could never be good enough in any way. When the negative is consistently focused on without any solutions, it is very damaging to a person's self-worth.

Another tactic that mental manipulators like to use is giving people the silent treatment. When you are trying to get ahold of somebody via a phone call, email, text message, or a variety of other ways and they deliberately don't respond, they gained power. This is due to the fact that they know that you are waiting on a response that they refuse to provide.

The intention is to place uncertainty in you.

They use silence as leverage, and it really is a head game that they are playing with you.

Mental manipulators are also fantastic at playing dumb. Feigning ignorance is one of their favorite tricks. They pretend that they have no idea what it is that you want or what it is that you are asking. When they do, this many people will take over the task themselves. We see children do this frequently so that they can talk their parents into doing the chore or task for them as they don't really want to do it. When adults use it, it is typically because they are trying to hide something or avoid an obligation.

The second to last tactic that emotional manipulators like to use is commonly referred to as guilt baiting. This is when a person targets another person's emotional weaknesses or vulnerabilities. It allows the manipulator to coerce someone into meeting their requests or demands. They frequently do this by blaming others. Additionally, if they know your soft spots, they will likely utilize them. You may even find that they make you feel responsible for their own happiness or their unhappiness.

The last trick that mental manipulators like to use is victimizing themselves. They will exaggerate their personal issues to get sympathy.

When the manipulator plays the role of the victim, it exploits the good nature of the person they are manipulating. Many people feel obligated to help others that are in need, and the manipulator knows this. They can reap the benefits of getting their own way by making you feel bad for them. You may even end up making concessions you would not normally make just to try and help them heal without ever realizing they are simply pulling one over on you.

How to Avoid Mental Manipulation

Now that we have looked at a variety of different tactics that the mental manipulator will try and use against you, we want to give you some tools to help you avoid it. Obviously, no one wants to be manipulated, and figuring out how to see what is happening and what to do about it can help ensure that you do not become a victim. There are so many different types of manipulation, and mental manipulation can be harder to see than others.

One of the tricks that are favored by the mental manipulator is denying things that they have said.

You can easily combat this behavior by simply taking notes. Whether you do this in a notebook or on your phone, it provides you with hard evidence if the subject comes back up. Certain phrases stand out when you are having a discussion with the manipulator and jotting them down puts some of the power back in your hands. This simple thing is very intimidating to the person trying to manipulate you, and it is likely they are going to become very defensive.

Chapter 10
Signs of Being Gas Lighted

Signs you're being manipulated with gas lighting

1. Tell shameless lies

We all tell a lie at some point in our lives.

But most of the time we don't do it with bad intentions. Apart from that we don't feel good about ourselves after such lies.

But for those who dominate gas lighting as a captain of their ship in a hurricane, telling lies intentionally is something they savor. They handle them with such precision that their lies are generally hard to believe.

They are able to lie with a look so serious and credible that everything inside you activates the red alert and you suspect that something stinks here.

And then you start wondering why they have done it, knowing very well that you are not buying their ridiculous tales.

It is because they are not fools. They know that for you their stories and lies are ridiculous and hard to believe, but with these kinds of lies, they keep you alert when it comes to them and their behaviors.

They know that with such a bold lie, you will find it very difficult to trust what they say and, therefore, you will always have to guess each of their movements.

Do you wonder what sense this makes?

Well ... the goal here is to keep you nervous. Because in this state you are more likely to make stupid mistakes and you lack judgment. And just this is what they then use as arguments against you.

2. They deny having said one thing, even in the presence of evidence

They are good at making a promise, but they will not keep their vows.

And they do it on purpose.

Imagine you hear someone say something, but you also find the same person vehemently denying having said it.

At first, this can be very irritating and annoying too, but over time you start to doubt yourself and what you heard.

"Maybe it's true that he didn't say it?"

All this is a plot to make you start questioning reality. And instead of what is real, you will choose what they say is real.

3. Attack your important things that give meaning to your existence

It could be your talent, your mission, your children and even your personality.

To take an example of my own experience, imagine that you have a dog that you want as your own child, and knowing that it is the center of your life and part of the family, they will proceed to make you feel sorry for having it.

And little by little you get emotionally away from your beloved dog until you no longer find sense in keeping it in your life.

They devalue your talents. Even if it had a social value and you were remarkably good at what you do, they will accuse you of being obsessed with your trade and yourself and have their ammunition to accuse you of abandoning or neglecting them.

Therefore, little by little they make you feel sorry for being who you are as a human being. They are cold and calculating efforts to shed your dignity and dilute your self-esteem as a human being.

Everything to make you more and more unstable.

4. Suck your energy on purpose

Gas lighting is a very efficient tactic to suck your energy and your efforts in a relationship. It is due to its regular and very powerful application or execution.

Gradually, they add abusive and degrading statements here and there.

Prick your bag of dignity here and there until all your self-confidence and self-awareness seeps into a thousand holes.

Before you know it, you're empty and you don't even know how you got to that situation.

This can happen even to the best of us. It's like the proverbial frog that doesn't realize that the gradual heating of the pan required that he should have jumped when he could because soon he wouldn't be able to do it.

If you are a victim of gas lighting, you can see the first warning signs and maybe take action. But most likely, you can't handle all that negative energy building up, just like the frog in the pan.

6. They can show some act of kindness to get you out of their evil stench

To avoid being labeled as the villain, they spray acts of kindness and affection here and there in all their terrible actions.

You find out that a person often humiliates you and says you have no courage and can also ignore you to praise you for something you did. It is essential that you do not fall for this deception.

They also intend to destabilize you by making you question the ability of perception to be right.

They are attacking your confidence in your visceral judgment. If they achieve this, they would proceed even more damage knowing very well that you have been completely brainwashed, without a reality of their own.

But, meanwhile, while throwing this inauthentic care here and there, everything plays in the plan of making you very unpredictable.

You are becoming unstable and nervous.

7. Use confusion as a weapon to make you vulnerable

For the one who loves gas lighting, his main means to an end is confusion.

Confusion has a way of weakening human beings. In general, most human beings thrive when they have some sense of purpose and sense of belonging.

That leads to productive work and some form of social interaction or social club.

All clubs or social services act as agents of stability, while the sense of purpose gives a sense of direction and value to life.

And they do it by attacking your value system, your work or your talent.

They intend to weaken you to the point where you need to overcompensate, because of the vacuum they created, with social ties.

But the manipulation does not end there completely.

While they manipulate you, they try to make you doubt what you perceive as reality so that it is much easier to control you.

Weak and manipulated that you already are, they can manipulate you even more easily until you think that the best social bond for you is with your abusive partner.

And when you are already at this point, when you try to leave the abusive partner, you end up running towards him/her for comfort.

What is a surprisingly bright system isn't it?

And when it is well-executed, it can cause a lot of damage to the victim.

If you are a victim in such a situation, it is a very hard job to heal the wounds of affliction.

8. They love to project their bad actions on you

A couple who loves gas lighting is also a perfectionist when it comes to projecting.

And it's not just the subject of the mirror. Because many times they accuse you of things, actions and attitudes that they are really doing. It's all a trick to keep you busy enough not to see that they are simply doing the things that accuse you of doing.

When you are in a relationship with these people, you will discover that they occasionally accuse you of ridiculous things. Things you don't even have any interest in.

It could be that your partner has accused you of using and abusing drugs, although they both know that you have never seen a gram of anything.

They even tell you that even if you "don't" use drugs, you act or behave like a drug addict.

Of course, you know you don't take drugs. But if they tell you that you behave like a madman or drug addict, you may start scratching your head, especially when this is repeated over and over again.

They also accuse you of being unfaithful and pretend disappointment, sadness, and helplessness in the look of your actions of injustice.

They would say that you are acting as if you are seeing someone else. That is the reason why you are not completely dedicated to the relationship and other external options are likely to distract you.

They do it so you don't end up looking for help outside. Because if they already accuse you of being unfaithful, you probably try to avoid absolutely everything that could give them arguments against you.

And in the end, you find that you always defend yourself against accusations of things you have never done.

9. They turn the world against you

Gas lighters are very good at creating illusions.

They are specialists to partner with people who know they would agree with whatever they do and what they say.

And then they would use the opinions of those people to unfairly condemn you. They are technicians in the orchestration of unfair trials.

They are also good at making those trails seem fair.

They may not even get that far; they can simply claim that someone they both respects would not be happy with the decisions you made.

They could also go further and subtly threaten to tell those people what you have said and done.

The result is that you are in constant fear and anxiety of being dishonored and publicly shamed.

They do all this just to make sure that, in the midst of their induced confusion; you are completely isolated from the world.

Therefore, you can only seek comfort in them, thus continuing the cycle of abuse.

10. You are publicly accused of insanity

This gas lighting technique is to stain your image in public.

If they get the public to see you as someone who is not able to make a good judgment, then that protects them from any attack that may arise when exposing their bad actions.

And when you ask for help, nobody will believe you. It is another important step to strengthen its power and control over you.

They have discovered their brainwashing spell is safe from all public criticism and, instead, they have punished you by the same public.

They also know that if you realize all this, do not try to expose their bad actions. At least they don't expect it from you because they know very well that you're cushioned.

Instead of shouting loudly and finally closing the door, it is very likely that you would decide to suffer in silence in that relationship.

This attitude will take you on the path of isolation and thus your perpetrator becomes even more powerful and will have all control over you.

Chapter 11
Strategies For Recognizing Manipulation and Gas Lighting

How can you tell when you're being manipulated? How can you tell when someone is messing with your mind and your emotions, hoping to exploit you for their own selfish, nasty benefit?

Sometimes you can almost swear that this person you're dealing with is up to no good. You have a nagging feeling in the back of your mind that something is not quite right here. It feels like nothing is as it seems every time you speak to this person. You want to give them the benefit of the doubt, but you just can't. You start to wonder if you're not really the crazy one here. After all, look at all the paranoid thoughts you have swimming around in your mind like a not-so-adorable school of fish!

When you're being manipulated psychologically, you feel as though your thoughts are being deliberately influenced toward the wrong conclusions and decisions. It feels as if your emotions are being taken advantage of, even if you're unable to put your finger on how and why it's working. You feel like you're losing control. You're not coming from a place of power in a manipulative interaction.

Aren't We Always Being Manipulated?

Now, it's easy to answer yes to this question. It would seem like there is a pretty thin line between innocent social influence and malevolent manipulation. The line is not really that thin. It's not unusual for people to socially influence one another. It's all a part of relating to one another in a healthy way. So how can you tell the difference between this healthy interaction and manipulation? Well, when you're being manipulated, it feels as if this person doing the manipulating is using you for their own benefit, at your own expense. They have an agenda, and you can feel it as they bend and twist you around to get what they want. The trouble is that they're so slick at it, you begin to doubt your gut feelings about what's going on — and that is just one of the goals of the manipulator.

How to find out if you're A Victim of Manipulation

Now, we're going to run through a list of questions you should ask yourself in order to figure out whether you're the victim of emotional and psychological manipulation. Call to mind the relationships or friendships which constantly leave you wondering about the other person's intentions, as you ask yourself these questions.

I want to make it clear that these questions are not necessarily the be-all and end-all when it comes to figuring out if you're a victim. However, they will let you see where, in your life. You're overtly or covertly manipulated. Please keep in mind that just because you recognize some things listed here, that does not automatically mean you're being manipulated. Sometimes, it's an innocent case where the person you're dealing with has a few unacceptable traits, and nothing more. It is important for you to recognize when you're being exploited and drained by the manipulative narcissist in your life.

Questions

1. Do you feel like you're never on equal footing with this person? You may have noticed that each time you interact with them, you feel like a fish out of water. It's almost like wherever the talk is happening, you're in their space, and not yours; not somewhere neutral where you feel like you have equal footing. You may have noticed that all your interactions take place, not just where they want it to, but when they want it to. There's never any thought given to what may be convenient for you. It feels as though you're always in their home, or their office, or their insert-random-place-here. You never feel like you're in a familiar, comfortable space physically or mentally when you interact with them.

2. Have you noticed that when you interact, you always must speak first? You may have noticed that when you meet, you're the first one to open your mouth. Inevitably, you feel vulnerable. You feel as if since you've had to speak first, you're basically being probed for weaknesses that can be exploited. You feel like they're working out what makes you tick so that they can hit you where it hurts. This is a great technique for making sales, but it has devastating effects when your narcissistic partner uses it against you.

3. When you interact with them, do you feel that they always find a way to bend or twist the facts? They tell a lie, and you feel confused because

you're not sure why they felt the need to lie. They make excuses, and while you feel like those are some terrible excuses, you don't want to be an inconsiderate bully by making them accountable for their actions. You want to make things work, but they choose to blame you — even if an objective third party, the United Nations, and everyone's grandma would attest to the fact that it was their fault, not yours. They say something that sounds like the truth, but history and your gut make you feel like it's not the truth. It's just their version of events. You've noticed that they only ever tell you things when they feel it will serve them, and they have a habit of keeping important information from you. You've noticed every time they open their mouth, they're either understating the facts so that you feel like you're just an overly dramatic nut-job making Mount Rushmore out of a pebble. When they're not understating things, they're exaggerating them, so that you feel like the lovechild of Frankenstein and the Loch Ness Monster!

4. Does this person weigh you down with their intellect and intelligence? You may have noticed that you always feel like a fool when you speak with them. They'll bully you intellectually as they dump all the stats and facts on you so that they can take advantage of you - since you only know so much. You feel like since they have all the facts, you have no choice but to go along with whatever agenda they are pushing. Sometimes it's for a specific goal. Other times, they just love to lord it over you.

5. When you talk, do they have a habit of always expressing negative emotions and yelling? Some manipulators use their voices to bully others so that they can get what they want. If you always tend to feel small, insignificant, and shut down because they're yelling at you, chances are it's no accident. Not only do they get louder and louder, they may become very theatrical with their bodies, as well. You feel like the only way to end that is to give in. They also have no issues doing this with others around, so that you feel embarrassed and ashamed. Others won't yell. They'll just be so obvious about their disappointment or pain that you won't submit to their will, that you begin to feel bad about standing up for yourself. This is a more subtle form of manipulation, with the end goal of forcing you to give them what they want.

6. Do you find yourself constantly surprised (in a bad way) and out of balance when you're with this person? Surprises can be nice. They can also be nasty. You may have noticed that this person is a huge fan of the nasty kind of surprises. They spring a "surprise" on you, and you feel off-balance immediately, as your mind struggles to make sense of things, and your emotions do exactly what the manipulator wants. You get these surprises, and you feel like you can't do anything to counter them. You can't make any plans to be able to deal with them.

7. Does this person always issue you ultimatums? You feel a lot of pressure to say or do something you otherwise wouldn't, because they've given you a directive: either do this, or you will have to do that. You know deep down that there are other options, but with them, it's either A or B. There are no other letters of the alphabet that they know! You feel the pressure to act, and you do, giving in to whatever they wanted from you.

8. Do they make a habit of making jokes at your expense? You may have noticed that this manipulative person loves to make wisecracks about you. They do this when there are others around you, making you feel incompetent or stupid. At times, they do it when it's just the two of you, to make you feel like you're making something into a big deal; never mind that it really is a big deal. Whatever the case may be, the jokes they make are designed to make you feel inferior. You feel insecure. You feel cut down, even if they're grinning. That's the plan. The end game is to be the top dog, psychologically speaking.

9. Do they criticize and judge you to no end? A true manipulator will do this, and not bother to offer you constructive feedback, or suggestions for how you can get better at whatever they're criticizing you for. You get the sense that they couldn't care less about helping you to become better. If they do, you will notice that you always feel "less than" around them. You feel like you're never good enough. They nitpick, and judge, and criticize, and they do it with a light tone of voice and a smile. Maybe they even throw in a warm, loving touch for good measure. However, you find yourself constantly feeling like you're being ridiculed. You feel your ideas and thoughts are being dismissed. You're marginalized into nothingness. You feel like you give a 110%, and no matter how hard you try or how much better you get, you're always going to be less than valuable in their eyes.

10. Do they give you the silent treatment until you do or say what they want? They stonewall you, and you feel powerless to do anything about the situation at hand. All attempts at communication on your part are ignored, making you feel even more helpless. The manipulator knows this. You feel like you're stuck waiting, and for what? You have no idea. The longer they make you wait, the more you feel uneasy, uncertain, and doubtful of your stance. They'll hold out if they need to, staying silent unless and until they feel like they have punished you enough, or until you cave in and give them what they want.

11. Have you noticed that this person is in the habit of playing dumb? They like to feign ignorance about what your wants and needs are — never mind that you've told them in 500, 2,500, 6.000 different ways and times! You feel exasperated by this, and you don't know what else to do, other than to put up and shut up.

12. Do most interactions with this person involve you being guilt-tripped? There are so many ways this can happen. The manipulator is great at shifting blame in such a way that if you're not careful, you really will take it on. You start to feel terrible for stuff that has nothing to do with you. Your weaknesses and soft spots are shamelessly exploited by the manipulator so that you have no choice but to do as they ask.

13. Does this person have a knack of playing the victim even when they clearly aren't? You may have noticed they just love to be the wounded puppy. This is a great cover-up for their nasty behavior. If they have health problems, rest assured they will play them up. If they don't have health problems, they will make them up. You feel like every word out of their mouth, every action they take is carefully crafted to pull you in, make you feel sorry for them, or make you want to do something for them.

Chapter 12
Dealing with Gas lighting: Dos and Don'ts

You are going to get the tools that you need to deal with the thorn in your flesh that is the narcissist.

Ideally, the best thing to do is go no contact, ditch them, and just leave. That's what a lot of books advocate, anyway. This advice, however sound, is sometimes just not practical. Sometimes, you just can't leave. You wonder if there's a way to make them change so that your life is a lot more manageable. It can be that the troublesome gas lighter is your manager, and you need to be on their good side, or you'll lose your job or get a slash in pay. It can be that the gas lighter is your significant other, and you've got kids, and you're not ready to disrupt the life the kids are comfy with.

Well, you'll be happy to know that there are other solutions besides simply running for the hills! You can't stop a narcissist from being a narcissist, but you can help them improve. Don't tell them that, though. They are flawless, like Beyoncé. Remember? So how exactly can we deal with these gas lighting devils?

A Little Bit of Sympathy

I know what you're probably thinking. "Wait. What?!" Hear me out, though. Narcissists can use some sympathy because we all, to one extent, have some narcissistic traits of our own. The difference is that with the narcissist, these traits occur in the extreme. These are traits that are good to have to certain degrees. If they didn't exist at all, we'd be living on a little blue dot full of low self-esteem.

Narcissism exists on a spectrum. Things only get worse the further down you go, where you've got the evil narcissist with the overly entitled attitude and zero consciences when it comes to exploiting others, being dishonest, and all that other horrible stuff.

To get deeper into this "a little bit of bad is good" line of thought, let's look at grandiosity. The fact is it's great for feeling happy, fulfilled, and healthy. A wee bit of narcissism in your adolescent years is also great because it allows you to survive all that usually accompanies that stage of life and living. Even as a teenager, it helps to be moderately narcissistic, as you have a smaller chance of suffering from depression and anxiety, and the quality of your relationships is significantly better than your self-aware, non-narcissistic peers, or your overly narcissistic ones. The surprising benefits of moderate narcissism do not just stop in school. It can be a big help when it comes to your career. The bosses who are a bit narcissistic are often seen by their employees as being better at getting things done when compared to the overly narcissistic or non-narcissistic leader. In other words, the only difference between the malignant narcissist and us is where we fall on the spectrum.When narcissism is on the furthest, malignant end of the spectrum, that's when it becomes a disorder. The only way that you can be of any help when it comes to making the narcissist a better person is to recall that this is a mental issue. In the heat of the moment, this is not an easy thing. All we can think of is the fact that this person is terrible. However, when we've been able to get away from their clutches, put some distance between you and their toxicity, and allowed ourselves to heal enough so that we can stand on our own two feet, we need to recall that just like we would show sympathy for sufferers of anxiety, borderline personality disorder, and depression, we should do the same for those with narcissism.

No Love

One common thing about most narcissists' childhoods is that they were never given true love when they were kids. They never knew the security of being shown, unconditional love. They were never shown any appreciation for simply being their authentic selves. Their parents and others in their lives only ever celebrated them when they achieved something. They never received any empathy, and on account of this, they learned to be distrustful of everyone. They learned to become ashamed of their authentic selves and to hide that self away.

Put yourself in the shoes of the narcissist like a child. Having tried and failed unsuccessfully, you decide that you're done trying to fulfill your emotional needs. You're done hoping you'll be loved for simply being you. The goal becomes apparent: You need to be more special than others. You need to do better than others. You've got to look better and be smarter. You choose to stop looking to people to help you feel validated, and instead, you focus on being the best at everything you do. You imagine a world where you are far better than everyone around you. Why am I having you look through the eyes of the narcissist like a child? It's simple: this is where the key to helping them lies.

Fixing Perfection

Let us revisit the issue of empathy when it comes to narcissists. It's a muscle they've never really had to flex for most of their lives. While the psychopath is a narcissist, the narcissist is not necessarily a psychopath. They can feel some empathy if they try. You can help them learn how.

If you resort to name-calling or criticism, all you do is make them even worse. The narcissist will simply resort to being more of what you hate. However, when you help them remember that relationships matter, in the most compassionate way that you can, you can help the narcissist in your life to do better. This is not wishful thinking. Studies have shown that simply teaching the narcissist to be more compassionate and caring is enough to reduce their narcissistic traits to somewhere near manageable if they are approached in a soft and gentle manner. The more you reflect secure love to them, the more they become comfortable with being loving and committed to you.

To fix your perfect narcissist, you don't berate them because of their many achievements, or their drive. You don't make them feel bad for having achieved so much. You don't criticize them for being manipulative and callous when it comes to other people's feelings. What you should do instead is let them see first-hand how it pays to be more understanding and to be willing to work well with others.

I ought to warn you that while this does have amazing results, you're not going to see changes overnight. They won't suddenly swing from being terrible and unpredictable to loving and stable. You'll need to give it time and use a very special technique.

Empathy Prompts

The way to reduce or get rid of narcissism is to use empathy prompts. First, you need to speak up about how your relationship is important, and then you need to speak up about the way you feel.

When you talk about why your relationship matters, you must make sure you use statements that are affirming and supportive. Tell, "I care about you deeply," or "You mean so very much to me," or "You're very important to me." When you use these affirmations, the narcissist gets the message that they do matter to you. They feel something they've not felt in a long time, if ever. They feel reassurance. As you use these affirmative statements, you will find that the narcissist will slowly but surely move from thinking about you and them as separate from each other, to think about you both as a team. They also get another message: They can get secure, safe, unconditional love from you. You can say to the narcissist, "Look, I feel like you're one person who matters the most to me in the world, so it really hurts when you're always suspicious of me. It makes me feel like I have failed you." You can say, "You're more important to me than you know. That's why it hurts when you refuse to return my messages and calls for days and even weeks."

Note that empathy prompts only really work with people who display narcissistic tendencies! If we're talking about someone with a clear case of Narcissistic Personality Disorder, you're probably not going to get very far without enlisting the help of a licensed psychotherapist. Don't let this get you down, though. You can still use empathy prompts to see if there's any hope at all when it comes to the narcissist in your life. Just make sure you are very sincere, and you don't raise your voice when you use the prompts. Also, don't covertly guilt trip them. If you do this right, you will notice that your narcissist will soften up.

Signs That Empathy Prompts are working

If you want to be certain that they're working, look out for the following responses from the narcissist:

● They'll want to clarify things. They'll do this by asking you questions like, "For how long have I been making you feel bad or sad?"

● They'll affirm you. In response to your empathy prompts, they will say, "You matter to me too. I don't want ever to hurt you." or something to that effect.

● They will validate your feelings. "I know, my sarcastic comments hurt you deeply."

● They will also apologize. "I'm sorry. I never wanted you to feel sad."

Note that all of this works great when you're dealing with your narcissistic lover. You most likely won't be getting this intimate with your manager or colleague at work.

The Narcissist at Work

Open any book, and they will most likely recommend that the only way to deal with the narcissist at work is to report them to the relevant authorities and get them fired. However, that just doesn't work as well as these books want you to believe they do? Research has shown that a measly 1.7% of such abusive cases get investigated, and lead to the abuser being punished accordingly. In 6.2% of the cases, the abuser is dealt with, but the target is not protected in any way. In 8.7% of the cases, the matter was investigated very unfairly, and there was no punishment to keep the abuser in check. 31% of these cases were never thoroughly investigated; there was no fair play, no punishment for the abuser, and a lot of punishment for the target. In 12.8 percent of reported cases, nothing was done, and the matter was simply ignored, with no punitive measures for either the target or the bully. In 15.7% of reported cases, nothing was done, but the target experienced retaliation from the abuser for reporting the matter while the target remained employed. Finally, in 24% of reported abuse cases at work, the employers simply fired the targets. What do all these stats mean? Reporting the abuser works only about 30% of the time. There's a 70% chance that you'll be the one run over when you do choose to report.

Dealing with the Workplace Narcissist

Reward the narcissist for good behavior. When the narcissist does something good, compliment them. When they act warmly, praise them for being warm — not for their performance at work. Only ever praise them when they show some sort of empathy or human kindness. Always be on the lookout for the chance to compliment them on being a more caring, cooperative coworker who cares about another people's happiness. Always compliment them when they act like a team player.

Chapter 13
Gas Lighting At Work, At Home, and In Society

The world of work is a competitive place. There are pressures to achieve our goals, meet deadlines, and get promoted. In this high-stress environment, it is very easy to ignore an incident of gas lighting or even continued manipulation by colleagues. Some gas lighters may be unintentionally driven to reach a once-off goal, such as achieving a promotion that you were also competing for. On a subconscious level (low level), you may wish to level the playing field if your colleague has got better qualifications than you. You may say to your colleague the morning before their interview, "Don't you think your outfit is a bit inappropriate for the position?" (And you may honestly think so.) However, your payoff is to undermine your colleague's confidence and sabotage their interview.

Gas lighting in the Home

Home is a place where we should be at peace, be able to let our guard down, and feel secure with our loved ones. Yet, it is also where we find relationships that contain narcissist traits and gas lighting. Any time that you want to make someone see something your way, you may be engaging in gas lighting. In fact, many people are "blissfully" unaware of the fact that they have been engaging in gas lighting themselves. Apart from messing around in their target's memories to instill doubt, gas lighters deny that they have acted maliciously. They will never own up to their abusive behavior unless it is to find another way to manipulate them by playing on your empathy (and sympathy).

On the low end of the spectrum, we might find a wife wanting to buy a new home entertainment center but needing to convince her husband to do so. She may say something like, "Honey, you like this brand. Remember that you said it's a reliable brand and that you think it's worth the money? You are so right!" There may be nothing apparently abusive or manipulative about this, but when we look closer, this is a moderated example of gas lighting. The wife establishes her power by pulling the husband in with endearing terms like "honey." She then lists the virtues of the brand she likes, but she falsely indicates that the husband had been in favor of it, and how can he not remember it? She sweetens the pot by flattering the husband—he's so wise. As a result of this gas lighting, the wife gets her home theater set while also feeling victorious in convincing her husband that it was his idea to get it. However, the husband feels manipulated, and he questions his memory since he doesn't remember having said those things, but surely, he must have since his wife (whom he trusts) says that he did? He doubts himself and willingly gives his power of choice to his wife.

On the high end of the spectrum, we may find a pathological narcissist who engages in intentional gas lighting to manipulate and disempower their family and, thereby, gain strength. An example of this may be a father who acts inconsistently towards his children. One day he might tell his children off for being noisy, while tomorrow he allows them to engage in noisy behavior in the house. He then tells his children that they made a noise on both days and that he will have to punish them. The father is in a position of power and gets the thrill of punishing his children, while the children feel uncertain about what was the right thing to do as they were punished. The children may refute the father and say that he gave them permission, which he will deny by saying that he is a strict father who has always avoided his children making noise. The children will begin to doubt that they heard their father correctly and fear the results of their displeasing him.

Gas lighting in Society

On the global stage, we will find many instances of gas lighting, where people have manipulated others to achieve their goals of self-empowerment and enrichment (emotionally and financially). Certainly, politicians are renowned for it, and it comes as no surprise to most of us that they would grandstand and manipulate, so why not gaslight? What is interesting to note is that what we would consider gas lighting in one culture may not be seen as such in another. Some cultures are more susceptible to gas lighting (and narcissism) than others. Webber (2016) indicates that cultures with a more collective identity such as some African cultures, where there is an emphasis on "we" and not "I" are less likely to engage in gas lighting and narcissism as power is shared among the whole tribe or family group. In large cities, there is also more pressure on people to reach individual excellence, which will encourage gas lighting, than in smaller towns or out in the rural countryside.

On the lower end of the scale, people worldwide will engage in gas lighting when it suits them and to attain a specific goal. They may do so to discipline and control their children by, for example, telling their child that they really do like going to school when the child hates it. The upper reaches of the scale for gas lighting globally may be best captured by referring to historical figures such as Hitler and Mussolini. They went from gas lighting (as Hitler did with his propaganda and speeches to draw in the crowds and convincing them of truths that they knew were false) before ending in a dictatorship. When looking at the strategies that Hitler used to gain prominence in German politics before World War II, it reads like the three stages of narcissist manipulations (or gas lighting) with Hitler wooing the people (idealization) and promising them everything their hearts desired, before suddenly changing to persecutions (devaluation), and, finally, death camps (discard). Granted, not all narcissists will engage in gas lighting to the point of being equivalent to Hitler; however, we may find the whole spectrum of emotional abuse in our lives if we look closely.

Chapter 14
Gas lighting in love

Gas lighting happens a lot in romantic relationships. First, the gas lighter will love-bomb you. This is called the idealization phase, where you're their one and only, and you could never do any wrong in their eyes. They will give you all the love you want and then some. Often, the narcissist will move way too fast and has no problems pursuing you relentlessly, getting you hooked on all the love and attention which they will only take away in the devaluing phase. Once they have you wrapped around their finger, they withdraw all that love which they've got you hooked on at this point. You'll do anything to get it back because you know that they've loved once, so if you try hard enough, maybe you can get them back. It won't happen, though. They'll start to treat you badly, instead. This is where the gas lighting comes in as they start with the lies, cheating, and violence, making you think it's all in your head, and you're nuts. In severe cases, you can have a nervous breakdown. There have been countless cases where gas lighting has led to suicide.

First, come the lies and exaggerations. What they do to you is to create false stories about you to make you look and feel bad. It's all set up to make you think that there's something about you that's just plain wrong. These stories are propped up by lies, accusations, and untrue assumptions, not facts that you can verify. This way, you're instantly forced to get on the defensive. For instance, a wife can say of her husband, "He was a terrible father, and I had to let him know that." A father can say to his daughter, "I hate it when you wear those off the shoulder tops! I've told you before: you look like a slut!" A manager could say to an employee, "You and your position are dispensable. I don't even know why we're still keeping you on."

Then come the repetitions. These lies and exaggerations need to be repeated often enough so that the gas lighter can keep you on the defensive, which allows them to dominate your relationship with each other, and dictate how all conversations go between you two.

Escalating in the face of a challenge. Did you just dare call the gas lighter out on their vicious lies? Then it's time for them to escalate! You'll never hear them acknowledge that you're right, and they lied. They will simply double down on their lies. Do you have evidence that they are lying? Good for you! Unfortunately, the evidence is only useful in a court of law. They will deny everything, blame you, and pile on more and more lies, bring in an issue that has nothing to do with the problem at hand, say stuff that makes others doubt you, add in more sauce to make you doubt yourself, and leave you in a tangled mess of confusion and frustration. "I moved in with my mother briefly, because she said she was depressed and needed company. When I moved in, I began to get sick. I don't fall ill that easily. One day, I walked into the kitchen and saw my mom putting rat poison into the pasta we'd just made together. She flat out denied it. I pushed, and she said she just keeps some spice in the box just as a gag. I acted like I bought her story. The first chance I got, I took that box and compared it to another from the store. I also went to get checked out in the hospital. My mother had been poisoning me in little doses."

Bring on the exhaustion! The gas lighter will keep attacking you nonstop until you feel completely worn down. At this point, you're so discouraged that you're resigned to your fate as a victim. Your happy self is gone, replaced by this fearful, pessimistic, self-doubting, self-loathing person. You're in a state of debilitation, wondering if you can trust your own perception, no longer able to recognize yourself, no longer sure who you are and what you want out of life.

Now comes the codependence. Now, you're in an even worse place in your relationship. You've become excessively reliant on your abusive partner for emotional and psychological support and guidance. You notice at this point that you are riddled with feelings of anxiety and insecurity, leaving you at the mercy of your abuser. Only they can give you the acceptance and approval you seek. They alone can make you feel safe, secure, and respected, as far as you're concerned. The gas lighter gives and the gas lighter teeth away, and there's not a thing you can do about it. You have become vulnerable. Fearful. Codependent.

A dose of false hope. There will be times when the gas lighter will be kind to you. They will treat you better, one way or another. However, it's really all for the show. You find yourself thinking, "Well, they're not as bad as I thought. I wonder why I ever thought they were terrible to me. Perhaps things can be better. Let me give this another chance." Aha! They have you right where they want you! The sudden change of heart is that it's all part of their manipulation to make you let your guard down and put you at ease. It's to dissuade you from taking any action to free yourself. Once the gas lighter notices that you've calmed down a bit, they will get right back to attacking you. This constant push and pull are how codependency and learned helplessness develop.

Dominate and instill control. The goal of the gas lighter is simple. It's to dominate, control, and milk others for what they are worth. By keeping up with the threats and lies, the gas lighter makes sure that you constantly feel afraid, in doubt, and insecure. When you feel this way, you're more vulnerable and open to them taking advantage of you whenever and however they like, all for their own selfish ends.

Chapter 15
Gas Lighting In Family

The Gas lighting mechanism is similar, in some ways, to some forms of pathological communication that are often found in families where there is a psychotic member or in any case with an important psychiatric pathology that is often discovered to be unconsciously maintained by the whole family system.

We are not talking about a conscious or deliberate violent behavior, but a completely unconscious, even if pathological, dynamic that can substantiate the parent-child relationship where the pathology of the latter more properly expresses the pathology and discomfort of whole family system, often unable to cope with the changes and processes of growth and release of its members.

These forms of paradoxical communications are often implemented with phenomenological similar mechanisms to the Gas lighting mode of operation.

The perceptions and communications of a child can be disconfirmed by the parent, even in spite of the evidence, and in such a systematic and pervasive way as to make the latter doubtfully affect the correctness of his reality test.

Gas lighting strictly describes a more deliberate and conscious behavior of violence and abuse, but this mechanism can be more generally traced in other types of intimate relationships often acted in ways that are not entirely aware or deliberate.

Psychosis indicates that group of disorders that impede normal mental function and that, unlike neuroses, are characterized by the loss of contact with reality. The term was introduced in 1845 by Ernst von Feuchtersleben and is the most serious form of psychiatric disorder.

The symptoms of psychosis are different and vary over time. The most frequent are:

- Confusing state and poor performance of daily mental functions (difficulty in expressing oneself, in remembering, etc.).

- Presence of "illusions" or false convictions, often of a paranoid type.

- Hallucinations (visual, auditory or olfactory).

- Altered and highly variable emotional states. The feeling of distance from reality is also associated with mood swings.

- Behavioral changes associated with previous symptoms (for example, execute orders of "items").

When due to the exposure to strong stress one witnesses the manifestation of symptoms, one speaks of an acute psychotic episode.

The symptoms of psychosis are combined in specific pathologies, some of which will be briefly described below. In schizophrenia, emotional and cognitive communication skills are compromised, and the subject is not able to distinguish between imagination and reality. Delusional disorders are episodes that last around a month characterized by tactile or olfactory hallucinations. Schizophreniform disorder is distinguished from schizophrenia for less than 6 months and for a good level of social functioning. In schizoaffective disorder, schizophrenic symptoms are associated with an episode of mood alteration, preceded by delusions and hallucinations. There are no disturbances in the affective-emotional sphere. Finally, there is talk of a shared psychotic disorder when symptoms appear in a person affected by another with a similar disorder.

Each form of psychosis involves a specific therapeutic treatment. In general, the first option is that of antipsychotic drugs, often in hospital settings, prescribed by a psychiatrist. The drugs greatly reduce the possible reappearance of psychotic symptoms. Among the short-term side symptoms are drowsiness, restlessness, spasms and blurred vision.

In the long term, however, there are more serious consequences that vary from person to person.

In some cases, there is a psychological or psychosocial therapy, in this case we think of a cognitive-behavioral or family therapy. Some also suggest animal-assisted therapy or the use of companion animals which should contribute to the well-being and rapprochement to the reality of patients.

We call love a generic feeling of attraction, not only physical but also emotional, which leads us to bind ourselves to a certain person, perhaps to see with it a certain intellectual or emotional affinity or, in the most extreme cases, to feel it as someone we understand each other with "On the fly" almost without speaking.

In one way or another, therefore, in the person we fall in love we feel we "recognize" something; somewhere we feel, implicitly and intuitively, that there is an alchemy that sounds both new and familiar to us.

However, what we recognize as love is not always a source of joy and gratification; sometimes it can be a feeling that ties us into a dysfunctional relationship in which we continue to suffer and be dissatisfied.

What is it that in these cases prevents us from binding ourselves to someone who can make us truly happy?

Try to do a little experiment for a moment: cross your arms as you spontaneously do; probably this is a posture that you take several times during the day, which you are used to and that you can perform practically "automatically", maybe it's a way to feel more comfortable and at ease and you could probably keep it for a long time, while you read on, almost forgetting about it while you immerse yourself again in reading.

Now try to free your arms and cross them in the opposite direction by reversing the arm that is above with the one below.

Well, maybe this is an unusual position that can be a little awkward for you and maybe it could distract you from reading. In other words, it is not the familiar position that you know and in which you are most comfortable.

In relationships, in some respects, we could say that it works in not very different ways: especially in love relationships we tend to find and reproduce patterns of the past, which have characterized relationships with some significant figures for defining our sense of security and identity ; we are so accustomed, by implication, to defining ourselves within these dynamics for us "family" to tend spontaneously and almost without notice to search for them and recreate them even with the partners we choose in adult life.

This is why, for example, love can be experienced as an emotionally ambivalent attraction in which the old and the new are mixed: a person he has just met whom we do not yet know and yet attracts us and makes us feel good in a way that it sounds "comfortable" because it has something familiar about it.

In a healthy love these aspects can be profitably integrated and, if the two partners have the emotional resources to accept also the mutual differences, it is possible that the encounter of love leads us to find something of the affections of the past but in the context of a new and more satisfying mode of relationship and emotional exchange.

In other words, the love relationship is not dysfunctional because it is able to help the two partners to grow and evolve with greater satisfaction for themselves and for the couple they have formed.

A love relationship can be dysfunctional when instead it holds the two partners united in a bond within which some unsatisfactory aspects of past emotional relationships are repeated, relationships that we do not recreate voluntarily, but that we reproduce almost automatically - like when we fold our arms, remember? - Because, although they cause us a lot of suffering, they are somehow "familiar" and emotionally adequate to assign us a role in which we implicitly recognize ourselves.

So then, even changing partners numerous times, we might be surprised to find ourselves in unsatisfactory sentimental situations and, from this point of view, painfully similar.

There has been so much talk in recent years of domestic violence and of couple unions based on violence where the reciprocal roles - the abuser and the victim - painfully confirm the partners in the belief that they cannot be defined psychologically if not in relation to another by to own and / or depend on.

Love can be dysfunctional even in less extreme forms of this, whenever we recognize, behind the failures and disappointments of which our emotional life can be studded, the same dissatisfactions, the same problems that have tormented a relationship that would otherwise had to provide us with serenity, joy and gratification.

The time has perhaps come to interrupt a cycle that tends to repeat itself too equal to itself. Sometimes this happens thanks to unexpected and particularly fortunate encounters that divert our emotional life towards unexpected turns. In other cases, it is necessary to repeatedly contact that same suffering to become aware of the price we pay and to undertake a change sometimes through a path of psychological counseling or psychotherapy. John Lubbock on the other hand wrote: "happiness is something to be practiced, like with the violin".

What is healthy love? When, on the other hand, does the couple's relationship because suffering or is it an indication of emotional dependency?

Similar questions are now widespread in the current culture where the couple's relationship does not exhaust its raison d'être in the construction of a family, but we expect personal and emotional satisfaction and fulfillment for both partners.A healthy love, however, is not an individual sentiment given once and for all, but a necessarily interpersonal dimension where the internal state of each one is regulated and influenced by the relationship that it has with the other.

Some psychoanalytic authors (Henry Dicks, Marital tensions, 1967) have identified in marriage a sort of natural therapeutic relationship where everyone would find compensation and reparation for those problematic relational dynamics lived in their own family of origin.

The two partners, in short, would represent for each other affective regulators for the management of their emotional life. This is not in itself pathological, but also occurs in a healthy love where in any case the couple's bond owes its stability to the mutual satisfaction of the emotional needs of both partners (Giulio Cesare Zavattini, Subjectivity and self-regulation of the couple's affections, 1995)

What makes the difference in a healthy love is in a certain sense the goal with which, unknowingly, we bind each other. In a healthy love the two partners trust each other aspects of their interiority and emotionality drawing from this energy and inner strength to grow and progress along their personal path of realization.

In a healthy love, we could say, the individuality of each one is enriched and improved by the dimension of a couple in a continuous exchange between these two dimensions: in a healthy love the individual nourishes the couple and vice versa.In pathological couple relationships, it is common for partners to bind themselves to perpetually perpetuate dysfunctional but habitual modes of relationship which, as a cause of suffering, paradoxically provide greater reassurance because they are predictable family members and, as such, able to confirm identity and the self-perception that one has of oneself.

Consider, for example, the wives of alcoholic men who are often already victims of fathers or other family members with a similar problem in their family of origin.

A healthy love is such if it solicits and promotes the growth of both partners; this implies that the couple's relationship is not sclerotic on a fixity of roles and mutual expectations but is able to evolve and adapt to changes.

A healthy love, in a certain sense, continually asks the two partners to try to be better and, therefore, a little different from how until then they were used to being.

This requires commitment and emotional fatigue in a process that is never given once and for all. For these reasons, a healthy love actually has little to do with the stereotypes with which the romantic love of fairy tales is banalized: there can be no "everyone lived happily ever after" not because happiness is not of this world, but because it is never given or reached once and for all, but continually sought, lost and rediscovered in an incessant path that we call life.

Choosing a partner is not a simple task, do you need to find someone who has our vision and perspective on life or are opposites attracting you?

What are the criteria for a winning selection? Literature suggests different points of reflection: natural selection would benefit successful males and fertile and healthy women.

SECTION III

Chapter 16
Practical Ways to Defend Against Gas Lighters

The gas lighter takes a single story from your whole life and repeats it over and over until you begin to believe it. By choosing one narrative (usually a negative one) and playing it in a loop, your focus and attention are glued to that negative aspect. Instances of where the gas lighter's malicious story seems to be true will start presenting themselves to you, and you will eventually start considering the validity of the story.

A gas lighter does not need to share a close connection with you to gaslight you. For example, they could be your boss, subordinate, or colleague but because these people can directly target your performance, the impact can create a lot of doubt in your abilities. In general, gas lighters do not engage in outright demolition of your perceptions, instead, they are likely to engage in the deconstruction of your views and beliefs. So, while someone may not directly put you down, they can achieve the same effect by "being realistic" about what you can and can't do. They will repeat the story of your inadequacy until you believe it.

The worst thing you can do to yourself when you suspect that someone is gas lighting you is to go into denial. You must listen to and trust your gut, which is exactly what the gas lighter never wants you to do.

Protecting yourself from a Gas lighting Coworker

If you suspect that someone is gas lighting you at work, your first line of action should be to establish that fact before taking any action. You don't want to act too quickly only to end up confirming that you are imagining things.

Here's how to know for sure that someone is trying to manipulate you using gas lighting in the workplace. If you find yourself constantly overworked either to prove yourself or because you are saddled with tasks that are outside your job descriptions (and sometimes belittling), you may be experiencing gas lighting at work. If someone makes you feel incompetent by deliberately sabotaging your work, giving you wrong due dates to make you miss deadlines, or you just can't figure out what is expected of you, they are showing strong signs of gas lighting.

One other subtle sign to look out for is turning down opportunities not because you don't like them or because you feel unqualified but because you want to avoid being put down. The coworker you think might be at loggerheads with you if you say yes to opportunities is probably gas lighting you. They may have been showing disgust at your progress at work, whispering abuse when they pass by your desk, ridicule you in front of other work colleagues, and try to make you look bad before your superior. To avoid further emotional attacks, you begin to pull back into your shell and let them control your behavior at work.

Here are some other things to be on the lookout for:

- excluding you (from important meetings or hangouts with colleagues).

- Continuously linking every other conversation to something you did wrong in the past.

- Making jabbing remarks at you when you make a complaint. For example, "Obviously, you have a problem with following instructions."

- Gossiping and spreading false rumors about you.

- Denying something they said.

If you establish a consistent pattern of undermining behavior from your direct report, coworker, boss, or someone else at work, it is safe to conclude that they are gaslighting you. Your next line of action should be to keep a record of your official interactions. Document every instruction and communication and make sure you have backup copies of both written and electronic communications. If the communication is verbal, you can get a witness or insist they put it in writing (where possible). For example, if your gas lighting boss, who happens to be in a good mood, says you can take a day off when you complete your current assignment, it will be a great idea to get them to put it in writing while they are still in a good mood. It is difficult for gas lighters to pull a fast one on you if you have such concrete evidence. If they deny or try to lie to confuse you, you have references to prove otherwise and maintain your sanity and self-trust.

If the gas lighter persists in their behavior, you can report to Human Resources or higher-level supervisors. But make sure you have irrefutable evidence (paper or digital proof) before making an official complaint. It is also crucial to follow laid-down procedures on making complaints in your organization. You don't want to be in violation of any official rule while trying to protect yourself. While talking to a few other colleagues at work to find out if they are experiencing the same thing can help, it may not always work out in your favor. Someone you talk to might snitch on you and make things messier. You could be accused of gossip and backbiting, and it won't be far from the truth. If you must speak with other colleagues about the situation, be sure of whom you are confiding.

One other effective thing you can do to shield yourself from further attacks from a gas lighter is to be straightforward with them. Let them know that you understand what they are trying to do, and you are not ready to play their games. Often, gas lighters try hard to hide their manipulation, so making them see that they are hiding in plain view can get them off your back. For example, instead of engaging in futile arguments by using defensive phrases such as "I did not," or "I am not," phrase your statements in empowering ways. You could say something along the lines of, "I refuse to argue with you. What exactly do you want and how can we achieve that together?"

Gas lighting is not limited to intimate relationships alone. It happens in the workplace more frequently than we care to admit. But don't accept it because you want to avoid conflicts. Put your foot down and don't allow someone else to make you think you are a pushover.

Protecting yourself from a Gas lighting Friend

Your circle of friends can be a formidable support system that upholds you when you are down. But they can also become the primary source of your feelings of confusion through a pattern of vilification, backbiting, harsh criticisms, shaming, and guilt-tripping. Since we are programmed to expect love, support and honesty from those closest to us, it can be difficult to quickly spot manipulation when it is coming from our friends.

Gas lighting friends can shame you for your choices and isolate you from others who can make you feel empowered. As long as they have you believing that your views are inferior to theirs, they can control you however they want. If you feel the need to make a friend like you although they consistently make you feel less, they are controlling you already.

If you find yourself always waiting for a friend to make choices for you, you always have to seek their approval before making personal decisions, or you feel you can't do anything socially acceptable (keeping up with the current trends) without them, although you're not truly happy when you're with them, you may be keeping a gas lighting friend or "frenemy."

You are dealing with a gas lighter friend if what you tell them in confidence becomes a subject for public consumption and ridicule. A friend who gets their kicks from gossiping about you and takes pleasure from your misfortunes is showing surefire signs of gas lighting. They would like to see you in a fight with other friends—a fight that they instigate.

So, what do you do if you have a gas lighting friend?

First things first, stay away from them. One way to do this is to be upfront about it and simply walk away. Cut off all ties, tell them you no longer want their company, and be firm about your decision. This may be a tough call, but if you must rid yourself of their toxic influence, it is crucial to let them out of your life. Don't wait until the gas lighter grows tired of manipulating you and dumps you. You are worth more than that! Why wait until they have no more use for you? Why let someone fill your life with unnecessary drama when you can actually do something about it?

Another way to end the friendship is to become very boring to hang out with so that the gas lighter walks away from the friendship. Gas lighters like to make people frantic and thrown off balance, but if you respond to them by being ambivalent, they can tire out quickly and take their sight off you. For example, instead of being defensive about an inflammatory remark by the gas lighter, you could respond with, "Oh, I see," "Maybe," "Okay," and so on. Be deliberate and consistent, and before long, your gas lighting friend will find you as boring as hell.

No matter how close you are with a gas lighting friend, if you decide to end the abuse, make up your mind never to borrow anything from them or lend them anything, especially money. Turn down any gift and all forms of assistance they offer you. A gas lighter will always find a way to make their so-called gifts come back to haunt you. They may go to the extent of accusing you of stealing it from them. This is one of their many tactics of getting even with you if they think that you have wronged them. Also, if you lend them anything, never expect to get it back. Stay away from exchanging anything with them to avoid a backlash.

A gas lighting friend does not truly care about you and anything that is of importance to you. Don't ever leave them in charge of your kids, pets, and belongings. Gas lighters can cause irreparable loss for you. Worst still, they can deny ever doing so and make you think it's all in your head. A gas lighting friend can blatantly deny being responsible for something you are sure they did and turn around to blame you for accusing them falsely. They could say things like, "How could you jeopardize our friendship with such grave accusations? You've allowed your crazy imaginations get out of hand, and I won't stand here listening to this nonsense!"

Protecting yourself from a Gas lighting Family Member

If you discover that you can never do anything right in your family no matter how hard you try, it is likely that someone (your parents, siblings, or other family members) is gas lighting you. This happens quite often in families with double standards for rewards and punishments. In such settings, a particular family member (usually a "golden child") gets the best treatment and even if they are wrong, they get a milder punishment. On the other hand, the "scapegoat child" always gets the worst treatments, and their achievements are hardly acknowledged. Instead, their inadequacies are often blown out of proportion to make them feel more out of place. And if the scapegoat child ever gets in a fight with the golden child, they usually take the fall for everything that went wrong. This can leave the scapegoat child wondering, "How exactly is this my fault? Am I missing something, is there a conspiracy here, or am I losing my mind?"

One common dynamic that plays out in gas lighting between family members is the drama triangle. It happens when there is a victim, a persecutor, and a rescuer. The persecutor (the gas lighter) can oppress the victim through bullying and threats.

Chapter 17
Recognize the Hidden Manipulation From Reading Body Language

We human beings are very positive. We like to think that most people are honest and nice and that is why many manipulators tend to strive in our society today. So, you really need to learn what to look out for, when you have a feeling that someone is a manipulator or that person is not telling the truth. This segment will talk about some of the manipulation techniques that narcissist uses to keep its victims sucked into their little game.

They use a mask all the time

First of all, you have to realize that most manipulate, tend to have a mask on because that way, it will be much harder for you not to know why your resistance to their influence. You will notice that manipulators tend to go the extra mile with everything because when someone tries to mask everything and cover-up over something, then they become extra friendly and out have a very strong smile. They will start telling off-color jokes and their behavior will be a little bit exaggerated, especially if they don't know you that well.

They also tend to use conviction bias to manipulate you. The conviction bias is meant to deceive you that they know what they're talking about. So, when you notice them talking with such exaggerated energy, then you should be aware that they are trying to manipulate you. Now sometimes someone might be generally friendly with you and be more enthusiastic with you, but if the person doesn't know who you're or you notice that the person is trying to hide something from you, then you should be more sensitive to their body language.

When they are trying to manipulate you, you will notice that one part of their body will be more expressive than the rest part of their body especially in their mouth area. You will see their super smiles and their exaggerated expressions because it is the easiest area to control. They will also try to use extreme hand gestures. As they use some part of their body exaggeratedly, and one part of their face will be relieving tension because it is impossible for anybody to control all of their muscles all at once. So, they might be smiling with you, but then the rest of their body will be unusually still. They might also be giving you some certain looks so that they will gain your sympathy, but their mouth will be quivering at the same time.

So, these are some signs that show that they are trying to control their body parts too hard. They won't be able to control all of their body so you should look out some signs of tension and anxiety in other parts of their body. Now, if they're trying to cover up for mischief that they did then their expression will become super serious and their body will be unusually still, and instead of denying something plainly, they will have a plausible explanation with a very thought Out chain of events and evidence to confirm it. Now you must keep in mind that real life is not very seamless.

Reality always includes some unexpected things that happen in between. So, whenever an explanation seems to deep or too professional, then you should be skeptical of it. So whenever you notice that somebody is trying to distract you from the truth, try not to confirm them. Instead you should encourage them to speak more. Because the more they speak, the more tension they will show. And then at the right moment pause and ask them questions that will make them uncomfortable and then when you ask them those question, you will notice their micro expression and their body language.

Most times they will have a frozen moment that throws them off and they will try to quickly mask it out. Also, try to notice how they give emphasis to the words they are saying through non-verbal cues. For instance, raising their eyebrows, using hand gestures, vocal pitch and a certain tone, widening of the eyes, and leaning forward. Normally we usually use this behavior whenever we are filled with emotions and when we want to add an exclamation point to what we are saying.

Now, whenever they emphasize anything, you will notice that the emphasis is not appropriate because it doesn't fit the context, or it comes a little bit late. Now manipulators range from different scale; some manipulate are better than others. Some will give you white lies every day by telling something like, "Hey you look good today, and I really like your outfit today, but then you can notice that their smile isn't telling you that." No, you don't have to acknowledge every plate on your life because that is usually draining for you because in social situations, they have a mask on whether you admit it or not. You should mostly pay attention to the non-verbal clues, especially whenever you need to that they want to harm you or take something away from you.

So, to sum up the signs of manipulation is exaggerated friendliness, they are trying really hard to gain your sympathy, and they want you to like them so that you will lower your resistance on them.

Use some part of their body in an exaggerated way

The second clue is that they use some part of their body in an exaggerated way, whereby some other parts of their body display anxiety and tension. Whenever they are trying to cover up something, they will usually have a perfect explanation for that, but since reality isn't seamless, then you should try to encourage them to talk more. Because the probability for them to make a mistake is bigger, and you should try to pose questions that will make them uncomfortable so that they can show more signs of tension.

Emphasize words

The next one is that when they emphasize some words a bit. And whenever they try to do that, it is either too late or too early. So, you have to pay attention to the narcissist's body language because people communicate a lot through their body language than through their words. So, it is totally wrong for you to believe what they are saying and ignore their body language, which is revealing stuff that they're not saying.

Observe what's going on

So, the best thing that you should do at first is to really observe what is going on in the office. You have to be so clever and also aware of how you feel about the narcissist so that you don't get sucked in the drama. You have to grey-rock them. This is very hard to do but it can be done, so try to observe without absorbing.

Try to observe the Dynamics and accept that the narcissist person is the way they are, and you cannot change them. So that you will no longer be in resistance to who that person is and what's going on. So that you will just accept that the person is a rock, and you will just accept that person is a tiger. And you will just accept that person is a Predator, but you are going to do everything you can to avoid that person.

Don't get into battles

So, try not to get into battles with this person because that is the last thing that you want to do. Try not to allow them to know that you have to figure them out because the minute they know that you have figured them out, then it is game on. Allow them to continue to believe that they are controlling you. To develop the skill to observe, not absorb. Do not engage in any battles with them and be very clever not to allow them to know that you already know what they are about. Because, once they understand that you are trying to manipulate them, they will try their possible best to dominate and Gain control over you.

Don't tangle with a narcissist person, just it let go. Now, if you are in a situation whereby you cannot leave the office, and you really need the job, then rather than going directly to the narcissist and having a blow-up with the person, just start documenting everything. Keep a journal of what the person said, what project got done what you did on a project. What the other person did and didn't do. When you completed the project, try to keep a log of the facts so that if you ever have to report to his superior about the facts, you will have proof to back you up. You don't want to go to the superior while being emotional because they are going to rely on the fact.

The more emotional you are, and the more factual you are about what is really happening and the clearer it is that there has been an atrocity taking place, either bullying or sexual harassment and also a clear attempt to sabotage you at work, the most serious that the people in the HR positions will take you. The more you know and understand who the narcissist is the easier it is for you to let go. It makes no sense to focus your energy on something you can't control.

Work on your triggers

The last thing you can do is to work on your own triggers and make sure that you are not over reactive. Make sure that you are accepting people for who they are, and if you get to a point whereby you have empathy for somebody who behaves this way and you can love this person, then good for you. however, you have to understand that when you are angry with someone, you're coming to that anger with you and it will make you feel as if you are securing yourself or as if you are stronger but at the end of the day, it is going to tear you apart. So, it is more important for you to focus on yourself and let go of what you can't control. Focus on the facts and remain engaged and non-emotional when dealing within narcissist person at work.

Chapter 18
Deal with the Effects of Gas lighting

Gas lighting (called "guéslaitin") is the term given to systematic manipulation that can occur within the family, professional, academic, religious, etc. Their practice is to convince the victim that she is forgotten, hysterical or crazy on several different occasions over time; with this, the person gains power and control over the victim.

A classic example is a partner who repeatedly repeats how you imagine things or distort facts while you clearly remember them. He can do this to get rid of issues he doesn't want to discuss, and over time, this repetition that you are irresponsible, overreacting, and always wrong can cause your self-esteem and confidence to break, both yourself and your others. To recover from gas lighting and in dealing with its effects, you must rebuild your self-esteem, gain your confidence back, and establish a support network.

1. Dealing with the effects of gas lighting

Getaway. This kind of manipulation is a mental and emotional abuse for the sole purpose of controlling and having power over you. In such a relationship, it is best to rethink it and decide if it's really worth continuing with someone who does it. Only then can you recover.

- For example, if you just realized that your partner does things on purpose to make you doubt yourself, this is the first sign that you should separate.

- Talk to someone intimate about how to escape from this situation. Tell someone like your brother that you are being manipulated by your partner and need to get out of this relationship.

- Ask a therapist or other mental health professional for help with how to finish.

- Contact a support network for victims of domestic violence. They will know how to guide you and will pass other contacts that may help.

Reduce your stress. Mental abuse can cause a lot of burnout and you may feel nervousness, tension, and fatigue, among other symptoms. One of the measures to become yourself is to strive to minimize these feelings and eliminate their sources. Some good ideas include meditation, yoga, breathing techniques, and visualization.

- There are several types of meditation to relieve stress; yoga, mindfulness, etc.

- Visualize yourself in a quiet place with details, such as an image of yourself with your forehead and chin totally relaxed. See the smile on your look and the happiness in your eyes.

Take care of your anxiety. Anxiety and nervousness are also the results of gas lighting. After all, you no longer trust yourself and spend all the time afraid of being accused of something you didn't do. This feeling can become a pattern and to get rid of it, you must find ways to calm down.

- For example, if you no longer know what looks good on you because your partner always criticizes your clothes, look your feelings and doubts, try to overcome this fear of displeasing him. It recovers its autonomy.

- When you realize that your nervousness is beating, try to calm down with the techniques of mindfulness; allow yourself to feel this tension temporarily, assume what you are feeling without judging yourself and let it go.

- Focus on your breathing and think "in" when you breathe in and "out" when you breathe out. This can be helpful in the midst of an anxiety attack.

Take care of depression. Being a victim of manipulation and mental abuse often brings depression as a consequence. However, know that you can fight it. Look for symptoms and try to reverse them.

- For example, note whether throughout the relationship you had difficulty completing simple tasks, fatigue, or lost energy and interest in life.

- Find out if you have physical symptoms that may be related to depression, even if you don't even suspect it. Things like changes in appetite or sleep, physical problems and unexplained pain, lack of concentration, etc. may be clues.

- Seek professional help for treatment and recovery from depression. It will help you decide if you should take medications or prefer alternative treatments.

- Develop ways to combat depression on a daily basis, such as creating an activity routine and not getting out of it. It is wise to stay away from alcohol and other substances.

2. Restoring Confidence in Yourself and Others

Listen to yourself. This will surely be one of the most difficult things during your recovery and also the most important. After being constantly manipulated, it is normal for you to simply ignore your intuition and it will disappear, but this is reversible.

- Start with small things, such as paying attention to your body; obey him if you feel hungry or sleepy and say to yourself, "I can trust myself to know when I need to eat or sleep. That may not seem like anything, but it's a big step towards my self-confidence. "

- When you need to make a decision, do not feel pressured or give this power to others. Say "I know my time and I prefer to find out what all my options are before I make a decision."

- Repeat "I can trust myself and my judgment" when you begin to doubt yourself.

Go to the source of the information. One of the effects of gas lighting is to doubt others and your own sanity as well. During manipulation, you may even go so far as to believe only what your partner says, no matter what others say. As you recover, try to regain your trust in others by checking the source of what people say.

- Begin by striving to believe in one or two close people. Choose someone intimate who has already gone through his highs and lows with you as a family member.

- Use these people to find out what is real and what is not. For example, if your sister says you look great, ask your mother if she is telling the truth or lying.

Have a diary. One way to recover from domination is to write whenever something that helps you believe in yourself happens. A journal filled with these experiences can help you see that others can be trusted.

- When you make a decision and it proves right, write it down! Write about when you decided to take an umbrella with you on a sunny day, which turned out to be a rainy day.

- Also write down when people give evidence that they are reliable. For example, when your friend promised something and did it to the letter.

Use affirmative sentences with yourself. It is not at all difficult for a gas lighting victim to feel worthless, hopeless and lost, as that was indeed the intention of the abuser. Work on your self-esteem with positive phrases about yourself.

- List your journal attributes and adopt some of the words used in the list when talking to yourself.

- Instead of repeating that you are lazy, lunatic, or forgetful, say that you are talented, creative, and hardworking, and repeat, "I can trust and like myself."

Spend your time doing things you enjoy. You may have even forgotten the things you always liked, especially if you had to do everything for your ex-partner. Try to resume the activities that interested you to heal.

- Take at least five minutes a day to do something that changes your mood, such as getting ready to sing in front of the mirror before work.

- Go after things you haven't done in a long time, like playing the piano; take a lesson or two to refresh your memory and find out if you still like it and resume where you left off.

Take care of your body. Suffering gas lighting can make you careless because the idea is to make you feel that it doesn't matter. You will need the energy, focus, and energy to recover, so take care of your health.

- Do some physical activity like yoga, martial arts, daily walks, etc.?

- Eat nutritious meals and snacks for energy and a good mood.

- Get plenty of rest. To be able to look the battle and regain confidence in yourself, believe in your instincts and make decisions safely, it is paramount to be rested. Only then will it be possible to maintain focus and willpower.

3. Creating a support network

Seek professional help. Recovery will be faster and more effective if you have a network of people you can count on. Psychologists and therapists will listen to what you have to say and can provide useful tools for dealing with the effects of gas lighting and have experience with patients with depression, anxiety, and stress.

- For example, if you were in a lasting relationship where you were consistently manipulated, a professional can help you identify the effects of these abuses and deal with them.

- Even if the relationship in question was brief, talking to a professional will help you figure out strategies to recover.

- Talk to someone you trust about what happened. Figures who can guide you, such as doctors, HR professionals, school principals, etc. may have good recommendations for you.

- In addition, they can also help you deal with symptoms of depression, anxiety or other disorders.

Trust your friends and family. This advice is particularly helpful if you have cut yourself off from socializing during gas lighting and think no one else cares about you. Often the abuser can convince the victim that only he knows what is best for her and this keeps her from relatives and friends. Resume these relationships and accept that they are part of your recovery and that you can trust these people.

- Call someone close to spending time with you. It doesn't have to be anything very elaborate like going out, but an invitation to spend the afternoon at your home doing nothing together.

- Accept invitations to social occasions from friends and family.

- Start by spending a short time in class. Going out for coffee or a snack is a great start.

Join a support group. Connect with other gas lighting victims, listen to the stories they have to tell (many similar to yours) and the tips they can give to deal with them during recovery. Positive interactions by a support group can improve their self-esteem and develop new relationships.

- Seek out groups of domestic abuse victims and the like in your area, ask for recommendations from people close to you, the psychologist, your religious leader, and so on.

- Join online groups and forums about it if you can't attend in person or if you can't find a group to attend.

Chapter 19
Ways to Stop a Gas lighter in Their Tracks

If you've read up to this point, then chances are you're probably thinking of a long list of people that have just got to be narcissists or gas lighters in your life. However, as a caution: Not everyone is a narcissist just because you have a little tiff here and there. Also, keep in mind that you might be recollecting past events through the narcissistic glasses, and so everyone might seem to be that way.

With that said, if you've asked yourself the questions listed in, and have observed for yourself that you really are dealing with a gas lighter, how do you deal with them? Let's get into that.

Putting an End to Gas lighting

Pay attention to the pattern. One of the major reason's gas lighting is so effective is that, for the most part, the target is completely ignorant of what's happening. The minute you move from ignorance to complete awareness, you will have successfully taken back some of your power. You will find it easier to shrug off the narcissist when they start playing games again.

Keep in mind that the gas lighter might never change, no matter what you do. Sometimes, the only way there can be any change is with the help of a professional. Gas lighting is all that the manipulator knows how to do, so you cannot expect them to give that up in favor of logic or reason. There is no other better coping mechanism that they know. This is not to say that they should not be held accountable for their actions. I'm just making sure you now not to hold on to the hope that they will change. They could, but don't hope for it. Accept that they're wired the way they are, and only professional therapy can help them become better people.

Remember that gas lighting behavior is not necessarily about you. It all really comes down to the fact that the gas lighter needs to feel like they're in charge. They need that rush of power. At their core, the gas lighter is riddled with insecurity. The only way they know how to get rid of that feeling is to make others feel less than they are, or at least give themselves the illusion that they are better than everyone else. Keep this in mind, and you will not bother internalizing anything they say or do anymore. You will be in a better position to manage the relationship you have with them or to end it altogether.

Create a support system that you can rely on. Dealing with a gas lighter on your own is no walk in the park. It helps to have other people that you can talk to, who will validate your perception of reality as well as your sense of self-worth. If you've noticed that ever since you got involved with the narcissist, you've somehow been cut off from the people that matter to you, then now is the time to reach out to them. Do not buy into the narcissist's lies about how no one else can love you the way they do. That is simply not true! Commit to spending time with your friends and family. Make appointments, if you must. Treat these appointments with as much commitment as you would a business meeting. The less isolated you are, the less of a hold the gas lighter can have on you.

Spend a long time thinking about whether you want to keep investing in the relationship. This is crucial, especially since having to deal with the gas lighter's shenanigans eats away at your peace of mind, self-worth - and even your health. Is the gas lighter your manager, or your boss? Then take proactive steps to find another job, making it a non-negotiable agreement with yourself that you're moving to a different, better and job. If the gas lighter is your lover and you'd like the relationship to continue, then keep in mind that you'll both be needing some therapy, and you will have to make that a non-negotiable aspect of your relationship if you decide to stay.

Start to build your self-esteem back up. Having been with a gas lighter for too long, it's easy to forget just how awesome you are! You need to take some time to remind yourself of everything about you that is amazing, no matter what the gas lighter has said to make you think otherwise. You might need to begin journaling so that at times when you are low or starting to buy into the insidious lies they have packed your head with, you can reopen that, and remind yourself of your awesomeness. Don't just write about the great things about you. Write about times when you felt the most alive, the most joyful. As you do this, you will naturally find yourself craving those times again, and taking action to liberate yourself and your mind.

Be open to getting professional help. It's difficult being the victim of gas lighting. Your self-esteem, sense of self, and sanity will have taken a beating. You might find that you're slow to make decisions, constantly unsure of yourself, and always wondering if you're good enough. You might even be suffering from depression or anxiety. If you find that you're overwhelmed by feelings of helplessness, uncertainty, hopelessness, and apathy, then chances are you need to seek the help of a professional psychotherapist right away, so that you can rebuild yourself after the devastating damage caused to you by the gas lighter.

Chapter 20
How to Avoid Falling for a Gas lighter

N ow you know why the narcissist acts the way they do, and you
know why they pick their targets. You know what to expect
from the gas lighter, and you completely grasp what gas
lighting behavior is. A critical question remains: How do you make sure
you never fall for the gas lighter ever again? You may have found
yourself always getting into relationships with this kind of person. How
do you put the kibosh on that, once and for all?

Steps for Protecting Your Heart from the Gas lighter

Don't be in a hurry to reveal personal information. When you're
tempted to share, ask yourself this: Would I feel okay telling my
colleagues at work? If the answer is no, then just don't do it! You see,
when you share private stuff, it often does a couple of things.

First, it makes you feel like you, and this person has some intimacy going
on. It makes you feel closer to the person you're sharing the info with.
Narcissists know this, and therefore, they do all they can to get you to
open up, so they can speed up the process of getting close to you. You
should never let people get too close until you know the sort of person
that they are.

Sharing too much too soon also leaves you vulnerable to the narcissist.
They can use what they have learned about you to attack you. You will
wish with all your heart that you'd kept your lips shut when you're
dealing with a narcissist.

The truth is that we all love the feeling of intimacy. It is this craving that
makes us so willing to reveal stuff to others, especially when they've just
laid themselves bare, too. There is nothing wrong with intimacy. Just
make sure it happens only with people you trust. That, by default, means
people that you've taken enough time to get to know.

During your initial conversations, ask as many questions as you're being
asked. When the narcissistic gas lighter is probing you, you don't know

- at the moment - which you're dealing with. The best way to be safe is to ask them just as many questions as they're asking you. Always wait until you get an actual answer. If what they say is very vague, then ask a more specific question.

Why does this matter? Narcissists will keep trying to draw information out of you. They move hard and fast so that they can learn all they can. When you ask them questions as well, you keep the playing field level. You get to learn about them, too, whether they want to let it out or not. Even their silence or shiftiness can tell you all you need to know about whether to move forward with this person. Also, as you ask questions too, you'll slow them way, way down.

For instance, if you tell them you're a fan of creamy alcoholic drinks, and they hit you with a "Me too!" you can follow that up with, "Really? What's your favorite bar?" Or you can ask them which kind of said creamy drinks they love the most. This follows up question will box them into having to be specific. In the process, it's not hard to tell if they're lying, since the more specific they must be, the more they will falter. This can also throw them off and make it less likely that they continue engaging with you. That's a win! Always more and more questions, even as they do. Reciprocity is a huge part of any relationship.

Keep your private time private. At the beginning of your relationship, you might notice that you're being bombarded with so much "love." You're not! The only reason you're getting all that love and attention is that the narcissist knows this is a very good way to control you. When you become accustomed to being the center of their universe, they immediately withdraw all that affection. What you should do in response to all the calls, messages, and texts, is nothing. Let your time be yours. Do not reply until you're good and ready to. When a narcissist always calls and texts you, it's no accident. It's a good way to keep you disconnected from those who really care about you and center your attention on them instead.

The narcissist needs attention. When they bombard you with all those calls and messages, they are trying to feel you out and see if you'll give them all the attention and narcissistic supply you need. When you don't give them what they want, they will have no choice but to give up on pursuing you. If someone really and truly cares about you, they will respect your privacy. They will understand that your time is yours to do with as you wish. They will not seek to eat into the time you could spend working on your own projects or building other beneficial relationships as well.

In the beginning, do not make the mistake of fighting for the relationship. Let's say you only just started dating this person, and they're already telling you that their family and friends do not approve of you or the relationship, or they tell you that they will be leaving town soon, or that they are concerned that you'll break up with them. All of these are red flags. What they're prodding you for is your word that you will never leave them. There's nothing wrong with seeking assurance, except that you've only both just started dating; it 'sway too soon for that. If they say something that indicates to you this relationship will crash and burn in no time, just get out.

When you date a narcissist, it's not unlike getting interviewed for a job. The narcissist wants to make sure you will rough it out with them for the rest of forever — however long forever is for them. They want to know that no matter how bad things get, you will do everything within your power to make sure that you both work as a couple. There's nothing wrong with all of this when your relationship has been going long and strong for a while. However, when you start declaring your undying devotion to early in the relationship, it tells them that you're desperate. Desperation is a weakness that they will not hesitate to exploit once they sense it in you. They want someone who is way too desperate to simply get up and get out of the relationship, no matter how bad things get.

If they know they would have to leave town, then why bother dating you, to begin with? If they are bothered by the fact that their loved ones do not approve of them being with you, then why bother continuing the relationship? A lot of the time, all of these seeming stumbling blocks don't exist. The narcissist is simply trying to get you to make a commitment. The thing about decent people is that when they commit or make a promise, it takes a whole lot to get them to break that promise. This is the one time it's okay to not stay true to your word. The narcissist is not worth losing your sanity and peace of mind over! If the narcissist gives you the impression that there is a lot keeping this relationship from lasting long, then see it for what it is: they are pressuring you to commit too much, too soon.

Keep Your Private Space Private. Don't be in a hurry to let someone move into your home immediately. You may have been in a situation where "just one night" became several months or years. When this happens, it is a major red flag. Do whatever you need to do in order to make sure that they don't stay at your home.

Why does this matter? That kind of major move is exactly what the narcissist does to control the way your life goes. The next thing you know, they are in your home and a part of it, just like furniture. The longer you let them stay, the more stressful it is when you need to keep your space as you'd like it to be. Don't be in a hurry to let them move in. You must first figure out your priorities, and then figure out where your relationship fits in. It's not unusual to love having other people around. After all, a good company is always great! However, the best friendships and relationships do not depend on spending a lot of time together over a short period of time. It's about respecting one another and honoring the other person's priorities as well.

Maintain your previous friendships and keep pursuing your hobbies and interests. If you're dating someone who must be with you every minute of every day, then this is not loving. This is not normal. It's a clear sign that something isn't quite working the way it should in their head. It's way too early to want to spend so much time with someone at the beginning of your relationship.

They start digging for too much detail. You can tell them you love clubbing with your friends, but then they might begin pressing you for more details, like, which friends? Which club? What time? How long will you be there? When you notice this, don't give them too much info. It will drive them up the wall — and as far from you as possible.

Understand that this is important because the narcissist does not want to share you with anyone. They want to have you completely to themselves. That's why they work tirelessly to cut you off from the people who love and support you. It's for this reason you need to keep engaging in hobbies that have you meeting new people and keep hanging out with your friends as well. If all you have in your life is the narcissist, then you will inevitably depend on them for all your social and emotional needs, and this means surrendering your power to them!

In a healthy relationship, your partner will respect the time you spend with others, and not ask you every five minutes via text when you're coming home. They will allow you to live and have some fun. If you think that you need to respond to that text, or you need to call it a night because they've said they miss you five times in a row, understand that it's not that you're a good lover; it's that you have been trained to obey. Break the chains!

Don't take care of people you only just met, no matter how badly you want to. If you notice that there is someone in your life who has hit a rough patch in life, and you feel the urge to help them out, take a moment to ask yourself why. Also, ask yourself if it's plausible that there's no one else they can look to for help. Do this all the time, no matter what. Here's why: You might be dealing with a narcissist who is trying to get as close as they can to you by putting themselves in a seemingly vulnerable position in your eyes. This way, you feel compelled to step in and be their savior. Do that, and they've gotten you right where they want you.

They can have very valid reasons for why they have no place of their own, or no job, or no money. With that said, you don't have to play Superman to their Lois. You don't need to save them because they just got out of an unhealthy relationship. Don't be the rebound! Move on. It will be difficult because you're in a battle against your natural instincts, which are to help others who are helpless get back on their feet, take care of them.

Chapter 21
Ways to Restore Your mentality, So You Can Think More Positively

How to recover from gas lighting

The answer to that is that it takes a very long time to recover from this. That's because gas lighting has lasting, real effects, and the abuse can last a long time. Here, we'll discuss how to recover from gas lighting in a way where you can feel liberated, and happy as well.

Understand What You're Dealing With

You need to identify what happened, and what's going on before you can do anything else. In many cases, people will not recognize it for what it is because you aren't really aware of what's going on, and you're confused. The confusion is purposeful because people will do it for the sole reason of making others feel terrible. When you do this, you won't understand as well because confusion is one of the symptoms of gas lighting. You need to understand the tactics, and you should make sure that you spend some time understanding the signs, and then go from there.

Get Out!

This is the next step, and while it's obvious, you need to do it. Understand that, until you're fully out of contact with them, if you're with the gas lighted, you'll be manipulated in some way since they know how to control you. If possible, break things off with the person if you can. If it is a family member or someone you've had an intimate relationship with, it's clearly nowhere near as easy, but it's very important to understand that the sooner you get out of there, the better.

If you can't fully break it off, you'll need to reduce your interactions and make it so that the interactions are practically nothing. But do understand that leaving any gas lighted can be dangerous, so understand that, if you think your life is in danger, call law enforcement and get support, and take the necessary.

How to Handle Yourself

When you are finally freed, or in the process of getting out, you should always be gentle with the way you handle yourself. You should make sure not to overly blame yourself for this and understand that it's hard to recognize gas lighting you should understand that self-criticism is very common, and it's a symptom of gas lighting. Letting go of this and acknowledging that this person is a total manipulator who used you is a good way to go about it. You need to accept it as a life lesson, and you should learn that, through recognizing, you gain an understanding of the experience, and get better about handling it too.

You need to start to love yourself too. Don't get upset about this, but instead, you need to learn from the experience, for the sole reason of recognizing the warning you didn't before.

When you do spend time working towards understanding yourself and getting better with gas lighting, you'll be able to get yourself properly equipped to learn from the mistakes of the past.

You may start to see everyone as a gas lighted for a while. This is the "once bitten, twice shy" mentality that you're going to develop, and oftentimes, you may not realize that you're being overly cautious. But, if you've been manipulated for so long, you're going to realize that this is a pattern that happens over a period of time, and the different settings. Learning from your mistakes is one of the best things to learn, and people don't realize that, while you can screw up every now and then, you're going to realize that this will only help you if you learn about the signs, but also move on.

Moving on is going to be hard. It won't be something that you're going to do right away. You may consider isolation for a bit, but it's not ideal. You should learn to love yourself again, learn to understand yourself and get a feel for yourself over time.

Surrounding Yourself with Love

Surrounding yourself with love is a big part. You should make sure that you have people that do and appreciate you. You need to surround yourself with positivity and make sure that you are surrounded by people that will love you.

You should talk to people that you trust about your fears and doubts that have been plaguing your life. This is something that is cathartic for you because even just an acknowledgment that you're not alone can be great for you.

But along with that, when you surround yourself with people that you love, you should also get people that will validate your reality as well. They may offer some advice, or just tell you that you understand what's going on. This will make you feel great.

Sometimes, you'll feel alone, and if the person who gas was lighting you were family, it can be very hard to overcome this. You'll realize that you aren't alone, and you can always go out and find some other groups out there, with people who are like-minded and can help. If you go to those group meetings, you'll be able to validate the experience and talk about the trauma.

And the best part about these groups is you can talk about people who also have gone through a similar experience can benefit from you talking to the other person about the issues at hand. You'll be able to be validated which is good if you feel the impact of the self-doubts that are there.

Self-doubts will happen, but you should have a support network. You should also if you have the wherewithal to do so, try and work on yourself. Consider some new hobbies to try and learn, because it will help with overcoming the trouble you've been through. Many don't realize just how helpful it can be to work on yourself.

Plus, if you're working on yourself during this point, you can take yourself back. Remember, it's hard to deal with the trauma of the past, but that doesn't mean you have to deal with it for the rest of your life. You can learn to be yourself, be the person that you want to be, and you'll be happier than ever before. Sometimes taking control of your life again will change things, so remember that.

Exercise Caution

So many who start to be themselves after all this time struggle with being willing to trust others. It will be hard to recover from the impact of gas lighting, but here's the thing: you should exercise caution when trying to pursue new relationships, whether it be an intimate relationship or otherwise, but you should also start to be yourself. Be willing to trust your judgment and the perception that you have.

If you are happy with the person, then that's fine. It's good to be happy with your choices. But also, be smart, and also understand that if you think there is something wrong, you should consult others about it.

If you get into a relationship with someone or are trying to repair a friendship, or maybe starting a new job after leaving your prior workspace, you should always be on the lookout for anything that seems off. However, you should also not let yourself be held back by the trauma of the past.

Talk to others if you have any suspicions of gas lighting, and if you notice that they're doing things that the person in the past did, such as love bombing and acting great, but then suddenly changes whenever you're closer to them, get out. You should see the red flags as soon as possible, and always be on the lookout.

Remember, you don't have to isolate yourself from relationships, but the smart thing to do is to work on trying to make sure that you understand what it is you're going through, and also, understand what it takes to learn to be trustworthy of yourself once again.

If you ever feel a bad gut feeling when you start to get into new relationships with someone, listen to it and don't think it's just your body trying to play tricks on you. Chances are, it's something that is amiss, and if you notice it, you should listen to it, and understand the truth of the matter.

Sometimes when you notice these things such as that gut feeling in your stomach, it's a sign that something is going on. But, other signs of anxiety also come up, and you should start to recognize them.

If you feel a bit of judgment when you notice it, you should acknowledge it, and actually, listen to it. That way, you'll be able to understand when that feeling comes about and become more knowledgeable of it.

Ignore the Motives

One thing to understand is that if you do wonder what the motives are, you should always make sure that you ignore it. Here's the thing, trying to understand why someone would gaslight you isn't going to help. In fact, it's going to make you feel as if you're going crazy. The problem with trying to find the answers to this is that if you continue to think about it, you're going to go crazy.

You should never try to figure it out, but instead, you should label the behavior that's there as what it is, and that's gas lighting. You should acknowledge that, and if your mind starts to wonder why it's happening, you should shut it down.

Understanding the motives of why someone would abuse you is only going to make you go crazy, and sometimes, it's better to just ignore the motives at hand, and from there, work to get out of the situation before it gets worse.

You don't' need to stay in a place that's abusing you, and you can recover. The reality of it is simple: gas lighting is terrible, is hurtful, and not good for you to deal with. If you continue to obsess love why someone does what they do, you're going to feel worse. But, instead you should be honest with why it's happening, and understand what is going on, but you should also take the time to recover and getaway.

Getting away is only the first step though. The road to recovery does take a long time. I highly recommend that, if you've been abused for a long time in this way or have a lot of hurt and trauma from this, you should see a therapist for this. The therapist can help you work out the trauma, so you're not facing it alone.

Remember, anyone can recover from the effects of gas lighting, and you should, with the right mindset and ideas, work towards a brighter future for yourself, and for your own life. You don't need to be the effect of your past, but instead, you can learn to embrace it, and build a future that helps you, and makes you happier as well.

Chapter 22
Why People That Are Empathy Often Get Gas Lighted

An empathy is an individual who is exceptionally touchy to the vitality of others. Empathy are known as vitality wipes since they ingest the passionate agony around them. Thus, empathy will in general be profoundly generous trying to improve everybody's lives.

With regards to gas lighting, empathy are obvious objectives since they regularly battle to separate themselves from their abusers. As such, while they are profoundly natural and discerning individuals, empathy regularly need individual limits and battle to state "no." And no limits = ideal prey for narcissistic gas lighting methods!

Gas lighting makes us question our own recollections, discernments, and decisions, startling us sincerely and mentally. In the event that you feel as if your confidence, certainty, and autonomy has wilted under the fire of gas lighting you are not the only one ... and there surely is trust!

Practically we all, including myself, have encountered some type of Gas lighting all through life. The issues emerge when Gas lighting is a continuous shadow that trails behind our connections and organizations. Fortunately, information and mindfulness is the initial step to recuperating your life and modifying the solid, insightful individual you are ... and you have just taken it!

While the facts demonstrate that in certain circumstances we truly may be going overboard, or may really be displaying silly conduct, it is additionally significant for you to tune in to your sense or instinct. Do you have an overwhelming inclination in the pit of your stomach? Do you feel overloaded and persecuted? Do you feel discouraged? These are signs that you have unknowingly gotten on duplicity and "unfairness." While we can deliberately be tricked, unwittingly we can't, and regularly we will have a waiting inclination that "something simply isn't right." Make sure that you tune in to this inclination and look for help, either expertly or socially (for example a believed gathering of companions or an encouraging group of people).

In reality, here are a few different ways to help yourself even with gas lighting:

1. Right off the bat explain to yourself how, when and who is gas lighting you. Consider what ways they cause you to feel unhinged and like you're losing it. Record whatever you can consider. You should have the option to affirm that you're being gas lighted before you can proceed onward with your life.

2. Focus on the indications of being gas lighted, such as feeling befuddled, put down, "insane" or controlled. Take a full breath, clear your brain, and focus yourself. Put in a safe spot standard time for establishing every day through contemplation or a care practice. These procedures will assist you with staying objective even in troublesome conditions.

3. Conclude whether it merits proceeding with your companionship or relationship. In case you're in a working relationship, consider whether it merits remaining in your activity or not. In the event that you need to remain, consider approaches to limit connection with the gas lighter until you feel grounded and certain.

4. Converse with confided in companions or friends and family about your concern. Then again, look for help from a guide or advisor who can assist you with accomplishing some shadow work.

5. Move your viewpoint from being a casualty to being a warrior/champ or whatever word feels the most enabling. You don't need to stay a casualty for a mind-blowing remainder, and by recovering your own capacity, you'll additionally have the option to help other people in comparable conditions.

What is the Opposite of Letting Go?

Something contrary to giving up is connection. At the point when we connect or relate to our musings, we endure. Then again, when we quit appending to our contemplations and just perceive the truth about them: vitality that we allocate importance to, we experience opportunity.

Basic contemplations that we append to which make feelings, for example, outrage, rage, sicken, dissatisfaction, uneasiness, dread, pain, and discouragement, include:

1. She ought to have been a decent mother.

2. In the event that he hadn't cheated, I would have been glad.

3. Things ought to have gone in an unexpected way.

4. I ought to have a lot more pleasant life at this point.

5. He/she shouldn't have passed on.

6. My supervisor ought to have advanced me.

7. In the event that I remain somewhat more, he will stop his drinking.

8. On the off chance that I did that another way, I would be a lot more joyful at this point.

9. She needs to change, or I won't discover harmony.

10. They are controlling my life.

11. Everything was greatly improved before.

12. I will be cheerful later on when I get what I need.

At the point when we append to our convictions about how life ought to go, we endure every single time since we are opposing what is directly here and at the present time. At the point when we oppose reality, we likewise will in general embrace the job of the person in question, which causes considerably more prominent affliction.

In all actuality by what method can we 100% realize that something is totally fortunate or unfortunate for us? While something like a separation or demise may quickly appear to be an awful thing, how would we realize that it is totally awful? Would we be able to see each conceivable future result and outcome of such an event right now? Obviously we can't. Is it conceivable that such an encounter could really bring forth beneficial things also? However, we proceed to accept and demand that it shouldn't have happened when actually what will be will be. With or without our contemplations it has still occurred.

Obviously, encountering a misfortune or injury doesn't mean we ought to overlook how we feel. It is consummately ordinary and imperative to permit ourselves to feel the annoyance, disarray, misery, dread, scorn, and harshness inside us. Be that as it may, when we begin connecting ourselves to these feelings, we experience languishing.

It is our connection and distinguishing proof with our considerations that is the sole reason for our affliction. As recently referenced, giving up is a procedure that requires some investment and exertion. There is no snappy and quick approach to relinquish all your difficult emotions. Notwithstanding, probably the quickest ways I have by and by found of giving up is addressing and distrusting musings. This strategy is known as self-request and assists with finding a good pace of your misery. You can choose to peruse increasingly about self-request.

Chapter 23
Narcissist Manipulation Techniques

• Cycle: idealization-devaluation-abandonment

A sudden transition from a fairytale love story, treating you like an ideal to subtle comments, constant criticism, often hidden, negating the legitimacy of your needs or preferences. In the idealization phase, you begin to feel that you have never felt/felt like this before and are as if on an emotional high.

A relationship with a narcissist is like a drug addiction. At first, it is great, and then the narcissus takes away your drug supply, i.e., your attention, feelings, become withdrawn for no apparent reason. It starts to give you less and less expecting more and more.

You will do everything to have at least a bit of the man he was (or rather, he was pretending) at the very beginning of the relationship. When the mask begins to fall, and you begin to orient yourself where you are, very often abandonment occurs.

Abandonment does not necessarily mean the end of the relationship, it is often a total physical and emotional withdrawal, ignoring you, so-called silent treatment (quiet days). Some narcissists at this stage give up completely, entering into another relationship, which they often began while still with you.

Very often, abandonment, offending at amen is also a reaction of narcissistic personalities to the opposition, to setting boundaries or paying attention to their unacceptable behavior.

This mechanism is not only found in relationships, but also in other relationships. Or draw attention to their unacceptable behavior. This mechanism is not only found in relationships, but also in other relationships. Or draw attention to their unacceptable behavior. This mechanism is not only found in relationships, but also in other relationships.

Narcissus often makes us feel guilty about this method of manipulation. This is to divert attention from his behavior and make us focus on our REACTION and feel guilty that, e.g., we reacted badly, too violently; we chose the wrong words, etc. The truth is that dysfunctional narcissus behavior is a problem, not your reaction to them. After narcissistic abandonment, the victim often feels worthless, drained of energy, lost and totally confused.

• Gas lighting

Is a technique used by violent people to convince you that there is something wrong with your perception? Narcissus will convince you that you perceive reality incorrectly, that something seems to you, May even support you with mental illness. In extreme cases, it can even especially store items at home or postpone and support you that you did it. As a result of gas lighting, the victim ceases to trust himself, his feelings, and he stops listening to intuition, he stops believing that what he sees and experiences is real. Gas lighting makes you start questioning yourself and believing that maybe it's wrong with you.

• Smear campaigns (slandering you behind your back)

Narcissus often holds up a whole harem of potential victims. These can be contacts to former partners or, e.g., an account on a dating site. Very often, being with you simultaneously smears you behind your back to your potential next goals or to family members/friends, etc. Of course, you do not know it. Very often, narcissus outside the house is a charming, almost flawless man. He tries to keep a circle of people who worship him or just like him. Prepare that in his circle you will always be bad/angry, and no one will believe you in what happened behind closed doors. You will be presented as a madwoman.

• Triangulation

Deliberately causing your jealousy and lack of stability and security by talking about your former partners, keeping in touch with them, comparing you to others. It can also be a deliberate placement of photos or items belonging to former partners or potential partners (e.g., friends) so that they are found. It evokes the feeling that there is still a third person in the relationship. Often, the narcissus's partner also begins to play detective because of the growing lack of trust.

• Two faces (or more)

You can't comprehend how it is possible that one person can be great at one moment and behave as if you were enemy No. 1 at another. You don't know what to expect, you tiptoe, live like a ticking bomb. Stress becomes an integral part of your everyday life. Outside, your partner praises you to the heavens and arranges hell for you at home. In the evening, he launches a real brawl for a trivial reason, and in the morning he asks as if nothing ever happened: "What are we doing there today?" or "What for breakfast?" It puts you in the light of total confusion, you feel like in a fog, you no longer know what is true and what is not, with whom are you actually in a relationship? Who is this? You can't define this man because he changes his face as often as he likes depending on the situation.

Signs of a Narcissist Person

• Admiration

Narcissists dominate the conversation. They like to talk about themselves, their exploits, and sometimes fix the truth by exaggerating their exploits. They give advice even when nobody asks them, and they feel superior to others. Nothing frustrates them more than waiting, and they believe that their needs should be considered a priority by their entourage, or even by society as a whole.

• The Ambition

Wanting to advance in his career and/or his private life is quite natural, but narcissists are much more ambitious than the rest of the population, says the site Health. They tend to believe that they are part of an elite that deserves only the best and that a bright future awaits them. For them, people are either winners or losers, and it goes without saying that they surround themselves only with the first ones.

• Manipulation

Despite their characteristics described above, narcissists are sometimes difficult to identify because they know how to charm their entourage. They manage to make others feel important. But at the slightest criticism against them, everything is destroyed. They cannot stand to receive judgments and tend to use their manipulative skills to get what they want or need. In question, explain the specialists cited by Health, a lack of deep empathy.

• The Grudge

Despite a very apparent self-confidence, narcissists are not indifferent to others. That is why, from the first signs of disapproval, they feel personally attacked. This injury will cause a lot of anger, grudge, and, in some cases, a desire for revenge. This problematic situation is compounded by the fact that narcissists refuse to be held responsible for their mistakes or bad behavior and tend to accuse others in their place.

Chapter 24
Affective Addiction

H owever, there are cases (and many statistics claim that women suffer more from it) where addiction becomes pathological; it happens in all those situations where the subject, by virtue of his way of being, depends emotionally on the partner, whose happiness and everything that revolves around him, represents the unique purpose of his existence.

Almost certainly this model has already been experimented (perhaps with its parents) and is characterized by the fear of being abandoned, anguish, low self-esteem, melancholy, etc. all things that "color" the trait as pathological. Affective dependence is an almost totally female pathology, with an age between 20 and 40-50 years.

The characteristics of these women is certainly the fragility, the need to be appreciated, very low self-esteem, an unmotivated fear of being abandoned.

In order to reach or fill this, they tend to do everything in a very responsible way, but their traits are characterized by exaggeration. The cause of this discomfort must be sought in the family of origin.

Symptoms of emotional addiction

There are so many, and I try to make a list of the most common ones:

1. Feeling unable to succeed in maintaining one's emotional relationship;

2. little self-esteem about one's intelligence, physical appearance and ability to arouse interest in others;

3. terror of solitude;

4. the person who is the object of our love is idealized beyond measure to the point of feeling good only if he is beside him;

5. stay with the "breath on the neck" up to suffocate the other;

6. be passive and subject to the negative characteristics of the person you love and therefore a profound sense of inadequacy and inferiority;

7. getting depressed, feeling anxious or suffering in an uncontrolled way with each detachment and the possibility of abandonment;

8. be guilty of any crisis and discussion within the relationship;

9. react to conflicts or possible crises in the context of the relationship with an excess of anxiety or even with a Panic Attack crisis;

10. hyper control of behaviors, both physical and mental, towards the loved person;

11. management of out of control jealousy, which can be morbid and manic;

12. moving away from all other relationships (emotional and social) about the relationship one is dependent on;

13. irritation, despair and anger if the other has fun or could have fun alone;

14. The loved one, by virtue of an exaggerated jealousy and possessiveness, becomes the object of stalking, threats, etc., if he tries to escape control, in particular the sentimental one.

The symptoms listed above, of which it is obviously desirable that there are not all of them together, the last of them, refers to people whose pathology is really serious, but which, fortunately, even if it exists is quite rare.

Now one wonders: does it really happen that the dependence on a person is so strong that it can be compared to drug addiction? The facts oblige us to answer affirmatively.

When we love in an obsessive way, when being in love translates into continuous suffering, when the obsession is constant in our acting and living the relationship, here we are in the situation of "emotional employees". This nosographic term can also be found under another term, not Italian but which is entering the common lexicon, namely, love addiction.

So, in other words, emotional dependence is a pathological trait that affects one of the main functions, feeling and in a more specific way is a pathology that distorts the natural flow of amorous behavior.

What differs from the normal way of experiencing falling in love? The time and intensity that grows more and more exacerbating the desire for fusion in and with each other.

Who offers, lives the relationship not for the relationship, but to give respite to their fears, ignores the real meaning of human relationships, exaggerates with their own needs to crystallize a situation thus avoiding (he believes) the risks of separation, abandonment, unhappiness, etc.). The evolution of this pathology may point towards anxiety disorders, depression, difficulty sleeping, disorders in the food and sexual sphere, etc.

At the base of this disorder, there is a very low self-esteem, the result of a childhood characterized by lack of love, abandonment, violence, deprivation, abuse of power, poor or absent emotional life; all experiences that have undermined the psyche of the child and that, in a certain sense, orient the personality on a front where reality is distorted, and everything is done to fill the self-esteem generated by the little consideration that is perceived.

These individuals do everything to appear amiable to be accepted and thus fill the profound sense of emptiness and lack of esteem that is absent. These people, therefore, will be victims and perpetrators at the same time as those who will take them into consideration in one way or another.

From all this, therefore, it becomes clear that these subjects 'fall in love' with other subjects who have complementary problems; subjects that is, with another type of dependence such as drugs, alcohol abuse, subjects with various compulsions (gambling, shopping, mobile phone, internet, pornography, etc.). This is because it is easier to project one's own problems on others and therefore delude oneself that by helping others, one becomes useful, but this is a wrong way because it is 'sick'. In this way a circuit is created that self-references the two subjects (the dependence of the first reinforces that of the other).

How to defeat emotional dependency

Psychotherapy provides the tools necessary to identify cognitive errors that fuel false beliefs and highlights real fragility, providing emotional tools that can remodel the perception of things and relationships sought and experienced. In the end, the objective of the journey focuses on the discovery of the sound bases on which to set an authentic desire to love.

You must know that there are different types of dependencies, which take their name from the way in which this dependency is exercised. For example, we have the Obsessive Affective Employee, whose obsession mainly affects the relationship with the partner; the Codependent Affective Employee, characterized by subjects with low self-esteem and who try in every way not to break away from the partner, becoming precisely codependent on the other; the Employee of the Report, who even though he is no longer in love with his partner, fails to break away from him because he cannot manage change; Affective Narcissistic Employees: the problem of co-dependencies in the couple base their actions on the principle that the other must be dominated and therefore implement every stratagem to exercise strong control; Ambivalent Affective Employees, who have an avoidant personality (perhaps linked to attachment patterns), would like a bond but fear it, avoid it; The Rejecters Seducers, seduce only by sex or by company, but if the anxiety takes possession of them, they refuse any relationship; The Romantic Employees, their dependence leads them to have more partners and therefore to depend on them and the immediate consequence is that in reality, doing so avoids having a real commitment.

Chapter 25
How To Stop Gas lighting Abuse

In every gas lighting abuse, there is a silver lining. In such a relationship, it takes two to tango. The power your gas lighter holds over you, his victim, is only true up to the extent you allow him. While it is definitely not easy to just break off from the relationship, it is exactly what you need to do. Gas lighters are not your regular diplomats. That is to say, they're not reasonable. So stop trying to reason with them. Also, while it may seem like you do not have a choice to walk away, please know that you certainly do. They may have told you how no one will accept you, how they're simply putting up with you. This is nothing but a trick to keep you in the relationship and under their control. Know this - You can simply opt-out. And if you choose to stay and fight off their gas lighting behavior, it should be done at your own terms.

Gas lighting abuse occurs because the victim wants to stay and get her gas lighter to see things from her own point of view. And why this desperate move to win the gas lighter to her side? Because she awfully wants to win his approval. It is life support for them. His approval would make her feel whole once more. Getting this approval means she finally gets to make him accede to her own sense of reality. It is a victory for her if she achieves this feat. After a series of distortions to her truth, it confirms she wasn't crazy or delusional like he made her look. Know this - this will never happen. The gas lighting effect came through because he succeeded in eroding your sense of reality. He just can't soft-pedal. That means his grip over you would be broken. Which Magician knowingly allows the spell over his victim to be broken? His agreeing to your sense of perception breaks off the whole control plot and power play he's engaged in.

You don't need his approval to feel whole. You are enough just as you are. You surely don't need anybody's approval to be human.

Again, you must stop making excuses for your gas lighter and do not accept any from them either. Do not rationalize their failings. If they've failed to act, then they must accept the responsibility.

Furthermore, you will have to set limits on what's acceptable to you, and what's not. These limits should never be toyed with. It gives you a sense of what you're willing to put up with, and puts in perspective how your gas lighter regards you. If he crosses this red line numerous times, without the slightest care in the world, then opt-out of the whole affair.

You can trust your own sense of reality. When your gas lighter does not agree with your point of view, take it with a pinch of salt. Trust what you see and hear and don't allow your gas lighter's opinion to overwhelm yours. When he sees you're not buying into his narratives anymore, he will begin to back-pedal. When this happens, he may leave the relationship on his own volition.

Finally, be honest with yourself. Access your relationship thoroughly to gauge what point it is right now. Do you need therapy? Is the abuse something you can handle on your own? Are you happy? Do you feel the need to put a stop to the way he constantly puts you down? Your answers to these and many more questions you will be raising is key to knowing the next steps to take. In all, never forget your one leverage - you can always walk away.

Chapter 26
How to Recognize Manipulation and Take Back Control

There will be many challenges that you will face, but in the long run, you will be in a better position. Many people struggle with how lonely it is after divorcing their partner. We are going to look over how you can overcome loneliness so that you do not get sucked back into a relationship with your ex.

Obviously, when you do start looking at getting into a new relationship, it is going to be extremely scary. It will likely take quite a while for you to truly open up and trust someone again. We're also going to look at what you can do to make sure that you are choosing a partner that is going to be healthy for you. Included in this, we will give you narcissistic traits to watch out for, so you don't end up making the same mistakes twice. Most people learn the lesson fairly quickly about what to avoid after being with a narcissist, but the more information you have the better off you will be.

Trust is going to be extremely difficult for you. It will take time for you to be able to open up and allow someone into your heart. This is completely normal as you have suffered mass devastation at the hands of someone who was supposed to love you. Make sure you are being patient with yourself. There is no rush. If you are having worries about entering into a relationship or trusting another person, it may be a clear sign that you're not quite ready to date again, and that is completely OK.

Letting go can be extremely hard when your relationship has been your sole focus for a long amount of time. Know that with perseverance, strength, and education, you will be able to come back and lead a healthy and fulfilling life that is free from the abuse of a narcissist.

Overcoming Loneliness

Regardless of if you were married to a narcissist or not, when you divorce someone, it is going to lead to feelings of loneliness. These feelings can be almost debilitating; they are so strong. Unfortunately, extreme loneliness could encourage you to go back to your toxic relationship so that you simply aren't alone. Obviously, this is something you should avoid at all costs, especially if you just divorced a narcissist.

Divorce can feel very isolating. When you divorce a narcissist, it can be even more so as they will likely do their best to turn everyone against you. You must remember that you are absolutely not alone and that there is a plethora of people that are working through the same hardships that you are. You must also remember that there are at least some people that can see your ex-spouse for who they are and will be ready to stand by your side at a moment's notice.

One great way to help you move on and combat the loneliness that comes from divorce is to join support groups that can help you work your way through it. You don't have to do this in the public eye if you don't feel ready as there are many online support groups that are available to help you heal and move past everything that has happened to you. These types of groups help you feel a sense of inclusion, and it can help combat the loneliness that you are currently experiencing.

A lot of the loneliness that you may be feeling could be due to the fact that you are isolating yourself. This is a common thing to happen once you have left a narcissistic relationship, as you will likely be working through a variety of different issues. Let's look at a three-step system that can help you get past your loneliness and isolation.

The first step is to allow yourself plenty of time to grieve. The grieving process can be quite lengthy, and it feels as if you are on an emotional rollercoaster. This makes many people want to speed past the grieving process, but it won't be beneficial if you do. The more you try to speed up the grieving process, the more you will actually be lengthening it. You should also be aware that you should avoid rushing into a new relationship. New relationships right after divorce may postpone the grieving process, but it will not stop it altogether. You really do need to allow yourself to grieve over the harm that has come to you and the loss of your marriage.

The next step is to not allow yourself to focus on the past longer than you need to. As you are grieving and healing, you will definitely need to spend some time looking over past experiences, but once you have accepted them and you understand them, you need to move on.

When you are constantly looking at the past, it can actually increase the loneliness, sadness, and anger that you feel. You are absolutely entitled to all of the negative feelings that you have experienced from your past, but if you hold on to them for a long amount of time, it can be very difficult to completely move on and find the ability to enjoy your life. You must always remember that the relationship you had with the narcissist is a thing of the past and life will improve as long as you dedicate yourself to healing.

The last step is to not be afraid to reach out for help. When you are trying to work through the pain that has been caused to you and the extreme heartache that you are feeling, a solid support system is exactly the right answer.

The people in life that are not afraid to reach out for help always seem to find a way to land on their feet. Choosing to try and do it alone tend to add to the suffering that an individual will feel. Additionally, it lengthens the time that you will feel extremely lonely and lost. Whether you choose to find support from friends, family members, therapists, or support groups, there is no wrong decision. In fact, the more people you have in your corner to help support you through this arduous journey, the better off you are.

Reaching out for support is probably one of the most important pieces when you are trying to shake the loneliness that comes after divorce. When we connect with other people that understand us and understand the situation that we have come from, it makes it easier to break free of isolation. There are some fabulous retreats and other activities that you can participate in with people that have similar experiences, and it can be extremely freeing.

Choosing a New Partner

Now that we have looked at a variety of ways to help you shed the loneliness factor, we want to discuss choosing a new partner and starting to date again. This can be utterly terrifying due to the fact that you were fooled once, and you will never want to be fooled in that way again. There are a lot of different things that you will need to learn, but there are also things that you will need to unlearn after being the victim of narcissistic abuse.

More often than not, people that have suffered from the hands of someone that has a personality disorder will want to learn about it.

Obviously, knowledge is power, so learning about personality disorders can help keep you safe from falling into a relationship with someone that has one.

You must understand that there are varying degrees of personality disorders and just because someone has 1 does not mean that they will not be a suitable fit for you. However, recognizing the signs of a serious personality disorder that will cause you to harm is a good way to ensure that you don't go back through the torture that was being in a relationship with a narcissist.

Not only will you have to learn a variety of different things before being comfortable stepping into a new relationship, but you are also going to need to unlearn some things. The narcissist in your life probably did a pretty good job at twisting and warping your reality. Undoing the damage that they have done will take time, but it is completely possible. You will likely need to take a step back from yourself and look at each experience with the narcissist individually so that you can see the truth of what actually happened. It is quite likely that you have already worked through that process if you are considering looking for a new partner at all.

Deciding to date after leaving a narcissistic relationship is something that can be extremely difficult as it can take years to truly heal and work through all of the obstacles that come along with narcissistic abuse. Don't be afraid to discuss what is on your mind with your friends, family, and therapist. It is fairly likely that your thoughts and ideas about love and relationships are still a little bit skewed and getting other's opinions on the situation can make it clearer as to what the right choice for you is.

When you are starting to consider dating again, you should take the time to brush up on the red flags that help you easily see that someone is a narcissist. You should also take the time to remember what your relationship with the narcissist was like in the beginning. More often than not, the beginning is a time that felt positive with your ex and examining it can show you some of the early signs pinpointing a person as a narcissist.

Let's take a look at a variety of different red flags that try to clue you in that someone is a narcissist. If you see these traits in someone you are considering dating, you are better off to run for the Hills rather than think it is a fluke or that you can change them.

One of the first red flags that you should watch out for is people that have a showy, flashy, or larger than life attitude. If you would make this statement about someone that you have never met anyone like them or it's like they are a magnet, you should be leery. If you genuinely like someone, you will be able to explain what it is about them that you like. So, the inability to explain what it is that draws you to a person is a red flag that they may not be relationship material.

Another huge red flag is when someone expresses their love for you after a short amount of time. If you have not been dating someone for very long, you should be concerned if they are committing themselves to you. It takes time for love and serious feelings to develop, so if you see that somebody is rushing in and telling you that they love you quickly, it is a pretty good clue that it will lead to an unhealthy relationship.

Love bombing is another major red flag that you absolutely need to pay attention to. If someone is showing you in an overwhelming amount of adoration or attraction without a core that is emotional, you should be concerned. Many narcissists use love bombing to manipulate and gain control over a person. It is actually quite surprising how often it works. If an alarm bell is setoff inside of you because someone is paying you an overwhelming amount of attention, you should listen to what your intuition is telling you and stay away from that person.

Chapter 27
How To Deal With The Effects of Gaslighting

The most insidious thing about gaslighting is that it denies the victim of reality, telling them they didn't see what they just saw with their eyes, or they didn't hear what they thought they heard by telling them their perceptions of what is right is wrong.

Countless people over the globe have fallen victims to this unique form of abuse at one point or the other in their lives and having survived the ordeal, they choose to share their experience with others, and by doing so, they disclose how they managed to cope with the awful situation.

Ariel Leve is a renowned survivor of narcissistic childhood abuse, and in her childhood memoir, she tells of how she grew up with a narcissistic mother and the horrible abuses she went through. She is just one of the countless people who have survived narcissistic abuse and manipulation.

In interviews and talks, she shares four strategies she used to deal with the abuse with others and we will further those strategies by adding plans from other survivors to throw light upon how to deal with gaslighting and help the victims cope with the situation.

    1.   Remaining Defiant.

Remaining defiant means holding on to your story of the abuse. It means trusting your own version of events and not allowing them to be altered on demand. A narcissist will try to bully you into accepting their own version of reality but trust your version of the real world.

Being defiant also means you realize what makes a difference to you, and you don't allow it to be adjusted or meddled with by anybody. It is tuning in to your own internal voice that knows better than anything said by another person.

You don't have to argue or contend with the narcissist —you just need to stand by your choices with absolute confidence.

Remaining defiant also makes you resilient in the face of abuse.

2. Accepting the fact that there will never be accountability on the part of a narcissist

There is no way the narcissist will ever take responsibility for their actions, as they don't know how to acknowledge their misdeeds as they are not people who can apply logic and reason to a situation.

You on your own part should keep a good record of events as they happen, for a narcissist will never acknowledge the fact that they are using gaslighting tactics to manipulate you.

If you speculate you are a victim of gaslighting, recording everything that has been said and done to you by the abuser is an excellent method for knowing who is truly right and what is truly right.

Writing things down, particularly exchanges that occur between you and the narcissist provides a solid defense for you when you are being manipulated to think against what is right.

Written proof of any faulty exchange is solid protection against anybody attempting to pull the wool over your face and will enable you to comprehend reality when you're being questioned.

3. Letting go of the wish for things to be different

Your hope for the narcissist to change can never prevail. Wishing for things to be changed is hoping that after a while, the narcissist will come to use reason and logic in dealing with you.

Also, after cycles of failed promises, a narcissist will still come around to promise that the bad things they do will never happen again. If you truly wish for things to be different, you'd see how the narcissist is manipulating you with the promises.

A gaslighting narcissist will always move the ground you stand on, and you have to stop wishing they would change their nature or events will turn out differently later. You have got to accept the situation and assess the ways you can seek to empower yourself.

4. Developing a healthy detachment

Detaching from the gaslighting situation doesn't mean total detachment from real life, it just recognizes the difference in the world of the narcissist and the real world.

A healthy detachment means you don't need the narcissist to validate what reality is for you, and it involves developing healthy coping mechanisms, and writing is one of the ways to do this. Sure, some certain circumstances will make you remain in close association with a narcissist, but really, the best choice for you might be to abandon the relationship altogether. You can't change a narcissist, and if there is a chance that the gaslighting narcissist doesn't alter their injurious conduct, then leaving the relationship for your psychological and emotional wellbeing is your best choice.

Try not to let the narcissist persuade you that things will be extraordinary if you stay or that you are just overreacting to issues. Once again asking you to stay might be another pointer to gaslighting as a person who truly wants to change will recognize their wrongdoings and apologize for their bad behavior and will be willing to put efforts into making the relationship work.

5. Confiding in a Trusted Support System

You can always count on a trusted friend, a loved one or a professional if you suspect a narcissist is gaslighting you. By opening up to someone, you get to check and validate your reality.

Not only is opening up to a trusted person an added form of documentation, opening up to trusted people can help you understand what is happening to you better and also help you gain the courage to walk away.

Build up your own emotionally supportive network.

You need other individuals throughout life who can affirm your reality and self-worth. Gaslighting narcissists often try to isolate their victims to remain in charge.

Gaslighting narcissists might even go further into manipulating you to think they are the only people who care about you and understand you perfectly. Don't believe their lies. Spend time with loved ones. Check out your thoughts, feelings, and perceptions by talking to them.

Get professional help in the event that you need it. Victims of gaslighting frequently lose trust in their own thoughts and emotions and end up apprehensively double-checking themselves all the time.

Sometimes, you may sink into depression, and you will definitely need the help of a licensed professional to help you recover from the insidious effects of gaslighting.

6. Dismissing Self-blame

It is imperative to know that narcissists have psychological issues they are not willing to address and thus can project their wounds onto other people and become harmful and harsh to them. It is pertinent to note that how they treat you is an impression of how they feel about themselves.

The dismal truth is that your abuser may never acknowledge or concede what they were doing. For the most part since they don't believe they're doing anything incorrectly.

All you can do is recall that there's nothing you could've done any other way. Rational thinking doesn't work with a gaslighter.

You should not bear the responsibility. Comprehend that their wrong ways aren't your shortcoming.

While the reason for gaslighting is to wear you out, it's essential to remain as defiant and careful as you can. When you truly understand what gaslighting is, you also get to know your options, and you're nearer to the enlightening reality of your circumstance so you can choose what's best for you.

The essence of these strategies is for you to realize that the narcissist eventually needs control of your life, and this is the reason why they seek to keep you away from making your life as autonomous and independent as could be expected under the circumstances.

Put the time into your own interests and friends. Be as dedicated to your own life as you are with your relationship.

Conclusion

There is no place in a loving relationship for manipulation of any kind. Far too many people stay in manipulative and abusive relationships out of fear of the future, but the future can only be brighter than the present day. Staying in this type of relationship will turn you into a shell of the person you were before. Breaking free will allow you to return to that person, but with an added element of strength and fearlessness.

We've covered a lot of ground, but the content will always be there if you need to go back over anything and refresh your memory.

To an outsider looking in, a manipulative relationship is cut and dried. You walk away because you're not being treated correctly. For the person in the middle of the relationship, it's never that easy. Emotions are involved, thoughts and perceptions are twisted, control is exerted, and confidence is shattered. All of this happens over time, and the slow drip of manipulation is one of the most effective methods of control there are.

There isn't one particular type of person who is more likely to be more vulnerable to manipulation than another, but narcissists are very good at identifying people who may be a little lacking in confidence or going through an especially hard time. Those people may be more vulnerable in some ways, but that doesn't mean that a person who seems very strong and confident on the outside can't be subjected to manipulation too.

If there is one message, we want you to take away from this book, it's that any type of manipulation is wrong. Even if the manipulation is from a narcissist who has a specific personality disorder, none of this is an excuse. Treating other people with no care, thought, or emotion is always something that should never be tolerated. Finding the strength to walk away will be the best thing you ever do.

Of course, it could be that you are watching a close friend or family live their lives under the clutches of a manipulative partner. We hope that this book has educated you on what that person might be going through and feeling. As a result, you're in a much better position to help them deal with the situation and hopefully break free from it in time.

Narcissism is difficult to explain to someone who has never been affected by it. This is a personality disorder that may cause extreme distress to other people, but at the heart of it all, the narcissist isn't happy either. All you can do in any situation is look after yourself, and that means breaking free, looking to the future, and finding a situation that makes you happy, free from manipulation of any sort.

It is not only children in the formative ages who can be influenced by their environment. Even as adults, the people we spend time with can affect us positively or negatively. Living, working and associating with someone who constantly reminds you of how incompetent, weak, and unfit you are is not healthy for your emotional health. Surrounding yourself with positivity is not merely a New Age gibberish. The implication of doing the opposite can be quite devastating. Unfortunately, even if you inadvertently stick with negative people, it will still wreak its havoc.

For this reason, if you discover that someone is gas lighting you, your best option would be to discontinue your relationship with them. You may be in a position where cutting off all ties may not be immediately practicable, but you should work toward that end.

Don't let past good experiences blind you from the unpleasant experiences an abusive person is presently putting you through. You need to move past sentimentalism and be more decisive to regain your freedom and rebuild your life again.

If you have suffered emotional abuse, especially gas lighting, you may conclude that you are frail, pathetic, and won't be able to take on the challenge of doing without the gas lighter in your life. Don't believe that lie. It is the gas lighter's spiteful narrative that is trying to trick you into losing faith in yourself. You are not frail or pathetic. Instead, you are strong because it takes a strong individual to survive gas lighting abuse. Don't let anyone tell you otherwise!

And no, you are not paranoid or too sensitive if you think that your colleague or business partner is undermining you. You are also not mistrusting if you think that your spouse or romantic partner is being unfaithful. If you have a hunch, follow it without making accusations. The gas lighter may have tricked your conscious mind, but they can't squelch your unconscious mind. This is why even though you may buy into their lies you still feel an inner discordance with your truth. Trust your gut. Many mysteries have been unfolded and cases have been solved based on nothing but a hunch. You may not be right all the time, but the more you listen to your intuition, the stronger it gets and the more you trust yourself.

Ridding yourself of a gas lighter creates a vacuum in your life that needs to be filled. I am not suggesting that you should jump from an abusive relationship into the next available relationship. However, as you eliminate the bad influence from your life, it is wise to replace it with something empowering. Never neglect the need to stay in constant touch with a support system that will help to boost your sense of self. Get connected to support groups, trusted friends, and dependable family members who you can draw inspiration from. Leaving an abusive person without finding a positive substitute does little to speed up your recovery and makes you vulnerable. Your journey to recovery is only assured with the help of positive reinforcements.

Remember that the bulk of your work is internal and intangible but carries a lot of impacts. Ending your relationship or friendship is necessary in most cases, but it is physical and external. Blocking an abuser's phone number, deleting their contact details, and severing all forms of communication is necessary, but there are all physical and external. You can still undo these things. But recognizing your true self-worth, building your self-esteem, learning to love and trust yourself more are intangible, internal, and have more influence in your behavior. You can physically end a relationship but still want to be with the person despite causing you so much pain. But if you learn to recognize your worth, you would not desire to be with someone who treats you with disdain. They are your bedrock for recovery.

It is time to bid farewell to the confusion, self-doubt, and people-pleasing behavior forced down on you by the gas lighter. No one deserves to go through such insidious psychological torture—not you, not anyone!

CPSIA information can be obtained
at www.ICGtesting.com
Printed in the USA
LVHW080424171020
668893LV00001B/16

9 781801 093118